Adkisson's Captive Insurance Companies

Adkisson's Captive Insurance Companies

*An Introduction to Captives,
Closely-Held Insurance Companies,
and Risk Retention Groups*

Jay D. Adkisson

iUniverse, Inc.
New York Lincoln Shanghai

Adkisson's Captive Insurance Companies
An Introduction to Captives, Closely-Held Insurance Companies,
and Risk Retention Groups

iUniverse books may be ordered through booksellers or by contacting:

iUniverse
2021 Pine Lake Road, Suite 100
Lincoln, NE 68512
www.iuniverse.com
1-800-Authors (1-800-288-4677)

The views expressed in this work are solely those of the author and do not
necessarily reflect the views of the publisher, and the publisher hereby disclaims
any responsibility for them.

ISBN-13: 978-0-595-42237-1 (pbk)
ISBN-13: 978-0-595-86574-1 (ebk)
ISBN-10: 0-595-42237-3 (pbk)
ISBN-10: 0-595-86574-7 (ebk)

Printed in the United States of America

Table of Contents

Chapters

Appendices

About the Author

Few people know more about structuring captives than Jay Adkisson. As one of the founders of Manchester Strategic Advisors, one of the original CHIC and small captive consulting firms, and as an owner of Trafford Insurance Services, an insurance management firm in the British Virgin Islands, Jay has been intimately involved in the formation and management of literally dozens of captives from 1998 until 2003, when the partners of Manchester and Trafford decided to go their own ways and those firms were wound up.

Following the 2004 publication of their best-selling book, "Asset Protection: Concepts and Strategies" by the McGraw Hill Companies, Jay and Chris Riser formed the law firm of Riser Adkisson LLP, which provides business, tax and estate planning services to business owners and affluent individuals. Even before Jay became involved with captives, he had a national reputation as an asset protection planner and this reputation has continued today. Jay is a regular speaker at events of the American Bar Association and various state and county bar associations. He is also regularly quoted by such publications as the Wall Street Journal on asset protection and related topics.

In addition to his law practice, Jay is a registered options principal for Securities Equity Group, a securities broker-dealer. He is also the Director of Private Client Services of Select Portfolio Management Inc., a registered investment advisory firm. A regular speaker at events sponsored by financial and insurance companies, Jay is also the author of "Equity Indexed Annuities: The Smart Consumer's Guide". He also has a life agent license in California.

Notwithstanding all the foregoing, Jay is probably best known internationally as the creator of Quatloos.com, a very popular website that educates the public about tax and financial scams and frauds. Jay has been the feature of an article in Forbes and has appeared on ABC's 20/20. He is also a regular lecturer to the Internal Revenue Service about tax frauds.

Jay earned his Juris Doctor degree from the University of Oklahoma, and is admitted to practice law in Oklahoma and Texas, and before various federal district and appellate courts nationwide. He currently lives in Southern California, and is an avid private pilot.

Contact the Author

Jay Adkisson regularly consults with new clients nationwide on captive insurance structuring and creation. He can be contacted at the following:

Nationally Toll-Free at 888-359-8851

Orange County, California: 949-607-0952

Dallas, Texas: 214-459-6272

E-Mail: jay@captivebook.com

URL: http://captiveinsurancecompanies.com

Postal Mail: P.O. Box 7088, Laguna Niguel, CA 92677

Jay is also a regular speaker on captive insurance topics, in addition to general business, estate and asset protection planning topics, to both public and private groups.

Acknowledgements

Thanks go to my father Ron Adkisson for his editing and suggestions. Thanks also go to Joe Petrucelli for his comments and suggestions on the tax treatment of captives. And as always, thanks must go to Karen for putting up with me during the writing of this book.

Introduction

A captive insurance company is, in a nutshell, an insurance company formed by a business owner to insure the risks of the operating business. The operating business pays premiums to the captive, and the captive insures the risks of the operating business. A captive is much more than an exotic form of self-insurance: It is the creation of a new insurance company that has the potential to grow from being a mere captive into a full-blown insurance company seeking to profit from underwriting the risks of others.

In just the last decade, the captive industry has grown substantially. From an estimated 1,000 captives in 1980 to over 5,000 by 2006, captives now account for more than 10% of all commercial insurance premiums collected worldwide. In the U.S. alone, captives were responsible for over $9 billion in premiums in 2005.

The U.S. dominates the captives market. Fully 30% of all captives are domiciled in the U.S., and even most of the offshore captives have U.S. parents. Doubtless, this is due to the peculiarities of the U.S. tax code which disallows an ordinary company from accruing reserves against future claims, but allows another company within the same economic family (the captive) to do precisely that. The point is that captives are a recognized and established planning tool for U.S. businesses.

In 1958, an engineer by the name of Fred Reiss created American Risk Management for the purpose of assisting U.S. corporations in setting up their own insurance companies. Because at the time the U.S. insurance commissioners did not differentiate between captives and ordinary insurance companies, most captives were formed outside the United States, usually in a debtor haven where no or low taxes were charged locally. After the U.S. passed the Tax Reform Act in 1962, which for the time being eliminated the benefits of captive arrangements for U.S. companies, Reiss moved to Bermuda and formed International Risk

Management. Thus, Bermuda and the other offshore domiciles would dominate the worldwide captive market for the rest of the century.

Several IRS rulings and court cases decided in the 1970's and 1980's started to define situations in which captive arrangements would be respected in the U.S. More and more major U.S. corporations started forming captives. By 1981, Vermont passed its captive legislation and the domestic captive sector began to grow. All of this lead to more court cases, more challenges by the IRS, and more defining of when captives were or were not permissible.

Eventually, by the mid-1990s the tax laws relating to captives had matured to the point that tax planners could be comfortable knowing that premium payments to the captive would be deductible in appropriate instances. The captive business literally exploded as even mid-sized and privately held businesses started forming captives to manage their insurance risks. The number of captive domiciles also exploded, and today more than half of the U.S. states now have captive enabling legislation.

Captives are great planning tools and there is now a whole industry that supports them. Yet, captives are poorly understood by both business owners and business planners. Those who know the most about captives are doing planning for large multi-national corporations. But the planners who are advising the smaller businesses and their owners who might benefit from a captive usually know very little if anything about them.

There are some insurance brokers who now set up captives, but their knowledge is limited to the insurance issues and many of the potential tax and wealth transfer advantages of a good captive structure are simply missed. The tax and estate planners who could do this ancillary structuring to make the captive really work usually know little or nothing about captives or the insurance issues that are involved. Because of this, there are very, very few planners (a handful nationwide) who really offer the "whole package" to clients that fully exploit all the potential advantages of a captive.

I came into the captive business from the business and estate planning side, and not from the commercial insurance side. I had been practicing law in Oklahoma and Texas for nearly a decade, mostly in commercial litigation and asset protection planning, when I had the opportunity to move to California and join a new consulting company being formed to create small captives for small- to medium-sized businesses. My partners, another lawyer and a CPA, had substantial experience in insurance and taxes respectively, which gave me the great luxury of learning the intricacies of the captive business for the next five years while integrating captives into my own unique estate and asset protection planning. Many of the strategies that we came up with remain unique and unparalleled within the captive and estate planning worlds.

Whether or not you are ever involved with captives, they are an interesting business topic. The purpose of this book is to provide readers with a general overview of captives and their benefits, plus a description of the captive formation process and the main captive domiciles. While captive formations are extremely complicated and must be left to planners who are experienced with them, readers should be able to take away a feeling of what captives are all about and how they can help certain businesses and their owners. I have also sought to familiarize readers with some of the unique terminology of the captive business.

Jay Adkisson
Orange County, California, 2006

Chapter 1

Captive Benefits

A *captive insurance company*—known simply as a "captive"—is a real insurance company with reserves, surplus, policies, policyholders, and claims. It is licensed as an insurance company in the domicile where it is formed, foreign or domestic, and may later be licensed to conduct the business of insurance by other jurisdictions as well.

The main purpose of a captive is to insure the risks of other companies that are also owned by the captive's owner, the *parent*. These other companies are sometimes referred to as *brother-sister companies* of the captive, or more often as the *operating companies*. They make premium payments to the captive in exchange for the captive issuing insurance for the risks of these companies. See Figure 1.1.

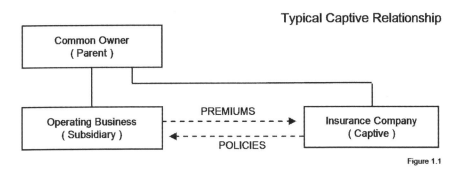

Figure 1.1

You must think of a captive as an insurance company, because that is what it is and that is how it must be operated. If you do not want to own an insurance company, then you do not want to own a captive. The relationship between the insurance company and the operating business whose risks it is underwriting should be, for the most part, an arms-length relationship where each entity operates independently of the other, except for the exchange of risk and premium. The captive should have its own business plan and goals for becoming successful. At the same time, for the arrangement to be efficient it should be tightly integrated into the owner's overall business plan.

As a captive matures, opportunities may develop for it to become a *profit center* that actually makes money and adds to the bottom line of the entire economic family, and thus becomes independently valuable in its own right. But when the captive is initially formed, its primary function is usually to operate as a *cost center*—meaning a tool to reduce the insurance costs of the operating business.

There are several compelling reasons to consider a captive, including the following.

Stabilize Insurance Budgets

Insurance companies are very similar to banks in that their profitability is determined by their investment income. When the investment markets do well, commercial insurance companies will lower their premiums to attract more dollars. In fact, commercial insurance companies may actually lower their premiums below what should be the correct actuarially-determined underwriting price so as to attract more premium dollars for investment. This means that when the investment markets are doing well, insurance premiums may be artificially low.

Conversely, when the investment markets do poorly, insurance companies will raise their premiums to try to recoup their losses, making their premiums artificially high. It is because of these artificial highs and lows that insurance premiums sometimes wildly fluctuate, even though the claims made against issued policies were relatively steady during the same time period. In other words, higher premiums do not mean the plaintiffs' lawyers suddenly began winning a bunch of cases—it usually just means that the insurance company didn't do well on Wall Street.

Captives help to level out insurance costs in at least three ways.

First, to the extent that the captive is used to underwrite risks, the captive can charge premiums based on claims experience and actuarial predictions instead of investment profits or losses. This means that the premiums paid to the captive should be much more consistent than those charged in the commercial insurance markets.

Second, the captive can reserve premium payments in those years when the commercially-obtained insurance is cheap, and use those reserves in years when the commercial insurance becomes expensive. When the insurance market becomes more expensive, the captive owner then has the option of raising deductibles for his existing coverages (thus lowering the insurance cost), and having the deductibles covered by the captive. The owner could alternatively have the captive make a refund of premiums which is then used to pay the higher insurance costs, or have the captive purchase the insurance through reinsurance contracts, if such is available.

Third, since a captive can earn investment income on the premiums paid to it (instead of to a third-party commercial insurance company), there will be more dollars available to pay claims or earn profits. In other words, instead of the premiums earning investment income for somebody else's insurance company, the premiums will go to work earning investment returns within the captive.

Reduce Insurance Administrative Costs

When you pay your commercial insurance premiums, you are not paying for the true cost of insurance. In addition to a spread that the insurer usually builds in for underwriting profit, your premiums include the administrative costs of your commercial insurer. These costs include your agent's commissions, advertising costs, costs of compliance with state and federal regulation, and general administrative costs such as office space and salaries for the insurance company's officers and employees. Although these costs are spread over a large number of insureds, they can still be substantial.

While a captive insurance company has its own administrative costs, these costs are relatively low—usually around $50,000 per year for most small captives. When you consider that on a $1 million premium, a 3% agent's commission can be $30,000 by itself, you can see the potential for a captive to significantly reduce the administrative costs that are built into commercial premiums. This means that more dollars can be available for investing and ultimately to pay claims. You probably strive to reduce overhead in your operating business—with a captive you have the possibility of reducing your insurance overhead too.

Negotiation Tool

A hidden benefit of a captive is the effect that it can have in negotiating commercial insurance rates. Since the commercial insurer knows that the captive owner can forego buying a commercial policy and simply keep the risk in house, the commercial insurer may be motivated to offer competitive prices in order to keep the business. The same is true of an agent, who can sometimes reduce (known as *dialing down*) their commissions to further incentivize the sale of commercial insurance.

In other words, a captive creates a powerful bargaining chip: "Lower your rates or I will insure it myself." The agent and the commercial insurer will be concerned that once a customer shifts a particular risk to a captive, the customer will always be out of the market for that type of insurance.

Utilize Own Experience

Once upon a time, insurance companies actually sent underwriters out into the field to conduct detailed inspections of a client's assets and business operations so as to best determine that client's particular risk exposure. The underwriters would go into a business and spend hours, if not days, pouring through books and records, examining physical facilities and workplaces, and talking with management and employees to understand exactly what the business was doing, its procedures for mitigating risks, and the extent of the insurance company's potential liability.

Those days are long gone. Today, the underwriter is a computer program. The agent acts as sort of a field underwriter but very little actual inspection, other than obtaining asset lists or the employee census, and gathering other mundane information, is done. Modern underwriting is now done at the insurance company's office by business classification, meaning that a business in a particular class will be imputed to have an experience rate roughly equal to all the other businesses in that class, without much regard to whether a company has better or worse loss experience. The agent cranks in the data, and the computer cranks out the rate based on the experiences of similar businesses.

This is great if your business has worse than average loss experience, since it means that you are getting your insurance more cheaply than you should be getting it and everybody with better experience is subsidizing you. But it also means that if your business has better than average loss experience, you are effectively paying higher premiums because you are subsiding competitors with worse loss experience.

A captive allows its owner to set premiums based upon the actual loss experience of the operating business, without regard to how other businesses of the same class are rated or any industry-wide losses or experience. If the claims history of the captive's insured is better than those in the industry, then the captive works to prevent you from subsidizing businesses with worse claims experience.

Premium Flexibility

Commercial insurance companies are typically inflexible as to how premium payments are made. Most companies require the full amount of the premium to be paid up-front, while others may allow premiums to be spread over some period (often for a slight additional charge). In either case, the customer has little flexibility when premiums are to be paid. This can contribute to occasional but sometimes severe cash crunches for many businesses.

A captive allows much greater flexibility when premiums are to be paid. For instance, a captive may require the payment of premiums only at year's end which can give the operating business a direct cash flow advantage. It can also aid in timing deductions for tax purposes.

Policy Terms

One of the biggest advantages of a captive is the ability to dictate the terms of coverage. For instance, a captive policy can be written as a *litigation expense policy* that is limited to paying for attorney fees and other litigation costs but does not pay claims—thus giving the owner a war chest to fight claims without creating a pot of money for claimants to chase. This is discussed further in Chapter 7 relating to policies.

Increased Claims Control

A commercial insurance company gives its customers almost no say in how claims are resolved. Questions as to whether to litigate or settle, what attorneys to hire, and decisions made about the course of the litigation are made by the commercial carrier.

Some would argue that control over claims is the best reason for using a captive. Decisions as to whether to settle claims early to avoid expense, or to not settle claims so as to deter other plaintiffs, are strictly those of the captive's owner. The captive can choose to hire the lawyers who are the best at resolving certain types of claims, instead of ordinary insurance defense counsel who handle a wide variety of claims. Strict control can also be had of litigation costs and expenses, such as to whether to take the deposition of a particular witness or hire the best expert in the field.

A captive will not fight with you about coverage questions, either. You will never get a *reservation of rights letter* from your captive that says that it will defend you for now, but may in the future go to court to fight over whether your policy covers the particular claim. Thus, you will never have to worry about your captive trying to wiggle out from paying the claim based on some technicality.

Recapture Underwriting Profits

Commercial insurance companies do not operate with the intention of doing so at a loss, nor do they provide charity to their customers. Underwriters want to make a profit on each and every policy that they issue and so they often build a spread into their premiums charged. This spread artificially increases the true price of insurance paid by customers.

The companies that will benefit the most from a captive are those with a good loss experience, *i.e.,* a better loss experience than others in the same industry. Companies with a good loss experience are effectively subsidizing the insurance costs of others with poorer experience. The use of a captive severs these hidden subsidies and returns them to the economic family as the captive's profits.

The investment returns earned by the captive are another form of profit. Instead of a commercial carrier earning investment returns from the premiums until claims are paid, the captive can instead earn those returns.

One of the benefits of a captive is to recover all of these profits (premiums, investments, loss control, etc.), and make them profits of the captive and not of some commercial insurer. These profits can then be used to either reduce future premiums or be distributed to the owner as dividends. In either case, these profits stay within the owner's economic family.

Accept Greater Deductibles

Many captive owners will have types of risk that they desire to shift to others and not maintain within their business or captive. These are typically risks of a catastrophic nature, i.e., claims that could wipe out the business and for which it would not make sense to use a captive to insure. Sometimes too, the pricing of commercial insurance means that the operating business should purchase insurance with higher deductibles.

In both of these situations, the captive insurance company could be used to insure the deductibles of commercially obtained insurance, thus allowing the operating business to accept a higher deductibles and either reduce the cost of the commercially obtained insurance or obtain higher claims limits.

The insuring of deductibles is known as *risk retention* or sometimes just *retention*, since by covering the deductibles those risks are effectively retained within the economic family and not transferred to a commercial insurer. Typically, using the captive to insure deductibles is a good idea when there is good claims experience data and the amount of the claims are relatively consistent from year to year.

Access to Reinsurance Markets

A *reinsurance company*, or *reinsurer*, is one that predominantly sells insurance only to other insurance companies. Often, reinsurance companies have restricted licenses that allow them to sell insurance only to other insurance companies. Reinsurance licenses usually do not allow them to offer insurance to the general public.

Reinsurance companies can often offer insurance at much cheaper "wholesale" prices than front-line or retail insurers because they have much lower administrative expenses, much lighter regulation to contend with, and almost no sales or advertising budgets. Also, reinsurance companies can spread risks over much larger pools than retail insurers which allow them to underwrite particular categories of risk more cheaply.

Because captives are licensed insurance companies, reinsurance companies can sell reinsurance to captives. This means that captives have access to the wholesale reinsurance markets that ordinary businesses do not have. Since multiple reinsurers can sometimes be put together to insure a particular risk, it may also allow the captive to obtain much higher coverage limits than would ordinarily be commercially available to the operating business.

A caveat here is that reinsurance companies will only participate in risks where significant premiums will be paid for the reinsurance coverage. The physician who attempts to form a captive with the idea of obtaining medical malpractice reinsurance for a $25,000 premium will be disappointed. Few if any reinsurance companies will be interested in less than a six-figure reinsurance premium, and many will not be interested until the premiums are in the seven- or eight figure range.

Customized Coverage

Insurance coverage that is purchased from commercial insurance companies is typically inflexible. Like going to a fast food restaurant, you have your choice of a few items from a menu and you might even be able to choose some of the accompaniments such as "hold the onions," but it is impossible to change the base product. Commercial coverage utilizes standardized policies with standardized terms covering standardized risks, and getting a commercial insurance company to significantly vary any of this is like ordering a crepe suzette at a fast-food hamburger franchise—they may have the ingredients and the ability to make the crepe, but it isn't going to happen.

The type of coverage that a captive can write is, in stark contrast, limited only by your needs, imagination, and good common sense. Policies can cover multiple, unrelated risks if you desire, and they can cover risks that no commercial insurance company would touch. Such things as premium payments, claims administration, and what type of coverage is afforded can easily be altered or changed. In other words, a captive gives complete flexibility to custom tailor coverage that specifically fits the needs of the operating business.

As importantly, coverage can be tailored to meet the needs of third-parties that may require an insurance certificate for the operating company or be drafted in a way to make the risks more attractive to reinsurers. This also goes to efficiency, since with a captive you can create only the precise coverages that the operating business needs: Nothing more, nothing less.

The types of policies that can be written by a captive are discussed more fully in Chapter 7.

Underwrite Exposed Risks

Every business has some risks for which it has no insurance. In the industry vernacular, this is known as a *naked risk*. For instance, a business may carry general liability coverage, but this coverage might exclude intentional acts by management employees. Since a claim of sexual harassment would be considered an intentional act, it might be excluded by the general liability insurance policy thus leaving the business vulnerable to such a claim. Insuring exclusions is one of the best uses of a captive.

Another similar situation is where insurance is commercially available but too expensive. This is often the case with such coverages as environmental insurance. If the business has no environmental insurance, the business is exposed to environmental claims and is thus effectively self-insuring itself against such claims.

A captive allows a business to insure itself against exposed risks and formalize the *de facto* self-insurance in a tax efficient way within the captive. Since the owner has full control over the policies and terms, these exposed risks can be dealt with through individual policies or by way of a business umbrella policy issued by the captive.

Enhance Loss Prevention

If a business is insured by a commercial insurer, it may have little more incentive to take additional steps to reduce claims or losses other than to avoid premium hikes. A captive, however, helps the business owner to focus on risks and loss control, since claims payments by the captive are effectively a loss of wealth.

The use of a captive places a greater emphasis on the development and utilization of loss prevention programs. If losses are reduced, then greater profits for the owner results. The captive thus works to positively influence the operational behavior of the entire business family.

Along these lines, a captive can be used to better accumulate and analyze claims and loss data so as to enhance loss prevention programs. By developing better data about certain types of risks, it may be easier to obtain commercial insurance or reinsurance at more favorable prices.

Profit Center

So far, we have only discussed the captive as a cost center, *i.e.*, a vehicle to reduce insurance costs within the business family. For those starting a new captive, control of insurance costs is usually the major factor. However, a captive has the potential to become a profit center—an independent business unit that yields net profits towards the overall bottom line.

Most captives will eventually mature into ordinary insurance companies that will charge premiums from and underwrite the risks of third-parties. These third-party customers will most often be in similar businesses and the captive will already be familiar with their risks. By capturing the underwriting profits on these new customers and generating investment returns on the additional reserves and surplus, the captive can go from merely a cost center to an independently profitable and valuable business for the owner.

Liability and Wealth Transfer

A captive insurance company can help to clean up the balance sheet of the operating business by shifting contingent liabilities to the captive. This can improve the looks of the operating business for purposes of selling the business.

Similarly, a captive insurance company can operate as a wealth-transfer vehicle to shift value out of the operating business. This can be important where the operating business is subject to catastrophic claims that could entirely eliminate its wealth, or where it is desired to shift wealth to other family members for estate planning purposes as we will next discuss.

Chapter 2

Wealth Transfer, Accumulation and Preservation

A captive should be much more than just a loss control vehicle. A captive should be a vehicle for transferring wealth out of the operating business so that wealth is not trapped and exposed to higher taxation or to creditors. A captive should also be a vehicle for accumulating and preserving the wealth for future generations.

Sadly, captives are rarely any of these things for the reason that they are usually created by those in the property-casualty insurance business, such as insurance agents and risk managers, who simply are not aware of advanced estate planning concepts. The owners of such captives may continue on for years blissfully unaware of the tremendous unused advantages of their captives.

Wealth Transfer

By paying premiums to the captive, wealth is effectively transferred out of the operating business and into the captive. Since the premiums are paid with pre-tax dollars by the operating business, it means that this amount of wealth will avoid taxation within the operating business. Because the captive has the insurance company benefit of being able to accrue reserves tax-free and other tax advantages peculiar to insurance companies, any taxes paid on the money transferred will be much easier to mitigate or manage within the captive.

It also means that this amount of wealth will be removed from the reach of creditors of the business. If the operating business later becomes financially troubled or is the target of a large lawsuit, the amount of premiums that have been paid to the captive will be out of the reach of the creditors. This can be a significant benefit for operating businesses that face significant lawsuits, such as a property development company that may be exposed to an environmental or construction defects lawsuit.

Note that not only is wealth transferred to the captive, but also risk is transferred to the captive. This is why it is critically important that policies be meticulously drafted to limit the liabilities of the captive instead of (as most insurance managers unfortunately do) simply copying boilerplate policies from the formbook.

If the captive is owned by the children of the business owner, and the children are over the age of 21, then the activities of the captive are not attributed to the owner for federal gift and estate tax purposes. This means that if the captive is owned by the children, every premium dollar paid passes outside the parent's estate and to the children without creating any federal gift or estate taxes.

Where the children over 21 own the captive and the captive is designed to serve an intergenerational wealth transfer role in addition to an insuring role, the captive is known as a *closely-held insurance company* (CHIC).

The children should not be allowed to own the CHIC directly, but instead the CHIC should be owned by a trust for the children's benefit. There are several reasons for this. First, so long as the CHIC is held by a trust, the value of the CHIC and the wealth within it will be protected from the children's creditors, such as future ex-spouses. Second, the use of a trust may allow further intergenerational transfers to grandchildren and their heirs with lower gift and estate taxes.

The typical CHIC relationship is shown in Figure 2.1.

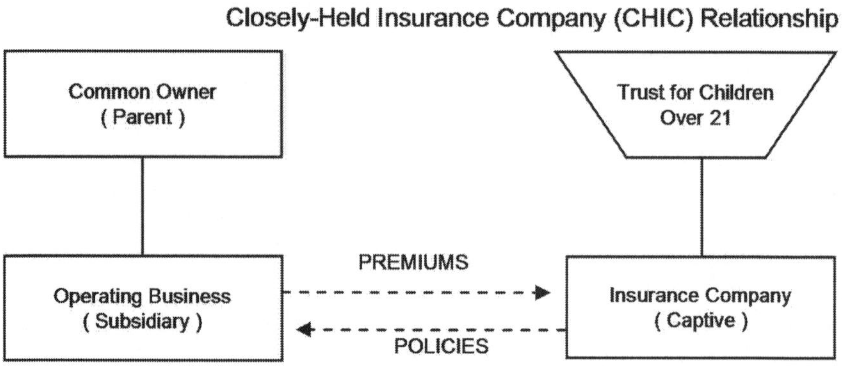

Closely-Held Insurance Company (CHIC) Relationship

Figure 2.1

CHICs are one of the most widely misunderstood forms of captives. Some captive advisors who simply cannot comprehend the wealth transfer aspect blandly tell their clients that a CHIC is merely a captive owned by an individual instead of a publicly-traded conglomerate. As the person who created the concept of the CHIC and coined the term in 1998, I continue to be amazed at the number of captives that are still formed in the name of the parent when they should have been formed in a trust for the children.

New estate planning techniques, such as the *beneficiary-taxed trust* (BETIR Trust), are now being used with CHICs to super-charge their tax and estate planning benefits. To realize the fullest potential of a CHIC as a wealth transfer vehicle, the involvement of a tax attorney familiar with captives and the latest estate planning techniques is essential. It is also very important that the captive and estate planning structure be periodically reviewed in view of changes in circumstances, growth of wealth in the captive, and tax law changes.

Note that the wealth transfer ability of captives can go in reverse when needed, by the captive variously paying claims of the operating business, refunding its unearned premiums, or making loans to the parent which then uses the money for additional capital to the operating business. For tax reasons, however, loans should not be made directly from the captive to the parent.

Wealth Accumulation

Captives, like all insurance companies, have the very powerful tax advantage in that they can accrue reserves, *i.e.*, take a current-year tax deduction for contributions to their reserves. This lowers the insurance company's apparent profitability, but also allows them to accumulate wealth on a long-term tax-deferred basis. This gives rise to the saying, "Insurance companies never seem to make any money, but always seem to own everything." Because of this, captives are perfect vehicles for intergenerational and even dynastic wealth accumulation.

The ability to accrue reserves can give the insurance company the unique ability to create deductions, defer taxes, and time taxes for years when the insurance company is otherwise unprofitable. Thus, by manipulating its reserves, an insurance company can sometimes create current-year deductions that can offset its investment gains.

Having assets held in a captive as opposed to a trust can be very advantageous from a tax standpoint. As discussed, a captive has many inherent abilities to mitigate or defer taxes on its investment income. By contrast, a trust has no ability to mitigate or defer taxes and because of what is known as *compressed trust tax rates*, the highest income tax brackets for trusts start at a very low amount of income. This requires close management of the taxable investment returns of the trust, which the captive can soak up to the extent those returns are in the captive. Thus, in addition to its other benefits, a captive can act in a tax management role for the trust which owns it.

Often a captive can be structured to operate as a *family bank* in the sense that the captive funds a limited liability company (LLC) which then makes loans to family members instead of the family members simply receiving outright cash gifts from a trust. The advantages of this concept are compelling. First, by making loans and requiring the repayment of loans to the LLC, the family's wealth remains intact and is not dissipated by gifts. Second, when the loan is secured against the family member's other assets, it can act as a *friendly lien* that will deter creditors or, in the worst case, can allow the LLC to liquidate the family member's wealth to the extent of the loan plus interest and return it to the LLC. The third advantage is that by making loans to the family member, instead of outright gifts from a trust, the family member is taught to conserve the loan proceeds and use them wisely or else future loans will not be extended (and the LLC will always have the right to collect against the loans if the family member goes too far astray).

Wealth Preservation

Because the captive is not a subsidiary of the operating business, it is not directly subject to claims against the operating business. The liability of a captive is usually limited to its exposure on the policies that it underwrites. So long as the policies are carefully drafted—usually as litigation expense policies, policies of limited indemnification, and the like—while the captive will pay claims it will never be directly sued for anything.

Claims against the parent of the captive put the captive at risk of being seized by the parent's creditors. Ownership of a captive by a properly-structured trust is a good solution. Since the trust probably isn't going to do anything that will give rise to claims against it, the captive itself should be protected.

Another way to protect the captive's stock is to have the captive owned by a limited partnership (LP) or limited liability company (LLC) which are entities that provide *charging order protection* for the assets of the entity against the creditors of a member. The entities do this by taking advantage of the statutory provisions that limit a creditor's rights to a charging order (sort of a cross between a lien and an assignment of income) on the member's economic right to distributions. This prevents a creditor from getting the assets of the entity itself. In other words, the most a creditor could get would be profit distributions (if any) from the LP or LLC but not the stock of the captive held by the LP or LLC.

Having the captive's surplus (and reserves to the extent allowed by the Insurance Commissioner) held in an LP or LLC is a good idea also. There are two reasons for this, the first being that if something bad happens within the captive (such as a CPA seriously messes up the tax treatment or some claimant tries a bad-faith lawsuit against the captive) the assets are protected from the captive itself by way of the charging order protection of the LP or LLC.

Second, if the assets are of the type that could generate liabilities (such as commercial property), they should be separated from the captive's non-liability producing assets. Indeed, it is very important that liability-producing assets not be mixed with passive assets such as cash, equity investments, or bonds, etc. that have no chance of creating liabilities.

Note that charging order protection may not be effective where there is only one member holding an interest, because charging order protection is really meant to protect members from being forced into a partnership with another member's creditors. Also, if the debtor member has management rights, there is an outside chance that a creditor might somehow be able to force a distribution of assets of the entity. The better structural designs involving charging order protection often utilize a management company owned by the family trust to act as the only managing member and thus shut out creditors from any management participation.

The effect of using one LP or LLC to hold the captive's stock to protect it from creditors, and another (or several) LP or LLC to hold the assets of the captive, is to insulate the captive and its assets from its creditors as well of the creditors of its owners. Since the most common entity used is an LLC, this is known as *sandwiched LLC protection*, as illustrated in Figure 2.2.

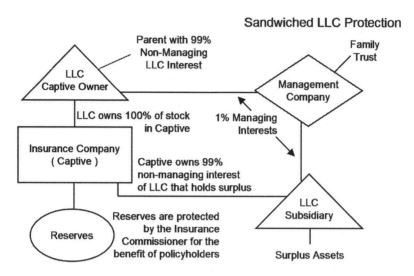

Figure 2.2

This structure has many benefits. Because an LLC owns the captive, ownership can be easily changed at the LLC level rather than at the captive level. Shares of the LLC which owns the captive can be gifted or sold to other family members or a family trust, sometimes with a valuation discount to further lower taxes. Similarly, the use of the management company allows the control of the captive's assets to change without the ownership of the captive itself changing. It may also be easier from a tax perspective for the LLC, which holds the assets, to make loans to related parties than for the captive to make those loans directly.

Example: Property Developers

Some of the best captive structures that I have put together were for property developers. The reason is that property developers have lots of risks that they are typically exposed to, such as construction defects, environmental, flood and earthquake risks. Some of these risks can last for years and sometimes decades, thus allowing the developer's captive to maintain reserves against these risks for a long period of time.

Developers also usually have 11 or more projects going such that, if properly structured, the captive can take the position that it is within the 11 insureds safe harbor (discussed in Chapter 5) and thus can avoid underwriting any third-party risks. Also, by choosing which risks to underwrite in which projects, the developer has the flexibility to transfer money out of certain projects by way of paying premiums and leave money in others. The captive thus becomes the vehicle for consolidating the profits of all the developer's projects.

If the captive qualifies as an 831(b) company, this creates the potential for up to $1.2 million per year to be moved out of each project (creating an expense deduction) and moved into the captive tax-free. If the captive is owned by a trust for the children over 21 years of age, it also potentially means that each dollar paid in premiums passes outside of the developer's estate for estate tax planning purposes.

The property developer's captive structure is illustrated in Figure 2.3.

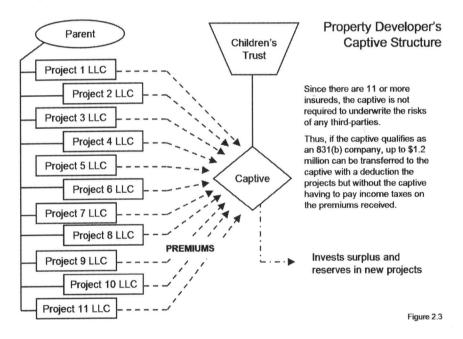

Property Developer's Captive Structure

Since there are 11 or more insureds, the captive is not required to underwrite the risks of any third-parties.

Thus, if the captive qualifies as an 831(b) company, up to $1.2 million can be transferred to the captive with a deduction the projects but without the captive having to pay income taxes on the premiums received.

Invests surplus and reserves in new projects

Figure 2.3

The long term benefits of this structure are tremendous. Over five years, this structure has the potential to move $6 million in premiums out of the projects without tax to the captive, to create deductions within the project entities ($2.16 million at the highest federal rate), and to avoid gift and estate taxes ($2.4 million assuming a 40% federal rate). In this case, the total combined tax savings would be $4.56 million—or 76% of each dollar paid to the captive!

Compare the combined tax savings of $4.56 million against the total costs of $100,000 to form the captive and $50,000 per year to operate the captive, and you can see the tremendous potential net benefits of an advanced captive structure as a wealth transfer and accumulation tool. When you consider that $6 million has also been transferred out of the reach of creditors of the projects and has created a large war chest for the developer to fight claims, the wealth preservation advantages of the captive structure become very clear.

And Even More Sophisticated Structures

The top tax and estate planners can be very creative in their use of captives, including using segregated cell captives to hold assets for individual family members, using the captives to issue annuity and life insurance policies to family members and trusts, and using the new *Series LLC* to help segregate reserve pools for specific risks.

The problem is that there are very, very few planners who are familiar with these techniques and how to implement them—probably less than a half-dozen such planners nationwide. Again, most captives are formed by insurance managers, property-casualty brokers, and risk managers who simply have no understanding of these techniques. While these captives may be effective from a pure underwriting standpoint, without knowledgeable planning they will miss some of the outstanding wealth planning advantages available to the owner.

Chapter 3

Basic Concepts

Like all insurance companies, a captive insurance company is primarily a creation of the tax laws. An ordinary business cannot take deductions for reserves that it sets aside for future claims, but an insurance company is allowed to take those deductions. If it were not for the special tax treatment given to insurance companies, businesses would not form captives but instead would simply set aside reserves to pay claims in a separate account or form a special purpose vehicle like an LLC. See Figure 3.1.

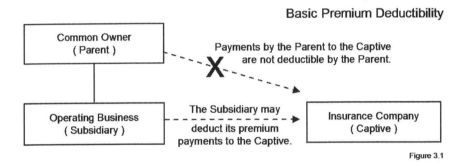

Figure 3.1

A captive takes advantage of this special tax treatment that allows the parent to set aside the funds to self-insure with its own insurance company. While the premiums paid by the parent to the captive will not be deductible, the premium payments from the operating business to the captive will be deductible. This is discussed more fully in Chapter 5.

Insurance Companies as Banks and Wealth Transfer Vehicles

Insurance companies are very similar to banks. A bank takes in deposits and eventually pays out withdrawals. In the meantime, a bank earns revenue by investing the deposits. Even when the bank is paying interest on deposits, it makes money by investing those deposits and achieving a higher rate of return than the interest paid on those deposits. It is all just a numbers game: The more money the bank takes in, the more earnings it makes on its deposits. The more premiums that an insurance company takes in, the more it increases its reserves and surplus.

Insurance companies operate the same way as banks. Insurance companies take in premium payments (deposits) and eventually pay out claims (withdrawals). In the meantime, the insurance company makes money by investing its reserves and surplus. An insurance company is better than a bank because it does not have to pay any interest on the premiums; however, it is worse than a bank because the amount of its exposure to claims is not limited to a set rate as if it had mere deposits to return with interest. Instead, an insurance company's exposure can vary widely depending on the policies that it writes and whether Lady Luck creates few or many claims against those policies.

As an insurance company, a captive has the same advantage as all other insurance companies in that it is receiving premiums, paying claims, and making investment returns on the often lengthy time between when premiums are paid and claims are resolved. But a captive has a very important advantage over ordinary insurance companies: It can act as a wealth-transfer tool for its owner.

The use of a captive allows a business owner to bleed wealth out of the operating company by way of premium payments. This reduces the balance sheet of the operating company for tax and other purposes, such as reducing its profile to creditors or for federal estate and gift tax purposes. Wealth is thus accumulated in the captive instead of in the operating business. Where a family owns a number of businesses, the captive can bleed wealth out of each of the businesses and consolidate that wealth in the captive—thus making the captive the equivalent of a family bank. At the same time, the captive's exposure can be significantly limited by conservative underwriting and careful policy drafting.

Control and Capitalization

Like any insurance company, a captive is controlled by its owners. That means that the owners can make all underwriting decisions, set premium amounts, dictate policy limits and terms, and choose investments.

There are very few limitations set by the Insurance Commissioner (or equivalent), for the reason that the Insurance Commissioner knows that the captive is being used in relation to the owner's other companies. It is only when the captive starts underwriting insurance to third-parties that the Insurance Commissioner will start caring about such things as limits or policy terms.

The Insurance Commissioner does care that the captive is adequately funded and sufficient reserves are set aside for the risks that it is going to underwrite. Like all bureaucrats, a primary motivation of the Insurance Commissioner is to avoid unnecessary work and the last thing the Commissioner wants to do is to waste time liquidating a captive, or having the reputation of the jurisdiction sullied by repeated insurance company failures. Thus, in addition to minimum capitalization requirements that are set by statute in each domicile (rarely less than $100,000 and often more), the Commissioner may require that additional capital be infused into the captive from time to time so that it remains solvent.

Reserves and Surplus

The assets of a captive are considered either reserves or surplus. *Reserves* constitute the portion of the captive's assets that back its issued policies. The amount of reserves that a captive is required to keep is determined by the insurance company's actuaries based on anticipated claims. The insurance commissioner will often review the actuaries' estimates to make sure they are realistic.

Surplus is all the other assets of the insurance company that are not reserves. Think of surplus as "stand-by reserves" that are available to back risks should the insurance company issue new policies. Surplus also measures the capacity of the insurance company to underwrite new risks. See Figure 3.2.

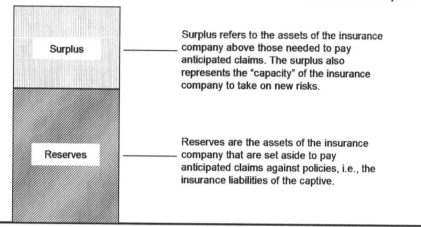

Figure 3.2

What part of the captive's assets constitutes reserves and what part constitutes surplus can have significant consequences. The captive's addition to reserves can in some events generate a current-year tax deduction for the amount of the addition. As policies expire, the reserves are freed up and become surplus—this can result in current year income to the insurance company if they were previously deducted. Of course, the portion of the reserves used to pay claims do so without creating income to the captive.

Because reserves back policies, they are often subject to strict investment guidelines by the Insurance Commissioner. Only some types of assets can be reserves; these are known as *permitted assets*. For instance, an Insurance Commissioner may require that some part of the reserves be in U.S. Treasuries, or may only credit 50% of the value of commercial real estate held by the captive for reserve purposes

By contrast, surplus does not back any claims and thus there are few (if any) restrictions on the types of assets that can be held as surplus. However, once policies are written and the surplus becomes reserves then the permitted asset restrictions apply.

Limitations of Captives

Although captives are insurance companies and have licenses to conduct the business of insurance, these licenses are typically restricted so that the insurance company can only sell insurance to:

- The owner of the captive;
- Businesses that are owned by the owner of the captive;
- Other insurance companies (in this capacity, the captive operates as a *reinsurance company* or *reinsurer*); and
- Certain other businesses in the same or similar line of business, only as specifically designated in the captive insurance license or as allowed by the Insurance Commissioner.

In other words, a captive does not have anything like a general insurance license to sell insurance policies willy-nilly to whoever it chooses. For the captive to do this would violate both the laws of the domicile where the captive is formed as well as the laws of the jurisdiction where the insurance is sold. A captive license is thus a *restricted license*.

For a captive to sell insurance in any jurisdiction other than its domicile of formation will require it to qualify to do business in the other jurisdiction, which means obtaining an insurance license in the other jurisdiction. This is typically not a limitation on the owner's other companies buying insurance from the captive because most states have laws that allow such a purchase from a captive, or they have laws that allow so-called *surplus lines* (read: "difficult to obtain") insurance. Other exceptions may apply in particular states. But it is a significant limitation to the captive selling insurance to third-parties.

An exception to this limitation is where the captive is organized as a Risk Retention Group (RRG), which is discussed more fully in Chapter 4.

Captives are also typically restricted to non-life insurance business, meaning that they cannot be used to issue life insurance or annuity contracts to the general public. However, a captive may be able to obtain an exemption from the insurance commissioner for single life insurance contracts sold to family members to further advanced estate planning strategies.

Captives and Bad Risks

As discussed in the next chapter, captive insurance companies have many unique and substantial benefits such that they should at least be considered by businesses with significant insurance risks. Captives are at their best, for instance, in taking advantage of pricing disparities where the business is paying much more in premiums than its loss history and potential for future losses justify. But there is one thing that a captive cannot do: A captive cannot magically transform a bad risk into a good one.

The most common misconception of those who are exploring captives is that a captive can always offer insurance more cheaply for a significant risk. While it is true that you can set your own premiums with a captive, within reason, the other truth is that because captive insurance is a form of self-insurance, the risk stays with you. If you have a bad loss, the money is going to come out of the captive and not from the commercial insurance company that you would have transferred the risk to had you paid for coverage.

Because a captive is a tremendous wealth transfer and wealth accumulation tool, probably the last place that you will want a large loss to be paid from is the captive. It doesn't make sense to accumulate money in a captive just to see it all paid out on a big claim. Therefore, the smart use of the captive will keep third-party insurance in place (maybe with higher deductibles) for significant risks, and instead use the captive to underwrite risks that, while real, will hopefully never materialize.

A similar misconception is that a captive will automatically be able to obtain reinsurance much more cheaply than if the owner purchased insurance directly. While sometimes this is true, with significant risk potential it is less likely to be the case. The underwriters of significant reinsurers—at least those whom you would be comfortable expecting them to actually pay claims—are very sophisticated and know a bad bet when they see one. Reinsurance companies are not formed to lose money. Thus, if you have a significant risk, you can expect to pay a reinsurance premium in relation to that risk.

Another limitation is that reinsurance can only rarely be acquired for premium amounts of less than $1 million. The doctor who forms a captive in the hopes that he can acquire a $1 million/$3 million medical malpractice policy more cheaply by way of a $20,000 reinsurance premium will be sadly disappointed to find out that there is no market for micro-premium reinsurance.

Minimum Costs and Break-Even

To have it done correctly, the turnkey formation and licensing of a custom-tailored captive insurance company will cost in the range of $100,000 for simple captives and much more for complex captives. That is only to get it up and running. The annual management, actuarial and accounting costs will be at least another $50,000 per year for anything like quality services. If you are paying less than this for formation and annual management, then you must wonder whether it is being done correctly.

Because of these costs, captives do not even begin making financial sense unless the premiums paid by the operating business to the captive exceed $300,000 per year—probably $500,000 per year is a more realistic figure. But for the company that can justify at least $500,000 per year in premiums, a captive will likely offer tremendous long-term advantages.

Reinsurance

Reinsurance is where one insurance company acts to insure the risks of another insurance company. If you think of the insurance company that sells directly to customers as the "retail" insurer, and the reinsurance company as the "wholesale" insurer, then you wouldn't be too far off the mark.

Because captive insurance companies are usually thinly-capitalized, they cannot retain much risk. Captives often must lay off the risk to somebody else who has the capital to back the risk—meaning a reinsurer. Sometimes, reinsurance can be purchased much more cheaply than retail insurance and the captive can be used as a conduit to obtain the reinsurance.

The typical reinsurance relationship involving a captive is shown in Figure 3.3 as follows:

Reinsurance Relationship

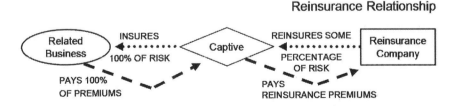

Figure 3.3

The reinsurance markets have been around literally for centuries, and the business of reinsurance is very sophisticated and has its own concepts and terminologies. Key to this is the concept of buying and selling risks. Those who run reinsurance companies are out to make a profit, and so they look for risks that are unlikely to materialize or where the premiums-to-expected-claims ratio are very favorable for them.

The company that buys reinsurance or sells the risk, depending on how you look at it, is known as the *ceding company* or sometimes the *cedant*, and the agreement by which the risk is transferred to the reinsurance company and premiums are paid to the ceding company is known as a *cessation agreement*. The company that sells the reinsurance or buys the risk is known as the *reinsurance company* or *reinsurer*.

When the captive keeps a part of the risk for itself, it is known as *retention* of the risk. The captive can also cede to the reinsurer the total risk over a certain amount thus relieving the captive from having to pay any losses over this amount; this is called *stop-loss reinsurance*.

Sometimes the reinsurance company will reserve the right to choose or reject certain risks that are being underwritten by the captive. Where the reinsurer has this right, it is said to have given *facultative reinsurance* to the captive and the reinsurer may further change the policy terms or charge higher or lower premiums for the risk.

Several reinsurance companies may get together to offer reinsurance on a large risk. How they divide or share risks, costs, and expenses, is determined by way of an agreement between them which is known as a *reinsurance treaty*. Where each reinsurer accepts a stated percentage of each and every risk within a certain category on a pro rata basis, the agreement is known as a *quota share treaty*.

Retrocession occurs when a reinsurance company itself seeks reinsurance from another reinsurer. This is actually a common occurrence in the reinsurance markets, with the last levels of risk gravitating towards the largest reinsurance companies who can spread them over many insureds. The premium and loss data provided by the first reinsurance company to the second reinsurance company is contained in a report called a *Bordereau*.

When an insurance company wants to close its books and wind down its affairs, it will purchase a *policy to close* whereby all of its open risks are taken over by a reinsurer. This allows the insurance company being closed to show that it no longer has any outstanding policy liabilities to which it is exposed.

Premiums Withheld Reinsurance

The last thing that an insurance company wants to do is to pay money to a reinsurance company only to later find out that the reinsurance company doesn't have the ability to pay claims. *Premiums withheld reinsurance* is where the insurance company that is buying the reinsurance does not release the premiums paid to the reinsurer until claims are resolved.

In other words, the insurance company buying reinsurance holds on to its money until it knows the profit or loss on the reinsurance agreement. If claims are lower than the reinsurance premiums and the reinsurer makes a profit, the insurance company cuts a check to the reinsurer for the amount of the profit. But if claims are higher than the reinsurance premiums and the reinsurer takes a loss, the insurance company keeps the premiums and the reinsurer must make up the difference. In addition to premiums withheld reinsurance, or sometimes as an alternative, the reinsurer is required to place an irrevocable *letter of credit* (LOC) with the insurance company being reinsured, which the insurance company can tap to pay claims as set forth in the reinsurance agreement.

Where a captive is used as a reinsurance company it may be required to post a LOC with the insurance company that it is reinsuring. Similarly, where the captive is itself purchasing reinsurance, it should normally require a LOC from the reinsurer. The point is that letters of credit are often used with captives as they buy and sell reinsurance.

Fronting

Captives have very limited insurance licenses, and are usually not *admitted carriers* (i.e., licensed insurance companies) in the jurisdictions they need to sell insurance. Often, the local jurisdiction by statute will allow the captive to sell insurance to a related business or it will give an exception for insurance that is not commercially available within the state, known as *surplus lines insurance*.

But sometimes there is no exception and the insurance simply cannot be written directly by the captive. This is often the case with workers compensation insurance and other types of insurance seen as necessary to protect workers or the public good.

There are also situations where a Certificate of Insurance is required from a licensed insurance company, and the captive doesn't qualify for this purpose. A health care facility may not accept, for example, a Certificate of Insurance from a non-admitted carrier for purposes of extending hospital privileges to a physician.

When the captive cannot sell insurance directly, the captive will have to make use of a *fronting arrangement* whereby a locally-licensed insurance company (known as the *fronting company*) sells the policy, collects premiums, and administers claims, and the captive is used strictly as a reinsurer of the insurance company. For its fee, the fronting company retains some percentage of the premium, such as 10% to compensate it for its risks and administrative expenses. The fronting relationship is shown in Figure 3.4.

Typical Fronting Relationship

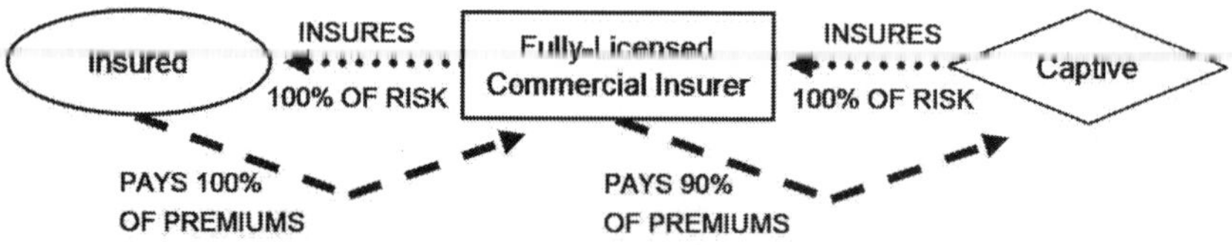

Figure 3.4

The fronting company will also likely require that the captive place a letter of credit to ensure that moneys are available to pay claims. The fronting company will also likely withhold the payment of premiums to the captive until all claims are resolved.

It is very important that a fronting arrangement be a long-term relationship, or else the captive will constantly be scrambling to find a company willing to provide fronting services. The availability of fronting arrangements should be determined during a feasibility analysis that evaluates the prospect of a captive.

Chapter 4

Types of Captives

There are many variations of captive structures, and multiple ways to categorize them. A *single-parent captive* is a captive with a single owner or is controlled by a small group of owners. A *multiple-parent captive* is a captive with many owners and is also known as a *group captive*.

Another categorization could be made based on the captive's customers. A *pure captive* only underwrites the risks of its owners. A captive that underwrites risks that are unrelated to the captive's owners (whether single-parent or group), or which participates in reinsurance business on the open market, is known as a *diversified captive*.

Pure Captive a/k/a Single-Parent Captive

The most straightforward captive structure is that of the pure captive, which primarily insures only the risks of other businesses owned by its owner. Most captives could be classified as pure captives. Because the captive has only one owner (or a close group of owners sharing the same business interests), the profits or losses of the captive are kept within the economic family.

Corporate Captive

The most traditional form of a pure captive is the *corporate captive*, which term usually refers to a captive that is owned by a large conglomerate or other publicly-traded company. Most of the world's largest companies have one or more captive insurance companies—for instance, the captive used by United Parcel Service was the subject of a court opinion that is provided in Appendix S, *infra*.

Special issues arise in the structuring of a corporate captive to make sure that the entity is fully transparent to auditors and that it is the shareholders and not a small group of insiders who are benefited. There can be significant issues under the Sarbanes-Oxley legislation that can affect the reporting of the captive insurance company's activities and its effect on the consolidated balance sheet of the publicly-traded parent.

MicroCaptives, MiniCaptives, and CHICs

Starting in the late 1990s, a new type of captive structure appeared that was aimed at wealthy private individuals and privately-held businesses. This structure is known as a *microcaptive* or a *501(c)(15) captive* and involves a captive that is designed to take in less than $350,000 per year in total premiums.

The growth of the microcaptive coincided with the stock market boom of the late 1990s and the desire of wealthy individuals with appreciated property to take advantage of special tax benefits offered to a small insurance company. This was a form of insurance company recognized as qualifying under section 501(c)(15) of the U.S. tax code that allowed the company to have totally unlimited untaxed investment income. These companies were used in part to avoid taxes on highly appreciated assets. Because of abuses (real and perceived), Congress effectively terminated those benefits as of the end of 2003.

Slightly larger than the microcaptive is the form of insurance company which takes in less than $1.2 million in premiums, and which is known as a *minicaptive* or *831(b) Captive*. This amount corresponds with the provisions of Section 831(b) of the U.S. tax code, which allows a company making less than $1.2 million in premiums per year to receive that premium without taxes so long as an election is made and certain other conditions are met. This is discussed in much more detail in Chapter 5 in relation to 831(b) captives.

A variation of a pure captive is where the captive is owned by the business owner's children or grandchildren, but is still used to underwrite the risks of the business. This type of structure is known as a *closely-held insurance company* (CHIC, pronounced "chick").

There are two primary advantages to the CHIC arrangement. First, all the insurance underwritten can, in some instances, be considered third-party insurance for purposes of determining certain tax treatment. Second, the payment of premiums from the business to the captive effectuates a generational wealth transfer that is not subject to any federal gift or estate taxes.

Group Captive

A captive that is used to underwrite the risks of a number of persons or businesses that are members of an organization or have similar interests is known as a *group captive.* Since these risks are the same for each member, they are said to be *homogeneous risks* (as opposed to be *heterogeneous risks* which encompass a range of diverse risks).

A group captive may insure certain risks of individuals and are usually formed to increase the members' buying power. For instance, a yacht club's captive that offers hull and loss insurance to its members is a type of group captive known as an *association captive.*

A group captive may also insure the risks of businesses. They are often created to obtain insurance that is otherwise unobtainable in the open market or is overpriced. An example of this would be a captive formed by a group of mining companies that offers insurance to members of the group. A captive that offers insurance primarily to businesses in the same or similar trade is known as an *industry captive.*

The organization of a group captive is usually as either a *stock company* with each member-insured owning some shares of stock in the captive, or as a *mutual company* with each member-insured owning an interest in the company based on some calculation. Because the profits and losses of a group captive are considered those of the member-insureds in the aggregate and of no one member-insured in particular, the activities of a group captive are reported independently.

Because group captives sell insurance to so many people or businesses, they are much more tightly regulated than single-parent captives. The insurance commissioner will require significant additional capitalization (usually a minimum of $1 million) and much higher reserves. Similarly, the investment of the reserves will be more tightly regulated since significant investment losses could expose the insureds.

There are many types of group captives; we'll discuss some of the most popular ones.

Agency Captives and PORCs

An *agency captive* is, simply enough, a captive insurance company owned by insurance brokers or agents to provide insurance to their clients. This gives the brokers or agents the chance to capture a share of the underwriting profit that would ordinarily by kept by the commercial insurer.

Often, the clients of the brokers or agents will not even realize they are dealing with a captive because a *fronting company* is used, i.e., a commercial insurer issues the policies and collects premiums, but the risks are actually shifted to the broker's or agent's captive as reinsurance. This type of captive is sometimes called a *producer-owned reinsurance company* (PORC), and is often seen with insuring relationships involving automobile warranty companies.

Branch and Sponsored Captives

Sometimes a foreign captive cannot insure risks domestically, such as where employee benefit risks regulated under ERISA are involved. The solution is for the offshore captive to create and own a domestic captive, known in this context as a *branch captive*, to cover the special risk. The characteristic of such a captive is that it is owned by the foreign captive and not by the parent directly.

Sometimes several insurance or reinsurance companies will get together and capitalize a captive to serve a special purpose, such as to segregate certain types of risks or the risks of a particular insured. Such a captive is referred to as a *sponsored captive*, and is often implemented by a captive with segregated cell provisions that theoretically limits the liability of each sponsoring insurer.

Rent-A-Captive

Sometimes businesses are too small to justify forming their own captive. In an attempt—and I stress "attempt"—to provide these businesses with captive-like benefits, the concept of the *rent-a-captive* was created in the late 1990s. The rent-a-captive simply involves an insurance company that accepts the insured's risk, provides capital to back the risk, and then pays the insured a percentage of the underwriting profits or charges the insured for underwriting losses (usually against a letter of credit that the insured places with the insurance company when the policy is issued).

Types of Captives   33

The upside of a rent-a-captive is that there are no captive start-up costs and no capital is required (though, as mentioned, the insured will usually be required to place a letter of credit with the insurance company to protect it against any losses). The downside of a rent-a-captive is that all of the control is with the insurance company, the insurance company will charge a substantial percentage of the premiums paid to use the insurance facility, and—most importantly— nobody really knows how well a rent-a-captive structure will stand up for U.S. tax purposes as to deductibility of premiums paid.

Many rent-a-captive insurance companies are created as *segregated cell companies*, which are insurance companies created in a jurisdiction that recognizes so-called "series" or "cell" legislation that allows for internal separation of liability for each cell within the company from the others. Think of a segregated cell company as a honeycomb, where specific risks are placed in each cell to the exclusion of the others. In the rent-a-captive context, each cell is "rented" out to a particular insured who pays for the use of the cell but receives back underwriting profits.

While a rent-a-captive appears to be a group captive, when the structure is collapsed it is apparent that a rent-a-captive relationship is much more like that of a Pure Captive, i.e., having only one insured. Because of this, there may not be sufficient risk-sharing and risk-shifting to satisfy the IRS test for whether a recognizable insurance relationship exists. Another downside of a rent-a-captive is that it really is true self-insurance in the sense that the insurance company being used is not actually covering any risks. Finally, there is always the concern of what happens if the insurance company being used gets hit with a big claim— the creditor might clean out all of the assets of the insurance company including those being used to back individual risks.

Risk Retention Group (RRG)

Very similar to a group captive is the *risk retention group* (RRG) which is an insurance licensed in at least one U.S. state and which meets certain requirements under the Federal Liability Risk Retention Act (LRRA), see Appendix A, the most important of which is that it underwrites insurance for its insureds/owners for homogeneous risks. The primary benefit of an RRG is that once it has been licensed in a state and qualifies under the LRRA, it can operate in any other state without additional licensing—effectively, a nationwide captive insurance company.

An RRG is a member-owned business association that is formed specifically for the purpose of pooling and sharing similar business risks. Originally passed by Congress as the Product Liability Risk Retention Act of 1981, it was drafted to help manufacturers survive the product liability crisis which existed then. The Act was later expanded into the LRRA and renamed in 1986 to allow RRGs to cover a much broader range of risks. In recent years, RRGs have been used by physician groups and hospital associations to attempt to alleviate the medical malpractice insurance crisis in many states.

RRGs must be licensed in at least one state or the District of Columbia, but once licensed they are allowed under the federal Liability Risk Retention Act of 1986 (which specifically preempts contrary state laws) to underwrite the insurance risks of its members nationwide, including giving preferential rates, terms and conditions to groups seeking liability insurance coverage.

The members of an RRG must be engaged in the same or similar businesses, at least so far as the liability exposures are concerned. Interestingly, insurance companies are forbidden from being members of an RRG unless all the other members are insurance companies. RRGs are exempt from federal and state securities registration but must make full disclosures of all their operations to their members.

RRGs are effectively exempt from state law except that the states can still collect premium and surplus taxes, force compliance with unfair claim settlement practices, and follow a few other requirements common to insurance companies. The states may not, however, dictate rates, coverages, forms, methods of operations or investment activities, loss control or claims, etc. RRGs can thus underwrite most types of general liability policies, such as Errors & Omissions and Products Liability insurance, etc., but RRGs are not allowed to underwrite insurance relating to employees, such as workers' compensation, or personal lines insurance to consumers, such as auto insurance.

A key benefit to the use of RRGs is that, because each policyholder is also a member who participates in profits, each policyholder has substantial incentive to engage in proactive risk management to try to avoid claims, instead of just "let the insurance company take care of it." The members also can adopt better loss-control and more quickly identify other members whose risk-management is lax, and either assist them in upgrading their risk management or else invite them to take their insurance business elsewhere. Indeed, it is the fact that the members of an RRG know their business better than anybody else that often gives the RRG an underwriting edge over insurance companies.

RRGs are commonly used in conjunction with its members' captive insurance companies. The idea is that the RRGs pool a certain layer of risk, and then each member's captive reinsures the RRG for the remaining layers. Captives are also used to reinsure the particular risks of the members who own the captives. This arrangement may be necessary if the member's captive insurance company is domiciled outside the United States and is not admitted to underwrite business in the states where the RRG is operating. When used in this fashion, the RRG effectively becomes, quite legally, the fronting company for the members' captives.

For example, assume that Members A, B, and C form a Risk Retention Group to offer products liability insurance coverage of up to $1 million for each of the members. Historically, the losses of each member have averaged about $50,000 per year. Members A, B, and C each also have captive insurance companies, and their captives reinsure the RRG for their own annual claims exceeding $100,000 per member. Thus, the members have pooled their risks for their first $100,000 losses each per member, and have accepted the risks of losses exceeding this amount. Members B and C now need not worry if Member A has losses of $1 million in a given year, since their exposure as to Member A's liability is capped at $100,000 by the reinsurance policy given by Member A's captive.

Physician Groups

Many physicians would like to create a captive to reduce their medical malpractice insurance costs. In the years that I have been putting together captives, I have probably had no less than 500 physicians contact me about a captive. Most of them have the misconception that for a few thousand dollars they can form a captive, easily access the reinsurance markets, and reduce the premiums for their liability insurance from $60,000 to $30,000 or some number.

Of course, these physicians don't realize the cost of forming and annually running the captive, and their assumptions about obtaining cheap reinsurance deflate when they learn that the reinsurance companies usually will not have an interest in reinsuring a single policy. I've had a few physicians go forward and form single-parent captives, but these were for things such as issuing product liability coverage on patents they own and other things outside of their medical malpractice coverage.

What has proven to work for larger groups of physicians are risk retention groups. Recall that a risk retention group is much like a mutual insurance company, where the insureds own the RRG and share in any underwriting profits by way of dividends. An RRG allows physicians to set up their own insurance company relatively cheaply and with light regulation. RRGs work best when the physicians impose strict risk management requirements upon the physician insureds.

Physicians' RRGs are typically bundled with a captive that acts as a reinsurer. The underwriting profits are thus shifted in substantial part to the captive, which is owned by trusts set up for the physicians' children. This allows the underwriting profits to both pass outside the physicians' estate for tax purposes and away from the physicians' ownership in case a creditor (such as a medical malpractice plaintiff) obtains a judgment against a particular physician. This structure is shown in Figure 4.1.

Physicians' RRG-Captive Structure

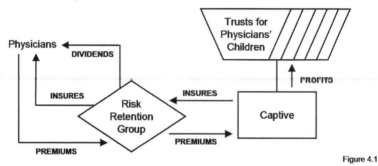

Figure 4.1

A physicians' RRG can be a good investment for the several physicians who initially form it, since they can earn officers' and directors' fees for participating in management and also own the captive that is used for reinsurance and charge a fee to use it. The physicians' RRG concept is so attractive that they constitute a large percentage of nationwide RRG formations.

To get a physicians' RRG together, at least $1 million in capital is required. It is usually better if several physicians put up this capital, but it could, for instance, be spread over a group of 20 who put up $50,000 each.

Chapter 5

Captive Taxation

Captives are inherently creatures of the tax laws. Were it not for the tax laws, most businesses would simply keep internal reserves against future claims. The tax laws, however, prevent an ordinary business from accruing such reserves, yet they allow the parent to set up a captive to insure the risks of the business owned by the parent.

The taxation of captives is something that is poorly understood by even many of those who are involved with the industry—primarily the insurance managers and insurance agents who have little background or experience in complex tax matters. Thus, many captives are formed and maintained in a defective fashion as it relates to taxes and their owners will be blissfully unaware of any problems until a terse letter shows up from the IRS.

That is why it is critically important that competent tax counsel be retained at the outset to review the proposed captive arrangement, to make necessary adjustments, and then to be available to periodically review the arrangement to ensure compliance. It is also very important that a competent CPA firm specifically experienced in captive insurance taxation be retained to do the company's tax returns. There are relatively few CPA firms that are familiar with captives, but these firms are worth their weight in gold since their advice can head off problems before they materialize.

Until several years ago, the tax laws relating to captive insurance companies were uncertain. The IRS attempted to ignore captives for years, arguing only in a few cherry-picked cases that since the captive was owned by the same parent as the operating business, there was no true insurance so far as the parent was concerned. In effect, the IRS argued, the parent was simply using the captive as a sham to create tax-deductible reserves in the captive where it couldn't create them in the operating business.

This was the so-called "economic family" challenge against captives. The IRS tried it in a bunch of cases, and usually lost. In the biggest "economic family" challenge, the IRS lost a case against United Parcel Service's captive where over $500 million in deductions were in dispute. After that, the IRS abandoned the economic family challenge and instead started concentrating on the definition of "insurance".

So how is "insurance" defined for tax purposes? The primary authority on what constitutes "insurance" is a single sentence in a short U.S. Supreme Court opinion decided on the eve of World War II and does not having anything to do with captive insurance where it was said: "Historically and commonly insurance involves risk-shifting and risk-distributing."[1]

So there you have it. Insurance means that you have (1) a risk transferred from one party to another, *i.e., risk shifting*; and (2) a risk that is spread over some undefined number of claims, *i.e., risk-distributing*. As we've already discussed, the IRS first attempted to claim that there is no risk shifting in a captive insurance situation because both the insured and insurer are in the same economic family. Later, after losing on that theory in nearly every court case, the IRS finally abandoned that position.

One thing that was established in the IRS's favor, however, is that there is no insurance when a subsidiary (such as a captive) insures the parent. Thus, a captive only works when it is used to insure other businesses owned by the same parent, but not the parent itself. Insurance premiums paid by the parent to the captive will not be deductible.[2]

The IRS's primary challenge is now on risk-distribution. In other words: Is the captive issuing enough policies to different insureds such that the risk is sufficiently spread around to constitute "insurance" for tax purposes?

---

[1]   *Helvering v. Le Gierse*, 312 U.S. 531, 61 S.Ct. 646 (1941).

[2]   *Stearns-Roger Corp. v. U.S.*, 774 F. 2d 414 (1985); *Beech Aircraft Corp. v. U.S.*, 797 F. 2d 920 (1986); Gulf Oil Corporation v. U.S., 89 T.C. No. 70 (1987).

At the risk of over-simplifying, there are basically two ways that the test for risk distribution can be met:

(1) by assuring a certain minimal percentage of the captive's underwriting is *third-party risk*, i.e., risks of insureds that are not directly or indirectly affiliated with the captive or

(2) by underwriting a minimal number of insureds, such as 11 or more insureds, even if they are affiliated with the captive.

The Percentage Safe Harbor

The first possible way of meeting the test—underwriting a minimal percentage of third-party risk—is the most uncertain of the two tests for the reason that nobody knows exactly what the minimal percentage is. The court in *Gulf Oil*, Appendix M, found risk distribution unacceptable where the percentage of third-party risk was a mere 2%. For years, there was an unofficial safe harbor established by off-the-record statements by IRS officials that they would not challenge captives that were underwriting at least 30% third-party risks.

The new safe harbor is 50% third-party risks. So long as the captive is underwriting at least 50% of the risks of unaffiliated third-parties, the IRS will typically not challenge the captive relationship.

Captives usually satisfy the 50% third-party risks by finding quality reinsurance risks to underwrite. In other words, the captive sells reinsurance to another insurance company and receives a premium in return. This allows the other insurance company to lay off a part of its risk to the captive, and gives the captive both a chance to make a profit from the risk and satisfy the 50% third-party risk requirement.

Typically, the captive's insurance manager will help the captive's owners to identify quality reinsurance risks for the captive to underwrite. These risks will normally be safe risks in the sense that the loss ratio will be very predictable and the odds of the captive suffering a net loss will be low, but it also usually means that the captive's profits for selling reinsurance will be limited.

The 11 Insureds Safe Harbor

By far, most single-parent captives qualify under the percentage safe harbor test because the parent doesn't have 11 or more subsidiaries for the captive to offer insurance to. But where there are 11 or more subsidiaries for the captive to underwrite, the third-party insurance can be dispensed with.

The second possible way of meeting the risk distribution test is for the captive to have at least 11 or more insureds. This test can be met even if every insured is an affiliated company. However, entities that are disregarded for tax purposes, such as a single-member LLC, do not count towards the 11 and are instead treated as if they are the parent.

For instance, assume that a real estate development company has 11 projects and each of these projects is in an LLC. The LLCs are not single-member LLCs and are not disregarded for tax purposes. In this case, the risk-distribution requirements would be met to validate the captive relationships and make the premiums paid to the captive fully deductible. But if the LLCs were single-member LLCs, they would be disregarded and treated as if they were the parent (and it will be recalled that the parent's premium payments to the captive are not deductible)

The 11 Insureds Safe Harbor is set out in Revenue Ruling 2005-40, which is Appendix K to this book. This Revenue Ruling was actually a godsend to the U.S. captive community, since it finally set out guidelines that captive arrangements could safely follow to qualify for the deductibility of premiums paid.

Other Factors Still Important

Even if a captive qualifies under the safe harbor provisions of Revenue Ruling 2005-40, it does not mean that the captive relationship will be automatically validated. Instead, the captive may still have to prove the following:

- The insured parties truly face hazards;
- Premiums charged by the captive are based on commercial rates;
- The risks are shifted and distributed to the insurance company, since the entities are commercially and economically related;
- The policies contain provisions such that the covered risks may exceed the amount of premiums charged and paid;

- The validity of claims are established before payments are made;
- The premiums of the operating subsidiaries were determined at arms-length;
- The premiums were pooled such that a loss by one operating subsidiary is borne, in substantial part, by the premiums paid by others; and,
- The captive and its insureds conducted themselves in all respects as unrelated parties would in a traditional relationship.

Is the Captive an Insurance Company for Tax Purposes?

In addition to challenges to the deductibility of insurance premiums paid to the captive, the IRS may also challenge the captive itself to determine whether it qualifies as an insurance company. Merely having an insurance license does not mean that the captive will be treated as an insurance company for tax law purposes. Instead, the captive must be prepared to prove all of the following:

- The captive is regulated as an insurance company wherever it does business;
- An adequate amount of capital was present within the insurance company;
- The insurance company is able to pay claims;
- The insurance company's financial performance is adequate;
- The captive's business operations and assets are kept separate from the business operations and assets of its shareholders; and
- The captive maintains separate financial reporting from the parent and any affiliated companies.

These are not the only factors that the IRS will look at, but they are some of the most important factors. What the IRS wants to see is a real insurance company acting like, well, a real insurance company. What the IRS doesn't want to see is a thinly-capitalized corporate shell masquerading as an insurance company so that a nice fat deduction is artificially created without any real risks actually being underwritten. The IRS has effectively conceded the legitimacy of true captive arrangements, but will aggressively challenge shams.

Again, it is a common mistake for planners to presume that because the captive has a license to act as an insurance company, it is *ipso facto* an insurance company for tax law purposes. While the fact of the insurance license is a helpful factor, it is not at all dispositive.

The 953(d) Election

Certain insurance companies domiciled outside the U.S. may qualify under the tax code for the 953(d) election. This would allow the captive to be taxed as a domestic company and avoid most of the foreign company reporting requirements. Once the election is made, it is good for all subsequent tax years, unless terminated.

Most offshore captives that have onshore risks will make the 953(d) election to avoid the 4% federal excise tax (FET) on premiums paid to the captive (or 1% for reinsurance premiums), as set out in section 4371. If the 953(d) election has been made, then section 4371 does not apply because the insurance company will be treated as a domestic company.

501(c)(15) MicroCaptives

Once upon a time, there was a type of insurance company that was totally free of all taxes, including any taxes on investment income, and with few limitations. This was the 501(c)(15) insurance company, sometimes known as a *microcaptive* or an *exempt captive*. Unfortunately, it was abused by some advisors who used it primarily to avoid the capital gains on appreciated assets.

In one well-publicized case, a 501(c)(15) captive was set up and capitalized with over $100 million in appreciated stock while the captive was only receiving a few thousand dollars a year in premiums. The taxpayer was able to use the captive to liquidate the appreciated stock without any immediate capital gains taxes being due.

Similarly, 501(c)(15) was misused by auto dealers who attempted to transform their warranty operations into tax-free income streams by way of what was called a *producer owned reinsurance company* (PORC). For about a year, PORCs were on the list of transactions that the IRS considered to be abusive tax shelters. The IRS later took PORCs off the list when section 501(c)(15) changed so as to eliminate the concept.

The abuses of 501(c)(15) caused Congress to change the provision as of the end of 2003 so as to limit the entity to $600,000 in gross receipts, 50% of which must be insurance premiums. The effect is that no 501(c)(15) company can have more than $300,000 in investment income per year. This, of course, killed off 501(c)(15) for all but the smallest insurance companies.

Surprisingly, even at the time of the writing of this book four years after Congress changed the law, some captive owners and advisors had still not gotten the word about the changes to 501(c)(15) and were attempting to form and run their captives as if the law had not changed. They will be in for an unpleasant surprise when the inevitable audit comes. The importance of having good tax counsel and a good CPA firm to keep up with changes in the tax laws is once again illustrated.

The 501(c)(15) companies contributed to a significant degree to the overall numbers of captive insurance companies formed. From an estimated 690 tax-exempt captives in 1995 to an estimated 1,600 such companies in 2002, the 501(c)(15) companies helped to create captives as an industry even though many of these companies did not survive the changes to the tax code.

831(b) MiniCaptives

After the demise of the 501(c)(15) microcaptives, those who were interested in forming new and smallish captives turned to the provisions of 831(b). The 831(b) election is an incentive given by Congress to encourage the formation of new insurance companies, and add competition into the insurance marketplace. Whereas the investment income of a 501(c)(15) company was tax exempt, an 831(b) company is not so lucky and its investment income is taxed like any other non-life insurance company. By way of partial compensation, an 831(b) company can accept up to $1.2 million of premium income each year totally tax-free by electing to be taxed on its investment income only.

An election of 831(b) treatment must be timely made. Without this election, there can be no 831(b) treatment. Once the election has been made, it can only be revoked with the approval of the Secretary of the Treasury. This latter restriction was doubtless meant to prevent an insurance company from jumping back-and-forth to 501(c)(15) treatment every so often.

A strange quirk of an 831(b) company is that it must take in at least $350,000 in premiums to qualify for that treatment. This is a statutory rule that is left over from when the upper limits of premiums allowed in a 501(c)(15) company was that amount. This minimum limit to 831(b) companies should have been discarded when 501(c)(15) was gutted but, due to careless legislative drafting, it survived.

That an 831(b) company can take in up to $1.2 million per year tax-free is still a significant advantage, since the operating company being underwritten will have a deduction for that amount for the insurance premiums paid. In other words, an 831(b) company has the ability to legally shelter—without having to file a tax-shelter registration statement—up to $1.2 million per year, each and every year. When claims are paid, they are paid with pre-tax dollars and are not recaptured as income.

Chapter 6

Formation and Licensing

The captive markets are well-developed and the procedures and pricing models for forming and licensing captives are also well-developed. The best model follows a three-phase approach that allows a prospective owner to incrementally approach the captive concept without committing all resources at once.

Phase One involves an initial feasibility study by an attorney or captive consultant to determine if a captive is indeed a good fit for the prospective owner. Preliminary tax and asset protection planning issues are addressed in this stage as well. This is where the captive is creatively designed to fit within the owner's overall wealth transfer and preservation plan.

Phase Two is the actuarial study, which reviews the anticipated coverages that the captive will underwrite, and also makes estimates as to what capitalization the new captive will require, how premiums will be priced, and what risks will be covered. The actuarial study is usually required to be submitted with the insurance license application, so the study necessarily precedes the application process (although often the study is conducted concurrently with the creation of the application to save time).

Phase Three is the actual submission of the insurance application to the Insurance Commissioner, the formation of the company, and all necessarily ancillary planning such as creating trusts or LLCs to hold the shares of the captive. Most of the labor-intensive work in creating a captive is here in Phase Three.

The following chart illustrates the typical cost of each of these phases, and thus the total cost for a turnkey captive structure:

Phase	Typical Cost
Initial Feasibility Study & Planning	$10,000
Actuarial Study	$25,000
Application, Formation, Licensing and Ancillary Business/Estate Structuring	=======
TOTAL	$100,000

The all-inclusive turnkey cost for a small, non-corporate captive is around $100,000. The fees for application and formation, etc., are often split one-half to start the application process and the other half due when the authorization to form the captive is given by the insurance commissioner.

This $100,000 fee could easily vary as much as $20,000 towards the cheap and $50,000 for the expensive, depending on the complexity of the situation and other factors. But if a captive provided on a turnkey basis costs less than $80,000 then you must really wonder about the quality of the planning and work you are getting, i.e., are you getting the captive equivalent of a Yugo. Likewise, if the estimated bill for a captive exceeds $150,000 then you should get a clear explanation of why the fees are so high.

The real key to finding efficiency in pricing versus quality is to have a good attorney or captive consultant who has experience with the better managers and other necessary team members, and who does enough work in this area that he or she can beat down the providers on costs for you. One of the worse things you can do is to find somebody with only slight experience in captives and does not make it a regular part of their practice. There could be significant additional costs if important issues are not resolved in advance.

Team

Very few captive insurance companies, and especially the smaller ones, have any regular employees. Instead, all the services that would have been provided by the captive's employees are outsourced to various service providers, such as actuarial, underwriting and accounting services. These providers, along with the estate and tax planning counsel that provide the ancillary structuring, constitute the *captive team* and allow the parent to own a captive without having to spend substantial time running it themselves.

The success or failure of a captive is often determined very early in the process when the team that will assist in the evaluation, formation and operation of the captive is put together. Assembly of a competent and cohesive team of planners is one of the most important parts of the captive formation process. Moreover, the more impressive the team, the more quickly the insurance application is apt to be granted.

Some team members are mandatory in most jurisdictions; usually, these are the local insurance manager, auditor, and actuary. These three are usually required to be licensed or qualified to perform their respective roles in the jurisdiction where the captive is formed. The most common additional team members include the attorney/consultant who is involved in the initial feasibility study and the ancillary trust and corporate planning, an investment advisor to address the captive's assets, and a tax attorney to opine on the deductibility of premiums and to insure the captive arrangement qualifies as an insurance company for tax purposes.

Feasibility Study

Creating a captive is so much more than simply obtaining a license and writing insurance. To form a captive means to create a new and valuable asset, one that will serve the insurance needs of the related businesses for years and potentially be a generational wealth transfer tool for the family. A captive should not be viewed as a loophole tax shelter or as a temporary bandage against high current insurance costs. Instead, it must be considered as a long term and independently valuable asset and tool for wealth accumulation and preservation.

The creation of an effective and efficient captive structure requires a great deal of forethought and creativity before the application process even begins. Issues such as how the captive will be owned, how it will be capitalized, what risks will be covered, and how much capital will be required are all questions that must be answered before the application process starts in earnest.

There is also the fundamental question that must be answered: Does a captive make sense in this case? The main purpose of a feasibility analysis is to determine if there are any significant roadblocks to the formation or successful operation of the captive. To this end, a feasibility analysis is also a fact-gathering process. The prospective captive owner will need to provide full coverage and loss experience information, as well as information necessary for a tax analysis—usually the last several years' business and personal tax returns.

My personal experience is that captives do not always work for those who believe they need one. The numbers simply do not work out, they do not have the requisite capital and cash flow, or they do not understand that what they will end up with is an operating insurance company that must be managed and treated as an operating insurance company to be effective.

These questions should be answered by way of a pre-application *feasibility analysis* that lays out the general diagram for the overall captive structure and the strategy for using it effectively to serve the purposes for which it will be formed. The suggested team members (captive managers, actuaries, accountants) should be identified, and capitalization, coverage, and governance issues should be addressed. The analysis should also give a comparison of insurance costs and tax costs of the economic family both with and without the captive.

While the feasibility analysis is the first, smallest, and least expensive part of the puzzle—it is by far the most important. With a good feasibility analysis, the rest of the captive formation should thereafter be a connect-the-dots experience.

The cost of a quality feasibility analysis is currently in the $10,000 range, although most attorneys or consultants who perform the analysis will return all or a significant part of this fee if it ultimately leads to a "no go" recommendation. This allows a prospective captive client to obtain quality help in making an initial evaluation without committing the total fees required through formation and licensing.

For instance, my personal practice is to not even start the feasibility analysis unless I believe there is a better-than-not chance that the captive will make sense for a client, and then to refund anywhere from one-half to all of the fee (depending on how much time I have spent) if my ultimate recommendation is that the captive would not work in the particular client's case. I also bill to conduct a feasibility analysis on a one-half up front and the other one-half due when the completed *planning memo* setting forth my findings and recommendations is presented to the client.

Some insurance managers will perform a cheapie feasibility analysis for free that considers only the formation of the captive and insurance costs, but does not look at the larger business structure. Such planning may ultimately lead to the successful creation of a captive, but it is doubtful that the arrangement will be anywhere near optimally efficient within the economic family because insurance managers tend to look at captives in isolation to the exclusion of other business, tax, estate planning and asset protection planning needs.

Actuarial Study

After the feasibility analysis is completed, the next step is to have an *actuarial study* performed. This is a detailed study by an accredited actuary of the proposed risks to be underwritten by the captive, what range of premiums should be charged for that insurance, and what capital and reserves will be necessary to adequately back those risks.

While not strictly required to obtain a captive license, some jurisdictions strongly suggest that an actuarial study be performed in advance of the insurance application. A detailed actuarial study will leave the insurance commissioner with a good impression and possibly speed the licensing process. Certainly, for purposes of justifying the captive relationship to the IRS it is strongly suggested that an actuarial study be done before the captive is formed.

The actuarial study usually requires that detailed loss information be made available to the actuary, who will use this information along with relevant industry data to reach conclusions. The more detailed information given to the actuary, the better the evaluation will be. The materials reviewed include historical loss patterns, loss exposures, and instances of large or unusual losses.

The price for a quality actuarial study for a small captive is currently around $25,000 although more complex studies can easily run into the six-figures. Studies can take six weeks or longer, although this time delay usually seems to be more a function of the prospective owner getting loss data to the actuary than anything else. Some actuaries who limit their services to the captive market can often produce a quality study in much less time.

Application

The application for an insurance license is submitted to the Insurance Commissioner where the captive is to be formed. The application will normally be required to present the following information:

Personal information about the company's shareholders, directors and officers. This is to determine their reputation, credibility and trustworthiness, and what experience they have or do not have in the insurance business. Automatic disqualifiers are criminal records and recent bankruptcies. Often, a current resume is required. It is not unusual for insurance commissioners to hire private investigators to check the backgrounds of those making an application for a captive and to obtain additional information such as creditworthiness.

The persons who will be affiliated with the insurance company in an ownership or management capacity will usually be required to provide *letters of references* from a bank and two professionals. The letters must be provided on the bank's or professionals' letterhead and will blandly and simply recite, "X has kept an account for Y years and has managed it satisfactorily," or "I have known X for Y years and she has managed her affairs satisfactorily".

Where a captive has a corporate owner, the financial statements of the parent must usually be provided to demonstrate that the parent has the financial strength to properly support the captive.

Information about the company to be formed. This part requests information such as the number and class of shares to be authorized and issued, and how much capital will be initially injected into the company.

Some insurance commissioners require that copies of the Articles of Incorporation and Bylaws to be provided.

The name of the company is also requested, which is an oddity because the company usually hasn't been formed yet. Typically, a particular name for the company will be reserved before the application process starts and this is the name used in the application.

Business Plan. By far the largest and most difficult part of the insurance application is the business plan, which describes for the commissioner how the company will conduct the business of insurance for which it seeks licensure.

Although the strict requirements vary from jurisdiction to jurisdiction, the following information will either be required or strongly suggested to be contained in the business plan:

- **Structure of Governance**—Identifies the ultimate beneficial owners of the captive, how they will elect directors, the initial directors, how the board of directors will function, and how officers will be elected.

- **Management**—The persons who will have day-to-day control over issuing policies, investing reserves and surplus, and paying claims, etc., will be identified.

- **Service Providers**—Designates the local firms that will act as the insurance manager and auditor, both of which are usually required to be licensed or approved in the local jurisdiction, as well as actuaries, underwriters, attorneys, and any other necessary professionals which the insurance company may be required to hire. These firms will often be required to give a written statement or letter for attachment to the application which says that they have been formally retained.

- **Capital Requirements**—Based upon the actuarial study, the plan will set forth the amount of capital to be contributed to the captive, and the type of assets to be contributed (stock, land, etc.), if not cash.

- **Investment Policies**—Describes where and how the reserves and surplus of the captive are to be held and invested.

- **Pro Forma Financial Statements**—Spreadsheets are attached to the application, based on actuarial and other assumptions, that make at least a five-year estimate of the captive's cash flow, rate of return on investments, effects on the parent's consolidated earnings before income tax, interest, depreciation and amortization, and similar factors.

- **Design and Purpose of the Captive**—An overview of the type of insurance business that the captive intends to conduct should be given, i.e., construction defects insurance, environmental insurance, etc., and how the captive's insurance program has been designed to conduct that business.

- **Coverage and Limits**—The coverage to be extended, the type of coverage, deductibles, and any coverage limits should be described.

- **Insureds**—Identifies who will be insured by the captive, i.e., other businesses held by the owner of the captive, group members, etc., which is very important to make sure that the captive stays within its very limited license and does not intend to sell insurance directly to the general public.

- **Fronting Requirements**—Describes those situations where the captive will need to use the services of a front company, which is an insurance company licensed to conduct insurance business in the jurisdiction where the captive wants to sell insurance but has no license.

- **Reinsurance Requirements**—This section discusses the captive's need for reinsurance, such as stop-loss coverage.

- **Risk Management and Claims Practices**—Details the procedures the insurance company will take to minimize risks and pay claims.

- **Economic Impact Statement**—Sometimes called an application for a *Certificate of Public Good*, this is an informational filing that describes how the local jurisdiction will be benefited by the captive, which usually means how many people will be hired locally to assist with the captive operation.

- **Fees**—The last thing that is enclosed with the application is a check for the application fee and any review fees or other expenses. The total fees typically range between $3,000 to as much as $12,000 for a simple captive license depending on the domicile chosen and the class of the license.

A good captive manager will assemble the application and hand-deliver it to the Commissioner along with a personal explanation of any highlights or unusual issues. By advising the Commissioner in advance of special issues, the issues tend to be resolved much more quickly leading to a more expeditious granting of the application.

Meeting with the Insurance Commissioner

Most jurisdictions require some sort of interview with the Insurance Commissioner before the application is granted. Usually, this is done by the local insurance manager who physically takes the application over to the Commissioner's office and explains to the Commissioner the purpose of the captive and the highlights of the application.

Some U.S. jurisdictions require a personal meeting between the owners of the prospective captive and the Commissioner, and strongly suggest that the meeting take place before the captive application is submitted. Personally, I have found that the application tends to be granted more quickly if it is filed first and then the meeting with the Commissioner takes place, since then the meeting is fresh on the Commissioner's mind and the processing of the application can begin immediately.

Formation and Licensing

It is important to understand the order in which an insurance company is formed and licensed. Because the jurisdiction will not allow the formation of a company with "Insurance Company" in its name unless it will be a licensed insurance company, the company does not even exist at the time the insurance application is submitted. Instead here are the steps:

1. The insurance application is approved by the Insurance Commissioner, who issues a Statement of Authority that allows the formation of the insurance company;

2. The Statement of Authority is taken to the Secretary of State or Financial Services office and a Certificate of Incorporation that forms the captive is issued;

3. The captive is capitalized by depositing cash into a bank account in the name of the captive; and,

4. Upon proof of the Certificate of Incorporation and capitalization, the Commissioner then issues the insurance license to the captive and it is thereafter in business.

The original corporate books and records, and usually the insurance license as well, are often required to be kept in the jurisdiction of formation. Usually, the insurance manager keeps the books and records, as well as audited financial statements and information relating to current underwriting activity, claims, reserves, etc., available for the Insurance Commissioner to inspect at any time. But many captives will keep a duplicate set of books and records with their accounting firm.

Capitalization

Before the insurance license will be issued, the insurance company must be capitalized. Usually, this means little more than setting-up a bank account for the captive and wire-transferring money to it. But it may also mean transferring stock accounts or real property to the captive, which is often a more difficult task requiring the assistance of an experienced tax attorney.

A caution that the minimum reserve requirements set forth in the various captive statutes are just that—minimums. Depending on what the captive will be doing, the Commissioner often requires additional capitalization. The Commissioner will also require that a certain amount of the captive's reserves be kept in cash or equivalents and immediately available to administer claims; this amount is rarely less than $100,000.

Ancillary Structuring

Once the decision to form the captive has been made, the creation of trusts and other entities, such as a limited liability company to hold and protect the shares in the captive, should be substantially completed while the actuarial study is being made and the application is being processed. Typically, this planning must be substantially completed before the captive is formed. Trying to do it after formation can lead to serious tax headaches, unnecessary expenses, and the loss of valuable opportunities.

Ongoing Management

Formation is just one piece of a successful captive, and arguably the least important piece. While proper planning is critical, the ongoing management of the captive will ultimately be determinative of the captive's failure or success.

After the captive is up and running, the role of the insurance manager is arguably the most important for it will be the insurance manager that determines what risks to underwrite and drafts policies. While actuarial assistance in evaluating risks and setting premiums and reserves will be important, it will be the insurance manager that takes a leadership role for the captive and insures that the captive stays in compliance with the terms of its license and meets all regulatory requirements and deadlines.

Nearly all jurisdictions require that the captive be audited on an annual basis by an accounting firm that has been approved by the Insurance Commissioner. The accounting firm should be one that specializes in captive insurance and can steer the captive away from the numerous tax landmines hidden in the Internal Revenue Code.

If there will be many claims, such as where the captive has insured a deductible, they should be handled by a *third-party administrator* (TPA), which is a company that specializes in risk management and claims resolution.

The captive program should be constantly reevaluated to determine whether additional risks could be underwritten or whether existing risks being covered have become more cheaply insured by commercial insurance. Where the captive will make a significant change to its operations or ownership structure, the Insurance Commissioner must typically be notified.

Chapter 7

Policies

Captives offer two huge advantages over buying insurance from a commercial insurance company. First, you can create whatever type of coverage for the operating business that you can dream up. Second, you can draft the policies according to whatever terms you desire. The only limits to these two advantages is that they must fall within the minimal bounds of commercial reasonableness, i.e., don't think that you can create coverage for falling space junk and thereby create a valid deduction for your business.

Business Liability

Liability policies cover claims that would be made against the operating business by third-party claimants. Every company is exposed to various types of liabilities. Obviously, some companies more than others depending on the nature of the business. Most businesses have insurance coverage against the most common liabilities for businesses of that type, but are "naked" on other risks. Against these risks, it is possible to draft several different types of policies, such as:

- **Direct Policies.** These are policies which would directly pay claimants and pay your legal defense fees and expenses. These types of policies are not preferred for captives since they potentially create an asset for plaintiffs to chase.

- **Policies of Indemnification.** These are policies that would indemnify you for claims only (only you could decide whether to make a claim) and pay your legal defense fees and expenses. In other words, the insured business pays the claim and then requests reimbursement from the captive. If drafted correctly, such policies could effectively cover the claim without creating an asset for plaintiffs to chase. However, a court might force the debtor business to make a claim for indemnification from the captive.

- **Litigation Expense Policies.** Policies which would pay your legal defense fees and expenses only. The *litigation expense policy* ("LEP") is frequently used with captives so that no large asset becomes available to creditors. These are the best types of policies for captives, since they do not create any rights in favor of third-party claimants.

Sadly, many insurance managers simply copy their policies from a form book or copy commercial policies without giving any thought to the peculiar needs of a particular captive to restrict what the policies cover.

There are many types of liabilities for which policies may be issued. Common liabilities covered by captives include:

- **Advertising Liability.** This is a liability to the business which arises as a result of the business' advertising. This includes administrative liability for false advertising, as well as civil liability to other businesses for trade libel arising out of the advertising. Punitive damages are often awarded in this area.

- **Antitrust & Unfair Competition—Liability For.** The competitive activities of a business can result in liability for over-competitive or unfair conduct. Regulatory liability, such as to the Federal Trade Commission, can also arise. Litigation of these issues is typically both protracted and expensive because of the complicated economic issues and need for expert witnesses. This litigation can also be "offensive" in nature, insofar as it is not uncommon for companies to bring this type of litigation to discredit or harass their competitors to gain a business advantage. Damages in these sorts of cases can rise to the level of extreme because of inflated claims for lost profits and the possibility of treble damages under the Sherman Act.

- **Commercial Vehicle Insurance.** A steady source of litigation for most businesses arises from their employees' use of company vehicles. These claims can arise both from employees directly against the company and from third-parties who are injured by the employees' allegedly negligent driving. Punitive damage claims are possible.

- **Construction and Design Defects.** A company can be liable for construction defects for many years after a project is completed. Often it is difficult to mount a defense to such claims because, although the plaintiff may prove his case by merely proving the existence of the loss or defect by way of the doctrine of res ipsa loquitur, the defendant may be hard-pressed to locate key witnesses (or to have such witnesses remember the facts) or documents which will likely have been administratively destroyed.

- **Copyright Infringement—Claims Against.** A business can be liable for its unwitting use of copyrighted materials. While many such claims arise because of "offensive" litigation by the business's competitors, such claims also occasionally arise merely because of employee negligence or malfeasance. Insurance purchased against this risk can indemnify the business for legal and other costs related to the defense of such claims, and indemnify the business for successful claims made against it.

- **Deceptive Trade Practices.** A company can have both civil and regulatory liability for certain business practices which are alleged to be deceptive in nature. For example, if a company advertises Product A but because of manufacturing delays or overwhelming demand runs out of Product A and starts selling Product B, the company can be alleged to have engaged in "bait-and-switch" tactics, irrespective of the company's innocent intentions. Similar theories of liabilities arise because of products which fail to measure up to the perception created by marketing. Additionally, in many states (such as Texas) the tort of Deceptive Trade Practices is so broadly defined that it can encompass many different types of alleged wrongs, including many torts which have nothing whatsoever to do with business or trade. Punitive damages are often awarded for these torts.

- **Directors & Officers Liability.** A business can be liable for actions taken by the directors and officers of the company, for both intentional acts and negligence. Insurance purchased against this risk can indemnify the business for the legal and related expenses incurred in defending both the business as well as the directors and officers, indemnify the business for successful claims against the business as a result of actions of the directors or officers, and indemnify the business for successful claims for indemnification asserted by the directors and officers when they have been successfully sued.

- **Employment Practices.** A business can be liable for a wide variety of employment practices, including sex, age, and racial discrimination, as well as failure to comply with the Americans with Disabilities Act.

- **Environmental.** Environmental liability exists for all businesses which own real property, or which conduct business operations involving the use of chemicals and solvents. Liability can also arise for businesses whose operations can affect ground water, such as drilling operations, etc. It is important to note that environmental liability can even accrue to innocent businesses, simply by owning contaminated property if measures are not taken to prevent existing contamination from flowing to adjacent property.

- **Errors & Omissions.** Businesses can be liable for the failure of their officers and employees to take some action. This is a very common business liability, and can encompass many acts (or non-acts). Liability under Sarbanes-Oxley may exist as well. Most businesses maintain "E&O" insurance against claims of this type, but often that insurance is insufficient and additional insurance is sometimes necessary.

- **Libel & Slander (& Trade Libel).** Businesses can be liable for misstatements of fact by their officers and employees which allegedly cause harm to its competitors. Businesses can also face litigation costs as a result of baseless suits brought by competitors.

- **Malpractice.** Professionals face many types of negligence liability as a result of their professional practice. While most professionals keep some level of malpractice insurance, it may be advisable for these professionals to maintain excess malpractice insurance against the possibility of an unusually large claim.

- **Performance Liability.** Businesses are required to perform under their contracts, and the failure to perform will often result in liability to the business.

- **Product Liability.** Manufacturers can be liable for injuries and losses caused by their products. Manufacturers can also be liable for frivolous lawsuits brought about by public misperception and driven by class-action plaintiffs lawyers—the silicon breast implant litigation being a good example of this.

- **Structural Defects.** Architects, engineers, builders, contractors, and even materials suppliers can be liable for structural defects in homes, building, and other structures. This type of liability can also arise where the project does not strictly meet specifications, and where negligence by another involved professional (for example, the project geologist) has caused failure.

- **Title Insurance.** Companies and partnerships which deal in real property are commonly exposed to the risks of a flaw in the chain-of-title.

- **Trademark Infringement—Claims Against.** The information age has created new problems for businesses which may unwittingly utilize someone else's trademark. Additionally, trademark litigation is occasionally brought for collateral reasons, such as to force a competitor to incur legal fees and generally disrupt the operations of the competitor.

Business Casualty

The best type of policy for a captive to issue is a business loss or casualty policy, since then it is only the business that is asserting the claim and no third-party claimants are involved. Indeed, businesses are at risk of suffering their own losses, whether from their own miscalculations, miscalculations of others, bad acts by competitors, or just plain bad luck. Many businesses are essentially self-insured whether they realize it or not, since the money to pay for uncovered losses will come from the business owner's pocket. The following types of insurance protect businesses against these losses.

- **Administrative Action.** A business can suffer losses because of the unforeseen administrative action of a governmental body. For instance, if OSHA enacts new rules that apply to a manufacturer, the manufacturer will have costs in complying with the new rules, such as issuing protective gear to employees. A business can also be liable for fines because it has failed to keep up with the myriad of regulations issued by a variety of federal, state, and local governmental agencies. Administrative action insurance protects against business losses caused by governmental rule changes, and also against fines which are imposed against businesses as a result of those new rules.

- **Advertising and Marketing Failure.** Many businesses are reliant upon successful advertising and marketing campaigns. The failure of such campaigns can be devastating to a business, and can have long term effects. Marketing efforts can fail for a variety of reasons, including inability to secure commercial air time or newspaper space at a reasonable price, or a miscalculation by the business's marketing firm. Advertising and marketing failure insurance protects a business against advertising campaigns gone bad, and reimburses the business for losses caused by such failure.

- **Antitrust and Unfair Competition.** A business is susceptible to monopolistic conduct by its largest competitors, as well as to unfair competition by all its competitors of any size. Because of litigation costs and uncertainty, it might not make sense to attempt to sue for redress so the business will simply have to suffer the loss. The captive can insure against such losses.

- **Business Credit Cover.** Businesses can suffer serious losses if they lose their creditworthiness, or even if a regular lender fails to extend credit in a timely fashion. This insurance covers business losses caused by the loss of credit or the inability to obtain credit.

- **Business Dirty Tricks.** Businesses are susceptible to the dirty tricks of their competitors—especially in highly-competitive business environments dominated by only a few companies. This insurance compensates the business for any losses occasioned by any unusual conduct of a competitor aimed directly at the business.

- **Business Document Forgery & Counterfeiting.** Businesses can suffer losses because their business documents (such as checks) are forged, or key contractual documents, etc., are counterfeited.

- **Business Extortion.** Even today, businesses can suffer losses by extortion—both violent and non-violent. For instance, a city counsel-person may require that the business enter into unfavorable contracts with his brother-in-law in exchange for support of street improvements in front of the business. This extortion by its nature may be impossible for the business to prove to law enforcement, yet it may still cause losses.

- **Business Interruption.** Interruption of business operations can occur for a wide variety of reasons, few of which can be foreseen, including labor problems, administrative problems, embargoes, etc. Interruptions may also be caused by the necessity of a business to change its operations, for instance to re-tool its assembly line. This insurance compensates the business for losses caused by interruptions in its operations for whatever reason.

- **Business Reputation.** Most businesses are dependent upon their reputation and the goodwill they have developed with their customers and suppliers. Unfortunately, there are many ways that a businesses reputation can be tarnished (such as by false claims of a disgruntled employee or statements of a competitor), causing losses to the business.

- **Cargo Consequential Loss.** Most businesses will purchase insurance for cargo which is lost during shipping. However, few businesses will purchase insurance to cover their "consequential losses" meaning losses occasioned by the loss of the cargo above the value of the cargo itself. For instance, a business may require a certain part in its assembly line. Loss of the part during shipment is measured not only by the value of the part, but also by shutting down the assembly line until the replacement part is received. This insurance covers such losses.

- **Cash In Transit.** A business can suffer losses from cash lost in transit, and not just by armed robbery. Misdrafted wire-transfer instructions, banker errors, and the like can all result in losses.

- **Commercial Crime.** So called "white collar crime" poses serious concerns for business, especially in this electronic age where a company's most important assets can be transmitted away in less than a second. Commercial crime insurance can cover not only common embezzlement, but also theft of source computer code, customer lists, and other trade secrets. This insurance compensates the business for such losses.

- **Communications Breakdown or Interruption.** Today's businesses are heavily reliant on their communications. A lost telephone line may be more than an inconvenience, it may cause a business-wide shutdown of all operations. This insurance compensates the business for failures in its communications infrastructure.

- **Computers: Dissemination of Data.** E-mail has greatly helped to make businesses efficient. At the same time, the click of a key can inadvertently transmit a business's entire business strategy to all customers and competitors. This insurance covers losses to the businesses by an unforeseen dissemination of data, whether negligent or otherwise.

- **Computers: Loss of Data.** The "paperless office" age is upon us. Few businesses reduce their business data to hard copy form, instead relying on disk and tape date to store this information. Unfortunately, the risk of permanently losing this information, by an inadvertent erasure or otherwise, can lead to significant losses for the businesses, as well as in administrative fines and penalties.

- **Computers: Software Liability.** Many businesses have developed proprietary computer codes for their own use, and also for the use of franchisees, joint venturers, etc. However, the authoring business may retain liability for losses caused by the failure of such software.

- **Computers: Virus Losses.** A new threat faced by business is the computer virus, which can in seconds literally wipe out the electronic infrastructure of a business. The loss is measured not only in the loss of the computer code which is corrupted, but also in the disrupted operations of the business.

- **Confiscation and Expropriation.** All businesses run the risk of having their property confiscated or expropriated. At the mild end of the spectrum, a company employee may utilize a company car to solicit illegal activity resulting in confiscation of the vehicle. At the other end of the spectrum, changes in the political climate may cause a business or its subsidiary to be nationalized.

- **Contract Frustration.** Various factors may contribute to frustration of a business's key contract: for example, an early onset of winter might frustrate construction activity. Losses to the business are not confined to contract payment, but may also manifest in loss to the company's reputation, devaluation of goodwill, being barred from future projects, etc. This insurance compensates the business for all losses caused directly or indirectly by contract frustration.

- **Copyright Infringement—By Another.** Businesses may develop significant assets in their proprietary intellectual property, but these are difficult assets to protect and defend. Even if a copyright case is won, it may take years and, in the meantime, the value to the business can be lost or substantially decreased. This insurance compensates the business for losses caused by the copyright infringements of others.

- **Currency Risks.** Companies conducting business internationally run the inherent risk of currency fluctuations. This insurance compensates the business for any significant losses occasioned by such currency fluctuations.

- **Delay Start-Up.** Businesses can suffer losses because of unforeseen delays in the start-up or success of new ventures.

- **Eminent Domain.** Businesses that own property are at risk of having their property condemned at a rate substantially less than the potential fair market value of the property. For example, if a business owns property in a development area and a renewal bill passes, the business may receive compensation measured by the value of the property before passage of the bill, when obviously the market value of the property will be much higher when the neighborhood renewal is completed.

- **Employee HIV Contamination.** Some businesses, especially medical clinics and hospitals, face potential liability from accidents which have the effect of contaminating employees with the HIV virus.

- **Financial Crime.** Businesses can be victimized by a wide range of financial crimes, including insider trading, counterfeiting of stock shares, unauthorized financial account access, churning of the business's stock and financial account, malfeasance by the custodian of the company's shares, and other acts. This insurance compensates the company for all losses caused by such acts.

- **Force Majeur.** Business operations can be disrupted by a wide variety of unexpected natural phenomena, including floods, hurricanes, etc. The potential also exists for consequential damages, i.e., a U.S. business with a Taiwan supplier may face losses when earthquakes disrupt the Taiwan supplier's manufacturing plant. This insurance covers all losses, direct and consequential, arising from any force majeur.

- **Foreign Operations.** Foreign operations pose unique problems for businesses. For example, miscommunications because of language barriers, failure to understand foreign markets, currency fluctuations, etc., may result in losses to the domestic business.

- **Judicial/Administrative Delay.** A business may suffer losses because of the failure of a court or administrative agency to act quickly. For instance, the FDA might delay approval of a new drug, causing lost profits to a business. Or a court could fail to act quickly to prevent a competitor from stealing key employees. This insurance covers the actual and consequences losses caused by judicial or administrative delay.

- **Insurance Failure & Bad-Faith.** A business's insurance carrier may fail to pay legitimate claims because of insolvency or bad-faith of the insurer, leaving the business "naked" to the very liabilities for which it had purchased coverage. This insurance covers such failures or bad faith, and often can be tailored so that it not only indemnifies the business for losses, but also funds litigation to pursue the errant insurer.

- **Knock-Off Lost Profit.** Businesses may suffer losses when their product is replicated ("knocked-off") by a competitor. Whether this activity is legal, or in violation of copyright or patent laws, still results in losses to the business.

- **Lawsuit Interruption.** This insurance compensates the business for significant interruptions due to the involvement of the business in defending a lawsuit or administrative hearing, etc. Covered losses could include the time value of key employees while preparing for depositions, gathering documents under subpoena, testifying at depositions, trial preparation, and time testifying at trial.

- **Labor Costs.** Businesses can suffer losses because of unforeseen and dramatic increases in their labor costs.

- **Legal Expenses.** Legal expense policies cover all legal expenses, not otherwise covered by other policies, resulting from defending against litigation. Often, legal expense policies will be available even though no coverage is purchasable against the particular liability itself.

- **Lender Failure.** A business may rely upon a key lender to extend financing to the business. This insurance covers any losses to the business caused by any failure of the lender to extend promised financing, including insolvency of the lender, bad-faith refusal to extend financing, change in management of the lender, significant change in lending policies of the lender, etc.

- **Loss of Key Customer.** This coverage compensates the business for consequential damages occasioned by the loss of a large customer.

- **Loss of Talent.** The loss of certain talented employees may cripple a business. An example would be a tech company's loss of a majority of its programmers. This insurance covers a business for the loss of a number of talented employees that are not otherwise covered by key man insurance.

- **Machinery Breakdown.** Some businesses are reliant upon particular pieces of equipment, the loss of which necessarily halts the operations of the business.

- **Market Flooding.** Some businesses risk the flooding of their goods into the marketplace by competitors seeking to establish a market foothold, or to eliminate the business as competition. This insurance compensates the business for all losses, direct and consequential, caused by market flooding.

- **Market Risks.** All businesses have exposure to various market forces. Where these market forces can be specifically identified, insurance coverage can be underwritten to protect the business against their adverse turns.

- **Patent & Trademark Infringement—Claims Against.** A business may bear liability to others for alleged patent & trademark infringement, as well as liability costs for defending against such claims.

- **Political Risk.** Some businesses, particularly those with operations abroad, face certain risks due to changes in local politics. When specifically identifiable, these risks can be underwritten to protect the business in case those politics turn adverse to the business. These risks can also be domestic in nature, i.e., a real estate developer facing a developmental commission that has been filled with environmentalists, etc.

- **Product Launches.** Businesses can suffer substantial direct and consequential economic losses due to failed launches of new products.

- **Product Tampering.** The intentional or negligent tampering of products by an employee can cause tremendous damage to a business.

- **Production Benchmarks.** A business that bases its business plan on certain production benchmarks or completion points may suffer losses, including potential loss of financing or customers, if those benchmarks are not met.

- **Property Damage.** Businesses typically have many exposures to losses due to property damage, whether occasioned by weather, vandalism or theft, fire, and other events.

- **Revelation of Trade Secrets.** A business can suffer dramatic losses and lose its ability to compete by the intentional or negligent revelation of its trade secrets to competitors and customers.

- **Strike and Labor Unrest Insurance.** Labor strikes and "go slow" events may temporarily cripple a business and cause long-term damage to the reputation of the business and other harms.

- **Terrorism.** Some businesses are particularly susceptible to losses due to terrorism or the threat of terrorism.

- **Theft.** A business faces a variety of risks due to the possible theft or embezzlement by its employees.

- **Trade Credit.** The loss of trade credit to a business by its suppliers (for instance, as occasioned by an industry downturn that makes suppliers nervous) could cause serious harm to the business.

- **Trade Good Will.** Various unforeseeable factors could cause a business to lose good will within its particular trade.

- **Patent and Trademark Infringement—By Another.** A business with intellectual property risks the expropriation of that intellectual property by competitors. This insurance may indemnify the business for losses due to such expropriation, and pay litigation expenses to pursue the expropriating competitors for injunctive relief and damages.

- **Transit Risk.** Businesses that ship goods or materials, or require the safe transit to them of raw materials to be used in manufacturing, may bear substantial transit risks.

- **Unfair Calling of Guarantees.** Businesses that issue guarantees risk those guarantees being unfairly called by customers or consumers, i.e., the guarantees may be called even though the work or product is not defective.

- **Weather Risks.** Certain types of business, such as farmers and real estate developers, have exposure to weather risks.

Excess Insurance

Although a business may have coverage against certain losses and liabilities, that coverage will almost always have upper limits as defined by the issuing insurance company. If there is a risk that the losses or liabilities will exceed that coverage, the purchase of excess insurance coverage should be considered. Umbrella liability indemnifies the business for all business losses that are otherwise uncovered.

Bonds

Captives can also underwrite bonds in some circumstances, thus saving the business owner money having to obtain bonds commercially. Bonds are a recognized form of an insurance contract which can serve a wide variety of legitimate business purposes. Bonds can be issued directly by an insurance company to a business, to the business's commercial partners and customers, and to lenders, etc. An insurance company may also reinsure the bonds issued by others.

- **Buyer-Credit.** These bonds back the purchasing power of a business, and are often required by sellers to ensure payment on contracts.

- **Customs Duty Bonds.** These bonds back the payment of customs duties in international transactions. While these bonds are rarely large, companies which engage in substantial international transactions can be liable for substantial amounts under the aggregate bonds issued. Typically, there are also currency risks involved with these bonds.

- **ERISA.** These bonds back the payment of employee retirement and related benefits under the Employee Retirement Income Security Act. A domestic captive may be required to issue bonds of this type.

- **Fidelity & Surety.** These bonds back the fiduciary and similar responsibilities of a business.

- **Performance.** These bonds back the performance of contracts and other obligations.

In summary, it is not difficult to find some significant risks to which a business is currently exposed but is not covered by insurance. By using a captive, policies can be drafted that will allow these risks to be covered and reserved against in a tax efficient fashion.

Chapter 8

Domiciles

The term *domicile* relates to where the captive is formed and initially licensed as an insurance company. Once formed and licensed, a captive may then become an *admitted carrier* in any other jurisdiction where it applies for an insurance license.

Where to form the captive is one of the most important issues in planning; however, it should be one of the last issues to be resolved. This is because other issues involving tax, capitalization, structuring and the like must be resolved first, and only then should issues of domicile be considered. Unfortunately, many people desiring to form a captive start thinking of domicile first. This is putting the cart before the horse.

The cold hard truth is that the laws of most domiciles are all about the same on paper. Each domicile usually copycats everybody else's statutes and adopts any new and attractive provisions quickly to stay competitive. This is particularly true of the most popular and aggressive captive domiciles. If one domicile comes up with something that is truly unique and advantageous, that edge rarely lasts more than a couple of months past when the other domiciles find out about and adopt the new feature.

Because the statutes of the captive domiciles are so similar, decisions regarding the selection of the right location for a particular captive are often made on the basis of the insurance consultant's personal experience with particular domiciles, anecdotal information obtained from clients and captive managers about what the local insurance commissioner is like, and how quickly applications are processed and issued are resolved.

Permitted Assets—A Moving Target

Different insurance commissioners will have different standards as to what may be used for reserves. The assets that are allowed to be counted towards reserves are known as *permitted assets*.

For example, one insurance commissioner may recognize 100% of the value of a parcel of commercial property towards reserves, while another insurance commissioner may only recognize 20% of the value for the same parcel, and yet another commissioner might not give any credit for the value of commercial property. If the client desiring to form a captive is heavily into real estate, the domicile that gives the highest credit towards commercial property may be the most desirable domicile. Conversely, the one that gives the lowest credit will be the least desirable.

A particular insurance commissioner's restrictions on permitted assets can sometimes create negative tax issues or eliminate potential tax benefits, such as where the captive owner seeks to capitalize the company with an appreciated or leveraged asset.

Because what will or will not qualify as permitted assets are only vaguely described by statute, it means that captive owners may be subject to the whims of who the insurance commission is in a particular domicile. Like any other bureaucratic position, insurance commissioners tend to change every few years and what may constitute permitted assets today may change tomorrow, depending on a particular commissioner's view of the issue.

Some domiciles have been relatively stable in their treatment of permitted assets over the years. Bermuda and the Cayman Islands come to mind when one thinks of consistency in the treatment of permitted assets. By contrast, the British Virgin Islands (BVI) has been all over the board in its treatment of permitted assets, with different insurance commissioners taking wildly different positions to the frustration of captive owners and insurance managers.

Maturity and Conservatism

When a domicile first starts attracting captive business, the attitude of the insurance commissioner will usually be along the lines of "anything goes" just to increase the number of captives being formed. However, as the domicile gains a number of captives and matures, the primary motivation of the insurance company is not to increase the raw number of captives being formed, but rather to increase the quality of the new captives and enhance the reputation of the domicile for attracting high-end business.

Similarly, when a domicile first starts offering captives, there is little or no bureaucracy and each new company is reviewed on an individual basis. By the time a domicile has dozens of captives, administrative procedures (a/k/a red tape) have been created so that lower-level employees within the insurance commissioner's office can process the new captive applications. This results in little individual consideration of the needs of a particular captive's owners. These jurisdictions will usually resolve ordinary issues more efficiently, but they may be inflexible in the handling of extraordinary situations.

The upshot of this is that persons desiring to form a new captive should consider new and hungry domiciles in addition to the established domiciles. As the new domiciles are eager for any business, they will usually offer a much greater degree of flexibility than those jurisdictions where the insurance commissioners have become set in their ways.

The inflexibility of an established jurisdiction can manifest itself in overly strict permitted asset rules. But inflexibility can also be found in regard to the types of policies that the insurance company can underwrite and the terms of the policies. Since captives are often only underwriting other companies owned by the same parent, the insurance commissioner shouldn't normally care what policies are being issued, the terms of the policies, or the rates being charged. However, the insurance commissioners of some domiciles feel compelled for whatever reasons to meddle in these issues.

Records and Meetings

Most domiciles require that the captive's records be kept in the domicile. This is so that the Insurance Commissioner can take possession of the records and inspect them at any time and take control of the captive if necessary. Where the captive is offshore, keeping the records there isn't a bad idea since it helps to protect the documents from disclosure in discovery or otherwise. The downside is that if the records are needed elsewhere for bookkeeping purposes, a duplicate set of records must be maintained.

All captive statutes require that the captive's shareholders or directors have regular meetings, usually at least annually. However, not all captive statutes require that the meeting be physically held in the domicile. Most domiciles allow the meetings to be attended telephonically or by proxy, but a few do not. With some domiciles, attending the annual meeting might be more of a pleasure than a chore which doubtlessly contributes to the popularity of the Cayman Islands and Hawaii.

Licensing Fees, Annual Fees and Premium Taxes

All domiciles charge *licensing fees* to grant the captive's initial application of an insurance license. These fees can sometimes significantly vary depending on the type of business the captive will be conducting.

All jurisdictions also charge *annual fees* to renew licenses. These fees can significantly vary from domicile to domicile. Some jurisdictions also charge *premium taxes*, which are calculated as a percentage of the premiums earned by a captive. The annual fees and premium taxes must factor into a calculation of the total expenses of operating the captive, and thus whether it will make economic sense for the owner to form.

Offshore or Onshore?

For years, the only realistic option for those who wanted a captive was to form it offshore. This is because the state insurance commissioners simple did not understand the concept of a captive and its peculiarities. It makes absolutely no sense for a captive, for instance, to be subjected to rate filing requirements or to have its policies approved by the Insurance Commissioner. In stark contrast, the offshore domiciles understood the captive game and the need for a light regulatory hand.

At some point, a few of the states, primarily Vermont, wised up to the concept of captives and decided that they could be a good revenue earner. The states then started passing legislation that enabled captives and by the time of the writing of this book more than half the states have such legislation.

A few of the states, most notably Vermont, South Carolina, Hawaii, and Utah, now aggressively compete against each other for captive business. This competition helps to keep the bureaucracy light and the fees low among all the states. These states also still compete, of course, with the offshore domiciles.

Thus, in recent years, a planning question is whether the captive should be formed onshore or offshore. To give the standard lawyer's answer: It depends. Resolution of the issue depends on a variety of factors, mostly involving certain complex tax issues. Onshore and offshore captives both offer certain advantages or disadvantages that may or may not be important in particular cases. So, it depends.

Chapter 9

Domestic Domiciles

As a rule of thumb, I think it should be presumed that a captive formation will be domestic, and that a decision to form an offshore captive should only be made in special circumstances. This is in part because domestic captives are more easily recognized by the state insurance commissioners, and the Certificates of Insurance that they issue are much more likely to be respected. It is also because the U.S. tax code creates numerous impediments, landmines, and onerous reporting requirements for offshore captives—including a deep suspicion by IRS agents that captives are often used to facilitate offshore tax evasion.

The domestic domiciles simply are more advantageous than the offshore domiciles for captives involving U.S. businesses. These advantages include:

- **No Foreign Entity Tax Reporting.** The U.S. tax reporting of foreign entities has become extremely onerous, with significant non-waivable penalties for even innocently missed returns. This can significantly increase the overall administrative cost of the captive.

- **Fewer Audits or Inquiries.** An offshore captive may (depending on the domicile) require the offshore transfer of funds that may automatically generate a *suspicious activity report* (SAR) from the transmitting U.S. bank pursuant to the Patriot Act and likely trigger an audit or other scrutiny of the offshore captive's affairs. Even if the captive's affairs are totally innocent, there will be costs to responding.

- **Less Heat from State Regulators.** A captive formed in a state and subject to regulation of a state insurance commissioner is much less likely to run into difficulties with the insurance commissioner of another state for the unauthorized sale of insurance.

- **Domestic Domicile Sometimes Required.** Some types of insurance companies, such as Risk Retention Groups, can only be formed domestically, and some types of policies or benefits can only be written by domestic insurance companies. Similarly, some third parties will not accept a Certificate of Insurance or a bond from an offshore captive.

- **Higher Efficiency and Lower Costs.** The domestic captive domiciles are typically more efficient than their offshore counterparts (see *Junkanoo*, supra), and overall costs seem to be higher offshore.

- **Greater Accessibility.** Travel is easier, quicker, and less expensive to the domestic domiciles. This can be important if personal contact with the insurance manager is important, or the shareholders or directors will have regular meetings in the domicile.

More than half of the U.S. states now have captive enabling legislation, but relatively few states are making a strong attempt to market themselves as captive domiciles. The "big three" as far as the U.S. is concerned are Vermont, South Carolina, and Hawaii. These three jurisdictions probably account for more than half of the domestic captive formations in any year. But other jurisdictions are aggressively marketing themselves as captive-friendly domiciles, including Arizona, Montana, Nevada, New York, and Utah.

Vermont

Estimated Captives: 750

The first true domestic captive insurance domicile was Vermont, which passed its Special Insurers Act in 1981. Now, Vermont is not just the most popular onshore captive domicile, but it is also the second-ranked domicile in the world in terms of assets within its captives and the third-ranked domicile in the sheer number of captives formed.

Vermont's popularity as a captive domicile has significantly benefited the state. Vermont captives hold over $1 billion in Vermont's banks and financial companies, and the industry generates over 1,500 jobs and more than $20 million annually to the state in premium taxes. Because of this, Vermont is very protective of its captive industry and its reputation for efficiency.

Captives are regulated by the Captive Insurance Division of the Vermont Department of Banking, Insurance, Securities and Health Care Administration

(BISHCA). The Division coordinates with the Vermont Captive Insurance Association (VCIA) and captive service providers in the state.

Vermont's fees are relatively low, and include $200 for an application fee, $300 for a license fee, and $3,200 for an actuarial review. There are also incorporation fees that can vary depending on the circumstances. Vermont does charge a premium tax, which rate starts at 0.38% for direct insurance ($3,800 per million) and 0.21% for reinsurance. The rate decreases as the amount of premiums increases, and there is a $200,000 maximum.

Vermont has no investment restrictions for pure captives. The investment restrictions for association captives and risk retention groups are the same as for other insurance companies. Captives are required to provide the Insurance Division with an Annual GAAP financial statement, as well as an actuarial opinion on reserves.

Typically, the Insurance Commissioner desires to personally meet with applicants to discuss the proposed captive. The idea here is to identify and resolve any special issues in advance so that the application is not slowed down. Captive applicants are also required to provide a *Certificate of Public Good* that describes how Vermont will be benefited by the formation of the captive (usual answer: Local manager will be hired).

South Carolina

Estimated Captives: 120

The Palmetto State went into the captive business in 2000 and started aggressively marketing for new business. By attracting the smallish captive market with very low capitalization requirements, South Carolina soon built a captive market that effectively competes with Vermont for new domestic captives.

Of course, as South Carolina's captive market matured, regulators became more picky about the types of captives they would accept. Now, South Carolina no longer looks for the smallest captives or offers the lowest capitalization requirements, but has instead turned its focus (like Vermont) to quality formations instead of sheer numbers. This is good for South Carolina, but perhaps not so good for those with limited capital resources who are struggling to get a smallish captive up and running.

South Carolina's statute allows stock captives, mutual captives and reciprocal captives. Licenses are granted for all forms of insurance except workers' compensation and consumer-type insurance (auto or homeowners, etc.). Captives may not directly insure the risks of other than affiliated or similarly controlled companies, but reinsurance can be freely written.

South Carolina charges a minimal premium tax of 0.4% on the first twenty million of direct premiums, graduating to 0.075% after sixty million in premiums. There is also a reinsurance tax of 0.225% on the first twenty million of reinsurance premiums, graduating to 0.025% after sixty million in premiums. However, there is no tax on premiums between affiliated captives.

South Carolina has very liberal permitted asset rules. The insurance statute does not restrict the type of investments the captive can make, unless they threaten the solvency or liquidity of the captive. By statute, only $250,000 initial capitalization is required ($100,000 for reserves and $150,000 for surplus), although the Director may, of course, require a higher amount.

Like many (but not all) domestic domiciles, South Carolina effectively requires a meeting with the Director to pre-approve the start of the application process. Otherwise, the captive application and approval process is about the same as other domiciles. The captive must retain an approved CPA to perform audits and a qualified actuary to calculate reserve requirements. By March 1 of each year, at least two directors must certify the financial condition of the captive under oath.

The South Carolina captive legislation is very favorable to alternative risk structures, such as allowing protected cell captives. There are no policy or rate filing requirements. Also, there is a very active and effective South Carolina Captive Insurance Association (SCCIA) that works to protect the interests of captives in that state.

Hawaii

Estimated Captives: 150

An unlikely candidate for an international insurance center, Hawaii has actually been in the captive business since 1987 and boasts over 150 captives. Many of these are for owners in the western United States or for those who are conducting business in the Pacific Rim. Hawaii's unique location allows it to communicate with both the West Coast and the Far East during the same workday to resolve claims and other insurance issues.

Hawaii requires an introductory meeting with the Captive Insurance Administrator of the Insurance Division. The purpose of the meeting is to explain who is behind the captive, how it will be capitalized and operated, and what its purpose will be. Hawaii also requires that the Insurance Commissioner issue a Certificate of Public Good based on how the captive will benefit the state.

A traditional captive is required to be capitalized for at least $250,000 although the Insurance Commissioner is likely to require more. A general rule in Hawaii is that net premiums cannot exceed capital by more than a 3 to 1 ratio, i.e., a captive having only $250,000 in capital could only receive up to $750,000 in annual premiums. Hawaii has relatively low capitalization requirements for risk retention groups of only $750,000.

Hawaii has relatively low fees, and minimal premium tax rates that start at 0.25% for the first $25 million and go downwards to only 0.05% for premiums over $50 million. Annual GAAP financial statements are required. One of the innovative features of Hawaii's captive law is to allow the formation of not-for-profit captives, which can be useful for educational and healthcare related institutions.

Chapter 10

Offshore Domiciles

Domiciles outside of the United States are referred to as *offshore domiciles*. The most popular jurisdictions include Bermuda, the Cayman Islands, and the British Virgin Islands, but there at least a dozen other significant offshore domiciles worldwide, such as Ireland and Hong Kong. Some of the offshore domiciles have insurance commissioners who are very efficient; others are not.

Sometimes an offshore domicile is a better fit for a particular captive. The advantages of "going offshore" with the captive formation include the following.

- **Occasional Tax Advantages.** Where the captive is being capitalized with appreciated assets, there may be a tax advantage in using an offshore captive in case the captive is not treated as an insurance company for U.S. tax purposes. An offshore captive may also sometimes be used to legitimately defer the payment of U.S. taxes on other true foreign business activities.

  Note that nearly all captives owned by U.S. persons or businesses will choose U.S. taxation anyway, by what is known as the *953(d) election*, so there is no generalized tax advantage for offshore captives. Beware that the 953(d) election might in some cases operate to prevent a captive's parent from using any net operating loss of the captive.

- **Less Bureaucracy.** Some, but certainly not all, offshore domiciles offer significantly less bureaucracy than the U.S. captive domiciles, including more lax requirements for capitalization and permitted assets. (Caution that some offshore domiciles, such as the British Virgin Islands, have a very intense bureaucracy that is probably worse than that of any U.S. state.) Also, most offshore domiciles will rely on CPA audits instead of requiring regulatory examinations.

- **Asset Protection Advantages.** An offshore captive may offer certain unique asset protection advantages if properly structured, since creditors may have great difficulty in enforcing judgments abroad.

- **Access to Foreign Investments.** An offshore captive may allow access to certain foreign investments, such as European mutual funds, that are not available domestically.

- **Exotic Locales.** Some offshore domiciles are a highly desirable place to regularly visit (Grand Cayman, for instance).

Whether to form onshore or offshore will depend on these and other factors that are identified while the captive is being planned and the pro forma and business plan are being drafted. This is why the choice of domicile is one of the last issues that are resolved, instead of one of the first.

Junkanoo

The term *Junkanoo* officially refers to the street parades and festivals that are held at the end of the year in the Bahamas. But the term Junkanoo is also slang for the culture of apathy and slowness that permeates the Caribbean financial centers. Some exemplary translations that show the effect of Junkanoo follow:

Statement	Meaning
It will be done today.	*With luck we might get to it by the end of next week.*
It will be done by the end of this week at the latest.	*Remind me next month.*
It may take a week or two to get this done.	*I have no idea; you'll just have to wait for it to happen.*
It will take 60 to 90 days.	*You'll be lucky to get it done within a year, if ever.*

The Junkanoo effect is due to a variety of factors, including often poorly-educated staffs who have a poor understanding of what they are doing and supporting personnel with little or no work ethic. It is also due to the general slowness that follows "island time" generally.

The Junkanoo effect is mostly due to the insurance commissioners themselves, who have the irritating habits of taking off for vacations lasting several months or to hawk the benefits of the domicile on the seminar circuit while all processing work comes to a screeching halt in his absence. When this happens, all of the advertisements of the offshore domicile ("We can approve applications in 60 days!") go out the window, and you will have to wait until the insurance commissioner both returns and works through the backlog of pending matters until he gets to yours. This can be a nightmare if your client needs to complete some action quickly for regulatory or tax reasons.

Of the "big three" offshore domiciles that primarily cater to the U.S. captive business, Bermuda (which is not in the Caribbean anyway) seems to be immune from the Junkanoo effect, it infects the Caymans only rarely. The BVI could be the posterchild for the Junkanoo effect, with inexplicable delays, decisions by the Insurance Commissioner that defy common sense, and a general inability to get anything important done in a timely fashion.

Bermuda

Estimated Captives: 1,000

The tiny mid-Atlantic outpost of Bermuda is home to what many would consider as the world's premiere captive jurisdiction. It was to Bermuda that many of the Lloyds of London syndicates migrated in the 1990s, and many of the captives owned by the largest corporate conglomerates are domiciled in Bermuda.

The Bermuda captive market traces its roots to several insurance companies that sold excess liability insurance in the mid-1980's. In 1992, Mid Ocean Re was formed as a property catastrophe reinsurer in response to Hurricane Andrew. Within a couple of years, Bermuda had attracted over $4.5 billion in capital for several reinsurance companies created there. More recently, Hurricane Katrina brought an additional $18 million into the Bermuda insurance market.

The point is that Bermuda caters primarily to the large (and mega-large) captive market. More than 100 of its insurance companies have financial strength ratings, and many are publicly traded. But therein is the rub for smallish captives: They are not Bermuda's primary business and almost an afterthought within the hugeness of Bermuda's overall insurance marketplace.

Bermuda also has a reputation of being an expensive domicile. Costs and fees that a $1 billion captive would not blink at can seem much more significant to a $1 million captive.

There are four classes of insurance companies under the Bermuda regulatory scheme, and these categories dictate how much capital is minimally required. A class I insurance company only requires $120,000 in capital (although of course the insurance commissioner is likely to require more depending on the business to be conducted) up to $100 million minimum capital for a class IV insurance company.

The initial incorporation expense is a minimum of $4,200 and greater depending on the amount of capital up to $9,000. The captive is granted an exemption from local Bermuda taxes through at least 2016. The annual fees start at $800 and can go as high as $15,000.

Bermuda allows a *segregated account company* (SAC), which can be thought of as an insurance company with segregated mini-insurance companies within it. The liabilities of each account are limited to the assets in that account and in theory do not spill over to other accounts or the general assets of the insurance company. Bermuda SACs are commonly used for so-called rent-a-captives.

The Insurance Act of 1978 controls Bermuda's captive industry. Enforcement of the Act is by the Supervisor of Insurance, who is appointed by the Minister of Finance. Bermuda has an Insurer's Admissions Committee which (allegedly) meets weekly to advice the Supervisor on new applications.

One quirk of Bermuda law is that if more than 30% of a captive's gross premiums are for professional liability insurance (such as medical malpractice coverage), the captive must appoint a Loss Reserve Specialist to annually certify the adequacy of the captive's reserves.

Cayman Islands

Estimated Captives: 700

The Cayman Islands are located due south of Cuba, and are directly accessible by jet service from Miami and Houston. Best known as an international financial center, the Cayman Islands seem to about sink under the weight of major international banks that have branches there.

The Caymans are probably the preferred offshore captive domicile for U.S. business owners seeking to form a small- to medium-sized captive. The Caymans have the efficiency and sophistication of Bermuda, but typically are not as expensive. And while the Caymans are slightly more expensive than the BVI, the Caymans are much more efficient, accessible, and have the advantage of numerous banks on-island to choose from.

A single-parent captive may be issued a Restricted Class B license that requires no minimum capitalization. This makes a lot of sense considering the nature of a captive, where the owner is simply self-insuring. An Unrestricted Class B license requires only $120,000 minimum capital.

Where the Caymans are more expensive is that they currently have a $8,333 annual licensing fee. But this is more than offset by the fact that the Caymans impose no investment restrictions on Class B companies (whether restricted or not-restricted). The Caymans also have a reputation of being one of the most efficient offshore domiciles.

The Caymans also have the advantage of being a wonderful place to visit. With world-class resorts, the beautiful Seven Mile Beach, and world-class diving, the Caymans compete with Hawaii as the most desirable captive location to visit.

British Virgin Islands

Estimated Captives: 350

The *British Virgin Islands* (BVI) are located immediately east of Puerto Rico in the British West Indies, and adjacent to the U.S. Virgin Islands. The Insurance Commissioner's office is in Road Town on the main island of Tortola. Access to the BVI is usually by flying a jet into San Juan and then taking a puddle-jumper to Tortola.

When I first started in the captive business, the BVI was a very attractive domicile. Insurance Supervisor Nigel Bailey aggressively pursued new captives and exercised a very light regulatory touch. The next Supervisor, Bill McCullough, also exercised a very light touch and was extremely reasonable in his decisions. Bailey and McCullough put the BVI on the map for captive formations and made it one of the most desired domiciles.

After McCullough left, the BVI turned into a regulatory nightmare for captive owners. The BVI is now jokingly referred to throughout the captive community as "Bureaucracy Very Intense". Sadly, the BVI has lost sight of the main advantage of an offshore domicile: Less regulation, not more. Yet, the BVI now seems determined to compete for the most rigid, inflexible and slow place to form a captive.

Although the BVI continues to advertise efficiency and the quick granting of applications, the reality is very different. Applications take seemingly forever to grant and the Insurance Supervisor is notorious for asking all sorts of inane questions and requesting irrelevant information. Be prepared to be told "No" (or worse, "we'll look into it next week") repeatedly before the application is finally granted.

The BVI's permitted asset rules are a constantly moving target that confound common sense and frustrate all who want to keep something other than cash in their captive. For instance, the BVI only credits up to 20% of securities, including blue-chip stocks. The BVI gives little or usually no credit for the value of real estate. Never mind that commercial real estate is the predominant asset held by major insurance companies.

When Nigel Bailey was the insurance commissioner, the BVI was a very innovative domicile and was one of the first to allow segregated cell captives. When Bill McCullough left, apparently all the innovative spirit left with him as the BVI has not introduced any new features to its laws since.

These days, the only thing that the BVI has to offer is that they are relatively cheap compared to Bermuda and the Cayman Islands—at least in terms of fees. However, when delays and the additional time-costs of professionals are figure in the expense calculation, the BVI's supposed advantage deteriorates.

Another problem with the BVI is that except for the captive industry, there is not much there in terms of a financial center. Unlike the Caymans which have many multinational banks, the BVI has few banks and only a couple that are worth consideration. This creates the peculiar situation for an offshore domicile in that you will need to keep the captive's assets elsewhere.

What the BVI does have is a terrible reputation for money laundering and fostering the activities of criminals. Many notorious fraudsters such as Marc

Harris have used BVI captives as part of fraudulent schemes, and the BVI has been a hotbed of those promoting aggressive tax evasion schemes. These days, BVI captives are regarded with suspicion by some law enforcement agents and domestic insurance regulators, and not without good reasons.

So, for all these reasons, the BVI should no longer be considered a desirable domicile for captives except for those owners who desire to swim through a sea of red tape, be constantly frustrated, and suffer the stigma of the bad acts of others. I only mention the place as an example of how a domicile may look good on paper, but actually be a nightmare. The BVI is also an example of how a jurisdiction can start out as a good one but sour as a choking bureaucracy takes over.

The BVI statute provides for minimum capitalization of $100,000 for most captives. Annual license fees are $2,000 per year for typical captives. The BVI imposes no premium, income or capital gains taxes on captives formed there. No extra charge for the red tape or mind-numbing delays. *Junkanoo*!

Appendices

Appendix A

Risk Retention Statute

15 U.S.C. Ch. 65—Liability Risk Retention

Section 3901. Definitions

(a) As used in this chapter—

    (1) "insurance" means primary insurance, excess insurance, reinsurance, surplus lines insurance, and any other arrangement for shifting and distributing risk which is determined to be insurance under applicable State or Federal law;

    (2) "liability"—

        (A) means legal liability for damages (including costs of defense, legal costs and fees, and other claims expenses) because of injuries to other persons, damage to their property, or other damage or loss to such other persons resulting from or arising out of—

            (i) any business (whether profit or nonprofit), trade, product, services (including professional services), premises, or operations, or

            (ii) any activity of any State or local government, or any agency or political subdivision thereof; and

        (B) does not include personal risk liability and an employer's liability with respect to its employees other than legal liability under the Federal Employers' Liability Act (45 U.S.C. 51 et seq.);

    (3) "personal risk liability" means liability for damages because of injury to any person, damage to property, or other loss or damage resulting from any personal, familial, or household responsibilities or activities, rather than from responsibilities or activities referred to in paragraphs (2)(A) and (2)(B);

(4) "risk retention group" means any corporation or other limited liability association—

(A) whose primary activity consists of assuming, and spreading all, or any portion, of the liability exposure of its group members;

(B) which is organized for the primary purpose of conducting the activity described under subparagraph (A);

(C) which—

(i) is chartered or licensed as a liability insurance company under the laws of a State and authorized to engage in the business of insurance under the laws of such State; or

(ii) before January 1, 1985, [omitted]

(D) which does not exclude any person from membership in the group solely to provide for members of such a group a competitive advantage over such a person;

(E) which—

(i) has as its owners only persons who comprise the membership of the risk retention group and who are provided insurance by such group; or

(ii) has as its sole owner an organization which has as—

(I) its members only persons who comprise the membership of the risk retention group; and

(II) its owners only persons who comprise the membership of the risk retention group and who are provided insurance by such group;

(F) whose members are engaged in businesses or activities similar or related with respect to the liability to which such members are exposed by virtue of any related, similar, or common business, trade, product, services, premises, or operations;

(G) whose activities do not include the provision of insurance other than—

(i) liability insurance for assuming and spreading all or any portion of the similar or related liability exposure of its group members; and

(ii) reinsurance with respect to the similar or related liability exposure of any other risk retention group (or any member of such other group) which is engaged in businesses or activities so that such group (or member) meets the requirement described in subparagraph (F) for membership in the risk retention group which provides such reinsurance; and

(H) the name of which includes the phrase "Risk Retention Group".(!1)

(5) "purchasing group" means [Omitted]

(6) "State" means any State of the United States or the District of Columbia; and

(7) "hazardous financial condition" means that, based on its present or reasonably anticipated financial condition, a risk retention group is unlikely to be able—

  (A) to meet obligations to policyholders with respect to known claims and reasonably anticipated claims; or

  (B) to pay other obligations in the normal course of business.

(b) Nothing in this chapter shall be construed to affect either the tort law or the law governing the interpretation of insurance contracts of any State, and the definitions of liability, personal risk liability, and insurance under any State law shall not be applied for the purposes of this chapter, including recognition or qualification of risk retention groups or purchasing groups.

Section 3902. Risk retention groups

(a) Exemptions from State laws, rules, regulations, or orders

Except as provided in this section, a risk retention group is exempt from any State law, rule, regulation, or order to the extent that such law, rule, regulation, or order would—

(1) make unlawful, or regulate, directly or indirectly, the operation of a risk retention group except that the jurisdiction in which it is chartered may regulate the formation and operation of such a group and any State may require such a group to—

  (A) comply with the unfair claim settlement practices law of the State;

  (B) pay, on a nondiscriminatory basis, applicable premium and other taxes which are levied on admitted insurers and surplus lines insurers, brokers, or policyholders under the laws of the State;

  (C) participate, on a nondiscriminatory basis, in any mechanism established or authorized under the law of the State for the equitable apportionment among insurers of liability insurance losses and expenses incurred on policies written through such mechanism;

  (D) register with and designate the State insurance commissioner as its agent solely for the purpose of receiving service of legal documents or process;

  (E) submit to an examination by the State insurance commissioners in any State in which the group is doing business to determine the group's financial condition, if—

    (i) the commissioner of the jurisdiction in which the group is chartered has not begun or has refused to initiate an examination of the group; and

(ii) any such examination shall be coordinated to avoid unjustified duplication and unjustified repetition;

(F) comply with a lawful order issued—

(i) in a delinquency proceeding commenced by the State insurance commissioner if there has been a finding of financial impairment under subparagraph (E); or

(ii) in a voluntary dissolution proceeding;

(G) comply with any State law regarding deceptive, false, or fraudulent acts or practices, except that if the State seeks an injunction regarding the conduct described in this subparagraph, such injunction must be obtained from a court of competent jurisdiction;

(H) comply with an injunction issued by a court of competent jurisdiction, upon a petition by the State insurance commissioner alleging that the group is in hazardous financial condition or is financially impaired; and

(I) provide the following notice, in 10-point type, in any insurance policy issued by such group:

-HEAD-

"NOTICE

"This policy is issued by your risk retention group. Your risk retention group may not be subject to all of the insurance laws and regulations of your State. State insurance insolvency guaranty funds are not available for your risk retention group."

(2) require or permit a risk retention group to participate in any insurance insolvency guaranty association to which an insurer licensed in the State is required to belong;

(3) require any insurance policy issued to a risk retention group or any member of the group to be countersigned by an insurance agent or broker residing in that State; or

(4) otherwise, discriminate against a risk retention group or any of its members, except that nothing in this section shall be construed to affect the applicability of State laws generally applicable to persons or corporations.

(b) Scope of exemptions

The exemptions specified in subsection (a) of this section apply to laws governing the insurance business pertaining to—

(1) liability insurance coverage provided by a risk retention group for—

(A) such group; or

(B) any person who is a member of such group;

(2)   the sale of liability insurance coverage for a risk retention group; and

(3)   the provision of—

    (A)   insurance related services;

    (B)   management, operations, and investment activities; or

    (C)   loss control and claims administration (including loss control and claims administration services for uninsured risks retained by any member of such group);

for a risk retention group or any member of such group with respect to liability for which the group provides insurance.

(c)   Licensing of agents or brokers for risk retention groups

A State may require that a person acting, or offering to act, as an agent or broker for a risk retention group obtain a license from that State, except that a State may not impose any qualification or requirement which discriminates against a nonresident agent or broker.

(d)   Documents for submission to State insurance commissioners

Each risk retention group shall submit—

(1)   to the insurance commissioner of the State in which it is chartered—

    (A)   before it may offer insurance in any State, a plan of operation or a feasibility study which includes the coverages, deductibles, coverage limits, rates, and rating classification systems for each line of insurance the group intends to offer; and

    (B)   revisions of such plan or study if the group intends to offer any additional lines of liability insurance;

(2)   to the insurance commissioner of each State in which it intends to do business, before it may offer insurance in such State—

    (A)   a copy of such plan or study (which shall include the name of the State in which it is chartered and its principal place of business); and

    (B)   a copy of any revisions to such plan or study, as provided in paragraph (1)(B) (which shall include any change in the designation of the State in which it is chartered); and

(3)   to the insurance commissioner of each State in which it is doing business, a copy of the group's annual financial statement submitted to the State in which the group is chartered as an insurance company, which statement shall be certified by an independent public accountant and contain a statement of opinion on loss and loss adjustment expense reserves made by—

    (A)   a member of the American Academy of Actuaries, or

(B) a qualified loss reserve specialist.

(e) Power of courts to enjoin conduct

Nothing in this section shall be construed to affect the authority of any Federal or State court to enjoin—

(1) the solicitation or sale of insurance by a risk retention group to any person who is not eligible for membership in such group; or

(2) the solicitation or sale of insurance by, or operation of, a risk retention group that is in hazardous financial condition or is financially impaired.

(f) State powers to enforce State laws

(1) Subject to the provisions of subsection (a)(1)(G) of this section (relating to injunctions) and paragraph (2), nothing in this chapter shall be construed to affect the authority of any State to make use of any of its powers to enforce the laws of such State with respect to which a risk retention group is not exempt under this chapter.

(2) If a State seeks an injunction regarding the conduct described in paragraphs (1) and (2) of subsection (e) of this section, such injunction must be obtained from a Federal or State court of competent jurisdiction.

(g) States' authority to sue

Nothing in this chapter shall affect the authority of any State to bring an action in any Federal or State court.

(h) State authority to regulate or prohibit ownership interests in risk retention groups

Nothing in this chapter shall be construed to affect the authority of any State to regulate or prohibit the ownership interest in a risk retention group by an insurance company in that State, other than in the case of ownership interest in a risk retention group whose members are insurance companies.

Appendix B

Vermont Captive Statute

TITLE 8 VERMONT STATUTES ANNOTATED

CHAPTER 141. CAPTIVE INSURANCE COMPANIES

CHAPTER 142. RISK RETENTION GROUPS AND PURCHASING GROUPS

CHAPTER 142A. RISK RETENTION MANAGING GENERAL AGENTS AND REINSURANCE INTERMEDIARIES

Section 6001. Definitions

As used in this chapter, unless the context requires otherwise:

(1) "Affiliated company" means any company in the same corporate system as a parent, an industrial insured, or a member organization by virtue of common ownership, control, operation, or management.

(2) "Association" means any legal association of individuals, corporations, limited liability companies, partnerships, associations, or other entities that has been in continuous existence for at least one year, the member organizations of which or which does itself, whether or not in conjunction with some or all of the member organizations:

   (A) own, control, or hold with power to vote all of the outstanding voting securities of an association captive insurance company incorporated as a stock insurer; or

   (B) have complete voting control over an association captive insurance company incorporated as a mutual insurer; or

   (C) constitute all of the subscribers of an association captive insurance company formed as a reciprocal insurer.

(3) "Association captive insurance company" means any company that insures risks of the member organizations of the association, and their affiliated companies.

(4) "Captive insurance company" means any pure captive insurance company, association captive insurance company, sponsored captive insurance company, industrial insured captive insurance company, or risk retention group formed or licensed under the provisions of this chapter. For purposes of this chapter, a branch captive insurance company shall be a pure captive insurance company with respect to operations in this state, unless otherwise permitted by the commissioner.

(5) "Commissioner" means the commissioner of the department of banking, insurance, securities, and health care administration.

(6) "Controlled unaffiliated business" means any company:

   (A) that is not in the corporate system of a parent and affiliated companies;

   (B) that has an existing contractual relationship with a parent or affiliated company; and

   (C) whose risks are managed by a pure captive insurance company in accordance with section 6019 of this title.

(7) "Excess workers' compensation insurance" means, in the case of an employer that has insured or self-insured its workers' compensation risks in accordance with applicable state or federal law, insurance in excess of a specified per-incident or aggregate limit established by the commissioner.

(8) "Industrial insured" means an insured:

   (A) who procures the insurance of any risk or risks by use of the services of a full-time employee acting as an insurance manager or buyer;

   (B) whose aggregate annual premiums for insurance on all risks total at least $25,000.00, and

   (C) who has at least 25 full-time employees.

(9) "Industrial insured captive insurance company" means any company that insures risks of the industrial insureds that comprise the industrial insured group, and their affiliated companies.

(10) "Industrial insured group" means any group of industrial insureds that collectively:

   (A) own, control, or hold with power to vote all of the outstanding voting securities of an industrial insured captive insurance company incorporated as a stock insurer;

   (B) have complete voting control over an industrial insured captive insurance company incorporated as a mutual insurer; or

   (C) constitute all of the subscribers of an industrial insured captive insurance company formed as a reciprocal insurer.

(11) "Member organization" means any individual, corporation, limited liability company, partnership, association, or other entity that belongs to an association.

(12) "Mutual corporation" means a corporation organized without stockholders and includes a nonprofit corporation with members.

(13) "Parent" means a corporation, limited liability company, partnership, other entity, or individual, that directly or indirectly owns, controls, or holds with power to vote more than 50 per centum of the outstanding voting:

   (A) securities of a pure captive insurance company organized as a stock corporation; or

   (B) member interests of a pure captive insurance company organized as a nonprofit corporation.

(14) "Pure captive insurance company" means any company that insures risks of its parent and affiliated companies or controlled unaffiliated business.

(15) "Risk retention group" means a captive insurance company organized under the laws of this state pursuant to the Liability Risk Retention Act of 1986, 15 U.S.C. § 3901 et seq., as amended, as a stock or mutual corporation, a reciprocal or other limited liability entity.

Section 6002. Licensing; authority

(a) Any captive insurance company, when permitted by its articles of association, charter, or other organizational document, may apply to the commissioner for a license to do any and all insurance comprised in subdivisions (1), (2), (3)(A)-(C), (E)-(R) and (4)-(9) of subsection 3301(a) of this title and may grant annuity contracts as defined in section 3717 of this title; provided, however, that:

   (1) no pure captive insurance company may insure any risks other than those of its parent and affiliated companies or controlled unaffiliated business;

   (2) no association captive insurance company may insure any risks other than those of the member organizations of its association, and their affiliated companies;

   (3) no industrial insured captive insurance company may insure any risks other than those of the industrial insureds that comprise the industrial insured group, and their affiliated companies;

   (4) no risk retention group may insure any risks other than those of its members and owners;

   (5) no captive insurance company may provide personal motor vehicle or homeowner's insurance coverage or any component thereof;;

   (6) no captive insurance company may accept or cede reinsurance except as provided in section 6011 of this title;

(7) any captive insurance company may provide excess workers' compensation insurance to its parent and affiliated companies, unless prohibited by the federal law or laws of the state having jurisdiction over the transaction. Any captive insurance company, unless prohibited by federal law, may reinsure workers' compensation of a qualified self-insured plan of its parent and affiliated companies; and

(8) any captive insurance company which insures risks described in subdivisions (1) and (2) of section 3301(a) of this title shall comply with all applicable state and federal laws.

(b) No captive insurance company shall do any insurance business in this state unless:

(1) it first obtains from the commissioner a license authorizing it to do insurance business in this state;

(2) its board of directors, or committee of managers or, in the case of a reciprocal insurer, its subscribers' advisory committee, holds at least one meeting each year in this state;

(3) it maintains its principal place of business in this state; and

(4) it appoints a registered agent to accept service of process and to otherwise act on its behalf in this state

(A) provided that whenever such registered agent cannot with reasonable diligence be found at the registered office of the captive insurance company, the secretary of state shall be an agent of such captive insurance company upon whom any process, notice, or demand may be served.

(c)

(1) Before receiving a license, a captive insurance company shall:

(A) file with the commissioner a certified copy of its organizational documents, a statement under oath of its president and secretary showing its financial condition, and any other statements or documents required by the commissioner;

(B) submit to the commissioner for approval a description of the coverages, deductibles, coverage limits, and rates, together with such additional information as the commissioner may reasonably require. In the event of any subsequent material change in any item in such description, the captive insurance company shall submit to the commissioner for approval an appropriate revision and shall not offer any additional kinds of insurance until a revision of such description is approved by the commissioner. The captive insurance company shall inform the commissioner of any material change in rates within thirty (30) days of the adoption of such change.

(2) Each applicant captive insurance company shall also file with the commissioner evidence of the following:

(A) the amount and liquidity of its assets relative to the risks to be assumed;

(B) the adequacy of the expertise, experience, and character of the person or persons who will manage it;

(C) the overall soundness of its plan of operation;

(D) the adequacy of the loss prevention programs of its insureds; and

(E) such other factors deemed relevant by the commissioner in ascertaining whether the proposed captive insurance company will be able to meet its policy obligations.

(3) Information submitted pursuant to this subsection shall be and remain confidential, and may not be made public by the commissioner or an employee or agent of the commissioner without the written consent of the company, except that:

(A) such information may be discoverable by a party in a civil action or contested case to which the captive insurance company that submitted such information is a party, upon a showing by the party seeking to discover such information that: (i) the information sought is relevant to and necessary for the furtherance of such action or case; (ii) the information sought is unavailable from other nonconfidential sources; and (iii)   a subpoena issued by a judicial or administrative officer of competent jurisdiction has been submitted to the commissioner; provided, however, that the provisions of this subdivision (3) shall not apply to any risk retention group; and

(B) the commissioner may, in the commissioner's discretion, disclose such information to a public officer having jurisdiction over the regulation of insurance in another state, provided that: (i) such public official shall agree in writing to maintain the confidentiality of such information; and (ii) the laws of the state in which such public official serves require such information to be and to remain confidential.

(d) Each captive insurance company shall pay to the commissioner a nonrefundable fee of $200.00 for examining, investigating, and processing its application for license, and the commissioner is authorized to retain legal, financial and examination services from outside the department, the reasonable cost of which may be charged against the applicant. The provisions of section 3576 of this title shall apply to examinations, investigations, and processing conducted under the authority of this section. In addition, each captive insurance company shall pay a license fee for the year of registration and a renewal fee for each year thereafter of $300.00.

(e) If the commissioner is satisfied that the documents and statements that such captive insurance company has filed comply with the provisions of this chapter, the commissioner may grant a license authorizing it to do insurance business in this state until April 1 thereafter, which license may be renewed.

Section 6003. Names of companies

No captive insurance company shall adopt a name that is the same, deceptively similar, or likely to be confused with or mistaken for any other existing business name registered in the state of Vermont.

Section 6004. Minimum capital and surplus; letter of credit

(a) No captive insurance company shall be issued a license unless it shall possess and thereafter maintain unimpaired paid-in capital and surplus of:

(1) in the case of a pure captive insurance company, not less than $250,000.00;

(2) in the case of an association captive insurance company, not less than $750,000.00;

(3) in the case of an industrial insured captive insurance company, not less than $500,000.00;

(4) in the case of a risk retention group, not less than $1,000,000.00; and

(5) in the case of a sponsored captive insurance company, not less than $500,000.00.

(b) The commissioner may prescribe additional capital and surplus based upon the type, volume, and nature of insurance business transacted.

(c) Capital and surplus may be in the form of cash or an irrevocable letter of credit issued by a bank chartered by the state of Vermont or a member bank of the Federal Reserve System and approved by the commissioner.

Section 6005. Dividends

No captive insurance company may pay a dividend out of, or other distribution with respect to, capital or surplus, without the prior approval of the commissioner. Approval of an ongoing plan for the payment of dividends or other distributions shall be conditioned upon the retention, at the time of each payment, of capital or surplus in excess of amounts specified by, or determined in accordance with formulas approved by, the commissioner. Notwithstanding the provisions of chapter 13 of Title 11B, a captive insurance company organized under the provisions of Title 11B may make such distributions as are in conformity with its purposes and approved by the commissioner.

Section 6006. Formation of captive insurance companies in this state

(a) A pure captive insurance company may be incorporated as a stock insurer with its capital divided into shares and held by the stockholders, as a nonprofit corporation with one or more members, or as a manager-managed limited liability company.

(b) An association captive insurance company, an industrial insured captive insurance company, or a risk retention group may be:

(1) incorporated as a stock insurer with its capital divided into shares and held by the stockholders;

(2) incorporated as a mutual corporation;

(3) organized as a reciprocal insurer in accordance with chapter 132 of this title; or

(4) organized as a manager-managed limited liability company.

(c) A captive insurance company incorporated or organized in this state shall have not less than three incorporators or three organizers of whom not less than one shall be a resident of this state.

(d) In the case of a captive insurance company:

(1)

(A) formed as a corporation, before the articles of incorporation are transmitted to the secretary of state, the incorporators shall petition the commissioner to issue a certificate setting forth the commissioner's finding that the establishment and maintenance of the proposed corporation will promote the general good of the state. In arriving at such a finding the commissioner shall consider: (i) the character, reputation, financial standing and purposes of the incorporators; (ii) the character, reputation, financial responsibility, insurance experience, and business qualifications of the officers and directors; and (iii) such other aspects as the commissioner shall deem advisable.

(B) the articles of incorporation, such certificate, and the organization fee shall be transmitted to the secretary of state, who shall thereupon record both the articles of incorporation and the certificate.

(2) formed as a reciprocal insurer, the organizers shall petition the commissioner to issue a certificate setting forth the commissioner's finding that the establishment and maintenance of the proposed association will promote the general good of the state. In arriving at such a finding the commissioner shall consider the items set forth in subdivisions (1)(A)(i)-(iii) of this subsection.

(3) formed as a limited liability company, before the articles of organization are transmitted to the secretary of state, the organizers shall petition the

commissioner to issue a certificate setting forth the commissioner's finding that the establishment and maintenance of the proposed company will promote the general good of the state. In arriving at such a finding, the commissioner shall consider the items set forth in subdivisions (1)(A)(i)-(iii) of this subsection.

(e) The capital stock of a captive insurance company incorporated as a stock insurer may be authorized with no par value.

(f) in the case of a captive insurance company:

    (1) formed as a corporation, at least one of the members of the board of directors shall be a resident of this state;

    (2) formed as a reciprocal insurer, at least one of the members of the subscribers' advisory committee shall be a resident of this state;

    (3) formed as a limited liability company, at least one of the managers shall be a resident of this state.

(g) Other than captive insurance companies formed as limited liability companies under chapter 21 of Title 11 or as nonprofit corporations under Title 11B, captive insurance companies formed as corporations under the provisions of this chapter shall have the privileges and be subject to the provisions of Title 11A as well as the applicable provisions contained in this chapter. In the event of conflict between the provisions of said general corporation law and the provisions of this chapter, the latter shall control.

(h) Captive insurance companies formed under the provisions of this chapter:

    (1) as limited liability companies shall have the privileges and be subject to the provisions of chapter 21 of Title 11 as well as the applicable provisions contained in this chapter. In the event of a conflict between the provisions of chapter 21 of Title 11 and the provisions of this chapter, the latter shall control; or

    (2) as nonprofit corporations shall have the privileges and be subject to the provisions of Title 11B as well as the applicable provisions contained in this chapter. In the event of conflict between the provisions of Title 11B and the provisions of this chapter, the latter shall control.

(i) The provisions of subchapter 3, and subchapter 3A of chapter 101 of this title, pertaining to mergers, consolidations, conversions, mutualizations, redomestications, and mutual holding companies, shall apply in determining the procedures to be followed by captive insurance companies in carrying out any of the transactions described therein, except that:

    (1) the commissioner may, upon request of an insurer party to a merger authorized under subsection (i) of this section, waive the requirement of subdivision (6) of section 3424 of this title;

(2) the commissioner may waive or modify the requirements for public notice and hearing in accordance with rules which the commissioner may adopt addressing categories of transactions. If a notice of public hearing is required, but no one requests a hearing, then the commissioner may cancel the hearing;

(3) the provisions of subsections 3423(f) and (h) of this title shall not apply, and the commissioner may waive or modify the requirement of subdivision 3423 (b)(4) of this title, with respect to market value of a converted company as necessary or desirable to reflect applicable restrictions on ownership of companies formed under this chapter; and

(4) an alien insurer may be a party to a merger authorized under this subsection; provided that the requirements for a merger between a captive insurance company and a foreign insurer under section 3431 of this title shall apply to a merger between a captive insurance company and an alien insurer under this subsection. Such alien insurer shall be treated as a foreign insurer under section 3431 and such other jurisdictions shall be the equivalents of a state for purposes of section 3431.

(j) Captive insurance companies formed as reciprocal insurers under the provisions of this chapter shall have the privileges and be subject to the provisions of chapter 132 of this title in addition to the applicable provisions of this chapter. In the event of a conflict between the provisions of chapter 132 and the provisions of this chapter, the latter shall control. To the extent a reciprocal insurer is made subject to other provisions of this title pursuant to chapter 132, such provisions shall not be applicable to a reciprocal insurer formed under this chapter unless such provisions are expressly made applicable to captive insurance companies under this chapter.

(k) The articles of incorporation or bylaws of a captive insurance company formed as a corporation may authorize a quorum of its board of directors to consist of no fewer than one-third of the fixed or prescribed number of directors determined under section 8.24(a) of Title 11A, or under section 8.24 of Title 11B.

(l) The subscribers' agreement or other organizing document of a captive insurance company formed as a reciprocal insurer may authorize a quorum of its subscribers' advisory committee to consist of no fewer than one-third of the number of its members.

(m) With the commissioner's approval, a captive insurance company organized as a stock insurer may convert to a nonprofit corporation with one or more members by filing with the secretary of state an irrevocable election for such conversion, provided that:

(1) the irrevocable election shall certify that, at the time of the company's original organization and at all times thereafter, the company conducted its business in a manner not inconsistent with a nonprofit purpose; and

(2) at the time of its irrevocable election, the company shall file with both the commissioner and the secretary of state amended and restated articles of incorporation consistent with the provisions of this chapter and with Title 11B, duly authorized by the corporation.

(n) The following provisions of Title 11B shall not apply to captive insurance companies which are nonprofit corporations:

(1) subsection 2.02(c) (relating to the signing of articles of incorporation by directors);

(2) section 11.02, in the case of any merger in which a captive insurance company merges with and into a captive insurance company organized as a nonprofit corporation under Title 11B where the latter is the surviving corporation.

Section 6007. Reports and statements

(a) Captive insurance companies shall not be required to make any annual report except as provided in this chapter.

(b) Prior to March 1 of each year, each captive insurance company shall submit to the commissioner a report of its financial condition, verified by oath of two of its executive officers. Each captive insurance company shall report using generally accepted accounting principles, unless the commissioner approves the use of statutory accounting principles, with any appropriate or necessary modifications or adaptations thereof required or approved or accepted by the commissioner for the type of insurance and kinds of insurers to be reported upon, and as supplemented by additional information required by the commissioner. Except as otherwise provided, each association captive insurance company and each risk retention group shall file its report in the form required by section 3561 of this title, and each risk retention group shall comply with the requirements set forth in section 3569 of this title. The commissioner shall by rule propose the forms in which pure captive insurance companies and industrial insured captive insurance companies shall report. Subdivision 6002(c)(3) of this title shall apply to each report filed pursuant to this section, except that such subdivision shall not apply to reports filed by risk retention groups.

(c) Any pure captive insurance company or an industrial insured captive insurance company may make written application for filing the required report on a fiscal year-end. If an alternative reporting date is granted:

(1) the annual report is due 60 days after the fiscal year-end; and

(2) in order to provide sufficient detail to support the premium tax return, the pure captive insurance company or industrial insured captive insurance company shall file prior to March 1 of each year for each calendar year-end, pages 1, 2, 3,

and 5 of the "Captive Annual Statement; Pure or Industrial Insured", verified by oath of two of its executive officers.

Section 6008. Examinations and investigations

(a) At least once in three years, and whenever the commissioner determines it to be prudent, the commissioner shall personally, or by some competent person appointed by the commissioner, visit each captive insurance company and thoroughly inspect and examine its affairs to ascertain its financial condition, its ability to fulfill its obligations and whether it has complied with the provisions of this chapter. The commissioner may enlarge the aforesaid three-year period to five years, provided said captive insurance company is subject to a comprehensive annual audit during such period of a scope satisfactory to the commissioner by independent auditors approved by the commissioner. The expenses and charges of the examination shall be paid to the state by the company or companies examined and the commissioner of finance and management shall issue his or her warrants for the proper charges incurred in all examinations.

(b) The provisions of section 3576 of this title shall apply to examinations conducted under this section.

(c) All examination reports, preliminary examination reports or results, working papers, recorded information, documents and copies thereof produced by, obtained by or disclosed to the commissioner or any other person in the course of an examination made under this section are confidential and are not subject to subpoena and may not be made public by the commissioner or an employee or agent of the commissioner without the written consent of the company, except to the extent provided in this subsection. Nothing in this subsection shall prevent the commissioner from using such information in furtherance of the commissioner's regulatory authority under this title. The commissioner may, in the commissioner's discretion, grant access to such information to public officers having jurisdiction over the regulation of insurance in any other state or country, or to law enforcement officers of this state or any other state or agency of the federal government at any time, so long as such officers receiving the information agree in writing to hold it in a manner consistent with this section.

Section 6009. Grounds and procedures for suspension or revocation of license

(a) The license of a captive insurance company may be suspended or revoked by the commissioner for any of the following reasons:

(1) Insolvency or impairment of capital or surplus;

(2) Failure to meet the requirements of section 6004 of this title;

(3) Refusal or failure to submit an annual report, as required by this chapter, or any other report or statement required by law or by lawful order of the commissioner;

(4) Failure to comply with the provisions of its own charter, bylaws or other organizational document;

(5) Failure to submit to or pay the cost of examination or any legal obligation relative thereto, as required by this chapter;

(6) Use of methods that, although not otherwise specifically prohibited by law, nevertheless render its operation detrimental or its condition unsound with respect to the public or to its policyholders; or

(7) Failure otherwise to comply with the laws of this state.

(b) If the commissioner finds, upon examination, hearing, or other evidence, that any captive insurance company has violated any provision of subsection (a) of this section, the commissioner may suspend or revoke such company's license if the commissioner deems it in the best interest of the public and the policyholders of such captive insurance company, notwithstanding any other provision of this title.

Section 6010. Legal investments

(a) Except as may be otherwise authorized by the commissioner, association captive insurance companies and risk retention groups shall comply with the investment requirements contained in sections 3461 through 3472, of this title, as applicable Section 3463a of this title shall apply to association captive insurance companies and risk retention groups except to the extent it is inconsistent with approved accounting standards in use by the company. Notwithstanding any other provision of this title, the commissioner may approve the use of alternative reliable methods of valuation and rating.

(b) No pure captive insurance company or industrial insured captive insurance company shall be subject to any restrictions on allowable investments whatever, including those limitations contained in sections 3461-3472; provided, however, that the commissioner may prohibit or limit any investment that threatens the solvency or liquidity of any such company.

(c) No pure captive insurance company may make a loan to or an investment in its parent company or affiliates without prior written approval of the commissioner, and any such loan or investment must be evidenced by documentation approved by the commissioner. Loans of minimum capital and surplus funds required by section 6004 of this title are prohibited.

Section 6011. Reinsurance

(a) Any captive insurance company may provide reinsurance, comprised in section 3301(a) of this title, on risks ceded by any other insurer.

(b) Any captive insurance company may take credit for the reinsurance of risks or portions of risks ceded to reinsurers complying with the provisions of subsections 3634a(a) through (f) of this title. Prior approval of the commissioner shall be required for ceding or taking credit for the reinsurance of risks or portions of risks ceded to reinsurers not complying with subsections 3634a(a) through (f) of this title, except for business written by an alien captive insurance company outside of the United States.

(c) In addition to reinsurers authorized under the provisions of section 3634a of this title, a captive insurance company may take credit for the reinsurance of risks or portions of risks ceded to a pool, exchange or association acting as a reinsurer which has been authorized by the commissioner. The commissioner may require any other documents, financial information or other evidence that such a pool, exchange or association will be able to provide adequate security for its financial obligations. The commissioner may deny authorization or impose any limitations on the activities of a reinsurance pool, exchange or association that, in the commissioner's judgement, are necessary and proper to provide adequate security for the ceding captive insurance company and for the protection and consequent benefit of the public at large.

(d) For all purposes of this chapter, insurance by a captive insurance company of any workers' compensation qualified self-insured plan of its parent and affiliates shall be deemed to be reinsurance.

Section 6012. Rating organizations; memberships

No captive insurance company shall be required to join a rating organization.

Section 6013. Exemption from compulsory associations

No captive insurance company, shall be permitted to join or contribute financially to any plan, pool, association, or guaranty or insolvency fund in this state, nor shall any such captive insurance company, or any insured or affiliate thereof, receive any benefit from any such plan, pool, association, or guaranty or insolvency fund for claims arising out of the operations of such captive insurance company.

Section 6014. Tax on premiums collected

(a) Each captive insurance company shall pay to the commissioner of taxes, in the month of February of each year, a tax at the rate of 38 hundredths of one percent on the first 20 million dollars and 285 thousandths of one percent on the next 20 million dollars and 19 hundredths of one percent on the next 20 million dollars and 72 thousandths of one percent on each dollar thereafter on the direct premiums collected or contracted for on policies or contracts of insurance written by the captive insurance company during the year ending December 31 next preceding, after deducting from the direct premiums subject to the tax the amounts paid to policyholders as return premiums which shall include dividends on unabsorbed premiums or premium deposits returned or credited to policyholders; provided, however, that no tax shall be due or payable as to considerations received for annuity contracts.

(b) Each captive insurance company shall pay to the commissioner of taxes in the month of February of each year a tax at the rate of 214 thousandths of one percent on the first 20 million dollars of assumed reinsurance premium, and 143 thousandths of one percent on the next 20 million dollars and 48 thousandths of one percent on the next 20 million dollars and 24 thousandths of one percent of each dollar thereafter. However, no reinsurance tax applies to premiums for risks or portions of risks which are subject to taxation on a direct basis pursuant to subsection (a) of this section. No reinsurance premium tax shall be payable in connection with the receipt of assets in exchange for the assumption of loss reserves and other liabilities of another insurer under common ownership and control if such transaction is part of a plan to discontinue the operations of such other insurer, and if the intent of the parties to such transaction is to renew or maintain such business with the captive insurance company.

(c) The annual minimum aggregate tax to be paid by a captive insurance company calculated under subsections (a) and (b) of this section shall be $7,500.00 and the annual maximum aggregate tax shall be $200,000.00. The maximum aggregate tax to be paid by a sponsored insurance company shall apply to each protected cell only and not to the sponsored captive insurance company as a whole.

(d) A captive insurance company failing to make returns as required by chapter 211 of Title 32 or failing to pay within the time required all taxes assessed by this section, shall be subject to the provisions of sections 5868, 5869, 5873 and 5875 of Title 32.

(e) Two or more captive insurance companies under common ownership and control shall be taxed, as though they were a single captive insurance company.

(f) For the purposes of this section common ownership and control shall mean:

    (1) in the case of stock corporations, the direct or indirect ownership of 80 percent or more of the outstanding voting stock of two or more corporations by the same shareholder or shareholders; and

    (2) in the case of mutual or nonprofit corporations, the direct or indirect ownership of 80 percent or more of the surplus and the voting power of two or more corporations by the same member or members.

(g) The tax provided for in this section shall constitute all taxes collectible under the laws of this state from any captive insurance company, and no other occupation tax or other taxes shall be levied or collected from any captive insurance company by the state or any county, city, or municipality within this state, except ad valorem taxes on real and personal property used in the production of income.

(h) Annually, ten percent of the premium tax revenues collected pursuant to this section shall be transferred to the department of banking, insurance, securities, and health care administration for the regulation of captive insurance companies under this chapter.

(i) Repealed.

(j) The tax provided for in this section shall be calculated on an annual basis, notwithstanding policies or contracts of insurance or contracts of reinsurance issued on a multiyear basis. In the case of multiyear policies or contracts, the premium shall be prorated for purposes of determining the tax under this section.

Section 6015. Rules and regulations

The commissioner may establish and from time to time amend such rules relating to captive insurance companies as are necessary to enable the commissioner to carry out the provisions of this chapter.

Section 6016. Laws applicable

No provisions of this title, other than those contained in this chapter or contained in specific references contained in this chapter, shall apply to captive insurance companies. Risk retention groups shall have the privileges and be subject to the provisions of chapter 142 of this title in addition to the applicable provisions of this chapter.

Section 6017. Captive insurance regulatory and supervision fund

(a)

    (1) There is hereby created a fund to be known as the captive insurance regulatory and supervision fund for the purpose of providing the financial means for the

commissioner of banking, insurance, securities, and health care administration to administer this chapter, chapter 142, and chapter 142A and for reasonable expenses incurred in promoting the captive insurance industry in Vermont. The transfer of ten percent of the premium tax under subsection 6014(h) of this title, and all fees and assessments received by the department pursuant to the administration of these chapters shall be credited to this fund. Of this amount, not more than two percent of the premium tax under Section 6014 may be transferred to the agency of commerce and community development, with approval of the secretary of administration, for promotional expenses. All fees received by the department from reinsurers who assume risk solely from captive insurance companies and are subject to the provisions of subsections 3634a(a) through (f) of this title, shall be deposited into the captive insurance regulatory and supervision fund. All fines and administrative penalties, however, shall be deposited directly into the general fund.

(2) All payments from the captive insurance regulatory and supervision fund for the maintenance of staff and associated expenses, including contractual services as necessary, shall be disbursed from the state treasury only upon warrants issued by the commissioner of finance and management, after receipt of proper documentation regarding services rendered and expenses incurred.

(b) At the end of each fiscal year, that portion of the balance in the captive insurance regulatory and supervision fund which exceeds $250,000.00 shall be transferred to the general fund.

(c) The commissioner of finance and management may anticipate receipts to the captive insurance regulatory and supervision fund and issue warrants based thereon.

Section 6018. Delinquency

Except as otherwise provided in this chapter, the terms and conditions set forth in chapter 145 of this title, pertaining to insurance reorganizations, receiverships and injunctions, shall apply in full to captive insurance companies formed or licensed under this chapter.

Section 6019. Rules for controlled unaffiliated business

The commissioner may adopt rules establishing standards to ensure that a parent or affiliated company is able to exercise control of the risk management function of any controlled unaffiliated business to be insured by the pure captive insurance company; provided, however, that, until such time as rules under this section are adopted, the commissioner may approve the coverage of such risks by a pure captive insurance company.

Section 6020. Conversion to or merger with reciprocal insurer

(a) An association captive insurance company, risk retention group, or industrial insured captive insurance company formed as a stock or mutual corporation may be converted to or merged with and into a reciprocal insurer in accordance with a plan therefor and the provisions of this section.

(b) Any plan for such conversion or merger shall provide a fair and equitable plan for purchasing, retiring, or otherwise extinguishing the interests of the stockholders and policyholders of a stock insurer, and the members and policyholders of a mutual insurer, including a fair and equitable provision for the rights and remedies of dissenting stockholders, members, or policyholders.

(c) In the case of a conversion authorized under subsection (a) of this section:

    (1) such conversion shall be accomplished under such reasonable plan and procedure as may be approved by the commissioner; provided, however, that the commissioner shall not approve any such plan of conversion unless such plan:

        (A) satisfies the provisions of subsection (b) of this section;

        (B) provides for a hearing, of which notice is given or to be given to the captive insurance company, its directors, officers, and policyholders, and, in the case of a stock insurer, its stockholders, and in the case of a mutual insurer, its members, all of which persons shall be entitled to attend and appear at such hearing; provided, however, that if notice of a hearing is given and no director, officer, policyholder, member, or stockholder requests a hearing, the commissioner may cancel such hearing;

        (C) provides a fair and equitable plan for the conversion of stockholder, member, or policyholder interests into subscriber interests in the resulting reciprocal insurer, substantially proportionate to the corresponding interests in the stock or mutual insurer; provided, however, that this requirement shall not preclude the resulting reciprocal insurer from applying underwriting criteria that could affect ongoing ownership interests; and

        (D) is approved: (i) in the case of a stock insurer, by a majority of the shares entitled to vote represented in person or by proxy at a duly called regular or special meeting at which a quorum is present; and (ii) in the case of a mutual insurer, by a majority of the voting interests of policyholders represented in person or by proxy at a duly called regular or special meeting thereof at which a quorum is present;

    (2) the commissioner shall approve such plan of conversion if the commissioner finds that the conversion will promote the general good of the state in conformity with those standards set forth in subdivision 6006(d)(2) of this title;

(3) if the commissioner approves the plan, the commissioner shall amend the converting insurer's certificate of authority to reflect conversion to a reciprocal insurer and issue such amended certificate of authority to the company's attorney-in-fact;

(4) upon the issuance of an amended certificate of authority of a reciprocal insurer by the commissioner, the conversion shall be effective; and

(5) upon the effectiveness of such conversion the corporate existence of the converting insurer shall cease and the resulting reciprocal insurer shall notify the secretary of state of such conversion.

(d) A merger authorized under subsection (a) of this section shall be accomplished substantially in accordance with the procedures set forth in sections 3424, 3426 and 3431 of this title, except that, solely for purposes of such merger:

(1) the plan of merger shall satisfy the provisions of subsection (b) of this section;

(2) the subscribers' advisory committee of a reciprocal insurer shall be equivalent to the board of directors of a stock or mutual insurance company;

(3) the subscribers of a reciprocal insurer shall be the equivalent of the policyholders of a mutual insurance company;

(4) if a subscribers' advisory committee does not have a president or secretary, the officers of such committee having substantially equivalent duties shall be deemed the president or secretary of such committee;

(5) the commissioner may, upon request of an insurer party to a merger authorized under subsection (a) of this section, waive the requirement of subdivision (6) of section 3424 of this title;

(6) subdivision (7) of section 3424 of this title shall not apply to such merger;

(7) the commissioner shall approve the articles of merger if the commissioner finds that the merger will promote the general good of the state in conformity with those standards set forth in subdivision 6006(d)(2) of this title. If the commissioner approves the articles of merger, the commissioner shall indorse the commissioner's approval thereon and the surviving insurer shall present the same to the secretary of state at the secretary of state's office;

(8) notwithstanding section 6004 of this title, the commissioner may permit the formation, without surplus, of a captive insurance company organized as a reciprocal insurer, into which an existing captive insurance company may be merged for the purpose of facilitating a transaction under this section; provided, however, that there shall be no more than one authorized insurance company surviving such merger; and

(9) an alien insurer may be a party to a merger authorized under subsection (a) of this section; provided, that the requirements for a merger between a domestic

and a foreign insurer under section 3431 of this title shall apply to a merger between a domestic and an alien insurer under this subsection. Such alien insurer shall be treated as a foreign insurer under section 3431 and such other jurisdictions shall be the equivalent of a state for purposes of section 3431.

(e)   A conversion or merger under this section shall have all of the effects set forth in subdivisions (3), (4) and (5) of section 3430 of this title, to the extent such effects are not inconsistent with the provisions of this chapter.

8 V.S.A. §§6021-6023 are recodified as 8 V.S.A. §§6034-6036.

Subchapter 2. Sponsored Captive Insurance Companies

Section 6031. Formation

(a)   One or more sponsors may form a sponsored captive insurance company under this chapter. In addition to the general provisions of this chapter, the provisions of this subchapter shall apply to sponsored captive insurance companies.

(b)   A sponsored captive insurance company shall be incorporated as a stock insurer with its capital divided into shares and held by the stockholders.

Section 6032. Definitions

As used in this subchapter, unless the context requires otherwise:

(1)   "Participant" mans an entity as defined in section 6036 of this title, and any affiliates thereof, that are insured by a sponsored captive insurance company, where the losses of the participant are limited through a participant contract to such participant's pro rata share of the assets of one or more protected cells identified in such participant contract.

(2)   "Participant contract" means a contract by which a sponsored captive insurance company insures the risks of a participant and limits the losses of each such participant to its pro rata share of the assets of one or more protected cells identified in such participant contract.

(3)   "Protected cell" means a separate account established by a sponsored captive insurance company formed or licensed under the provisions of this chapter, in which assets are maintained for one or more participants in accordance with the terms of one or more participant contracts to fund the liability of the sponsored captive insurance company assumed on behalf of such participants as set forth in such participant contracts.

(4)   "Sponsor" means any entity that meets the requirements of section 6035 of this title and is approved by the commissioner to provide all or part of the capital and surplus

required by applicable law and to organize and operate a sponsored captive insurance company.

(5) "Sponsored captive insurance company" means any captive insurance company:

(A) in which the minimum capital and surplus required by applicable law is provided by one or more sponsors;

(B) that is formed or licensed under the provisions of this chapter;

(C) that insures the risks only of its participants through separate participant contracts; and

(D) that funds its liability to each participant through one or more protected cells and segregates the assets of each protected cell from the assets of other protected cells and from the assets of the sponsored captive insurance company's general account.

Section 6033. Supplemental application materials

In addition to the information required by subdivisions 6002(c)(1) and (2) of this title, each applicant-sponsored captive insurance company shall file with the commissioner the following:

(1) materials demonstrating how the applicant will account for the loss and expense experience of each protected cell at a level of detail found to be sufficient by the commissioner, and how it will report such experience to the commissioner;

(2) a statement acknowledging that all financial records of the sponsored captive insurance company, including records pertaining to any protected cells, shall be made available for inspection or examination by the commissioner or the commissioner's designated agent;

(3) all contracts or sample contracts between the sponsored captive insurance company and any participants; and

(4) evidence that expenses shall be allocated to each protected cell in a fair and equitable manner.

Section 6034. Protected cells

A sponsored captive insurance company formed or licensed under the provisions of this chapter may establish and maintain one or more protected cells to insure risks of one or more participants, subject to the following conditions:

(1) the shareholders of a sponsored captive insurance company shall be limited to its participants and sponsors, provided that a sponsored captive insurance company

may issue nonvoting securities to other persons on terms approved by the commissioner;

(2) each protected cell shall be accounted for separately on the books and records of the sponsored captive insurance company to reflect the financial condition and results of operations of such protected cell, net income or loss, dividends or other distributions to participants, and such other factors as may be provided in the participant contract or required by the commissioner;

(3) the assets of a protected cell shall not be chargeable with liabilities arising out of any other insurance business the sponsored captive insurance company may conduct;

(4) no sale, exchange, transfer of assets, dividend or distribution may be made by such sponsored captive insurance company between or among any of its protected cells without the consent of such protected cells;

(5) no sale, exchange, transfer of assets, dividend or distribution may be made from a protected cell to a sponsor or participant without the commissioner's approval and in no event shall such approval be given if the sale, exchange, transfer, dividend or distribution would result in insolvency or impairment with respect to a protected cell;

(6) each sponsored captive insurance company shall annually file with the commissioner such financial reports as the commissioner shall require, which shall include, without limitation, accounting statements detailing the financial experience of each protected cell;

(7) each sponsored captive insurance company shall notify the commissioner in writing within 10 business days of any protected cell that is insolvent or otherwise unable to meet its claim or expense obligations;

(8) no participant contract shall take effect without the commissioner's prior written approval, and the addition of each new protected cell and withdrawal of any participant or termination of any existing protected cell shall constitute a change in the business plan requiring the commissioner's prior written approval; and

(9) the business written by a sponsored captive, with respect to each cell, shall be:

(A) fronted by an insurance company licensed under the laws of any state;

(B) reinsured by a reinsurer authorized or approved by the state of Vermont; or

(C) secured by a trust fund in the United States for the benefit of policyholders and claimants or funded by an irrevocable letter of credit or other arrangement that is acceptable to the commissioner. The amount of security provided shall be no less than the reserves associated with those liabilities which are neither fronted nor reinsured, including reserves for losses, allocated loss adjustment expenses, incurred but not reported losses and unearned premiums for business written through the participant's protected cell. The commissioner may require the sponsored captive to increase the funding of any security arrangement established under this subdivision. If the form of security is a letter of credit, the letter of credit must be established, issued or confirmed by a bank chartered in this state, a member of the Federal Reserve System, or a bank chartered by another state if such state chartered bank is acceptable to the commissioner. A trust maintained pursuant to this subdivision shall be established in a form and upon such terms approved by the commissioner.

Section 6035. Qualification of sponsors

A sponsor of a sponsored captive insurance company shall be an insurer licensed under the laws of any state, a reinsurer authorized or approved under the laws of any state, or a captive insurance company formed or licensed under this chapter. A risk retention group shall not be either a sponsor or a participant of a sponsored captive insurance company.

Section 6036. Participants in sponsored captive insurance companies

(a) Associations, corporations, limited liability companies, partnerships, trusts, and other business entities may be participants in any sponsored captive insurance company formed or licensed under this chapter.

(b) A sponsor may be a participant in a sponsored captive insurance company.

(c) A participant need not be a shareholder of the sponsored captive insurance company or any affiliate thereof.

(d) A participant shall insure only its own risks through a sponsored captive insurance company.

Section 6037. Investments by sponsored captive insurance companies

Notwithstanding the provisions of section 6034 of this title, the assets of two or more protected cells may be combined for purposes of investment, and such combination shall not be construed as defeating the segregation of such assets for accounting or other purposes. Sponsored captive insurance companies shall comply with the investment requirements contained in sections 3461 through 3472 of this title, as applicable; provided, however, that compliance with such investment requirements shall be waived for sponsored captive insurance companies to the extent that credit for reinsurance ceded to reinsurers is allowed pursuant to section 6011 of this title or to the extent otherwise deemed reasonable and appropriate by the commissioner. Section 3463a. of this title shall apply to sponsored captive insurance companies except to the extent it is inconsistent with approved accounting standards in use by the company. Notwithstanding any other provision of this title, the commissioner may approve the use of alternative reliable methods of valuation and rating.

Section 6038. Delinquency of sponsored captive insurance companies

In the case of a sponsored captive insurance company, the provisions of section 6018 of this title shall apply, provided:

(1) the assets of a protected cell may not be used to pay any expenses or claims other than those attributable to such protected cell; and

(2) its capital and surplus shall at all times be available to pay any expenses of or claims against the sponsored captive insurance company.

Subchapter 3. Branch captive insurance companies

Section 6041. Establishment of a branch captive

(a) A branch captive may be established in this state in accordance with the provisions of this chapter to write in this state only insurance or reinsurance of the employee benefit business of its parent and affiliated companies which is subject to the provision of the Employee Retirement Income Security Act of 1974, as amended. In addition to the general provisions of this chapter, the provisions of this subchapter shall apply to branch captive insurance companies.

(b) No branch captive insurance company shall do any insurance business in this state unless it maintains the principal place of business for its branch operations in this state.

Section 6042. Definitions

As used in this subchapter, unless the context requires otherwise:

(1) "Alien captive insurance company" means any insurance company formed to write insurance business for its parents and affiliates and licensed pursuant to the laws of an alien jurisdiction which imposes statutory or regulatory standards in a form acceptable to the commissioner on companies transacting the business of insurance in such jurisdiction.

(2) "Branch business" means any insurance business transacted by a branch captive insurance company in this state.

(3) "Branch captive insurance company" means any alien captive insurance company licensed by the commissioner to transact the business of insurance in this state through a business unit with a principal place of business in this state.

(4) "Branch operations" means any business operations of a branch captive insurance company in this state.

Section 6043. Security required

In the case of a branch captive insurance company, as security for the payment of liabilities attributable to the branch operations, the commissioner shall require that either a trust fund, funded by assets acceptable to the commissioner or an irrevocable letter of credit be established and maintained in the United States for the benefit of United States policyholders and United States ceding insurers under insurance policies issued or reinsurance contracts issued or assumed by the branch captive insurance company through its branch operations. The amount of such security may be no less than the amount set forth in subdivision 6004(a)(1) of this title and the reserves on such insurance policies or such reinsurance contracts, including reserves for losses, allocated loss adjustment expenses, incurred but not reported losses, and unearned premiums with regard to business written through the branch operations; provided, however, the commissioner may permit a branch captive insurance company that is required to post security for loss reserves on branch business by its reinsurer to reduce the funds in the trust account or the amount payable under the irrevocable letter of credit required by this section by the same amount so long as the security remains posted with the insurer. If the form of security selected is a letter of credit, the letter of credit must be established by, or issued or confirmed by, a bank chartered in this state or a member bank of the Federal Reserve System.

Section 6044. Certificate of general good

In the case of a captive insurance company licensed as a branch captive, the alien captive insurance company shall petition the commissioner to issue a certificate setting forth the commissioner's finding that, after considering the character, reputation, financial responsibility, insurance experience, and business qualifications of the officers and directors of the alien captive insurance company, the licensing and maintenance of the branch operations will promote the general good of the state. The alien captive insurance company may register to do business in this state after the commissioner's certificate is issued.

Section 6045. Branch captive reports

Prior to March 1 of each year, or with the approval of the commissioner within 60 days after its fiscal year-end, a branch captive insurance company shall file with the commissioner a copy of all reports and statements required to be filed under the laws of the jurisdiction in which the alien captive insurance company is formed, verified by oath of two of its executive officers. If the commissioner is satisfied that the annual report filed by the alien captive insurance company in its domiciliary jurisdiction provides adequate information concerning the financial condition of the alien captive insurance company, the commissioner may waive the requirement for completion of the captive annual statement for business written in the alien jurisdiction.

Section 6046. Examination of branch captives

(a) The examination of a branch captive insurance company pursuant to section 6008 of this title shall be of branch business and branch operations only, so long as the branch captive insurance company provides annually to the commissioner a certificate of compliance, or its equivalent, issued by or filed with the licensing authority of the jurisdiction in which the branch captive insurance company is formed, and demonstrates to the commissioner's satisfaction that it is operating in sound financial condition in accordance with all applicable laws and regulations of such jurisdiction.

(b) As a condition of licensure, the alien captive insurance company shall grant authority to the commissioner for examination of the affairs of the alien captive insurance company in the jurisdiction in which the alien captive insurance company is formed.

Section 6047. Taxation of branch captives

In the case of a branch captive insurance company, the tax provided for in section 6014 of this title shall apply only to the branch business of such company.

Section 6050. Purpose

The purpose of this chapter is to regulate the formation and operation of risk retention groups and purchasing groups in this state formed pursuant to the provisions of the federal Liability Risk Retention Act of 1986 ("RRA 1986"), to the extent permitted by such law.

Section 6051. Definitions

As used in this chapter:

(1) "Commissioner" means the commissioner of the department of banking, insurance, securities, and health care administration of this state, or the commissioner, director or superintendent of insurance in any other state.

(2) "Domicile", for purposes of determining the state in which a purchasing group is domiciled, means:

(A) for a corporation, the state in which the purchasing group is incorporated; and

(B) for an unincorporated entity, the state of its principal place of business.

(3) "Hazardous financial condition" shall have the same meaning as in 15 U.S.C. §3901(a)(7).

(4) "Insurance" shall have the same meaning as in 15 U.S.C. §3901(a)(1).

(5) "Liability" shall have the same meaning as in 15 U.S.C. §3901 (a)(2).

(6) "Personal risk liability" shall have the same meaning as in 15 U.S.C. §3901 (a)(3).

(7) "Plan of operation and feasibility study" means an analysis which presents the expected activities and results of a risk retention group as required by chapter 141 of this title.

(8) "Product liability" means liability for damages because of any personal injury, death, emotional harm, consequential economic damage, or property damage, including damages resulting from the loss of use of property, arising out of the manufacture, design, importation, distribution, packaging, labeling, lease, or sale of a product, but does not include the liability of any person for those damages if the product involved was in the possession of such a person when the incident giving rise to the claim occurred.

(9) "Purchasing group" has the same meaning as in 15 U.S.C. §3901(a)(5).

(10) "Risk retention group" shall have the same meaning as in 15 U.S.C. §3901(a)(4).

(11) "State" means any state of the United States or the District of Columbia.

Section 6052. Risk retention groups chartered in this state

(a) Pursuant to the provisions of chapter 141 of this title, a risk retention group shall be chartered and licensed to write only liability insurance pursuant to this chapter, must comply with all of the laws, rules, regulations and requirements applicable to such insurers chartered and licensed in this state under chapter 141 of this title, and with subdivisions (4), (5), (7), and (8) of section 6053 of this title. A risk retention group chartered in this state may provide coverage for payment of punitive damages, the multiplied portion of multiple damages, or other penalties in the nature of compensatory damages, and any such coverage shall be enforceable against such risk retention group in accordance with its terms.

(b) Before it may offer insurance in any state, each risk retention group shall also submit for approval to the insurance commissioner of this state a plan of operation and feasibility study which includes a description of the coverages, deductibles, coverage limits, rates, and rating classification systems for each line of insurance the group intends to offer, together with such additional information as the commissioner may reasonably require. The risk retention group shall submit for approval by the commissioner an appropriate revision in the event of any subsequent material change in any item of the plan of operation or feasibility study, including any material change in the information called for in subsection (c) of this section, but excluding the identity of policyholders and any changes in rates or rating classification systems. The group shall not offer any additional kinds of liability insurance, in this state or in any other state, until a revision of such plan or study is approved by the commissioner. The risk retention group shall inform the commissioner of any material changes in rates or rating classification systems, within thirty (30)   days of the adoption of such change.

(c)

(1) At the time of filing its application for charter, the risk retention group shall provide to the commissioner in summary form the following information:

(A) the identity of the initial policyholders or members of the group or if the identity is not known or cannot be determined, a description of who is eligible to be a policyholder or a member;

(B) the identity of the persons that organized the group;

(C) the identity of any persons that will act as a managing general agent or reinsurance intermediary for, provide other significant administrative services to, or otherwise influence or control the activities of, the group;

(D) summary descriptions of the services, described in subdivision (C) of this subsection, and of any contracts under which the services are to be performed, including the method of compensation therefor;

(E) the amount and nature of initial capitalization;

(F) plans for the payment of dividends or other distributions of members' capital and surplus; and

(G) the states in which the group intends to file.

(2) The applicant may bind separately any portions of the application or any amendment thereto that contain proprietary information or documents, and request confidential treatment of such portions. For the purposes of this section, "proprietary information or documents" means certain information or documents furnished by or pertaining to any of the persons specified above that would customarily be treated as confidential or sensitive and the disclosure of which could result in harm or prejudice to the person to whom the information or documents pertain or unfair advantage to another person. Such information includes, but is not limited to, trade secrets, historical or projected loss data or case reserves of members of policyholders, actuarial analyses which include such

data or reserves, historical or projected financial data not otherwise publicly available, and similar information or documents. The commissioner shall determine which portions specified by the applicant fall within the definition of proprietary information or documents and treat such portions as confidential. Provided, however, that nothing herein shall excuse the applicant from making any required disclosure under the RRA 1986, this chapter or chapter 141 of this title, or prohibit the commissioner from disclosing any proprietary information or documents in the furtherance of any legal or regulatory proceeding. Before using proprietary information or documents in a legal or regulatory proceeding that does not involve the applicant or any person named in the application or any amendment thereto, the commissioner shall first seek to obtain the same information from nonconfidential sources. If unavailable from nonconfidential sources, the commissioner shall seek to protect the confidential information or documents from unnecessary disclosure. Upon licensing, the commissioner shall forward to the National Association of Insurance Commissioners all information required under the RRA 1986 to be submitted to each state where the risk retention group proposes to operate and all other information not deemed confidential under this section. Providing notification to the National Association of Insurance Commissioners is in addition to and shall not be sufficient to satisfy the requirements of section 6053 or any other sections of this chapter.

(d) The provisions of section 6008(c) of this title shall apply to risk retention groups chartered in this state, except that such provisions shall not apply to final examination reports relating to risk retention groups.

Section 6053. Risk retention groups not chartered in this state

Risk retention groups chartered and licensed in states other than this state and seeking to do business, as a risk retention group in this state shall comply with the laws of this state as follows:

(1) Notice of operations and designation of secretary of state as agent. Before offering insurance in this state, a risk retention group shall submit to the commissioner:

(A) a statement identifying the state or states in which the risk retention group is chartered and licensed as a liability insurance company, charter date, its principle place of business, and such other information, including information on its membership, as the commissioner of this state may require to verify that the risk retention group is qualified under section 6051(11) of this title;

(B) a copy of its plan of operations and feasibility study and revisions of such plan or study submitted to the state in which the risk retention group is chartered and licensed; provided, however, that the provision relating to the submission of a plan of operation or feasibility study shall not apply with respect to any line or classification of liability insurance which:

(i)   was defined in the Product Liability Risk Retention Act of 1981 before October 27, 1986; and

(ii) was offered before such date by any risk retention group which had been chartered and operating for not less than three years before such date; and

(iii) the risk retention group shall submit a copy of any revision to its plan of operation or feasibility study required by section 6052(b) of this title at the time that such revision has become effective in its chartering state; and

(C)   a statement of registration, for which a filing fee shall be determined by the commissioner, which designates the secretary of state as its agent for the purpose of receiving service of legal documents or process.

(2) Financial condition. Any risk retention group doing business in this state shall submit to the commissioner:

(A)   a copy of the group's financial statement submitted to the state in which the risk retention group is chartered and licensed which shall be certified by an independent public accountant and contain a statement of opinion on loss and loss adjustment expense reserves made by a member of the American Academy of Actuaries or a qualified loss reserve specialist, under criteria established by the National Association of Insurance Commissioners;

(B)   a copy of each examination of the risk retention group as certified by the commissioner or public official conducting the examination.

(C)   upon request by the commissioner, a copy of any information or document pertaining to any outside audit performed with respect to the risk retention group.

(3) Taxation. Each risk retention group subject to the provisions of this section shall be liable for the payment of premium taxes and taxes on premiums of direct business for risks resident or located within this state as provided in section 8551 of Title 32, and shall report to the commissioner the net premiums written for risks resident or located within this state. Such risk retention group shall be subject to taxation, and any applicable fines and penalties related thereto, on the same basis as a foreign admitted insurer.

(4) Compliance with Unfair Claims Settlement Practices Law. Any risk retention group, its agents and representatives shall comply with the Unfair Claims Settlement Practices Act of this state, section 4724(9) of this title.

(5) Deceptive, false, or fraudulent practices. Any risk retention group shall comply with section 4724(1) through (5) of this title regarding deceptive, false or fraudulent acts or practices.

(6) Examination regarding financial condition. Any risk retention group may be required to submit to an examination by the commissioner to determine its financial condition if the commissioner of the jurisdiction in which the group is chartered and licensed has not initiated an examination or does not initiate an examination within 60 days after a request by the commissioner of this state. Any such examination shall be coordinated to avoid unjustified repetition and conducted in an expeditious manner and in accordance with the Examiner Handbook of the National Association of Insurance Commissioners.

(7) Notice to purchasers. Risk retention groups shall be required to notify purchasers as required by 15 U.S.C., §3902(a)(1)(I).

(8) Prohibited acts regarding solicitation or sale. The following acts by a risk retention group are hereby prohibited:

(A) The solicitation or sale of insurance by a risk retention group to any person who is not eligible for membership in such group; and

(B) The solicitation or sale of insurance by, or operation of, a risk retention group that is in hazardous financial condition or financially impaired.

(9) Prohibition on ownership by an insurance company. No risk retention group shall be allowed to do business in this state if an insurance company, other than an affiliated risk retention group, captive or other policyholder-owned insurance company or a risk retention group all of whose members are insurance companies, is directly or indirectly a member or owner of such risk retention group.

(10) Prohibited coverage. The terms of any insurance policy issued by any risk retention group shall not provide, or be construed to provide, coverage prohibited generally by statute of this state or declared unlawful by the highest court of this state whose law applies to such policy. This subsection shall not be construed to require the pre-approval of forms by the commissioner.

(11) Delinquency proceedings. After an examination under section 6052(6) of this title, a risk retention group not chartered in this state and doing business in this state shall comply with a lawful order issued in a voluntary dissolution proceeding or in a delinquency proceeding commenced by a state insurance commissioner if there has been a finding of financial impairment within the meaning of chapter 145 of this title.

(12) Penalties. A risk retention group subject to this section that violates any provision of this chapter will be subject to the fines and the penalties including revocation of its right to do business in this state, applicable to licensed insurers generally under this title.

(13) Operation prior to enactment of this chapter. In addition to complying with the requirements of this section, any risk retention group operating in this state prior to enactment of this chapter shall, within 30 days after December 31, 1992, comply with the provision of subsection (1)(A) of this section.

Section 6054. Compulsory associations

(a) No risk retention group shall be required or permitted to join or contribute financially to any insurance insolvency guaranty fund, or similar mechanism, in this state, nor shall any risk retention group, or its insureds or claimants against its insureds, receive any benefit from any such fund for claims arising under the insurance policies issued by such risk retention group.

(b) When a purchasing group obtains insurance covering its members' risks from an insurer not authorized in this state or from a risk retention group, no such risks, wherever resident or located, shall be covered by any insurance guaranty fund or similar mechanism in this state.

(c) When a purchasing group obtain insurance covering its members' risks from a licensed insurer, only risks resident or located in this state shall be covered by the state guaranty fund subject to chapter 112 of this title.

Section 6055. Purchasing groups; exemption from certain laws

A purchasing group and its insurer or insurers shall be subject to all applicable laws of this state, except that a purchasing group and its insurer or insurers shall be exempt from state laws as provided in 15 U.S.C. §3903(a)(1) through (a)(8).

Section 6056. Notice and registration requirements of purchasing groups

(a) A purchasing group intending to do business in this state shall, prior to doing business, furnish notice to the commissioner which shall:

(1) be as provided in 15 U.S.C. §3903(d);

(2) identify all other states in which the group intends to do business;

(3) specify the method by which, and the person or persons, if any, through whom insurance will be offered to its members whose risks are resident or located in this state; and

(4) provide such other information as may be required by the commissioner to verify that the purchasing group is qualified under subdivision 6051(9) of this title.

(b) The purchasing group shall register with and designate the secretary of state as its agent solely for the purpose of receiving service of legal documents or process, except for any groups exempted under 15 U.S.C. §3903(e). Service shall be effected in the manner provided in section 3383 of this title.

(c) Each purchasing group that is required to give notice pursuant to subsection (a) of this section shall also furnish such information as may be required by the commissioner to:

(1) verify that the entity qualifies as a purchasing group;

(2) determine where the purchasing group is located; and

(3) determine appropriate tax treatment under section 6058 of this title.

(d) Any purchasing group which was doing business in this state prior to the enactment of this chapter shall, within 30 days after December 31, 1992, furnish notice to the commissioner pursuant to the provisions of subsection (a) of this section and furnish such information as may be required pursuant to subsection (b) and (c) of this section.

Section 6057. Restrictions on insurance purchased by purchasing groups

(a) A purchasing group may not purchase insurance from a risk retention group that is not chartered in a state or from an insurer not admitted in the state in which the purchasing group is located, unless the purchase is effected through a licensed agent or broker acting pursuant to the surplus lines laws and regulations of such state.

(b) A purchasing group which obtains liability insurance from an insurer not admitted in this state or a risk retention group shall inform each of the members of such group which have a risk resident or located in this state that such risk is not protected by an insurance insolvency guaranty fund in this state in writing that such risk retention group or such insurer may not be subject to all insurance laws and regulations of this state.

(c) No purchasing group may purchase insurance providing for a deductible or self-insured retention applicable to the group as a whole; however, coverage may provide for a deductible or self-insured retention applicable to individual members.

(d) Purchases of insurance by purchasing groups are subject to the same standards regarding aggregate limits which are applicable to all purchases of group insurance.

Section 6058. Purchasing group taxation

Premium taxes and taxes on premiums paid for coverage of risks resident or located in this state by a purchasing group or any members of the purchasing groups shall be:

(1) imposed at the same rate and subject to the same interest, fines and penalties as that applicable to premium taxes and taxes on premiums paid for similar coverage from a similar insurance source by other insureds; and

(2) paid first by such insurance source, and if not by such source, by the agent or broker for the purchasing group, and if not by such agent or broker, then by the purchasing group, and if not by such purchasing group, then by each of its members.

Section 6059. Administrative and procedural authority regarding risk retention groups and purchasing groups

The commissioner is authorized to make use of any of the powers established under this title to enforce the laws of this state not specifically preempted by the Risk Retention Act of 1986 including the commissioner's administrative authority to investigate, issue subpoenas, conduct depositions and hearings, issue orders, impose penalties and seek injunctive relief. With regard to any investigation, administrative proceedings or litigation, the commissioner can rely on the procedural laws of this state. The injunctive authority of the commissioner, in regard to risk retention groups, is restricted by the requirement that any injunction be issued by a court of competent jurisdiction.

Section 6060. Duties of agent or brokers to obtain license

(a) Purchasing Groups.

   (1) No person, firm, association or corporation shall act or aid in any manner in soliciting, negotiating or procuring liability insurance in this state for a purchasing group from an authorized insurer or a risk retention group chartered in a state unless such person, firm, association or corporation is licensed as an insurance agent or broker in accordance with chapter 131 of this title.

   (2) No person, firm, association or corporation shall act or aid in any manner in soliciting, negotiating or procuring liability insurance coverage in this state for any member of a purchasing group under a purchasing group's policy unless such person, firm, association or corporation is licensed as an insurance agent or broker in accordance with chapter 131 of this title.

   (3) No person, firm, association or corporation shall act or aid in any manner in soliciting, negotiating or procuring liability insurance from an insurer not authorized to do business in this state on behalf of a purchasing group located in this state unless such person, firm, association or corporation is licensed as a surplus lines broker or excess line broker in accordance with chapter 131 of this title.

(b) For purposes of acting as an agency or broker for a purchasing group pursuant to subsection (a) of this section, the requirement of residence in this state shall not apply.

(c) Every person, firm, association or corporation licensed pursuant to the provisions of chapter 131 of this title, on business written through a purchasing group, shall inform each prospective insured of the provisions of the notice required by section 6057(c) of this title.

Section 6061. Binding effect of orders issued in United States district court

An order issued by any district court of the United States enjoining a risk retention group from soliciting or selling insurance, or operating in any state, or in all states or in any territory or possession of the United States, shall be enforceable in the courts of this state, upon a finding that such a group is in hazardous financial or financially impaired condition.

Section 6070. Application of chapter

This chapter applies to risk retention groups domiciled in this state operating under the provisions of chapters 141 and 142 of this title and to persons serving as managing general agents for such risk retention groups.

Section 6071. Definitions

As used in this chapter:

(1)

    (A) "Managing general agent" means any person who:

        (i) manages all or part of the insurance business of a risk retention group and acts as an agent for such risk retention group, and, who, either separately or together with affiliates, underwrites gross written premium in any one-quarter or year that exceeds the greater of: (I) 25 percent of the risk retention group's policyholder surplus or capital, or (II) $250,000.00; and

        (ii) adjusts or pays, on behalf of the risk retention group, with settlement authority, claims in excess of $25,000.00 per occurrence or $250,000.00 in the aggregate.

    (B) "Managing general agent" shall also mean a person who otherwise would be deemed as such, but for the fact that it underwrites gross written premium of less than the amounts specified above, but during the risk retention group's preceding fiscal year underwrote in excess of 10 percent of the risk retention group's gross written premium.

    (C) Notwithstanding the provisions of subdivisions (1) (A) and (B) of this section, the following persons shall not be considered as managing general agents of a risk retention group:

(i)   an officer, director or employee of the risk retention group or of any person described in subdivisions (ii) and (iii) of this subdivision (C), provided the officer or director is not individually licensed as a managing general agent hereunder;

(ii) a person affiliated with or under common control with the risk retention group;

(iii) an association, society, or other entity, or any person under common ownership or control therewith, that has, directly or indirectly, as its owners or members, persons who are policyholders or are eligible to become policyholders of the risk retention group; and

(iv) an attorney-in-fact of a risk retention group organized as a reciprocal, or any person affiliated with or under common control with the attorney-in-fact.

(2) "Reinsurance intermediary" has the same meaning as set forth in section 4815(9) of this title.

(3) "Risk retention group" means a company referred to in section 6070 of this title domiciled in this state.

(4) "Underwrite" means the authority to accept or reject risk on behalf of the risk retention group.

Section 6072. Licensure

(a) No person shall act in the capacity of managing general agent as defined in section 6071 (1)(A) of this title for a risk retention group unless such person is licensed under the provisions of this chapter. No person shall act in the capacity of managing general agent as defined in section 6071 (1)(B) of this title for a risk retention group unless within ninety (90) days of the end of the risk retention group's fiscal year in which such person became a managing general agent, such person becomes licensed under the provisions of this chapter. No officer, director or employee of a person licensed or exempt from licensure under this chapter shall be required to be licensed. The commissioner may exempt any other person upon a finding that the activities to be performed by such person on behalf of a risk retention group are not of the nature or magnitude requiring the protection of this chapter. A person shall not be required to obtain more than one license hereunder in order to serve as managing general agent for more than one risk retention group.

(b) No risk retention group shall employ the services of a reinsurance intermediary to solicit, negotiate or place reinsurance on its behalf, unless such person is licensed as a reinsurance intermediary under the provisions of chapter 131 of this title or under the provisions of another state's law governing reinsurance intermediaries or is licensed as a managing general agent under this chapter and is acting as such for the risk retention group.

(c) Application for a license under this section shall be made on a form prescribed by the commissioner and accompanied by a $30.00 fee plus the initial 12 months' licensing fee of $150.00.

(d) The commissioner shall issue a license to any person who has complied with the requirements of this chapter, unless the commissioner determines that the applicant, anyone named in the application, or any member, principal, officer or director of the applicant, is not competent or trustworthy, or that any controlling person of such applicant is not competent or trustworthy to act as a managing general agent or that any of the foregoing persons have given cause for revocation or suspension of such license, or have failed to comply with any prerequisite for the issuance of such license.

(e) If the applicant for a license is a nonresident that has not duly registered to do business in this state, such applicant, as a condition precedent to receiving or holding a license, shall designate the secretary of state as agent for service of process in the manner, and with the same legal effect, provided for by section 3370 of this title for designation of service of process upon unauthorized insurers; and shall also furnish the secretary of state with the name and address of a resident of this state upon whom notices or orders of the commissioner or process affecting such nonresident licensee may be served. Such licensee shall promptly notify the secretary of state in writing of every change in its designated agent for service of process.

(f) A license issued hereunder shall continue in force not longer than 12 months, but shall expire as of 12:01 a.m. o'clock on the first day of April of the year next following date of issuance unless the licensee prior thereto has filed with the commissioner, on forms prescribed and furnished by the commissioner, a request for renewal of such license for an ensuing 12-month period. Such request must be accompanied by payment of a renewal fee equal to the initial licensing fee for such license.

Section 6073. Contract required

(a) No risk retention group shall enter into a managing general agent relationship unless there is in force a written contract between the parties which sets forth the respective responsibilities of each party.

(b) The contract shall contain the following minimum provisions:

(1) The method for determining compensation and other amounts payable under the contract, and the terms for payment thereof shall be fair and reasonable.

(2) The contract may be terminated by the risk retention group for cause upon written notice.

(3) The authority to underwrite or settle claims may be suspended by the risk retention group during the pendency of any dispute regarding the cause for termination.

(4) The contract shall not result in the transfer of substantial control of the risk retention group or any of the powers vested in the members or board of directors, by statute, articles of incorporation or bylaws.

(5) Separate records of all business written under the contract shall be maintained. The risk retention group shall have access to and the right to copy all accounts and records related to its business in a form usable by the risk retention group.

(6) The required use of underwriting, rating and claims settlement and, if applicable, reinsurance cession standards and procedures approved by the risk retention group.

(c) Within 30 days of entering into a contract with a managing general agent, the risk retention group shall provide written notification thereof to the commissioner. Such notice of appointment shall include a statement of duties which the applicant is expected to perform on behalf of the risk retention group, the lines of insurance for which the applicant is to be authorized to act, a summary of the minimum contract provisions set forth in subsection (b) of this section and any other information reasonably requested by the commissioner. Information contained in such notification shall be entitled to confidential treatment in accordance with section 6052 of this title. The risk retention group shall give the commissioner notice of termination of a contract with a managing general agent within 10 days of termination.

Section 6074. Examination authority

(a) The commissioner may examine the books and records of a managing general agent or any affiliate thereof pertaining to or arising out of transactions with a risk retention group if the commissioner reasonably believes that such examination is necessary.

(b) All examination reports, work papers, recorded information, documents and copies thereof produced by, obtained by or disclosed to the commissioner or any other person in the course of an examination made under this section are confidential and are not subject to subpoena and may not be made public by the commissioner or any other person, except as otherwise provided in this section. The commissioner is authorized to use and make public any report, work paper or other documents, or any other information discovered or developed during the course of any examination conducted pursuant to this section in the furtherance of any legal or regulatory action.

Section 6075. Hearing; penalties

(a) If the commissioner determines, after notice and hearing, that any person licensed hereunder (i) has violated any provision of this chapter or rules promulgated hereunder, or (ii) is not competent or trustworthy, or (iii) has engaged in any activity or has failed to do any act that if known at the time of licensing would have been grounds to refuse licensing, the commissioner may impose one or more of the following penalties:

    (1) order the revocation, suspension or nonrenewal of the person's license;

    (2) order the termination, suspension or modification of the contract between such person and the risk retention group; or

    (3) impose an administrative penalty of not less than $100.00 nor more than $1,000.00 for each violation hereunder.

(b) In imposing any such penalty, the commissioner shall take into account the seriousness of the violation, whether or not it was willful, and the licensee's past record of compliance with this chapter.

(c) Any hearing conducted hereunder shall be conducted in accordance with chapter 25 of Title 3.

Appendix C

South Carolina Captive Statute

CHAPTER 90

Captive Insurance Companies

Section 38-90-10. As used in this chapter, unless the context requires otherwise:

(1) 'Alien captive insurance company' means an insurance company formed to write insurance business for its parents and affiliates and licensed pursuant to the laws of an alien jurisdiction which imposes statutory or regulatory standards in a form acceptable to the director on companies transacting the business of insurance in such jurisdiction.

(2) 'Affiliated company' means a company in the same corporate system as a parent, an industrial insured, or a member organization by virtue of common ownership, control, operation, or management.

(3) 'Association' means a legal association of individuals, corporations, partnerships, or associations that has been in continuous existence for at least one year:

    (a) the member organizations of which collectively, or which does itself;

        (i) own, control, or hold with power to vote all of the outstanding voting securities of an association captive insurance company incorporated as a stock insurer; or

        (ii) have complete voting control over an association captive insurance company incorporated as a mutual insurer; or

    (b) the member organizations of which collectively constitute all of the subscribers of an association captive insurance company formed as a reciprocal insurer.

(4) 'Association captive insurance company' means a company that insures risks of the member organizations of the association and their affiliated companies.

(5) 'Branch business' means any insurance business transacted by a branch captive insurance company in this State.

(6) 'Branch captive insurance company' means an alien captive insurance company licensed by the director to transact the business of insurance in this State through a business unit with a principal place of business in this State.

(7) 'Branch operations' means any business operations of a branch captive insurance company in this State.

(8) 'Captive insurance company' means a pure captive insurance company, association captive insurance company, sponsored captive insurance company, or industrial insured captive insurance company formed or licensed under this chapter. For purposes of this chapter, a branch captive insurance company must be a pure captive insurance company with respect to operations in this State, unless otherwise permitted by the director.

(9) 'Controlled unaffiliated business' means a company:

    (a) that is not in the corporate system of a parent and affiliated companies;

    (b) that has an existing contractual relationship with a parent or affiliated company; and

    (c) whose risks are managed by a pure captive insurance company in accordance with Section 38-90-190.

(10) 'Director' means the Director of the South Carolina Department of Insurance or the director's designee.

(11) 'Department' means the South Carolina Department of Insurance.

(12) 'Industrial insured' means an insured as defined in Section 38-25-150(8).

(13) 'Industrial insured captive insurance company' means a company that insures risks of the industrial insureds that comprise the industrial insured group and their affiliated companies.

(14) 'Industrial insured group' means a group that meets either of the following criteria:

    (a) a group of industrial insureds that collectively:

        (i) own, control, or hold with power to vote all of the outstanding voting securities of an industrial insured captive insurance company incorporated as a stock insurer; or

        (ii) have complete voting control over an industrial insured captive insurance company incorporated as a mutual insurer; or

    (b) a group which is created under the Product Liability Risk Retention Act of 1981, 15 U.S.C. Section 3901 et seq., as amended, as a corporation or other limited liability association taxable as a stock insurance company or a mutual insurer under this title.

(15) 'Member organization' means a individual, corporation, partnership, or association that belongs to an association.

(16) 'Parent' means a corporation, partnership, or individual that directly or indirectly owns, controls, or holds with power to vote more than fifty per cent of the outstanding voting securities of a pure captive insurance company.

(17) 'Participant' means an entity as defined in Section 38-90-230, and any affiliates of that entity, that are insured by a sponsored captive insurance company, where the losses of the participant are limited through a participant contract to the assets of a protected cell.

(18) 'Participant contract' means a contract by which a sponsored captive insurance company insures the risks of a participant and limits the losses of the participant to the assets of a protected cell.

(19) 'Protected cell' means a separate account established and maintained by a sponsored captive insurance company for one participant.

(20) 'Pure captive insurance company' means a company that insures risks of its parent and affiliated companies.

(21) 'Sponsor' means an entity that meets the requirements of Section 38-90-220 and is approved by the director to provide all or part of the capital and surplus required by applicable law and to organize and operate a sponsored captive insurance company.

(22) 'Sponsored captive insurance company' means a captive insurance company:

(a) in which the minimum capital and surplus required by applicable law is provided by one or more sponsors;

(b) that is formed or licensed under this chapter;

(c) that insures the risks of separate participants through the contract; and

(d) that segregates each participant's liability through one or more protected cells.

Section 38-90-20.

(A) A captive insurance company, when permitted by its articles of incorporation or charter, may apply to the director for a license to do any and all insurance, except workers' compensation insurance, authorized by this title; however:

(1) a pure captive insurance company may not insure any risks other than those of its parent and affiliated companies or controlled unaffiliated business;

(2) an association captive insurance company may not insure any risks other than those of the member organizations of its association and their affiliated companies;

(3) an industrial insured captive insurance company may not insure any risks other than those of the industrial insureds that comprise the industrial insured group and their affiliated companies;

(4) a captive insurance company may not provide personal motor vehicle or homeowner's insurance coverage or any component of these coverages;

(5) a captive insurance company may not accept or cede reinsurance except as provided in Section 38-90-110.

(B) To conduct insurance business in this State a captive insurance company shall:

(1) obtain from the director a license authorizing it to conduct insurance business in this State;

(2) hold at least one board of directors meeting, or in the case of a reciprocal insurer, a subscriber's advisory committee meeting, each year in this State;

(3) maintain its principal place of business in this State, or in the case of a branch captive insurance company, maintain the principal place of business for its branch operations in this State; and

(4) appoint a resident registered agent to accept service of process and to otherwise act on its behalf in this State. In the case of a captive insurance company:

(a) formed as a corporation, whenever the registered agent cannot with reasonable diligence be found at the registered office of the captive insurance company, the director must be an agent of the captive insurance company upon whom any process, notice, or demand may be served;

(b) formed as a reciprocal insurer, whenever the registered agent cannot with reasonable diligence be found at the registered office of the captive insurance company, the director must be an agent of the captive insurance company upon whom any process, notice, or demand may be served.

(C)

(1) Before receiving a license, a captive insurance company:

(a) formed as a corporation, shall file with the director a certified copy of its charter and bylaws, a statement under oath of its president and secretary showing its financial condition, and any other statements or documents required by the director;

(b) formed as a reciprocal shall: (i) file with the director a certified copy of the power of attorney of its attorney-in-fact, a certified copy of its subscribers' agreement, a statement under oath of its attorney-in-fact showing its financial condition, and any other statements or documents required by the director; and (ii) submit to the director for approval a description of the coverages, deductibles, coverage limits, and rates, and any other information the director may reasonably require. If there is a subsequent material change in an item in the description, the reciprocal captive insurance company shall submit to the director for approval an appropriate revision and may not offer any additional kinds of insurance until a revision of the description is approved by the director. The reciprocal captive insurance company shall inform the director of any material change in rates within thirty days of the adoption of the change.

(2) In addition to the information required by (C)(1), an applicant captive insurance company shall file with the director evidence of:

  (a) the amount and liquidity of its assets relative to the risks to be assumed;

  (b) the adequacy of the expertise, experience, and character of the person or persons who will manage it;

  (c) the overall soundness of its plan of operation;

  (d) the adequacy of the loss prevention programs of its parent, member organizations, or industrial insureds, as applicable; and

  (e) such other factors considered relevant by the director in ascertaining whether the proposed captive insurance company will be able to meet its policy obligations.

(3) In addition to the information required by (C)(1) and (C)(2) an applicant sponsored captive insurance company shall file with the director:

  (a) a business plan demonstrating how the applicant will account for the loss and expense experience of each protected cell at a level of detail found to be sufficient by the director, and how it will report the experience to the director;

  (b) a statement acknowledging that all financial records of the sponsored captive insurance company, including records pertaining to any protected cells, must be made available for inspection or examination by the director;

  (c) all contracts or sample contracts between the sponsored captive insurance company and any participants; and

  (d) evidence that expenses will be allocated to each protected cell in an equitable manner.

(4) Information submitted pursuant to this subsection is confidential and may not be made public by the director or an agent or employee of the director without the written consent of the company, except that:

  (a) information may be discoverable by a party in a civil action or contested case to which the captive insurance company that submitted the information is a party, upon a showing by the party seeking to discover the information that: (i) the information sought is relevant to and necessary for the furtherance of the action or case; (ii) the information sought is unavailable from other nonconfidential sources; and (iii) a subpoena issued by a judicial or administrative officer of competent jurisdiction has been submitted to the director; however, the provisions of subsection (C)(4) do not apply to an industrial insured captive insurance company insuring the risks of an industrial insured group; and

(b) the director may disclose the information to a public officer having jurisdiction over the regulation of insurance in another state if: (i) the public official agrees in writing to maintain the confidentiality of the information; and (ii) the laws of the state in which the public official serves require the information to be confidential.

(D) A captive insurance company shall pay to the department a nonrefundable fee of two hundred dollars for examining, investigating, and processing its application for license, and the director may retain legal, financial, and examination services from outside the department, the reasonable cost of which may be charged against the applicant. Section 38-13-60 applies to examinations, investigations, and processing conducted under the authority of this section. In addition a captive insurance company shall pay a license fee for the year of registration and a renewal fee of three hundred dollars.

(E) If the director is satisfied that the documents and statements filed by the captive insurance company comply with the provisions of this chapter, the director may grant a license authorizing the company to do insurance business in this State until March 1 at which time the license may be renewed.

Section 38-90-30.

A captive insurance company may not adopt a name that is the same as, deceptively similar to, or likely to be confused with or mistaken for any other existing business name registered in this State.

Section 38-90-40.

(A) The director may not issue a license to a pure captive insurance company, sponsored captive insurance company, association captive insurance company incorporated as a stock insurer, or industrial insured captive insurance company incorporated as a stock insurer unless the company possesses and thereafter maintains unimpaired paid-in capital of:

(1) in the case of a pure captive insurance company, not less than one hundred thousand dollars;

(2) in the case of an association captive insurance company incorporated as a stock insurer, not less than four hundred thousand dollars;

(3) in the case of an industrial insured captive insurance company incorporated as a stock insurer, not less than two hundred thousand dollars;

(4) in the case of a sponsored captive insurance company, not less than five hundred thousand dollars.

The capital may be in the form of cash or an irrevocable letter of credit issued by a bank chartered by this State or a member bank of the Federal Reserve System and approved by the director.

(B) The director may prescribe additional capital based upon the type, volume, and nature of insurance business transacted. This capital may be in the form of an irrevocable letter of credit issued by a bank chartered by this State or a member bank of the Federal Reserve System.

(C) In the case of a branch captive insurance company, as security for the payment of liabilities attributable to branch operations, the director shall require that a trust fund, funded by an irrevocable letter of credit or other acceptable asset, be established and maintained in the United States for the benefit of United States policyholders and United States ceding insurers under insurance policies issued or reinsurance contracts issued or assumed, by the branch captive insurance company through its branch operations. The amount of the security may be no less than the capital and surplus required by this chapter and the reserves on these insurance policies or reinsurance contracts, including reserves for losses, allocated loss adjustment expenses, incurred but not reported losses and unearned premiums with regard to business written through branch operations; however, the director may permit a branch captive insurance company that is required to post security for loss reserves on branch business by its reinsurer to reduce the funds in the trust account required by this section by the same amount so long as the security remains posted with the reinsurer. If the form of security selected is a letter of credit, the letter of credit must be established by, or issued or confirmed by, a bank chartered in this State or a member bank of the Federal Reserve System.

(D) A captive insurance company may not pay a dividend out of, or other distribution with respect to, capital or surplus, in excess of the limitations set forth in Section 38-21-250 through Section 38-21-270, without the prior approval of the director. Approval of an ongoing plan for the payment of dividends or other distributions must be conditioned upon the retention, at the time of each payment, of capital or surplus in excess of amounts specified by, or determined in accordance with formulas approved by, the director.

Section 38-90-50.

(A) The director may not issue a license to a captive insurance company unless the company possesses and thereafter maintains free surplus of:

(1) in the case of a pure captive insurance company, not less that one hundred fifty thousand dollars;

(2) in the case of an association captive insurance company incorporated as a stock insurer, not less than three hundred fifty thousand dollars;

(3) in the case of an industrial insured captive insurance company incorporated as a stock insurer, not less than three hundred thousand dollars;

(4) in the case of an association captive insurance company incorporated as a mutual insurer, not less than seven hundred fifty thousand dollars;

(5) in the case of an industrial insured captive insurance company incorporated as a mutual insurer, not less than five hundred thousand dollars; and

(6) in the case of a sponsored captive insurance company, not less than five hundred thousand dollars.

The surplus may be in the form of cash or an irrevocable letter of credit issued by a bank chartered by this State or a member bank of the Federal Reserve System and approved by the director.

(B) Notwithstanding the requirements of subsection (A) a captive insurance company organized as a reciprocal insurer under this chapter may not be issued a license unless it possesses and thereafter maintains free surplus of one million dollars.

(C) The director may prescribe additional surplus based upon the type, volume, and nature of insurance business transacted. This capital may be in the form of an irrevocable letter of credit issued by a bank chartered by this State, or a member bank of the Federal Reserve System.

(D) A captive insurance company may not pay a dividend out of, or other distribution with respect to, capital or surplus in excess of the limitations set forth in Section 38-21-270, without the prior approval of the director. Approval of an ongoing plan for the payment of dividends or other distribution must be conditioned upon the retention, at the time of each payment, of capital or surplus in excess of amounts specified by, or determined in accordance with formulas approved by, the director.

Section 38-90-60.

(A) A pure captive insurance company or a sponsored captive insurance company must be incorporated as a stock insurer with its capital divided into shares and held by the stockholders.

(B) An association captive insurance company or an industrial insured captive insurance company may be:

(1) incorporated as a stock insurer with its capital divided into shares and held by the stockholders;

(2) incorporated as a mutual insurer without capital stock, the governing body of which is elected by the member organizations of its association; or

(3) organized as a reciprocal insurer in accordance with Chapter 17.

(C) A captive insurance company may not have fewer than three incorporators of whom not fewer than two must be residents of this State.

(D) In the case of a captive insurance company formed as a corporation, before the articles of incorporation are transmitted to the Secretary of State, the incorporators shall petition the director to issue a certificate setting forth a finding that the establishment and maintenance of the proposed corporation will promote the general good of the State. In arriving at this finding the director shall consider:

(1) the character, reputation, financial standing, and purposes of the incorporators;

(2) the character, reputation, financial responsibility, insurance experience, and business qualifications of the officers and directors; and

(3) other aspects as the director considers advisable.

(E) The articles of incorporation, the certificate issued pursuant to subsection (D), and the organization fees required by Section 38-90-20(D) must be transmitted to the Secretary of State, who shall record both the articles of incorporation and the certificate.

(F) In the case of a captive insurance company formed as a reciprocal insurer, the organizers shall petition the director, to issue a certificate setting forth the director's finding that the establishment and maintenance of the proposed association will promote the general good of the State. In arriving at this finding the director shall consider:

(1) the character, reputation, financial standing, and purposes of the incorporators;

(2) the character, reputation, financial responsibility, insurance experience, and business qualifications of the officers and directors; and

(3) other aspects the director considers advisable.

(G) In the case of a captive insurance company licensed as a branch captive insurance company, the alien captive insurance company shall petition the director to issue a certificate setting forth the director's finding that, after considering the character, reputation, financial responsibility, insurance experience, and business qualifications of the officers and directors of the alien captive insurance company, the licensing and maintenance of the branch operations will promote the general good of the State. The alien captive insurance company may register to do business in this State after the director's certificate has been issued.

(H) The capital stock of a captive insurance company incorporated as a stock insurer must be issued at not less than par value.

(I) In the case of a captive insurance company formed as a corporation, at least one of the members of the board of directors of a captive insurance company incorporated in this State must be a resident of this State.

(J) In the case of a captive insurance company formed as a reciprocal insurer, at least one of the members of the subscribers' advisory committee must be a resident of this State.

(K) A captive insurance company formed as a corporation under this chapter has the privileges and is subject to the provisions of the general corporation law as well as the applicable provisions contained in this chapter. If a conflict occurs between a provision of the general corporation law and a provision of this chapter, the latter controls. The provisions of this title pertaining to mergers, consolidations, conversions, mutualizations, and redomestications apply in determining the procedures to be followed by a captive insurance company in carrying out any of the transactions described in those provisions, except the director may waive or modify the requirements for public notice and hearing in accordance with regulations which the director may promulgate addressing categories of transactions. If a notice of public hearing is required, but no one requests a hearing, the director may cancel the hearing.

(L)

   (1) A captive insurance company formed as a reciprocal insurer under this chapter has the privileges and is subject to Chapter 17 in addition to the applicable provisions of this chapter. If a conflict occurs between the provisions of Chapter 17 and the provisions of this chapter, the latter controls. To the extent a reciprocal insurer is made subject to other provisions of this title pursuant to Chapter 17, the provisions are not applicable to a reciprocal insurer formed under this chapter unless the provisions are expressly made applicable to a captive insurance company under this chapter.

   (2) In addition to the provisions of (L)(1), a captive insurance company organized as a reciprocal insurer that is an industrial insured group has the privileges and is subject to the provisions of Chapter 17 in addition to applicable provisions of this title.

(M) The articles of incorporation or bylaws of a captive insurance company may authorize a quorum of a board of directors to consist of no fewer than one-third of the fixed or prescribed number of directors as provided for in Section 33-8-240(b).

Section 38-90-70.

(A) A captive insurance company may not be required to make an annual report except as provided in this chapter.

(B) Before March 1 of each year, a captive insurance company shall submit to the director a report of its financial condition, verified by oath of two of its executive officers. Except as provided in Sections 38-90-40 and 38-90-50, a captive insurance company shall report using generally accepted accounting principles, unless the director approves the use of statutory accounting principles, with any useful or necessary modifications or adaptations required or approved or accepted by the director for the type of insurance and kinds of insurers to be reported upon, and as supplemented by additional information required by the director. Except as otherwise provided, an association captive insurance company and an industrial insured group shall file its report in the form required by Section 38-13-80, and each industrial insured group shall comply with the requirements set forth in Section 38-13-85. The director by regulation shall prescribe the forms in which pure captive insurance companies and industrial insured captive insurance companies shall report.

(C) A pure captive insurance company may make written application for filing the required report on a fiscal year-end that is consistent with the parent company's fiscal year. If an alternative reporting date is granted:

(1) the annual report is due sixty days after the fiscal year-end:

(2) in order to provide sufficient detail to support the premium tax return, the pure captive insurance company shall file before March 1 of each year for each calendar year end, pages 1, 2, 3, and 5 of the 'Captive Annual Statement: Pure or Industrial Insured', verified by oath of two of its executive officers.

(D) Sixty days after the fiscal year end, a branch captive insurance company shall file with the director a copy of all reports and statements required to be filed under the laws of the jurisdiction in which the alien captive insurance company is formed, verified by oath by two of its executive officers. If the director is satisfied that the annual report filed by the alien captive insurance company in its domiciliary jurisdiction provides adequate information concerning the financial condition of the alien captive insurance company, the director may waive the requirement for completion of the captive annual statement for business written in the alien jurisdiction. Such waiver must be in writing and subject to public inspection.

Section 38-90-80.

(A) At least once in three years, and whenever the director determines it to be prudent, the director personally, or by a competent person appointed by the director, shall visit each captive insurance company and thoroughly inspect and examine its affairs to ascertain its financial condition, its ability to fulfill its obligations, and whether it has complied with this chapter. The director upon application, in his discretion, may enlarge the three-year period to five years, if a captive insurance company is subject to a comprehensive annual audit during that period of a scope satisfactory to the director by independent auditors approved by the director. The expenses and charges of the examination must be paid to the State by the company or companies examined, and the department shall issue its warrants for the proper charges incurred in all examinations.

(B) All examination reports, preliminary examination reports or results, working papers, recorded information, documents and copies of documents produced by, obtained by, or disclosed to the director or any other person in the course of an examination made under this section are confidential and are not subject to subpoena and may not be made public by the director or an employee or agent of the director without the written consent of the company, except to the extent provided in this subsection. Nothing in this subsection prevents the director from using this information in furtherance of the director's regulatory authority under this title. The director may grant access to this information to public officers having jurisdiction over the regulation of insurance in any other state or country, or to law enforcement officers of this State or any other state or agency of the federal government at any time, so long as the officers receiving the information agree in writing to hold it in a manner consistent with this section.

(C)

    (1) This section applies to all business written by a captive insurance company; however, the examination for a branch captive insurance company must be of branch business and branch operations only, as long as the branch captive insurance company provides annually to the director, a certificate of compliance, or its equivalent, issued by or filed with the licensing authority of the jurisdiction in which the branch captive insurance company is formed and demonstrates to the director's satisfaction that it is operating in sound financial condition in accordance with all applicable laws and regulations of that jurisdiction.

    (2) As a condition of licensure, the alien captive insurance company shall grant authority to the director for examination of the affairs of the alien captive insurance company in the jurisdiction in which the alien captive insurance company is formed.

(D) To the extent that the provisions of Chapter 13 do not contradict the provisions of this section, Chapter 13 applies to captive insurance companies licensed under this chapter.

Section 38-90-90.

(A) The license of a captive insurance company to conduct an insurance business in this State may be suspended or revoked by the director for:

(1) insolvency or impairment of capital or surplus;

(2) failure to meet the requirements of Sections 38-90-40 or 38-90-50;

(3) refusal or failure to submit an annual report, as required by Section 38-90-70, or any other report or statement required by law or by lawful order of the director;

(4) failure to comply with its own charter, bylaws, or other organizational document;

(5) failure to submit to examination or any legal obligation relative to an examination, as required by Section 38-90-80;

(6) refusal or failure to pay the cost of examination as required by Section 38-90-80;

(7) use of methods that, although not otherwise specifically prohibited by law, nevertheless render its operation detrimental or its condition unsound with respect to the public or to its policyholders; or

(8) failure otherwise to comply with laws of this State.

(B) If the director finds, upon examination, hearing, or other evidence, that a captive insurance company has committed any of the acts specified in subsection (A) of this section, the director may suspend or revoke such license if the director considers it in the best interest of the public and the policyholders of the captive insurance company, notwithstanding any other provision of this title.

Section 38-90-100.

(A) An association captive insurance company, a sponsored captive insurance company, and an industrial insured group shall comply with the investment requirements contained in this title. Notwithstanding any other provision of this title, the director may approve the use of alternative reliable methods of valuation and rating.

(B) A pure captive insurance company or industrial insured captive insurance company is not subject to any restrictions on allowable investments contained in this title; however, the director may prohibit or limit an investment that threatens the solvency or liquidity of the company.

(C) Only a pure captive insurance company may make loans to its parent company or affiliates and only upon the prior written approval of the director and must be evidenced by a note in a form approved by the director. Loans of minimum capital and surplus funds required by Section 38-90-40(A) and 38-90-50(A) are prohibited.

Section 38-90-110.

(A) A captive insurance company may provide reinsurance, as authorized in this title, on risks ceded by any other insurer.

(B) A captive insurance company may take credit for reserves on risks or portions of risks ceded to reinsurers complying with the provisions of Sections 38-9-200, 38-9-210, and 38-9-220. A captive insurer may not take credit for reserves on risks or portions of risks ceded to a reinsurer if the reinsurer is not in compliance with Sections 38-9-200, 38-9-210, and 38-9-220.

Section 38-90-120.

A captive insurance company may not be required to join a rating organization.

Section 38-90-130.

A captive insurance company, including a captive insurance company organized as a reciprocal insurer under this chapter, may not join or contribute financially to a plan, pool, association, or guaranty or insolvency fund in this State, and a captive insurance company, or its insured or its parent or any affiliated company or any member organization of its association, or in the case of a captive insurance company organized as a reciprocal insurer, a subscriber of the company, may not receive a benefit from a plan, pool, association, or guaranty or insolvency fund for claims arising out of the operations of such captive insurance company.

Section 38-90-140.

(A) A captive insurance company shall pay to the director by March 1 of each year, a tax at the rate of four-tenths of one percent on the first twenty million dollars and three-tenths of one percent on the next twenty million dollars and two-tenths of one percent on the next twenty million dollars and seventy-five thousandths of one percent on each dollar thereafter on the direct premiums collected or contracted for on policies or contracts of insurance written by the captive insurance company during the year ending December 31 next preceding, after deducting from the direct premiums subject to the tax the amounts paid to policyholders as return premiums which shall include dividends on unabsorbed premiums or premium deposits returned or credited to policyholders.

(B) A captive insurance company shall pay to the director by March 1 of each year, a tax at the rate of two hundred and twenty-five thousandths of one percent on the first twenty million dollars of assumed reinsurance premium, and one hundred fifty thousandths percent on the next twenty million dollars and fifty thousandths of one percent on the next twenty million dollars and twenty-five thousandths of one percent of each dollar thereafter. However, no reinsurance tax applies to premiums for risks or portions of risks which are subject to taxation on a direct basis pursuant to subsection (A). A premium tax is not payable in connection with the receipt of assets in exchange for the assumption of loss reserves and other liabilities of another insurer under common ownership and control if the transaction is part of a plan to discontinue the operations of the other insurer and if the intent of the parties to the transaction is to renew or maintain business with the captive insurance company.

(C) If the aggregate taxes to be paid by a captive insurance company calculated under subsections (A) and (B) amount to less than five thousand dollars in any year, the captive insurance company shall pay a tax of five thousand dollars for that year.

(D) A captive insurance company failing to make returns or to pay all taxes required by this section, is subject to the relevant sanctions of this title.

(E) Two or more captive insurance companies under common ownership and control must be taxed, as though they were a single captive insurance company.

(F) For the purposes of this section, 'common ownership and control' means:

   (1) in the case of stock corporations, the direct or indirect ownership of eighty percent or more of the outstanding voting stock of two or more corporations by the same shareholder or shareholders; and

   (2) in the case of mutual corporations, the direct or indirect ownership of eighty percent or more of the surplus and the voting power of two or more corporations by the same member or members.

(G) In the case of a branch captive insurance company, the tax provided for in this section applies only to the branch business of the company.

(H) The tax provided for in this section constitutes all taxes collectible under the laws of this State from a captive insurance company, and no other occupation tax or other taxes may be levied or collected from a captive insurance company by the State or a county, city, or municipality within this State, except ad valorem taxes on real and personal property used in the production of income.

Section 38-90-150.

The director may promulgate and, from time to time, amend regulations relating to captive insurance companies as are necessary to enable the director to carry out the provisions of this chapter.

Section 38-90-160.

No provisions of this title, other than those contained in this chapter or contained in specific references contained in this chapter, apply to captive insurance companies.

Section 38-90-170.

The terms and conditions set forth in this title pertaining to insurance reorganizations, receiverships, and injunctions apply in full to captive insurance companies formed under this chapter.

Section 38-90-180.

(A) Except as otherwise provided in this section, the terms and conditions set forth in Chapter 27 pertaining to insurance reorganizations, receiverships, and injunctions apply in full to captive insurance companies formed or licensed under this chapter.

(B) In the case of a sponsored captive insurance company:

   (1) the assets of the protected cell may not be used to pay any expenses or claims other than those attributable to the protected cell; and

   (2) its capital and surplus at all times must be available to pay any expenses of or claims against the sponsored captive insurance company.

Section 38-90-190.

The director shall promulgate regulations establishing standards to ensure that a parent or affiliated company is able to exercise control of the risk management function of any controlled unaffiliated business to be insured by the pure captive insurance company; however, until such time as these regulations are promulgated, the director may by temporary order grant authority to a pure captive insurance company to insure risks.

Section 38-90-200.

(A) An association captive insurance company or industrial insured group formed as a stock or mutual corporation may be converted to or merged with and into a reciprocal insurer in accordance with a plan and the provisions of this section.

(B) A plan for this conversion or merger:

   (1) must be fair and equitable to the shareholders, in the case of a stock insurer, or the policyholders, in the case of a mutual insurer; and

   (2) shall provide for the purchase of the shares of any nonconsenting shareholder of a stock insurer of the policyholder interest of any nonconsenting policyholder

of a mutual insurer in substantially the same manner and subject to the same rights and conditions as are accorded a dissenting shareholder or a dissenting policyholder under Chapter 13, Title 33.

(C) In the case of a conversion authorized under subsection (A):

    (1) the conversion must be accomplished under a reasonable plan and procedure as may be approved by the director; however, the director may not approve the plan of conversion unless the plan:

        (a) satisfies the provisions of subsection (B);

        (b) provides for a hearing, of which notice has been given to the insurer, its directors, officers and stockholders, in the case of a stock insurer, or policyholders, in the case of a mutual insurer, all of whom have the right to appear at the hearing, except that the director may waive or modify the requirements for the hearing; however, if a notice of hearing is required, but no hearing is requested, the director may cancel the hearing;

        (c) provides for the conversion of existing stockholder or policyholder interests into subscriber interests in the resulting reciprocal insurer, proportionate to stockholder or policyholder interests in the stock or mutual insurer; and

        (d) is approved; (i) in the case of a stock insurer, by a majority of the shares entitled to vote represented in person or by proxy at a duly called regular or special meeting at which a quorum is present; (ii) in the case of a mutual insurer, by a majority of the voting interests of policyholders represented in person or by proxy at a duly called regular or special meeting at which a quorum is present;

    (2) the director shall approve the plan of conversion if the director finds that the conversion will promote the general good of the State in conformity with those standards set forth in Section 38-90-60(2);

    (3) if the director approves the plan the director shall amend the converting insurer's certificate of authority to reflect conversion to a reciprocal insurer and issue the amended certificate of authority to the company's attorney-in-fact;

    (4) upon issuance of an amended certificate of authority of a reciprocal insurer by the director, the conversion is effective; and

    (5) upon the effectiveness of the conversion the corporate existence of the converting insurer shall cease and the resulting reciprocal insurer shall notify the Secretary of State of the conversion.

(D) A merger authorized under subsection (A) must be accomplished substantially in accordance with the procedures set forth in this title except that, solely for purposes of the merger:

    (1) the plan or merger shall satisfy subsection (B);

(2) the subscribers' advisory committee of a reciprocal insurer must be equivalent to the board of directors of a stock or mutual insurance company;

(3) the subscribers of a reciprocal insurer must be the equivalent of the policyholders of a mutual insurance company;

(4) if a subscribers' advisory committee does not have a president or secretary, the officers of the committee having substantially equivalent duties are deemed the president and secretary of the committee;

(5) the director shall approve the articles of merger if the director finds that the merger will promote the general good of the State in conformity with those standards set forth in Section 38-90-60(D)(2). If the director approves the articles of merger, the director shall endorse his or her approval on the articles and the surviving insurer shall present the name to the Secretary of State at the Secretary of State's office;

(6) notwithstanding Section 38-90-40, the director may permit the formation, without surplus, of a captive insurance company organized as a reciprocal insurer, into which an existing captive insurance company may be merged for the purpose of facilitating a transaction under this section; however, there may be no more than one authorized insurance company surviving the merger;

(7) an alien insurer may be a party to a merger authorized under subsection (A) if the requirements for the merger between a domestic and a foreign insurer under Chapter 21 apply to a merger between a domestic and an alien insurer under this subsection. The alien insurer must be treated as a foreign insurer under Chapter 21 and other jurisdictions must be the equivalent of a state for purposes of Chapter 21.

(E) A conversion or merger under this section has all the effects set forth in Chapter 21, to the extent these effects are not inconsistent with this chapter.

Section 38-90-210.

(A) One or more sponsors may form a sponsored captive insurance company under this chapter.

(B) A sponsored captive insurance company formed or licensed under this chapter may establish and maintain one or more protected cells to insure risks of one or more participants, subject to the following conditions:

(1) the shareholders of a sponsored captive insurance company must be limited to its participants and sponsors;

(2) each protected cell must be accounted for separately on the books and records of the sponsored captive insurance company to reflect the financial condition and results of operations of the protected cell, net income or loss, dividends or

other distributions to participants, and other factors may be provided in the participant contract or required by the director;

(3) the assets of a protected cell must not be chargeable with liabilities arising out of any other insurance business the sponsored captive insurance company may conduct;

(4) no sale, exchange, or other transfer of assets may be made by the sponsored captive insurance company between or among any of its protected cells without the consent of the protected cells;

(5) no sale, exchange, transfer of assets, dividend, or distribution may be made from a protected cell to a sponsor or participant without the director's approval and in no event may the approval be given if the sale, exchange, transfer, dividend, or distribution would result in insolvency or impairment with respect to a protected cell;

(6) a sponsored captive insurance company annually shall file with the director financial reports the director requires, which shall include, but are not limited to, accounting statements detailing the financial experience of each protected cell;

(7) a sponsored captive insurance company shall notify the director in writing within ten business days of a protected cell that is insolvent or otherwise unable to meet its claim or expense obligations;

(8) no participant contract shall take effect without the director's prior written approval, and the addition of each new protected cell and withdrawal of any participant of any existing protected cell constitutes a change in the business plan requiring the director's prior written approval.

Section 38-90-220.

A sponsor of a sponsored captive insurance company must be an insurer licensed under the laws of any state, a reinsurer authorized or approved under the laws of any state, or a captive insurance company formed or licensed under this chapter. The business written by a sponsored captive insurance company must be fronted by an insurance company licensed under the laws of any state. A risk retention group may not be either a sponsor or a participant of a sponsored captive insurance company.

Section 38-90-230.

(A) An association, corporation, limited liability company, partnership, trust, or other business entity may be a participant in a sponsored captive insurance company formed or licensed under this chapter.

(B) A sponsor may be a participant in a sponsored captive insurance company.

(C) A participant need not be a shareholder of the sponsored captive insurance company or an affiliate of the company.

(D) A participant shall insure only its own risks through a sponsored captive insurance company.

Section 38-90-240.

A licensed captive insurance company that meets the necessary requirement of this title imposed upon an insurer must be considered for issuance of a certificate of authority to act as an insurer in this State."

Appendix D

Cayman Islands Insurance Law

INSURANCE LAW

(2004 Revision)

1. Short title

This Law may be cited as the Insurance Law (2004 Revision).

2. Definitions

In this Law—

"actuary" means a person who has qualified as an actuary by examination of the Institute of Actuaries in England or the Faculty of Actuaries in Scotland or the Society of Actuaries in the United States of America or Canada, and who is a current member of good standing of one of the above professional associations or a person of good standing with some other actuarial qualification who is recognised by the Authority as such for the purpose of this Law;

"approved external insurer" means an insurer licensed as such under section 4(7);

"auditor" means a person who has qualified as an accountant by examination of one of the Institutes of Chartered Accountants in England and Wales, Ireland and Scotland, or the Canadian Institute of Chartered Accountants or the American Institute of Certified Public Accountants, and who is a current member of good standing of one of the above Institutes or a person of good standing with some other accountancy qualification who is recognised by the Authority as such for the purpose of this Law;

"Authority" means the Cayman Islands Monetary Authority established under section 3(1) of the Monetary Authority Law (2004 Revision) and includes any employee of the Authority acting under the Authority's authorisation;

"contract" includes policy;

"domestic business" means insurance business where the contract is in respect of the life, safety, fidelity or insurable interest (other than in respect of property) of a person who at the time of effecting the contract is ordinarily resident in the Islands, or property that at the time of effecting the contract is in the Islands or, in the case of a vehicle, vessel or aircraft, or other movable property is ordinarily based in the Islands (but does not include re-insurance business);

"exempted company" has the meaning ascribed to it in the Companies Law (2004 Revision);

"exempted insurer" means an insurer which is—

    (a)   incorporated as an exempted company;

    (b)   a non-resident company which is either incorporated under the Companies Law (2004 Revision); or a foreign company registered under Part IX thereof; or

    (c)   constituted through partnership, shareholding or other acceptable mutual association by one or more members having a common trade, profession, affinity or other special interest;

"external insurer" means an insurer who is neither a local nor an exempted insurer;

"financial year" in relation to a licensee means the period not exceeding fifty-three weeks at the end of which the balance of the licensee's accounts is struck or, if no such balance is struck or if a period in excess of fifty-three weeks is employed, then a calendar year;

"general business" means insurance business other than long term business;

"Governor" means the Governor in Cabinet;

"insurance agent" means a person (not being an insurer) who solicits directly, or through representatives, advertising or other means, domestic business on behalf of not more than one insurer;

"insurance broker" means a person (not being an insurer) who negotiates directly, or through representatives or other means, contracts of insurance or of re-insurance on behalf of more than one insurer, or for placement with insurers or re-insurers;

"insurance business" means the business of effecting and carrying out contracts—

(a) protecting persons against loss or liability to loss in respect of risks to which such persons may be exposed; or

(b) to pay a sum of money or other thing of value upon the happening of an event,

and includes re-insurance business and running-off business including the settlement of claims;

"insurance manager" means a company operating in or from within the Islands which provides insurance expertise to or for insurers and which has in its bona fide employment a person who—

(a) is qualified by examination as a fellow or associate of the Chartered Insurance Institute of London, or who is a member of either the Society of Chartered Property and Casualty Underwriters or the American Society of Chartered Life Underwriters both of the United States of America; and who is either a current member of good standing of the applicable professional body or of some other professional insurance association recognised by the Authority for the purpose of this Law; or

(b) is a person of good standing with such insurance expertise as has been approved by the Authority.

"insurance sub-agent" means a person (not being an insurer, insurance agent or insurance broker) who solicits directly or through advertising or other means, domestic business on behalf of an insurance agent or on behalf of an insurance broker;

"insurer" means a person carrying on insurance business who is—

(a) a local insurer, an exempted insurer or an external insurer; or

(b) an association of individual underwriters including Lloyd's of London and other associations of underwriters recognised by the Authority and which comply with such laws as are enacted in their principal place of residence for their regulation and supervision;

"licence" and its cognates means a licence granted under this Law;

"local insurer" means an insurer, other than an exempted insurer, incorporated or constituted in and having its head office in the Islands;

"long term business" means insurance business involving the making of contracts of insurance—

(a) on human life or contracts to pay annuities on human life; but excluding contracts for credit life insurance and term life insurance other than convertible and renewable term life contracts;

(b) against risks of the persons insured sustaining injury as the result of an accident or of an accident of a specified class or dying as the result of an accident or of an accident of a specified class or becoming incapacitated in consequence of disease or diseases of a specified class, being contracts that are expressed to be in effect for a period of not less than five years or without limit of time and either not expressed to be terminable by the insurer before the expiration of five years from the taking effect thereof or are expressed to be so terminable before the expiration of that period only in special circumstances therein mentioned; and

(c) whether by bonds, endowment certificates or otherwise whereby in return for one or more premiums paid to the insurer a sum or series of sums is to become payable to the person insured in the future, not being contracts falling within paragraphs (a) or (b);

"net worth" means excess of assets (including any contingent or reserve fund secured to the satisfaction of the Authority) over liabilities other than liabilities to partners or shareholders;

"non-resident company" bears the meaning ascribed to that term in section 2(1) of the Local Companies (Control) Law (1999 Revision);

"policy holder" means the person with whom an insurer has effected a contract of insurance;

"prescribed" means prescribed by this Law or any regulations; and

"principal representative (insurance)" means a person operating in or from within the Islands who, not being a bona fide employee, maintains for an insurer full and proper records of the business activities of that insurer.

3. Insurance businesses to be licensed

(1) Whoever not being licensed in that behalf carries on insurance business is guilty of an offence.

(2) Whoever, not being licensed in that behalf, acts as—

(a) an insurance manager;

(b) an insurance broker;

(c) an insurance agent;

(d) an insurance sub-agent; or

(e) a principal representative (insurance),

is guilty of an offence.

4. Applications for licences

(1) Persons desiring to carry on insurance business in or from within the Islands may make application in writing to the Authority for the grant of a licence under one or more of the following categories—

(a) Class 'A' Insurer's Licence;

(b) Unrestricted Class 'B' Insurer's Licence;

(c) Restricted Class 'B' Insurer's Licence;

(d) Insurance Agent's Licence;

(e) Insurance Broker's Licence;

(f) Insurance Sub-Agent's Licence;

(g) Insurance Manager's Licence; and

(h) Principal Representative (Insurance)'s Licence.

(2) Applications shall be in the form prescribed, sent to the Authority and accompanied by the prescribed fee (to be forwarded by the Authority to the Financial Secretary for the benefit of the revenue, returnable if the licence is not granted) and the Authority, if satisfied that it will not be against the public interest, may grant a licence subject to such conditions as to the Authority appear necessary or desirable. Any decision to refuse to grant a licence is final and conclusive and not subject to any appeal to or review by, any court.

(3) It is a condition of every licence that the licensee shall notify the Authority forthwith of any change in the information supplied in the application.

(4) A Class 'A' Insurer's Licence permits a local or an external insurer to carry on insurance business generally in or from within the Islands.

(5) An Unrestricted Class 'B' Insurer's License permits an exempted insurer to carry on insurance business other than domestic business from within the Islands.

(6) A Restricted Class 'B' Insurer's Licence permits an exempted insurer only to accept insurance business other than domestic business from its member or members or such other persons as may be specifically approved by the Authority.

(7) An external insurer having its principal or registered office in a place outside the Islands where the legislation for the regulation and supervision of insurers is acceptable to the Authority may be licensed as an approved external insurer under Class 'A'.

(8) The Authority shall refuse to grant a licence if the Authority is of the opinion that the business to which the application relates would be carried on by persons who are not fit and proper persons to be directors or, as the case may be, managers or officers in their respective positions.

(9) No insurer's licence other than a Restricted Class 'B' Licence shall be granted to any person whose net worth—

  (a) in the case of an insurer effecting general business but not long term business, is less than one hundred thousand dollars;

  (b) in the case of an insurer effecting long term business but not general business, is less than two hundred thousand dollars; and

  (c) in the case of an insurer effecting long term business and general business, is less than three hundred thousand dollars.

(10) It is a condition of every insurer's licence that the licensee shall maintain his net worth at an amount not less than that prescribed by subsection (9).

(11) The Authority may revoke any licence—

  (a) if the licensee ceases to carry on insurance business;

  (b) if the direction and management of the licensee's insurance business has not been conducted in a fit and proper manner;

  (c) if a person holding a position as a director, manager or officer of the licensee's insurance business is not a fit and proper person to hold the respective position;

  (d) if the licensee becomes bankrupt or goes into liquidation or is wound up or otherwise dissolved; or

  (e) in the circumstances provided for in section 13.

(12) Every holder of a current licence shall on or before every 15th day of January during the currency of the licence pay to the Financial Secretary for the benefit of the revenue the annual fee prescribed in the Schedule in respect of each class of licence held.

(13) Without prejudice to subsections (1) to (12), if the annual fee referred to in subsection (12) is not paid by the holder of a current licence on or before every 15th day of January during the currency of the licence, the unpaid annual fee may be sued for by the Crown by action as a civil debt and the Crown may require, and the court may order, the payment of any penalties accrued in respect of the late payment of the fee.

(14) The Authority shall cause the granting of licences under this section to be gazetted.

(15) In determining for the purposes of this section whether a person is a fit and proper person, regard shall be had to all circumstances, including that person's—

(a) honesty, integrity and reputation;

(b) competence and capability; and

(c) financial soundness.

(16) In subsection (13)—

"court" means the Grand Court or a court of summary jurisdiction, as the case may be.

5. The Authority

(1) It is the duty of the Authority—

(a) to maintain a general review of insurance practice in the Islands;

(b) on its own motion to examine the affairs or business of any licensee or other person carrying on, or who has at any time carried on insurance business since the 17th June, 1980 for the purpose of satisfying itself that this Law has been or is being complied with, and the licensee is in a sound financial position and is carrying on his business in a satisfactory manner;

(c) to examine and report on the annual returns delivered to the Authority under sections 10 and 11; and

(d) to examine and make determinations with respect to—

(i) applications for approval, and the use of words or representations which require approval, under section 6(1);

(ii) proposals for the revocation of licences under section 6(3);

(iii) prescription of investments under section 7(1);

(iv) cases of suspected insolvency, and the exercise of powers under section 13;

(v) proposals for regulations to be made under section 18.

(2) The Authority may—

(a) examine and make determinations with respect to applications for licences under section 4; and

(b) take all necessary action to ensure the proper and just implementation of this Law.

(3) The Authority may authorise in writing any other person to assist it in the performance of its functions.

(4) For the purpose of performing its duties under subsection (1)(b), the Authority may in writing authorise any person, including an actuary approved by the Authority, at the expense of the licensee, to examine the affairs or business of any licensee or other person carrying on insurance business for the purpose of satisfying the Authority that this Law has been or is being complied with, and the licensee is in a sound financial position and is carrying on his business in a satisfactory manner, and to report to the Authority the results of every such examination.

6. Use of the word "insurance", etc.

(1) Whoever, not having the approval of the Authority or being a licensee—

(a) uses or continues to use the words "insurance", "assurance", "indemnity", "guarantee", "underwriting", "reinsurance", "surety", "casualty" or any other word which in the opinion of the Authority connotes insurance business or any of their derivatives in English or in any other language in the description or title under which he carries on business in or from within the Islands; or

(b) makes or continues to make any representation in any billhead, letter, letterhead, circular, paper, notice, advertisement or in any manner whatsoever that he is carrying on insurance business,

is guilty of an offence.

(2) Before giving its approval under subsection (1), the Authority may require of any person such references and such information and particulars as may be prescribed.

(3) The Authority may revoke the licence of any person who carries on insurance business, or acts as an insurance manager, an insurance broker, an insurance agent, an insurance sub-agent or a principal representative (insurance) under a name which—

(a) is identical with that of any other person, company, firm or business house whether within the Islands or not, or which so nearly resembles that name as to be calculated to deceive;

(b) is calculated falsely to suggest the patronage of or connection with some person of authority whether within the Islands or not;

(c) is calculated falsely to suggest that such person has a special status in relation to or derived from the Government of the Islands, or has the official backing of or acts on behalf of the said Government or of any department or official thereof or is recognised in the Islands as a national insurer, insurance broker, insurance agent or insurance manager; or

(d) is calculated falsely to suggest that the licensee is carrying on insurance business in a different category from that in respect of which he is licensed.

7. General requirements for licensed insurers

(1) A licensed approved external insurer that carries out domestic business shall, at all times—

    (a) in respect of its general business, deposit or maintain in a segregated account at a retail bank in the Islands which holds an "A" licence issued under section 6 of the Banks and Trust Companies Law (2003 Revision) funds in cash, short term securities or other realisable investments approved by the Authority, the total value of which shall at least equal the total of its—

        (i) unearned premium reserve;

        (ii) outstanding claims reserve;

        (iii) reserve for claims incurred but not reported; and

        (iv) unexpired risks reserve;

    (b) in respect of its long term business, deposit or maintain in a segregated account at a bank in the Islands which holds an "A" licence issued under section 5 of the Banks and Trust Companies Law (2003 Revision) funds in cash, short term securities or other realisable investments approved by the Authority, the total value of which shall at least equal its total actuarially determined policyholder liabilities in respect of its life and annuity business; and

    (c) vest such cash, securities or investments in a manner approved by the Authority.

(2) Every contract of domestic business shall be subject to the jurisdiction of the courts of the Islands, notwithstanding any provision to the contrary contained in such contract or in any agreement related to such contract. Every licensed insurer shall nominate at least one person resident in the Islands approved by the Authority who is authorised to accept on its behalf service of process in any legal proceedings on behalf of such insurer, and any notices required to be served on it.

(3) Licensed insurers, other than approved external insurers, may only carry on insurance business in accordance with the information given in their licence applications. Any proposed change in the nature of such business requires the prior approval of the Authority. Such insurers shall furnish annually to the Authority a certificate of compliance with this provision, in the prescribed form, signed by an independent auditor approved by the Authority, by a licensed insurance manager or by such other person as the Authority may approve.

(4) Every licensed insurer, other than an approved external insurer, shall prepare annual accounts in accordance with generally accepted accounting principles, audited by an independent auditor approved by the Authority.

Provided that the Authority may, in writing, exempt from this subsection any licensed insurer who pays an annual licence fee that has been reduced under paragraph (a) of the proviso to the Schedule.

(5) Every insurer licensed under Class 'A', other than an approved external insurer, who is carrying on general business shall, in addition, to the requirement in subsection (4), prepare annually a financial statement in the prescribed form, certified by an independent auditor approved by the Authority, to enable the Authority to be satisfied as to its solvency.

(6) Every insurer licensed under Class 'A' and Class 'B' who is carrying on long term business shall, in addition to subsection (4), prepare annually an actuarial valuation of its assets and liabilities, certified by an actuary approved by the Authority, so as to enable the Authority to be satisfied as to its solvency. Furthermore—

(a) every such insurer carrying on both long term business and general business shall keep separate accounts in respect of its long term business;

(b)

(i) all receipts, by any such insurer of funds in respect of its long term business shall be placed in a separate long term business fund; and

(ii) payments from the said long term business fund shall not be made directly or indirectly for any purpose other than those of the insurer's long term business, except insofar as such payments can be made out of any surplus disclosed on an actuarial valuation and certified by an actuary approved by the Authority to be distributable otherwise than to policyholders; and

(c) every such insurer carrying on long term business may establish any number of separate accounts in respect of contracts to pay annuities on human life and contracts of insurance on human life, the assets relating to which shall be kept segregated one from the other and independent of all other assets of the insurer, and, notwithstanding any other law to the contrary—

(i) separate accounts shall not be chargeable with any liability arising from any other business (including other types of long term business) of the insurer and no liabilities shall be satisfied out of the assets standing to the credit of the relevant separate account apart from those liabilities arising from the contract for which the separate account was established or liabilities relating specifically to the operation of the separate account;

(ii) the assets of a separate account shall include all premiums paid with respect to the contract for which the separate account was established and all interest, earnings and assets derived therefrom; and

(iii) any claim of the insurer under a contract of reinsurance taken out by the insurer in respect of a contract for which a separate account has been established shall be deemed to be an asset of the relevant separate account to the extent only that the insurer fails to meet its obligations under the relevant contract and upon payment of any amount due under such contract of reinsurance shall be immediately credited to the relevant separate account, whether the insurer is solvent or not.

(7) In respect of any insurer other than an approved external insurer or an insurer who, with the approval of the Authority, maintains permanently in the Islands a principal office and staff,—

   (a) each such insurer shall appoint an insurance manager resident in the Islands and maintain permanently at a designated principal office normally in the Islands (unless some other location is approved by the Authority) full and proper records of its business activities;

   (b) each such insurer carrying on besides insurance any other business shall keep separate accounts in respect of its insurance business and shall segregate the assets and liabilities of its insurance business from those of its other business;

   (c) the Authority may prescribe that any such insurer (other than a holder of a Restricted Class 'B' Insurer's Licence) shall not without the specific approval of the Authority make investments of a specified class and may in that case require such insurer to realise investments of that class within such period as may be prescribed; and

   (d) no such insurer shall without the sanction of the Authority—

      (i) amalgamate with any one or more insurers; or

      (ii) other than in the normal course of insurance business, transfer its insurance operations or a part thereof or accept transfer of the insurance operations or a part thereof from another insurer.

(8) An insurer licensed under Class 'B' may not carry on domestic business except to the extent that such business forms a minor part of the international risk of a policyholder whose main activities are in territories outside the Islands. Any such insurer shall forthwith give full particulars in writing to the Authority of any domestic business so carried on by the insurer.

(9) A licensed insurance broker may obtain a special dispensation from the Authority to place a policy or contract of domestic business with one or more unlicensed insurers where—

   (a) the said insurers have not been refused a licence under this Law;

   (b) the said insurers are approved by the Authority as being of sound reputation;

   (c) the Authority is satisfied that the proposed volume of domestic business to be placed with such unlicensed insurers is inadequate to support the payment of Class 'A' licence fees or that some other good and sufficient reason exists; and

(d) the said insurance broker can demonstrate to the satisfaction of the Authority an evident need (in terms of additional capacity or policy coverage, or otherwise) that the business be so placed.

Such dispensation, if granted, shall be subject to review at such intervals, if any, as the Authority may specify when granting the dispensation and there shall be no appeal against the refusal of any such dispensation or renewal thereof and the final sentence of section 7(2) shall apply to a policy placed under this subsection.

8. Shares not to be issued or transferred without approval of Authority

(1) No shares totalling more than five per cent of the issued share capital of a company which is a licensee under this Law shall be issued, and no issued shares totalling more than five per cent of the issued share capital of a company which is a licensee under this Law shall be transferred or disposed of in any manner, without the prior approval of the Authority.

(2) The Authority may exempt from subsection (1) a licensee whose shares or the shares of whose parent body, if any, are publicly traded on a stock exchange recognised by the Authority, and any such exemption—

   (a) shall be subject to a condition that the licensee shall, as soon as reasonably practicable, notify the Authority of—

       (i) any change in control of the licensee;

       (ii) the acquisition by any person or group of persons of shares representing more than ten per cent of the licensee's issued share capital or total voting rights; or

       (iii) the acquisition by any person or group of persons of shares representing more than ten per cent of the issued share capital or total voting rights of the licensee's parent company;

   (b) shall be subject to a condition that the licensee shall, as soon as reasonably practicable, provide such information to the Authority, and within such period of time, as the Authority may require for the purpose of enabling an assessment as to whether persons acquiring control or ownership of the licensee in the circumstances set out in paragraph (a) are fit and proper persons to have such control or ownership; and

   (c) shall be subject to such terms and other conditions as the Authority may deem necessary.

(3) In subsection (1), the reference to shares being transferred or disposed of includes not only the transfer or disposal of the legal interest in the shares but also the transfer or disposal of any beneficial interest in the shares.

9. General requirements for other licensees

(1) An insurance agent who acts on behalf of more than one insurer, is deemed for the purpose of this Law to be acting as an insurance broker.

(2) A licensed insurance broker shall maintain in force professional indemnity insurance in respect of his insurance broking activities, placed with an insurer licensed to carry on domestic business and for an indemnity of not less than one hundred thousand dollars for any one loss, or such other figure as may be prescribed by the Authority. Such professional indemnity insurance shall extend to include the activities on behalf of the broker or of his sub-agents, if any. In the event that such professional indemnity insurance be withdrawn, or cancelled, or the said insurance be not renewed, the said broker shall immediately notify the Authority and shall forthwith cease to solicit further insurance business until such professional indemnity insurance has been reinstated or replaced.

(3) A licensed insurance agent shall provide evidence satisfactory to the Authority of a power of attorney, agency agreement or guarantee satisfactory to the Authority, between the agent and the insurer for whom such agent acts. Such power of attorney, agency agreement or guarantee shall extend to include the activities on behalf of the insurer and the agent or his sub-agents, if any. In the event that such power of attorney, agency agreement or guarantee is withdrawn or such agreement is determined the said agent shall immediately notify the Authority and shall forthwith cease to solicit further insurance business until such power of attorney or guarantee has been reinstated.

(4) A licensed insurance agent may, as an alternative to meeting the requirement laid down in subsection (3), maintain in force professional indemnity insurance in like manner and for a like amount as if he had been a licensed insurance broker as in subsection (2).

(5) A licensed insurance sub-agent may not solicit or carry on insurance business on behalf of more than one insurance agent, or on behalf of more than one insurance broker. If the professional indemnity insurance or power of attorney, agency agreement or guarantee, as the case may be, referred to in subsections (2), (3) and (4), is for any reason withdrawn from the said sub-agent, then the licence of the said sub-agent is ipso facto suspended until such time as such professional indemnity insurance, power of attorney, agency agreement or guarantee, as the case may be, is reinstated.

(6) A licensed insurance manager or a licensed principal representative (insurance) shall use his best endeavours to carry on insurance and re-insurance business only with insurers of sound reputation. In the event that such insurance manager or a licensed principal representative (insurance) feels cause for concern regarding the probity or soundness of any insurer or re-insurer for whom or with whom he is carrying on business, he shall report the same forthwith to the Authority. In the event that either party to an agreement relating to representation between a Class 'B' insurer and an insurance manager or principal representative (insurance) intends to terminate the same, sixty days written notice of such proposed termination shall be given to the Authority by such insurance manager or principal representative (insurance).

(7) A licensed insurance manager or a licensed principal representative (insurance) who also carries on insurance business as an insurance broker or as an insurance agent is required to be licensed in respect of each such activity.

10. Annual returns by licensed insurers

(1) Each licensed approved external insurer who is carrying on domestic business shall furnish to the Authority within six months of the end of its financial year the following returns—

(a) a certificate of solvency or of compliance with insurance legislation specifically enacted in the country or place where the said external insurer is constituted for its supervision and regulation, or some equivalent document acceptable to the Authority;

(b) written confirmation that such certificate or equivalent document referred to in paragraph (a) embraces the said insurer's liabilities in respect of its domestic business;

(c) if the said insurer has a branch or other subsidiary activity in the Islands, written confirmation that the said insurer accepts responsibility for all contracts issued by such branch or subsidiary activity and also for all acts, omissions and liabilities of such branch or subsidiary activity;

(d) in respect of the said insurer's general domestic business, such information as the Authority may require concerning the availability of funds for prompt settlement of claims under such business;

(e) in respect of the said insurer's long term domestic business, such information as the Authority may require concerning the investment of premium income received by the said insurer from such business in prescribed investments within the Islands;

(f) if the said insurer is licensed under Class 'A' for long term business, an actuarial valuation of its assets and liabilities certified by an actuary approved by the Authority, in accordance with section 7(6);

(g) a list of insurance agents and insurance brokers who have the said insurer's authority to effect domestic business on its behalf; and

(h) written confirmation that the information set out in the application for the said insurer's licence, as modified by subsequent notifications of changes in accordance with section 4(3), remains correct, and gives a full and fair picture of the said insurer's business.

(2) Every insurer licensed under Class 'A' other than an approved external insurer shall furnish to the Authority within six months of the end of its financial year the following annual returns—

(a) written confirmation from an independent auditor approved by the Authority that annual accounts have been prepared as required under section 7(4) and whether or not the auditor's certificate for such accounts is unqualified;

(b) a certificate of compliance as required by section 7(3);

(c) if the said insurer is licensed under Class 'A' for general business, a financial statement in the prescribed form, certified by an independent auditor approved by the Authority, in accordance with section 7(5);

(d) if the said insurer is licensed under Class 'A' for long term business, an actuarial valuation of its assets and liabilities, certified by an actuary, approved by the Authority, in accordance with section 7(6);

(e) if the said insurer is an external insurer which has a branch or other subsidiary activity in the Islands which is constituted as a separate legal entity, written confirmation that the said insurer accepts responsibility for all contracts issued by such branch or subsidiary activity and also for all acts, omissions and liabilities of such branch or subsidiary activity;

(f) if the said insurer is licensed for general business, such information as the Authority may require concerning the availability of funds for prompt settlement of claims under general domestic business;

(g) if the said insurer is licensed for long term business such information as the Authority may require concerning the investment of premium income received from such domestic long term business in prescribed investments within the Islands; and

(h) a list of insurance agents and insurance brokers who have the said insurer's authority to effect domestic business on its behalf.

(3) Every insurer licensed under Class 'B' shall furnish to the Authority within six months of the end of its financial year the following annual returns—

    (a) written confirmation from an independent auditor approved by the Authority that annual accounts have been prepared as required under section 7(4) and whether or not the auditor's certificate for such accounts is unqualified; and

    (b) a certificate of compliance as required by section 7(3).

(4) The Authority may prescribe additions, deletions or modifications to the returns required to be made by licensees under this section.

(5) When a licensee changes its auditor, the Authority may require the former auditor to explain the circumstances responsible for such change.

11. Annual returns by other licensees

(1) Every licensed insurance agent shall furnish to the Authority within six months of the end of each calendar year the following returns in respect of his domestic business—

    (a) confirmation in writing that the said agent is acting for one insurer only and the name of that insurer;

    (b) evidence of the existence of a power of attorney, agency agreement or guarantee or professional indemnity insurance as required under section 9(3) or (4);

    (c) a list of the sub-agents, if any, authorised by the said agent to solicit domestic business on his behalf and on behalf of the insurer whom he represents; and

    (d) confirmation in writing that the information set out in the application for the said agent's licence, as modified by subsequent notifications of changes in accordance with section 4(3), remains correct and gives a full and fair picture of the said agent's business.

(2) Every licensed insurance broker shall furnish to the Authority within six months of the end of his financial year the following information in respect of his domestic business—

    (a) a list of all insurers for whom the said insurance broker is authorised to act, and the premium income to each such insurer during the last financial year;

    (b) evidence of the existence of professional indemnity insurance in respect of his activities as an insurance broker as required under section 9(2);

    (c) a list of the sub-agents, if any, authorised by the said insurance broker to solicit domestic business on his behalf and on behalf of the insurers whom he represents; and

    (d) confirmation in writing that the information set out in the application for the said insurance broker's licence, as modified by subsequent notifications of changes in accordance with section 4(3), remains correct and gives a full and fair picture of the said insurance broker's business.

(3) Every licensed insurance sub-agent shall furnish to the Authority before the renewal of his licence—

(a) confirmation in writing that the said sub-agent is acting for one insurance agent only, or for one insurance broker only, and the name of such insurance agent or insurance broker; and

(b) confirmation in writing that the information set out in the application for the said sub-agent's licence, as modified by subsequent notifications of changes in accordance with section 4(3), remains correct and gives a full and fair picture of the said sub-agent's insurance activities.

(4) Every licensed insurance manager shall furnish to the Authority within six months of the end of his financial year the following information—

(a) a list of all insurers for whom the said insurance manager acts; and

(b) confirmation in writing that the information set out in the application for the said insurance manager's licence, as modified by subsequent notifications of changes in accordance with section 4(3), remains correct and gives a full and fair picture of the said insurance manager's activities.

(5) The Authority may prescribe additions, deletions or modifications to the returns required to be made by licensees under this section.

12. Cease and desist orders

(1) Where the Authority is of the opinion that a licensee—

(a) is committing, or is about to commit, an act that is an unsafe or unsound practice in conducting the business of the licensee; or

(b) is pursuing, or is about to pursue, a course of conduct that is an unsafe or unsound practice in conducting the business of the licensee,

the Authority may direct the licensee—

(i) to cease or refrain from committing the act or pursuing the course of conduct; and

(ii) to perform such acts as in the opinion of the Authority are necessary to remedy or ameliorate the situation.

(2) Whoever, without reasonable cause, fails to comply with a direction given by the Authority under subsection (1) is guilty of an offence and liable on summary conviction to a fine of ten thousand dollars and on conviction on indictment to a fine of one hundred thousand dollars, and if the offence of which he is convicted is

continued after conviction he commits a further offence and is liable to a fine of ten thousand dollars for every day on which the offence is so committed.

13. Powers of Authority

(1) Whenever the Authority is of the opinion that—

(a) a licensee is or appears likely to become unable to meet its obligations as they fall due;

(b) a licensee is carrying on business in a manner detrimental to the public interest or to the interest of its creditors or policy holders;

(c) a licensee has contravened this Law;

(d) a licensee has failed to comply with a condition of its licence;

(e) the direction and management of a licensee's business has not been conducted in a fit and proper manner;

(f) a person holding a position as a director, manager or officer of a licensee's business is not a fit and proper person to hold the respective position; or

(g) a person acquiring control or ownership of a licensee is not a fit and proper person to have such control or ownership,

the Authority may forthwith do any of the following—

(i) require the licensee forthwith to take steps to rectify the matter;

(ii) suspend the licence of the licensee pending a full enquiry into the licensee's affairs made under section 5(1)(b);

(iii) revoke the licence;

(iv) impose conditions, or further conditions, as the case may be, upon the licence and amend or revoke any such condition;

(v) require the substitution of any director, manager or officer of the licensee;

(vi) at the expense of the licensee, appoint a person to advise the licensee on the proper conduct of its affairs and to report to the Authority thereon within three months of the date of his appointment;

(vii) at the expense of the licensee, appoint a person to assume control of the licensee's affairs who shall, with necessary changes, have all the powers of a person appointed as a receiver or manager of a business appointed under section 18 of the Bankruptcy Law (1997 Revision); and

(viii) require such action to be taken by the licensee as the Authority considers necessary.

(2) Notwithstanding section 16(1), a licensee may, within seven days of the decision, apply to the Authority for a reconsideration of its decision to revoke a licence under subsection (1)(iii).

(3) A person appointed under subsection (1)(vi) or (vii) or whose appointment has been extended under subsection (4)(b) shall, from time to time at his discretion and in any case within three months of the date of his appointment or of the extension of his appointment (as the case may be), prepare and furnish a report to the Authority of the affairs of the licensee and of his recommendations thereon.

(4) On receipt of a report under subsection (3), the Authority may—

(a) revoke the appointment of the person appointed under subsection (1)(vi) or (vii);

(b) extend the period of his appointment;

(c) subject to such conditions as the Authority may impose, allow the licensee to reorganise its affairs in a manner approved by the Authority; or

(d) revoke the licence and apply to the Grand Court for an order that the licensee be forthwith wound up by that Court in which case the provisions of the Companies Law (2004 Revision) relating to the winding up of a company by that Court shall, with necessary changes, apply.

(5) Notwithstanding any provisions herein, the Authority may revoke a licence if the licensee—

(a) has ceased to carry on insurance business; or

(b) goes into liquidation or is wound up or otherwise dissolved.

(6) Whenever the Authority suspends a licence under subsection (1)(ii) or revokes a licence under subsection (1)(iii), subsection (4)(d) or subsection (5), the Authority shall cause notice of such suspension or revocation to be gazetted, and may also cause such notice to be published (whether within the Islands or elsewhere) in such newspaper or other publication as the Authority may consider necessary in the circumstances.

14. Surrender of licence

A licensee may apply to the Authority to surrender its licence if it—

(a) has ceased to carry on the business in respect of which the licence was granted; or

(b) is being wound up voluntarily and produces evidence that it is solvent and able forthwith to repay all its creditors,

and the Authority may thereupon approve the surrender and cancel the licence.

15. Preservation of assets, etc.

(1) In any case where the Authority has suspended a licence under section 13(1), the Authority may apply ex parte to the Grand Court for an order that the assets, books or papers of the licensee be preserved, not moved or otherwise disposed of and the Grand Court may, if it is satisfied that such assets, books or papers are liable to be moved, destroyed or otherwise disposed of make an order that they shall be preserved, and not be moved or otherwise disposed of until a further order of that Court.

(2) Where an order has been made by the Grand Court under subsection (1), the licensee may apply to the Grand Court at any time for the discharge of such order and the Grand Court may thereupon discharge, vary or confirm the order.

16. Appeals

(1) An appeal shall lie to the Grand Court against any order of the Authority to suspend or revoke a licence under section 13(1).

(2) An appeal under this section shall not operate as a stay of any decision appealed against.

(3) The Rules Committee of the Grand Court may make Rules of Procedure governing the conduct of appeals under this section.

17. Application, etc.

(1) Nothing in this Law derogates from any provision of the Immigration Law (2003 Revision) relating to gainful occupation licences.

(2) No company which is licensed under this Law is required to be licensed under the Local Companies (Control) Law (1999 Revision) or the Trade and Business Licensing Law (2003 Revision).

(3) This Law has no application to or effect upon—

   (a) governmental pension arrangements;

   (b) the validity of policies of insurance in existence at the date of coming into effect of this Law;

   (c) the Friendly Societies Law (1998 Revision); or

   (d) pecuniary loss insurance provided by banks licensed under the Banks and Trust Companies Law (2003 Revision).

18. Regulations

The Governor may make regulations—

(a) prescribing anything by this Law required to be prescribed;

(b) exempting any person or class of persons or business or class of business from any provision of this Law;

(c) prescribing forms to be used;

(d) prescribing the format for any returns to be made under this Law;

(e) prescribing capital and liquidity margins and ratios to be maintained by licensees under this Law; and

(f) amending the Schedule save that any amendment increasing the scale of fees prescribed in the Schedule shall require the confirmation of the Legislative Assembly.

(g) providing for such matters as may be necessary or convenient for carrying out or giving effect to this Law and its administration.

19. Offences

(1) Whoever, for any purpose of this Law, makes any representation in the truth of which he does not believe (the onus of proof of his belief being upon him) is guilty of an offence and liable on summary conviction to a fine of ten thousand dollars and to imprisonment for two years.

(2) Whoever, by any act or omission, contravenes any requirement of this Law for which no specific penalty is provided, whether such contravention is or is not specifically stated to be an offence, is guilty of an offence and liable on summary conviction to a fine of five thousand dollars and to imprisonment for one year.

20. Savings

(1) Every application for the grant of a licence made under the old Law and wholly or partly heard by the Governor as at the 17th March, 2003, is to be continued and dealt with in all respects under the old Law.

(2) A licence granted as a result of an application determined under subsection (1) is to be granted on the same terms and conditions that would have applied under the old Law.

(3) Every application for the grant of a licence made under the old Law and not wholly or partly heard by the Governor as at the 17th March, 2003, is to be taken to be an

application made under this Revision of the Law and the provisions of this Revision are to apply accordingly.

(4) In the case of an appeal against any decision of the Governor that has been commenced but not finally determined before the 17th March, 2003, the Grand Court is to continue to deal with the appeal under the old Law; and when the appeal is finally determined, the old Law is to apply, subject to any necessary modifications, as if the appeal had been finally determined before the 17th March, 2003.

(5) Any licence granted under the old Law and in force immediately before the 17th March, 2003.—

   (a) shall have effect from that date, as if granted under this Revision of the Law; and

   (b) in the case of a licence for a specified period, shall remain in force, subject to the provisions of this Revision of the Law, for so much of that period as falls after that date.

(6) In this section—

Law 43 of 2001

2001 Revision

"old Law" means the Insurance Law (2001 Revision) as amended by the Insurance (Further Variation of Fees) Regulations, 2001, the Insurance (Amendment) Law, 2001 and the Insurance (Reduction of Fees) Regulations, 2002.

SCHEDULE

SCALE OF ANNUAL LICENCE FEES

(Section 4 (12))

   Class 'A' $30,000

   Class 'B' (Unrestricted) $7,000

   Class 'B' (Restricted) $7,000

   Insurance agent $400

   Insurance broker $4,500

   Insurance sub-agent $120

   Insurance manager—

acting for not more than 10 licensed insurers $15,000

acting for 11 to 50 licensed insurers $20,000

acting for 51 to 100 licensed insurers $25,000

acting for more than 100 licensed insurers $30,000

Principal representative (insurance)—for each insurer represented $1,500 (but subject to a maximum of $25,000):

Provided that—

(a) the amount of any annual licence fee hereinbefore prescribed to be paid by the holder of a Class 'A', Class 'B' (Unrestricted) or Class 'B' (Restricted) licence shall be reduced by one half if the Authority is satisfied that such holder has, prior to the date on which such fee becomes payable, ceased carrying on any insurance business other than that necessary to enable the performance of obligations of such holder under contracts of insurance in force at such date; and

(b) the amount by which any annual fee is reduced under paragraph (a) shall immediately become due and payable if the holder of the relevant licence effects any new contract of insurance during the year to which such fee relates.

(c) where a person applies for the grant of a Class 'B' (Unrestricted) or a Class 'B' (Restricted) licence and licence is granted in the month of December, the licence fee payable shall be one-twelfth of the annual licence fee hereinbefore prescribed:

And provided further that the Governor may, from time to time, waive or reduce any or all of the said licence fees in relation to any person or group of persons in Cayman Brac or Little Cayman.

Appendix E

26 U.S.C. § 831

Tax on insurance companies other than life insurance companies

(a) General rule.

Taxes computed as provided in section 11 shall be imposed for each taxable year on the taxable income of every insurance company other than a life insurance company.

(b) Alternative tax for certain small companies

(1) In general. In lieu of the tax otherwise applicable under subsection (a), there is hereby imposed for each taxable year on the income of every insurance company to which this subsection applies a tax computed by multiplying the taxable investment income of such company for such taxable year by the rates provided in section 11(b).

(2) Companies to which this subsection applies

(A) In general. This subsection shall apply to every insurance company other than life (including interinsurers and reciprocal underwriters) if—

(i) the net written premiums (or, if greater, direct written premiums) for the taxable year exceed $350,000 but do not exceed $1,200,000, and

(ii) such company elects the application of this subsection for such taxable year. The election under clause (ii) shall apply to the taxable year for which made and for all subsequent taxable years for which the requirements of clause (i) are met. Such an election, once made, may be revoked only with the consent of the Secretary.

(B) Controlled group rules

(i) In general. For purposes of subparagraph (A), in determining whether any company is described in clause (i) of subparagraph (A), such company shall be treated as receiving during the taxable year amounts described in such clause (i) which are received during such year by all other companies which are members of the same controlled group as the insurance company for which the determination is being made.

(ii) Controlled group. For purposes of clause (i), the term "controlled group" means any controlled group of corporations (as defined in section 1563(a)); except that—(I) "more than 50 percent" shall be substituted for "at least 80 percent" each place it appears in section 1563(a), and (II) subsections (a)(4) and (b)(2)(D) of section 1563 shall not apply.

(3) Limitation on use of net operating losses. For purposes of this part, except as provided in section 844, a net operating loss (as defined in section 172) shall not be carried—

(A) to or from any taxable year for which the insurance company is not subject to the tax imposed by subsection (a), or

(B) to any taxable year if, between the taxable year from which such loss is being carried and such taxable year, there is an intervening taxable year for which the insurance company was not subject to the tax imposed by subsection (a).

(c) **Cross references**

(1) For alternative tax in case of capital gains, see section 1201(a).

(?) For taxation of foreign corporations carrying on an insurance business within the United States, see section 842.

(3) For exemption from tax for certain insurance companies other than life, see section 501(c)(15).

Appendix F

Revenue Ruling 2001-31

Recent abuses of IRC §501(c)(15) companies have compelled the IRS to issue multiple Revenue Rulings, Procedures, Notices and Bulletins addressing various issues associated with the use of closely-held insurance companies. In addition, the IRS is closely scrutinizing companies organized pursuant to IRC §501(c)(15). Recently issued IRS publications include:

In Rev. Rul. 77-316, 1977-2 C.B. 53, three situations were presented in which a taxpayer attempted to seek insurance coverage for itself and its operating subsidiaries through the taxpayer's wholly-owned captive insurance subsidiary. The ruling explained that the taxpayer, its non-insurance subsidiaries, and its captive insurance subsidiary represented one "economic family" for purposes of analyzing whether transactions involved sufficient risk shifting and risk distribution to constitute insurance for federal income tax purposes. See Helvering v. Le Gierse, 312 U.S. 531 (1941). The ruling concluded that the transactions were not insurance to the extent that risk was retained within that economic family. Therefore, the premiums paid by the taxpayer and its non-insurance subsidiaries to the captive insurer were not deductible.

No court, in addressing a captive insurance transaction, has fully accepted the economic family theory set forth in Rev. Rul. 77-316. See, e.g., Humana, Inc. v. Commissioner, 881 F.2d 247 (6th Cir. 1989); Clougherty Packing Co. v. Commissioner, 811 F.2d 1297 (9th Cir. 1987) (employing a balance sheet test, rather than the economic family theory, to conclude that transaction between parent and subsidiary was not insurance); Kidde Industries, Inc. v. United States, 40 Fed. Cl. 42 (1997). Accordingly, the Internal Revenue Service will no longer invoke the economic family theory with respect to captive insurance transactions.

The Service may, however, continue to challenge certain captive insurance transactions based on the facts and circumstances of each case. See, e.g., Malone & Hyde v. Commissioner, 62 F.3d 835 (6th Cir. 1995) (concluding that brother-sister transactions were not insurance because the taxpayer guaranteed the captive's performance and the captive was thinly capitalized and loosely regulated); Clougherty Packing Co. v. Commissioner (concluding that a transaction between parent and subsidiary was not insurance).

EFFECT ON OTHER DOCUMENTS

Rev. Rul. 77-316, 1977-2 C.B. 53; Rev. Rul. 78-277, 1978-2 C.B. 268; Rev. Rul. 88-72, 1988-2 C.B. 31; and Rev. Rul. 89-61, 1989-1 C.B. 75, are obsoleted.

Rev. Rul. 78-338, 1978-2 C.B. 107; Rev. Rul. 80-120, 1980-1 C.B. 41; Rev. Rul. 92-93, 1992-2 C.B. 45; and Rev. Proc. 2000-3, 2000-1 I.R.B. 103, are modified.

DRAFTING INFORMATION

The principal author of this revenue ruling is Robert A. Martin of the Office of Associate Chief Counsel (Financial Institutions & Products). For further information regarding this revenue ruling, contact Mr. Martin at (202) 622-3970 (not a toll-free call).

Appendix G

Revenue Ruling 2002-89

ISSUE

Are the amounts paid by a domestic parent corporation to its wholly owned insurance subsidiary deductible as "insurance premiums" under section 162 of the Internal Revenue Code?

FACTS

Situation 1. P, a domestic corporation, enters into an annual arrangement with its wholly owned domestic subsidiary S whereby S "insures" the professional liability risks of P either directly or as a reinsurer of these risks. S is regulated as an insurance company in each state where S does business.

The amounts P pays to S under the arrangement are established according to customary industry rating formulas. In all respects, the parties conduct themselves consistently with the standards applicable to an insurance arrangement between unrelated parties.

In implementing the arrangement, S may perform all necessary administrative tasks, or it may outsource those tasks at prevailing commercial market rates. P does not provide any guarantee of S 's performance, and all funds and business records of P and S are separately maintained. S does not loan any funds to P.

In addition to the arrangement with P, S enters into insurance contracts whereby S serves as a direct insurer or a reinsurer of the professional liability risks of entities unrelated to P or S. The risks of unrelated entities and those of P are homogeneous. The amounts S receives from these unrelated entities under these insurance contracts likewise are established according to customary industry rating formulas.

The premiums S earns from the arrangement with P constitute 90% of S 's total premiums earned during the taxable year on both a gross and net basis. The liability coverage S provides to P accounts for 90% of the total risks borne by S.

Situation 2. Situation 2 is the same as Situation 1 except that the premiums S earns from the arrangement with P constitute less than 50% of S's total premiums earned during the taxable year on both a gross and net basis. The liability coverage S provides to P accounts for less than 50% of the total risks borne by S.

LAW AND ANALYSIS

Section 162(a) of the Code provides, in part, that there shall be allowed as a deduction all the ordinary and necessary expenses paid or incurred during the taxable year in carrying on any trade or business.

Section 1.162-1(a) of the Income Tax Regulations provides, in part, that among the items included in business expenses are insurance premiums against fire, storms, theft, accident, or other similar losses in the case of a business.

Neither the Code nor the regulations define the terms "insurance" or "insurance contract." The United States Supreme Court, however, has explained that in order for an arrangement to constitute insurance for federal income tax purposes, both risk shifting and risk distribution must be present. Helvering v. LeGierse, 312 U.S. 531 (1941).

Risk shifting occurs if a person facing the possibility of an economic loss transfers some or all of the financial consequences of the potential loss to the insurer, such that a loss by the insured does not affect the insured because the loss is offset by the insurance payment. Risk distribution incorporates the statistical phenomenon known as the law of large numbers. Distributing risk allows the insurer to reduce the possibility that a single costly claim will exceed the amount taken in as premiums and set aside for the payment of such a claim. By assuming numerous relatively small, independent risks that occur randomly over time, the insurer smooths out losses to match more closely its receipt of premiums. Clougherty Packing Co. v. Commissioner, 811 F.2d 1297, 1300 (9th Cir. 1987). Risk distribution necessarily entails a pooling of premiums, so that a potential insured is not in significant part paying for its own risks. See Humana, Inc. v. Commissioner, 881 F.2d 247, 257 (6th Cir. 1989).

No court has held that a transaction between a parent and its wholly-owned subsidiary satisfies the requirements of risk shifting and risk distribution if only the risks of the parent are "insured." See Stearns-Roger Corp. v. United States, 774 F.2d 414 (10th Cir. 1985); Carnation Co. v. Commissioner, 640 F.2d 1010 (9th Cir. 1981), cert. denied 454 U.S. 965 (1981). However, courts have held that an arrangement between a parent and its subsidiary can constitute insurance because the parent's premiums are pooled with those of unrelated parties if (i) insurance risk is present, (ii) risk is shifted and distributed, and (iii) the transaction is of the type that is insurance in the commonly accepted sense. See, e.g., Ocean Drilling & Exploration Co. v. United States, 988 F.2d 1135 (Fed. Cir. 1993); AMERCO, Inc. v. Commissioner, 979 F.2d 162 (9th Cir. 1992).

S is regulated as an insurance company in each state in which it transacts business, and the arrangements between P and S and between S and entities unrelated to P or S are established and conducted consistently with the standards applicable to an insurance arrangement. P does not guarantee S's performance and S does not make any loans to P; P's and S's funds and records are separately maintained. The narrow question presented in Situation 1 and Situation 2 is whether S underwrites sufficient risks of unrelated parties that the arrangement between P and S constitutes insurance for federal income tax purposes.

In Situation 1, the premiums that S earns from its arrangement with P constitute 90% of its total premiums earned during the taxable year on both a gross and a net basis. The liability coverage S provides to P accounts for 90% of the total risks borne by S. No court has treated such an arrangement between a parent and its wholly-owned subsidiary as insurance. To the contrary, the arrangement lacks the requisite risk shifting and risk distribution to constitute insurance for federal income tax purposes.

In Situation 2, the premiums that S earns from its arrangement with P constitute less than 50% of the total premiums S earned during the taxable year on both a gross and a net basis. The liability coverage S provides to P accounts for less than 50% of the total risks borne by S. The premiums and risks of P are thus pooled with those of the unrelated insureds. The requisite risk shifting and risk distribution to constitute insurance for federal income tax purposes are present. The arrangement is insurance in the commonly accepted sense.

HOLDINGS

In Situation 1, the arrangement between P and S does not constitute insurance for federal income tax purposes, and amounts paid by P to S pursuant to that arrangement are not deductible as "insurance premiums" under section 162.

In Situation 2, the arrangement between P and S constitutes insurance for federal income tax purposes, and the amounts paid by P to S pursuant to that arrangement are deductible as "insurance premiums" under section 162.

EFFECT ON OTHER DOCUMENTS

Rev. Rul. 2001-31, 2001-1 C.B. 1348, is amplified.

DRAFTING INFORMATION

The principal author of this revenue ruling is John E. Glover of the Office of the Associate Chief Counsel (Financial Institutions & Products). For further information regarding this revenue ruling contact Mr. Glover at (202) 622-3970 (not a toll-free call).

Appendix H

Revenue Ruling. 2002-90

ISSUE

Are the amounts paid for professional liability coverage by domestic operating subsidiaries to an insurance subsidiary of a common parent deductible as "insurance premiums" under section 162 of the Internal Revenue Code.

FACTS

P, a domestic holding company, owns all of the stock of 12 domestic subsidiaries that provide professional services. Each subsidiary in the P group has a geographic territory comprised of a state in which the subsidiary provides professional services. The subsidiaries in the P group operate on a decentralized basis. The services provided by the employees of each subsidiary are performed under the general guidance of a supervisory professional for a particular facility of the subsidiary. The general categories of the professional services rendered by each of the subsidiaries are the same throughout the P group. Together the 12 subsidiaries have a significant volume of independent, homogeneous risks.

P, for a valid non-tax business purpose, forms S as a wholly-owned insurance subsidiary under the laws of State C. P provides S adequate capital and S is fully licensed in State C and in the 11 other states where the respective operating subsidiaries conduct their professional service businesses. S directly insures the professional liability risks of the 12 operating subsidiaries in the P group. S charges the 12 subsidiaries arms-length premiums, which are established according to customary industry rating formulas. None of the operating subsidiaries have liability coverage for less than 5%, nor more than 15%, of the total risk insured by S. S retains the risks that it insures from the 12 operating subsidiaries. There are no parental (or other related party) guarantees of any kind made in favor of S. S does not loan any funds to P or to the 12 operating subsidiaries. In all respects, the parties conduct themselves in a manner consistent with the standards applicable to an insurance arrangement between unrelated parties. S does not provide coverage to any entity other than the 12 operating subsidiaries.

LAW AND ANALYSIS

Section 162(a) of the Code provides, in part, that there shall be allowed as a deduction all the ordinary and necessary expenses paid or incurred during the taxable year in carrying on any trade or business.

Section 1.162-1(a) of the Income Tax Regulations provides, in part, that among the items included in business expenses are insurance premiums against fire, storms, theft, accident, or other similar losses in the case of a business.

Neither the Code nor the regulations define the terms "insurance" or "insurance contract." The United States Supreme Court, however, has explained that in order for an arrangement to constitute "insurance" for federal income tax purposes, both risk shifting and risk distribution must be present. Helvering v. LeGierse, 312 U.S. 531 (1941).

Risk shifting occurs if a person facing the possibility of an economic loss transfers some or all of the financial consequences of the potential loss to the insurer, such that a loss by the insured does not affect the insured because the loss is offset by the insurance payment. Risk distribution incorporates the statistical phenomenon known as the law of large numbers. Distributing risk allows the insurer to reduce the possibility that a single costly claim will exceed the amount taken in as premiums and set aside for the payment of such a claim. By assuming numerous relatively small, independent risks that occur randomly over time, the insurer smooths out losses to match more closely its receipt of premiums. Clougherty Packing Co. v. Commissioner, 811 F.2d 1297, 1300 (9th Cir. 1987). Risk distribution necessarily entails a pooling of premiums, so that a potential insured is not in significant part paying for its own risks. See Humana Inc. v. Commissioner, 881 F.2d 247, 257 (6th Cir. 1989).

In Humana, the United States Court of Appeals for the Sixth Circuit held that arrangements between a parent corporation and its insurance company subsidiary did not constitute insurance for federal income tax purposes. The court also held, however, that arrangements between the insurance company subsidiary and several dozen other subsidiaries of the parent (operating an even larger number of hospitals) qualified as insurance for federal income tax purposes because the requisite risk shifting and risk distribution were present. But see Malone & Hyde, Inc. v. Commissioner, 62 F.3d 835 (6 th Cir. 1995) (concluding the lack of a business purpose, the undercapitalization of the offshore captive insurance subsidiary and the existence of related party guarantees established that the substance of the transaction did not support the taxpayer's characterization of the transaction as insurance). In Kidde Industries, Inc. v. United

States, 40 Fed. Cl. 42 (1997), the United States Court of Federal Claims concluded that an arrangement between the captive insurance subsidiary and each of the 100 operating subsidiaries of the same parent constituted insurance for federal income tax purposes. As in Humana, the insurer in Kidde insured only entities within its affiliated group during the taxable years at issue.

In the present case, the professional liability risks of 12 operating subsidiaries are shifted to S. Further, the premiums of the operating subsidiaries, determined at arms-length, are pooled such that a loss by one operating subsidiary is borne, in substantial part, by the premiums paid by others. The 12 operating subsidiaries and S conduct themselves in all respects as would unrelated parties to a traditional insurance relationship, and S is regulated as an insurance company in each state where it does business. The narrow question presented is whether P's common ownership of the 12 operating subsidiaries and S affects the conclusion that the arrangements at issue are insurance for federal income tax purposes. Under the facts presented, we conclude the arrangements between S and each of the 12 operating subsidiaries of S's parent constitute insurance for federal income tax purposes.

HOLDING

The amounts paid for professional liability coverage by the 12 domestic operating subsidiaries to S are "insurance premiums" deductible under section 162.

EFFECT ON OTHER DOCUMENTS

Rev. Rul. 2001-31, 2001-1 C.B. 1348, is amplified.

DRAFTING INFORMATION

The principal author of this revenue ruling is William Sullivan of the Office of the Associate Chief Counsel (Financial Institutions & Products). For further information regarding this revenue ruling contact Mr. Sullivan at (202) 622-3970 (not a toll-free call).

Appendix I

Revenue Ruling 2002-91

ISSUE

Whether a "group captive" formed by a relatively small group of unrelated businesses involved in a highly concentrated industry to provide insurance coverage is an insurance company within the meaning of section 831 of the Internal Revenue Code under the circumstances described below.

FACTS

X is one of a small group of unrelated businesses involved in one highly concentrated industry. Businesses involved in this industry face significant liability hazards. X and the other businesses involved in this industry are required by regulators to maintain adequate liability insurance coverage in order to continue to operate. Businesses that participate in this industry have sustained significant losses due to the occurrence of unusually severe loss events. As a result, affordable insurance coverage for businesses that participate in this industry is not available from commercial insurance companies.

X and a significant number of the businesses involved in this industry (Members) form a so-called "group captive" (GC) to provide insurance coverage for stated liability risks. GC provides insurance only to X and the other Members. The business operations of GC are separate from the business operation of each Member. GC is adequately capitalized.

No Member owns more than 15% of GC, and no Member has more than 15% of the vote on any corporate governance issue. In addition, no Member's individual risk insured by GC exceeds 15% of the total risk insured by GC. Thus, no one member controls GC.

GC issues insurance contracts and charges premiums for the insurance coverage provided under the contracts. GC uses recognized actuarial techniques, based, in part, on

189

commercial rates for similar coverage, to determine the premiums to be charged to an individual Member.

GC pools all the premiums it receives in its general funds and pays claims out of those funds. GC investigates any claim made by a Member to determine the validity of the claim prior to making any payment on that claim. GC conducts no other business than the issuing and administering of insurance contracts.

No Member has any obligation to pay GC additional premiums if that Member's actual losses during any period of coverage exceed the premiums paid by that Member. No Member will be entitled to a refund of premiums paid if that Member's actual losses are lower than the premiums paid for coverage during any period. Premiums paid by any Member may be used to satisfy claims of the other Members. No Member that terminates its insurance coverage or sells its ownership interest in GC is required to make additional premium or capital payments to GC to cover losses in excess of its premiums paid. Moreover, no Member that terminates its coverage or disposes of its ownership interest in GC is entitled to a refund of premiums paid in excess of insured losses.

LAW AND ANALYSIS

Section 162(a) of the Code provides, in part, that there shall be allowed as a deduction all the ordinary and necessary expenses paid or incurred during the taxable year in carrying on any trade or business.

Section 1.162-1(a) of the Income Tax Regulations provides, in part, that among the items included in business expenses are insurance premiums against fire, storms, theft, accident, or other similar losses in the case of a business.

Section 831(a) of the Code provides that taxes computed under section 11 are imposed for each tax year on the taxable income of every insurance company other than a life insurance company.

Section 1.801-3(a) provides that an insurance company is "a company whose primary and predominant business activity is the issuing of insurance or annuity contracts or the reinsuring of risks underwritten by insurance companies."

Neither the Code nor the regulations define the terms "insurance" or "insurance contract." The United States Supreme Court, however, has explained that in order for an arrangement to constitute insurance for federal income tax purposes, both risk shifting and risk distribution must be present. Helvering v. LeGierse, 312 U.S. 531 (1941).

Risk shifting occurs if a person facing the possibility of an economic loss transfers some or all of the financial consequences of the potential loss to the insurer, such that a loss by the insured does not affect the insured because the loss is offset by the insurance payment. Risk distribution incorporates the statistical phenomenon known as the law of large numbers. Distributing risk allows the insurer to reduce the possibility that a single costly claim will exceed the amount taken in as premiums and set aside for the payment of such a claim. By assuming numerous relatively small, independent risks that occur randomly over time, the insurer smooths out losses to match more closely its receipt of premiums. Clougherty Packing Co. v. Commissioner, 811 F.2d 1297, 1300 (9th Cir. 1987). Risk distribution necessarily entails a pooling of premiums, so that a potential insured is not in significant part paying for its own risks. See Humana, Inc. v. Commissioner, 881 F.2d 247, 257 (6th Cir. 1989).

No court has held that a transaction between a parent and its wholly-owned subsidiary satisfies the requirements of risk shifting and risk distribution if only the risks of the parent are "insured." See Stearns-Roger Corp. v. United States, 774 F.2d 414 (10th Cir. 1985); Carnation Co. v. Commissioner, 640 F.2d 1010 (9th Cir. 1981), cert. denied, 454 U.S. 965 (1981). However, courts have held that an arrangement between a parent and its subsidiary can constitute insurance because the parent's premiums are pooled with those of unrelated parties if (i) insurance risk is present, (ii) risk is shifted and distributed, and (iii) the transaction is of the type that is insurance in the commonly accepted sense. See, e.g., Ocean Drilling & Exploration Co. v. United States, 988 F.2d 1135 (Fed. Cir. 1993); AMERCO, Inc. v. Commissioner, 979 F.2d 162 (9th Cir. 1992).

Additional factors to be considered in determining whether a captive insurance transaction is insurance include: whether the parties that insured with the captive truly face hazards; whether premiums charged by the captive are based on commercial rates; whether the validity of claims was established before payments are made; and whether the captive's business operations and assets are kept separate from the business operations and assets of its shareholders. Ocean Drilling & Exploration Co. at 1151.

In Rev. Rul. 2001-31, 2001-1 C.B. 1348, the Service stated that it will not invoke the economic family theory in Rev. Rul. 77-316 with respect to captive insurance arrangements. Rev. Rul. 2001-31 provides, however, that the Service may continue to challenge certain captive insurance transactions based on the facts and circumstances of each case.

Rev. Rul. 78-338, 1978-2 C.B.107, presented a situation in which 31 unrelated corporations created a group captive insurance company to provide those corporations with insurance that was not otherwise available. In that ruling, none of the unrelated corporations held a controlling interest in the group captive. In addition, no individual corporation's risk exceeded 5 percent of the total risks insured by the group captive. The

Service concluded that because the corporations that owned, and were insured by, the group captive were not economically related, the economic risk of loss could be shifted and distributed among the shareholders that comprised the insured group.

X and the other Members face true insurable hazards. X and the other Members are required to maintain general liability insurance coverage in order to continue to operate in their industry. X and the other Members are unable to obtain affordable insurance from unrelated commercial insurers due to the occurrence of unusually severe loss events. Notwithstanding the fact that the group of Members is small, there is a real possibility that a Member will sustain a loss in excess of the premiums it paid. No individual Member will be reimbursed for premiums paid in excess of losses sustained by that Member. Finally, X and the other Members are unrelated. Therefore, the contracts issued by GC to X and the other Members are insurance contracts for federal income tax purposes, and the premiums paid by the Members are deductible under section 162.

GC is an entity separate from its owners. GC is adequately capitalized. GC issues insurance contracts, charges premiums, and pays claims after investigating the validity of the claim. GC will not engage in any business activities other than issuing and administering insurance contracts. Premiums charged by GC will be actuarially determined using recognized actuarial techniques, and will be based, in part, on commercial rates. As GC's only business activity is the business of insurance, it is taxed as an insurance company.

HOLDING

The arrangement between X and GC constitutes insurance for federal income tax purposes, and the amounts paid as "insurance premiums" by X to GC pursuant to that arrangement are deductible as ordinary and necessary business expenses. GC is in the business of issuing insurance and will be treated as an insurance company taxable under section 831.

DRAFTING INFORMATION

The principal author of this revenue ruling is Melissa Luxner of the Office of the Associate Chief Counsel (Financial Institutions & Products). For further information regarding this revenue ruling contact Ms. Luxner at (202) 622-3142 (not a toll-free call).

Appendix J

Notice 2003-34

I. PURPOSE

Treasury and the Internal Revenue Service have become aware of arrangements, described below, that are being used by taxpayers to defer recognition of ordinary income or to characterize ordinary income as a capital gain. The arrangements involve an investment in a purported insurance company that is organized offshore which invests in hedge funds or investments in which hedge funds typically invest. This notice alerts taxpayers and their representatives that these arrangements often do not generate the claimed Federal tax benefits.

II. BACKGROUND

The typical arrangement involves a Stakeholder, subject to U.S. income taxation, investing (directly or indirectly) in the equity of an enterprise (FC), usually a corporation organized outside the United States. FC is organized as an insurance company and complies with the applicable local laws regulating insurance companies.

FC issues insurance or annuity contracts or contracts to reinsure risks underwritten by insurance companies. Some of the contracts do not cover insurance risks. Other contracts significantly limit the risks assumed by FC through the use of retrospective rating arrangements, unrealistically low policy limits, finite risk transactions, or other similar devices.

FCs actual insurance activities, if any, are relatively small compared to its investment activities. FC invests its capital and the amounts it receives as consideration for its insurance contracts in, among other things, hedge funds or investments in which hedge funds typically invest. As a result, FCs portfolio generates investment returns that substantially exceed the needs of FCs insurance business. FC generally does not currently distribute these earnings to Stakeholder.

Stakeholder takes the position that FC is an insurance company engaged in the active conduct of an insurance business and is not a passive foreign investment company. Therefore, when Stakeholder disposes of its interest in FC, it will recognize gain as a capital gain, rather than as ordinary income.

III DISCUSSION

The business of an insurance company necessarily includes substantial investment activities. Both life and nonlife insurance companies routinely invest their capital and the amounts they receive as premiums. The investment earnings are then used to pay claims, support writing more business or to fund distributions to the company's owners. The presence of investment earnings does not, in itself, suggest that an entity does not qualify as an insurance company.

Treasury and the Internal Revenue Service are concerned that in some cases FC and its Stakeholders are inappropriately claiming that FC is an insurance company for Federal income tax purposes to avoid tax that otherwise would be due. The Service will challenge the claimed tax treatment in appropriate cases, as outlined below.

A. Definition of Insurance

For FC to qualify as an insurance company, FC must issue insurance contracts. Neither the Code nor the regulations define the terms Insurance or insurance contract. The United States Supreme Court, however, has explained that for an arrangement to constitute insurance for Federal income tax purposes, both risk shifting and risk distribution must be present. Helvering v. LeGierse, 312 U.S. 531 (1941). The risk shifted and distributed must be an insurance risk. See, e.g., Allied Fidelity Corp. v. Commissioner, 572 F.2d 1190 (7 th Cir. 1978), cert. denied, 439 U.S. 835 (1978); Rev. Rul. 89-96, 1989-2 C.B. 114.

Risk shifting occurs if a person facing the possibility of an economic loss resulting from the occurrence of an insurance risk transfers some or all of the financial consequences of the potential loss to the insurer. The effect of such a transfer is that a loss by the insured will not affect the insured because the loss is offset by the insurance payment. Risk distribution incorporates the law of large numbers to allow the insurer to reduce the possibility that a single costly claim will exceed the amount available to the insurer for the payment of such a claim. Clougherty Packing Co. v. Commissioner, 811 F.2d 1297, 1300 (9 th Cir. 1987). Risk distribution necessarily entails a pooling of premiums, so that a potential insured is not in significant part paying for its own risks. See Humana, Inc. v. Commissioner, 881 F.2d 247, 257 (6 th Cir. 1989).

Treasury and the Service are concerned that any risks assumed under the contracts issued by FC may not be insurance risks. Treasury and the Service are also concerned that the terms of the contracts may significantly limit the risks assumed by FC.

B. Status as an Insurance Company

A corporation that is an insurance company for Federal income tax purposes is subject to tax under subchapter L of the Internal Revenue Code. For this purpose, an insurance company is a company whose primary and predominant business activity during the taxable year is the issuing of insurance or annuity contracts or the reinsuring of risks underwritten by insurance companies. While a taxpayers name, charter powers, and state regulation help to indicate the activities in which it may properly engage, whether the taxpayer qualifies as an insurance company for tax purposes depends on its actual activities during the year. Section 1.801-3(a) of the Income Tax Regulations; 816(a) (which provides that a company will be treated as an insurance company only if more than half of the business of that company is the issuing of insurance or annuity contracts or the reinsuring of risks underwritten by insurance companies).

To qualify as an insurance company, a taxpayer must use its capital and efforts primarily in earning income from the issuance of contracts of insurance. Indus. Life Ins. Co. v. United States, 344 F. Supp. 870, 877 (D. S.C. 1972), affd per curiam, 481 F.2d 609 (4 th Cir. 1973), cert. denied, 414 U.S. 1143 (1974). To determine whether FC qualifies as an insurance company, all of the relevant facts will be considered, including but not limited to, the size and activities of its staff, whether it engages in other trades or businesses, and its sources of income. See generally Bowers v. Lawyers Mortgage Co., 285 U.S. 182 (1932); Indus. Life Ins. Co., at 875-77; Cardinal Life Ins. Co. v. United States, 300 F. Supp. 387, 391-92 (N.D. Tex. 1969), revd on other grounds, 425 F. 2d 1328 (5 th Cir. 1970); Serv. Life Ins. Co. v. United States, 189 F. Supp. 282, 285-86 (D. Neb. 1960), affd on other grounds, 293 F.2d 72 (8 th Cir. 1961); Inter-Am. Life Ins. Co. v. Commissioner, 56 T.C. 497, 506-08 (1971), affd per curiam, 469 F.2d 697 (9 th Cir. 1971); Natl. Capital Ins. Co. of the Dist. of Columbia v. Commissioner, 28 B.T.A. 1079, 1085-86 (1933).

In Inter-Am. Life Ins. Co., 56 T.C. at 506-08, the Tax Court applied the standard of section 1.801-3(a), and held that the taxpayer was not an insurance company because it was not using its capital and efforts primarily in earning income from the issuance of insurance. The court in particular noted the disproportion between investment income and earned premiums. The court also noted the absence of an active sales staff soliciting or selling insurance policies.

Even if the contracts qualify as insurance contracts as explained above, the character of all of the business actually done by FC may indicate that FC uses its capital and efforts primarily in investing rather than primarily in the insurance business.

C. Possible Tax Treatment of Stakeholder's Interest in FC

Sections 1291-1298 provide special rules for taxing an investment in a foreign corporation that is a passive foreign investment company (as defined in section 1297). These rules impose current U.S. taxation (or similar treatment) on U.S. persons that earn passive income through a foreign corporation. A foreign corporation is a passive foreign investment company if (1) 75 percent or more of the gross income of such corporation for the taxable year is passive income, or (2) the average percentage of assets (as determined in accordance with section 1297(e)) held by such corporation during the taxable year which produce passive income or which are held for the production of passive income is at least 50 percent. Section 1297(a). For these purposes, passive income generally means any income which is of a kind which would be foreign personal holding company income as defined in section 954(c). Foreign personal holding company income includes dividends, interest, royalties, rents, annuities, and gains from the sale or exchange of property giving rise to such types of income. Section 954(c)(1).

Section 1297(b)(2)(B) provides an exception to passive income for any income derived in the active conduct of an insurance business by a corporation which is predominantly engaged in an insurance business and which would be subject to tax under subchapter L if it were a domestic corporation (the insurance income exception). If FC would not be subject to tax under subchapter L if it were a domestic corporation (for the reasons discussed above), then the insurance income exception to passive income will not apply, and FC will be subject to the general income and assets tests described above. Additionally, even if FC would be subject to tax under subchapter L if it were a domestic corporation, the insurance income exception may not apply to FC because this exception is applicable only to income derived in the active conduct of an insurance business.

The Service will scrutinize these arrangements and will apply the PFIC rules where it determines that FC is not an insurance company for federal tax purposes.

IV. DRAFTING INFORMATION

The principal authors of this Notice are John Glover of the Office of Associate Chief Counsel (Financial Institutions & Products) and Theodore Setzer of the Office of Associate Chief Counsel (International). For further information regarding this notice contact Mr. Glover at (202) 622-3970 or Mr. Setzer at (202) 622-3870 (not a toll-free call).

Appendix K

Rev. Rul. 2005-40

Do the arrangements described below constitute insurance for federal income tax purposes? If so, are amounts paid to the issuer deductible as insurance premiums and does the issuer qualify as an insurance company?

FACTS

Situation 1. X, a domestic corporation, operates a courier transport business covering a large portion of the United States. X owns and operates a large fleet of automotive vehicles representing a significant volume of independent, homogeneous risks. For valid, non-tax business purposes, X entered into an arrangement with Y, an unrelated domestic corporation, whereby in exchange for an agreed amount of "premiums," Y "insures" X against the risk of loss arising out of the operation of its fleet in the conduct of its courier business.

The amount of "premiums" under the arrangement is determined at arm's length according to customary insurance industry rating formulas. Y possesses adequate capital to fulfill its obligations to X under the agreement, and in all respects operates in accordance with the applicable requirements of state law. There are no guarantees of any kind in favor of Y with respect to the agreement, nor are any of the "premiums" paid by X to Y in turn loaned back to X. X has no obligation to pay Y additional premiums if X's actual losses during any period of coverage exceed the "premiums" paid by X. X will not be entitled to any refund of "premiums" paid if X's actual losses are lower than the "premiums" paid during any period. In all respects, the parties conduct themselves consistent with the standards applicable to an insurance arrangement between unrelated parties, except that Y does not "insure" any entity other than X.

Situation 2. The facts are the same as in Situation 1 except that, in addition to its arrangement with X, Y enters into an arrangement with Z, a domestic corporation unrelated to X or Y, whereby in exchange for an agreed amount of "premiums," Y also "insures" Z against the risk of loss arising out of the operation of its own fleet in connection with the conduct of a courier business substantially similar to that of X. The amounts Y earns from its arrangements with Z constitute 10% of Y's total amounts earned during the taxable year on both a gross and net basis. The arrangement with Z accounts for 10% of the total risks borne by Y.

Situation 3. X, a domestic corporation, operates a courier transport business covering a large portion of the United States. X conducts the courier transport business through 12 limited liability companies (LLCs) of which it is the single member. The LLCs are disregarded as entities separate from X under the provisions of § 301.7701-3 of the Procedure and Administration Regulations. The LLCs own and operate a large fleet of automotive vehicles, collectively representing a significant volume of independent, homogeneous risks. For valid, non-tax business purposes, the LLCs entered into arrangements with Y, an unrelated domestic corporation, whereby in exchange for an agreed amount of "premiums," Y "insures" the LLCs against the risk of loss arising out of the operation of the fleet in the conduct of their courier business. None of the LLCs account for less than 5%, or more than 15%, of the total risk assumed by Y under the agreements.

The amount of "premiums" under the arrangement is determined at arm's length according to customary insurance industry rating formulas. Y possesses adequate capital to fulfill its obligations to the LLCs under the agreement, and in all respects operates in accordance with the licensing and other requirements of state law. There are no guarantees of any kind in favor of Y with respect to the agreements, nor are any of the "premiums" paid by the LLCs to Y in turn loaned back to X or to the LLCs. No LLC has any obligation to pay Y additional premiums if that LLC's actual losses during the arrangement exceed the "premiums" paid by that LLC. No LLC will be entitled to a refund of "premiums" paid if that LLC's actual losses are lower than the "premiums" paid during any period. Y retains the risks that it assumes under the agreement. In all respects, the parties conduct themselves consistent with the standards applicable to an insurance arrangement between unrelated parties, except that Y does not "insure" any entity other than the LLCs.

Situation 4. The facts are the same as in Situation 3, except that each of the 12 LLCs elects pursuant to § 301.7701-3(a) to be classified as an association. LAW

Section 831(a) of the Internal Revenue Code provides that taxes, computed as provided in § 11, are imposed for each taxable year on the taxable income of each insurance company other than a life insurance company. Section 831(c) provides that, for purposes of § 831, the term "insurance company" has the meaning given to such term by § 816(a). Under § 816(a), the term "insurance company" means any company more than half of the business of which during the taxable year is the issuing of insurance or annuity contracts or the reinsuring of risks underwritten by insurance companies.

Section 162(a) provides, in part, that there shall be allowed as a deduction all the ordinary and necessary expenses paid or incurred during the taxable year in carrying on any trade or business. Section 1.162-1(a) of the Income Tax Regulations provides, in part, that among the items included in business expenses are insurance premiums against fire, storms, theft, accident, or other similar losses in the case of a business.

Neither the Code nor the regulations define the terms "insurance" or "insurance contract." The United States Supreme Court, however, has explained that in order for an arrangement to constitute insurance for federal income tax purposes, both risk shifting and risk distribution must be present. Helvering v. Le Gierse, 312 U.S. 531 (1941).

The risk transferred must be risk of economic loss. Allied Fidelity Corp. v. Commissioner, 572 F.2d 1190, 1193 (7th Cir.), cert. denied, 439 U.S. 835 (1978). The risk must contemplate the fortuitous occurrence of a stated contingency, Commissioner

v. Treganowan, 183 F.2d 288, 290-91 (2d Cir.), cert. denied, 340 U.S. 853 (1950), and must not be merely an investment or business risk. Le Gierse, at 542; Rev. Rul. 89-96, 1989-2 C.B. 114.

Risk shifting occurs if a person facing the possibility of an economic loss transfers some or all of the financial consequences of the potential loss to the insurer, such that a loss by the insured does not affect the insured because the loss is offset by a payment from the insurer. Risk distribution incorporates the statistical phenomenon known as the law of large numbers. Distributing risk allows the insurer to reduce the possibility that a single costly claim will exceed the amount taken in as premiums and set aside for the payment of such a claim. By assuming numerous relatively small, independent risks that occur randomly over time, the insurer smooths out losses to match more closely its receipt of premiums. Clougherty Packing Co. v. Commissioner, 811 F.2d 1297, 1300 (9th Cir. 1987).

Courts have recognized that risk distribution necessarily entails a pooling of premiums, so that a potential insured is not in significant part paying for its own risks. Humana, Inc. v. Commissioner, 881 F.2d 247, 257 (6th Cir. 1989). See also Ocean Drilling & Exploration Co. v. United States, 988 F.2d 1135, 1153 (Fed. Cir. 1993) ("Risk distribution involves spreading the risk of loss among policyholders."); Beech Aircraft Corp. v. United States, 797 F.2d 920, 922 (10th Cir. 1986) ("'[R]isk distributing' means that the party assuming the risk distributes his potential liability, in part, among others."); Treganowan, at 291 (quoting Note, The New York Stock Exchange Gratuity Fund: Insurance that Isn't Insurance, 59 Yale L. J. 780, 784 (1950)) ("'By diffusing the risks through a mass of separate risk shifting contracts, the insurer casts his lot with the law of averages. The process of risk distribution, therefore, is the very essence of insurance.'"); Crawford Fitting Co. v. United States, 606 F. Supp. 136, 147 (N.D. Ohio 1985) ("[T]he court finds ... that various nonaffiliated persons or entities facing risks similar but independent of those faced by plaintiff were named insureds under the policy, enabling the distribution of the risk thereunder."); AMERCO and Subsidiaries v. Commissioner, 96 T.C. 18, 41 (1991), aff'd, 979 F.2d 162 (9th Cir. 1992) ("The concept of risk-distributing emphasizes the pooling aspect of insurance: that it is the nature of an insurance contract to be part of a larger collection of coverages, combined to distribute risk between insureds.").

ANALYSIS

In order to determine the nature of an arrangement for federal income tax purposes, it is necessary to consider all the facts and circumstances in a particular case, including not only the terms of the arrangement, but also the entire course of conduct of the parties. Thus, an arrangement that purports to be an insurance contract but lacks the requisite risk distribution may instead be characterized as a deposit arrangement, a loan, a contribution to capital (to the extent of net value, if any), an indemnity arrangement that is not an insurance contract, or otherwise, based on the substance of the arrangement between the parties. The proper characterization of the arrangement may determine whether the issuer qualifies as an insurance company and whether amounts paid under the arrangement may be deductible.

In Situation 1, Y enters into an "insurance" arrangement with X. The arrangement with X represents Y's only such agreement. Although the arrangement may shift the risks of X to Y, those risks are not, in turn, distributed among other insureds or policyholders. Therefore, the arrangement between X and Y does not constitute insurance for federal income tax purposes.

In Situation 2, the fact that Y also enters into an arrangement with Z does not change the conclusion that the arrangement between X and Y lacks the requisite risk distribution to constitute insurance. Y's contract with Z represents only 10% of the total amounts earned by Y, and 10% of total risks assumed, under all its arrangements. This creates an insufficient pool of other premiums to distribute X's risk. See Rev. Rul. 200289, 2002-2 C.B. 984 (concluding that risks from unrelated parties representing 10% of total risks borne by subsidiary are insufficient to qualify arrangement between parent and subsidiary as insurance).

In Situation 3, Y contracts only with 12 single member LLCs through which X conducts a courier transport business. The LLCs are disregarded as entities separate from X pursuant to § 301.7701-3. Section 301.7701-2(a) provides that if an entity is disregarded, its activities are treated in the same manner as a sole proprietorship, branch or division of the owner. Applying this rule in Situation 3, Y has entered into an "insurance" arrangement only with X. Therefore, for the reasons set forth in Situation 1 above, the arrangement between X and Y does not constitute insurance for federal income tax purposes.

In Situation 4, the 12 LLCs are not disregarded as entities separate from X, but instead are classified as associations for federal income tax purposes. The arrangements between Y and each LLC thus shift a risk of loss from each LLC to Y. The risks of the LLCs are distributed among the various other LLCs that are insured under similar arrangements. Therefore the arrangements between the 12 LLCs and Y constitute insurance for federal income tax purposes. See Rev. Rul. 2002-90, 2002-2

C.B. 985 (similar arrangements between affiliated entities constituted insurance). Because the arrangements with the 12 LLCs represent Y's only business, and those arrangements are insurance contracts for federal income tax purposes, Y is an insurance company within the meaning of §§ 831(c) and 816(a). In addition, the 12 LLCs may be entitled to deduct amounts paid under those arrangements as insurance premiums under § 162 if the requirements for deduction are otherwise satisfied.

HOLDINGS

In Situations 1, 2 and 3, the arrangements do not constitute insurance for federal income tax purposes.

In Situation 4, the arrangements constitute insurance for federal income tax purposes and the issuer qualifies as an insurance company. The amounts paid to the issuer may be deductible as insurance premiums under § 162 if the requirements for deduction are otherwise satisfied.

DRAFTING INFORMATION

The principal author of this revenue ruling is John E. Glover of the Office of the Associate Chief Counsel (Financial Institutions & Products). For further information regarding this revenue ruling contact Mr. Glover at (202) 622-3970 (not a toll-free call).

Appendix L

Humana Inc. v. C.I.R.

881 F.2d 247 (6th Cir. 1989)

Opinion of the Tax Court

Humana Inc. v. C.I.R., 88 T.C. No. 13, 88 T.C. 197 (1987)

United States Tax Court

HUMANA INC. AND SUBSIDIARIES, Petitioner

v.

COMMISSIONER OF INTERNAL REVENUE, Respondent

Docket No. 15292-80, 17130-82.[1]

Filed January 26, 1987.

GOFFE, JUDGE:

The Commissioner determined deficiencies in income tax against petitioner for the following taxable years:

Docket No.				Deficiency
TYE Aug. 31	1976	1977	1978	1979
15292-80	$4,615,905	9,409,814		
17130-82			7,723,542	20,460,078

---

[1] The cases were consolidated for trial, briefing and opinion.

After concessions by the parties, one issue remains for our decision, i.e., to what extent, if any, may petitioner deduct as ordinary and necessary business expenses amounts paid to a wholly owned captive insurance company which were treated as premiums for general liability and medical malpractice insurance.

We first decided the case in Memorandum Opinion, T. C. Memo. 1985-426. Petitioner filed a motion for reconsideration of the opinion pursuant to Rule 161.[2] The Court granted the motion and withdrew the opinion.

FINDINGS OF FACT

Some of the facts have been stipulated and are so found. The stipulations of facts and attached exhibits are hereby incorporated by reference.

Humana Inc. was incorporated under the laws of Delaware on July 27, 1964. At all pertinent times, the stock of Humana Inc. was publicly traded on the New York Stock Exchange, and its principal place of business was in Louisville, Kentucky.

Humana Inc. is the common parent of an affiliated group of corporations that filed consolidated Federal income tax returns for the taxable years ended August 31, 1976, through August 31, 1979, inclusive, with the Internal Revenue Service Center at Memphis, Tennessee. The parent and subsidiary corporations which filed the consolidated returns will sometimes be referred to collectively as 'petitioner.'

American Medicorp, Inc. (AMI), was incorporated under the laws of Delaware on January 11, 1968. It was primarily engaged in the business of operating general, acute care community hospitals offering a wide range of medical, surgical, and related services. On February 2, 1978, Humana Inc. acquired 53.4 percent of the common stock of AMI for $85.5 million and 2,849,567 shares of Humana Inc. preferred stock. On September 27, 1978, AMI merged with and into Humana Subsidiary, Inc., a wholly owned subsidiary of Humana Inc. that was incorporated for purposes of the merger. As a result of the merger, Humana Inc. became the owner of all of the outstanding common stock of AMI. The final short period taxable year of AMI ended on September 27, 1978. AMI was merged into Humana Inc. on December 21, 1978.

As of February 1978, AMI held two general liability insurance policies. The primary policy was provided by American Home Assurance Company (American Home), and an

---

2   All Rule references are to the Tax Court Rules of Practice and Procedure and all section references are to the Internal Revenue Code of 1954, as amended, and applicable to the taxable years in issue.

excess layer of insurance was provided by an industry pooling arrangement known as Hospital Underwriting Group, Inc. (HUG).

As of November 1976, petitioner operated 62 hospitals in 16 states and one foreign country, containing 8,586 beds. As of 1979, principally as a result of its acquisition of AMI, petitioner operated 92 hospitals in 23 states and one foreign country, containing 16,529 beds. Petitioner currently operates 87 hospitals owned by 36 corporations.

From 1972 until August 31, 1976, Continental Insurance Company (Continental) provided petitioner with general liability insurance, including malpractice liability and workers' compensation insurance. As early as 1973, however, there were signs that the availability of such coverage to hospitals was diminishing, and by the mid-1970's, this lack of availability became severe because of the long interval between setting the premium rate, collecting the premiums, and settling claims. During the intervals, loss reserves are established by use of actuarial accounting. Errors in such loss reserves have a strong impact on capital and earnings. Due to changing rules, economic inflation and misjudgments, insurers were adjusting their loss reserves and premiums in many lines of casualty insurance, including malpractice insurance. On May 7, 1976, Continental advised petitioner by letter that it would be unable to renew its insurance coverage when it expired on August 31, 1976.

Through the services of its insurance broker, Marsh & McLennan, Inc. (Marsh & McLennan), Humana Inc. attempted to obtain general and professional liability insurance from third-party insurers, but was unsuccessful. On June 1, 1976, Marsh & McLennan recommended that petitioner immediately take steps to establish a captive insurance company.

At the time that the Marsh & McLennan letter was received, petitioner was considering the following options:

(1) going uninsured;

(2) creating a trust fund or reserve for self-insurance;

(3) combining with other hospital companies in a 5-year insurance pooling arrangement; or

(4) establishing a captive insurance company.

Petitioner rejected Option (1) because it concluded that it was not strong enough to sustain the burden of catastrophic risk if it went uninsured. It rejected Option (2) because, first, it felt that this option would not allow it access to commercial insurance markets for certain excess protection which it regarded as essential; second, some 40 percent of its business was under Medicare and Medicaid, and at least the former would not permit reimbursement for additions to the reserves;[3] and third, it was clear that payments into such a reserve fund would not be deductible for Federal income tax purposes. Petitioner rejected Option (3) because, first, it had doubts about the financial viability of its potential affiliates in such a pooling arrangement; second, one such potential affiliate owned hospitals in what were regarded as the worst states for malpractice claims; and third, it was reluctant to bind itself to such an arrangement for a 5-year period. Option (4) was considered the most attractive because it possessed none of the perceived disadvantages associated with the other options and it would provide a regulated method of insuring risks which would both isolate funds for the settlement of claims and satisfy interested lenders, mortgagees, and securities analysts. In addition, Option (4) would provide access to world reinsurance and excess insurance markets.

On July 14, 1976, petitioner sought the approval of the Insurance Department of Colorado to establish a captive insurance company under Colorado law to insure against losses due to fire, general liability, medical malpractice, including hospitals, and other casualties.

On August 5, 1976, Health Care Indemnity, Inc. (HCI), was incorporated under the Colorado Corporation Act. The articles of incorporation of HCI state the following purposes for its incorporation:[4]

to conduct, engage in and carry on the business of making all kinds of insurance and reinsurance authorized to be made under the Colorado Captive Insurance Company Act * * * and to conduct, engage in and carry on all other activities incident to conducting such insurance and reinsurance business.

From August 20, 1976, to October 12, 1982, HCI qualified as a captive insurance company under Colorado law.

Humana Holdings, N.V. (HHNV), is a Netherlands Antilles corporation organized and incorporated on August 4, 1976. Humana Inc. purchased all of the capital stock of HHNV for $250,000, and continues to own it. The only business purpose for HHNV was to assist in the capitalization of HCI. Petitioner used the device of HHNV because it concluded that to do otherwise would have required the consolidation of HCI and

---

3   Prior to 1976, petitioner's insurance premiums were apparently considered an allowable cost for Medicare coverage, viz, Medicare would reimburse hospitals for the pro rata cost of certain expenditures, including insurance, for services provided to Medicare patients.

4   This excerpt is from the original articles filed on August 5, 1976, rather than the restated articles filed on December 24, 1981.

Humana Inc. for tax purposes, requiring Humana Inc. to abandon its fiscal year in favor of a calendar year.

At the time of the initial capitalization of HCI, 150,000 shares of preferred stock and 250,000 shares of common stock were issued. Of these, HHNV purchased the preferred stock for $250,000 in cash, which it still owns, and Humana Inc. purchased the common stock for $750,000, paid in irrevocable letters of credit issued in favor of the Commissioner of Insurance of the State of Colorado. At all times since such capitalization, each share of common stock of HCI has been entitled to five votes and each preferred share to one vote.

There were no agreements between HCI and Humana Inc. or its subsidiaries which would require the latter to contribute additional capital to HCI for the payment of any losses. However, on May 31, 1979, Humana Inc. contributed $1,323,000 to the capital of HCI. This represented a refund paid by HUG to Humana Inc. after AMI merged with Humana Subsidiary, Inc.

HCI issued the following policies during the taxable years in issue, identifying Humana Inc. and affiliated and subsidiary corporations, in the numbers shown, as named insureds:[5]

Policy No.	Coverage From	Coverage To	Number of corporations	Number of hospitals
1001	9/1/76	8/31/77	22	64
1003	9/1/77	9/1/78	22	59
HCI-90178	9/1/78	9/1/79	48	97

In addition, policy number HCI-60178, was effective from June 1, 1978, at which time Humana Inc. owned 53.4 percent of AMI's common stock, until June 1, 1979. HCI replaced AMI's primary policy with American Home, and incorporated by reference the terms of AMI's excess coverage under its policy with HUG.

The charges for the foregoing policies accrued ratably throughout the policy periods. During the taxable years in issue, the following amounts were paid by petitioner to HCI for such policies and were deducted on the consolidated Federal income tax returns:

---

[5]   While the policy entered into evidence reflects a commencement date of August 31, 1977, we have accepted the stipulation of the parties that it commenced on September 1, 1977.

TYE Aug. 31—

Policy No.	Payments
1977	
1001	$5,703,571[6]
1978	
1003	5,865,986[7]
1979	
HCI-90178	7,582,893[8]
HCI-60178	1,903,125[9]
	========
Total	21,055,575

The foregoing charges were developed by Marsh & McLennan pursuant to standard industry practice generally by applying to the average number of occupied beds, a composite rate developed by a rating organization known as Insurance Service Offices. The resulting amounts were billed by HCI to Humana Inc. on a monthly basis and were paid by Humana Inc. in a single payment representing the total premiums for all of the

---

[6]   The stipulation of the parties at one point describes this amount as $5,703,511. We agree with petitioner, however, that the record reflects that this was a computation error. At all times since 1971, Humana Inc. has owned only 62.35 percent of a corporation, Brentwood Hospital, Inc. ('Brentwood '). Brentwood has never been a part of the affiliated group which filed consolidated returns and respondent did not disallow the $89,460 attributable to it. When this sum is subtracted from the total amounts paid on policy number 1001, or $5,793,031, the difference is $5,703,571.

[7]   For reasons described in footnote 6 above, this amount is computed as the difference between total amounts paid on policy number 1003, or $5,963,006, and the payment by Brentwood, or $97,020.

[8]   For reasons described in footnote 6 above, this amount is computed as the difference between total amounts paid on policy number HCI-90178, or $7,663,533, and the payment by Brentwood, or $80,640.

[9]   This amount is computed as the difference between total amounts paid on policy number HCI-60178, or $2,878,125, and $975,000, which is the amount attributable to AMI and its subsidiaries prior to September 27, 1978, when AMI became a wholly owned subsidiary of Humana Inc. and which was not claimed by petitioner on the return for the taxable year ended August 31, 1979.

hospitals. Later, by means of an allocation formula, portions of the foregoing amounts were charged to the subsidiaries.[10]

Each of the policies provided three types of coverage: Coverage A-personal injury; Coverage B-property damage; and Coverage C-professional liability, including personal injury relating to certain professional services (i.e., malpractice). Each policy also included a 'good samaritan endorsement' under which professional employees, acting outside of their capacity as employees, were covered for certain occasional professional services not rendered for their personal benefit.

Under each of the four policies, the following were considered as 'an insured:'

a. The named insured;

b. Any officer, hospital administrator * * *, stockholder, or member of the Board of * * * Directors or Governors of the named insured while acting for * * * the named insured.

c. Under Coverages A and B, any employee, student or volunteer worker of the named insured while acting within the scope of his duties * * *;

* * *

f. Under Coverage C, any person included in any of the employee classifications for which coverage is afforded under this policy, as indicated in Item 5 of the Declarations, while such person is acting within the scope of his duties as an employee * * *.

Pursuant to Item 5 of the Declarations, any employee of the insured was covered, including those professional employees who were licensed residents, interns, physicians, surgeons, or dentists, except that physicians, surgeons, and dentists were excluded under policy number HCI-60178. Under such policy, however, coverage was extended to independent contractors licensed as physicians and practicing in the hospital emergency room or attending to emergencies on the hospital premises. After June 1, 1979, this coverage was also provided for those insured under policy number HCI-90178. Generally, no coverage was provided for non-employee physicians, since they carried their own insurance.

---

10   The amounts paid by Humana Inc.-representing the total of premiums for all the hospitals operated by Humana Inc. and its subsidiaries-were charged back to the subsidiaries based upon the number of occupied beds. Adjustments were made if, for example, a hospital operated by the subsidiary had a teaching program, an intern residence program, or nurse anesthetists as opposed to doctor anesthetists.

Humana Inc., on forms 10-K filed with the Securities and Exchange Commission for the taxable years in issue, described the coverage provided by HCI as follows: The Insurance Subsidiary will insure the risks of the Company only, and it will only provide insurance to physicians who are actually employed by the Company. In such documents, 'Company' is defined as Humana Inc. and its subsidiaries.

At all times pertinent in this case, payments for coverage of each of the categories described above were paid by petitioner and were not charged to the employee or other individual involved.

Pursuant to policies numbered 1001, 1003, and HCI-90178, the liability of HCI was limited to $2 million per occurrence under Coverages A, B, and C, $2 million in the aggregate under Coverages A and B, and $10 million in the aggregate under Coverage C.[11] Pursuant to policy number HCI-60178, the liability of HCI was limited to $500,000 per occurrence and $2.4 million in the aggregate for each category of covered risks.

The insurance coverage of petitioner during the taxable years in issue also included multiple layers of excess coverage placed with third-party insurance carriers, over and above the foregoing primary layer provided by HCI.

In policies numbered 1002 and 1004, HCI also provided certain excess comprehensive general coverage to petitioner for the respective periods September 1, 1976, to August 31, 1977, and September 1, 1977, to August 31, 1978. All of the liability under these policies was reinsured by HCI with third-party reinsurance companies. The Commissioner allowed petitioner to deduct the premiums for these policies. With the exception of these policies, during the taxable years in issue HCI did not reinsure the risks of losses with other insurance companies nor did petitioner obtain policies with third-party insurers which were reinsured by or with HCI.

At all times involved in this case HCI filed separate Federal income tax returns based upon a calendar year. The returns and its books and records were maintained using the accrual method of accounting

During the taxable years in issue, HCI had no employees other than its officers, most of whom were also officers of Humana Inc. By contract dated August 1976, Marsh & McLennan provided HCI with resident managing officers and a variety of administrative and management services, including consulting, underwriting, risk control, recordkeeping, and accounting services. At all times involved in this case, Underwriters

---

11   Effective June 1, 1979, the aggregate liability under Coverage C for policy number HCI-90178 was increased to $13 million.

Adjusting Co. provided, by written contract, claims administration and claims service for HCI.

After concessions, the sole issue for decision is whether the following amounts are deductible as insurance premiums:

TYE Aug. 31—	Amount
1977	$5,703,571
1978	5,865,986
1979	9,486,018
	========
Total	21,055,575

OPINION

We previously decided this case in Memorandum Opinion, T. C. Memo. 1985-426. Petitioner filed a motion for reconsideration, which the Court granted, and the Court withdrew the opinion.

Humana Inc. and its subsidiaries operated hospitals whose insurance coverage was cancelled. Humana Inc. incorporated a captive insurance subsidiary which it jointly owned with a wholly owned foreign subsidiary. The captive insurance subsidiary purported to provide insurance coverage for Humana Inc. and its other subsidiaries. Humana Inc. paid to the captive insurance subsidiary amounts which it treated as insurance premiums. It charged portions of these amounts to its operating subsidiaries.

Two issues are presented for our decision:

1. Are the sums paid to HCI by Humana Inc. on its own behalf deductible as ordinary and necessary business expenses for insurance premiums and

2. Are the sums charged by Humana Inc. to the operating subsidiaries deductible on the consolidated income tax returns as ordinary and necessary business expenses for insurance premiums.

For convenience the first issue may be described as the 'parent-subsidiary' issue and the second issue may be described as the 'brother-sister' issue. These represent the relationships between the entity which purports to be the insured and the captive insurance subsidiary which purports to be the insurer.

We have previously decided the parent-subsidiary issue in Carnation Co. v. Commissioner, 71 T.C. 400 (1978), affd. 640 F.2d 1010 (9th Cir. 1981), and Clougherty Packing Co. v. Commissioner, 84 T.C. 948 (1985), on appeal (9th Cir., Dec. 13, 1985). Our decision in Carnation has been followed in disallowing the deductions in Beech Aircraft Corp. v. United States, 797 F.2d 920 (10th Cir. 1986), Stearns-Roger Corp. v. United States, 774 F.2d 414 (10th Cir. 1985), and Mobil Oil Corp. v. United States, 8 Cl. Ct. 555 (1985). Carnation was applied, but with a different result, in Crawford Fitting Co. v. United States, 606 F. Supp. 136 (N.D. Ohio 1985). Our decision in Clougherty has been followed in Anesthesia Service Medical Group v. Commissioner, 85 T.C. 1031 (1985), on appeal (9th Cir., May 14, 1986), Stearns-Roger, and Mobil. Accordingly, we decide the parent-subsidiary issue in favor of respondent under the authority of Carnation and Clougherty, and it is unnecessary to restate our analysis.

Petitioner also contends that even if the subject payments failed to constitute deductible insurance premiums, they are nonetheless deductible under section 162 'because they are 'ordinary and necessary' business expenses 'paid or incurred' during the taxable years' in issue. In Clougherty we answered this argument by holding that in disallowing the payments as insurance premiums we reclassified them as nondeductible. 84 T.C. at 960. The Claims Court in Mobil followed this approach. 8 Cl. Ct. at 567.

Payments to a captive insurance company are equivalent to additions to a reserve for losses. Stearns-Roger Corp. v. United States, supra at 415; Mobil Oil Corp. v. United States, supra at 567. It has long been recognized that sums set aside as an insurance reserve are not deductible. Steere Tank Lines, Inc. v. United States, 577 F.2d 279, 280 (5th Cir. 1978), cert. denied 440 U.S. 946 (1979); Spring Canyon Coal v. Commissioner, 43 F.2d 78 (10th Cir. 1930), cert. denied 284 U.S. 654 (1931). If the payments to HCI are not deductible as insurance premiums, they are not deductible at all.

In addition, petitioner argues for deductibility of portions of the amounts paid by Humana Inc. to HCI. It contends that the expense of providing insurance to certain employees, officers, directors, and contractors covered under the policies in issue should be deductible. As to this argument, petitioner cites no authority to support its apparent contention that the risks, whether arising from purely corporate acts or acts of specific corporate employees, were other than the risks fully retained within the meaning of Carnation and Clougherty. Indeed, we believe that it would be difficult to find any such persuasive authority where, as here, the coverage of certain employees, officers, and others was clearly an integral part of the protection of the parent corporation. In this regard, on its forms 10-K filed by Humana Inc. with the Securities and Exchange Commission for the taxable years in issue, it described the coverage provided by HCI as follows: The Insurance Subsidiary will insure the risks of the Company only, and it will only provide insurance to physicians who are actually employed by the Company. In such documents, 'Company' is defined as Humana Inc. and its subsidiaries.

We turn now to the brother-sister issue, which is an issue of first impression in this Court. It has, however, been decided in favor of the government in Stearns-Roger and Mobil. Those cases extended the rationale of Carnation and Clougherty to the brother-sister factual pattern. We likewise extend the rationale to the brother-sister factual pattern of the instant case. We emphasize that our holding is based upon the factual pattern presented in this case. We recognize that corporate factual patterns may differ. See Crawford Fitting Co. v. United States, supra. In addition, other factors may be present, e.g., reinsurance agreements, guarantees, etc.

Petitioner, in support of its motion for reconsideration argues that in the Mobil case it has support for holding that the risk was shifted among the subsidiaries. We disagree. Mobil involved not only the deductibility of payments from the parent and the subsidiaries to the captive insurance subsidiary but also whether the payments from the subsidiaries to the captive insurance subsidiary resulted in constructive dividends to the parent. The Claims Court held that the arrangement did not cause the risk of loss to be shifted and the payments were, therefore, not deductible as insurance premiums. It also held that the payments did not result in constructive dividends to the parent. 8 Cl. Ct. at 568.

Petitioner relies upon the portion of the Claims Court opinion concerning constructive dividends in which the Court describes the business purposes involved. The business purpose for the payments is not relevant in deciding the deductibility of the payments as insurance premiums because the payments have been reclassified as nondeductible additions to a reserve for losses.

This is the first case on captive insurance arrangements in which expert testimony has been presented to this Court. Carnation was decided on the parties' motions for summary judgment and Clougherty was fully stipulated. In the instant case three expert witnesses testified and the Court received written reports of their opinions. Dr. Irving Pfeffer testified for petitioner and Dr. Irving Plotkin and Mr. Richard Edward Stewart testified on behalf of respondent. Dr. Plotkin testified in the Stearns-Roger, Beech Aircraft, and Mobil cases cited above. Dr. Pfeffer and Mr. Stewart did not testify in any of the previously decided cases.

The opinion of Dr. Pfeffer provides little reasoning and is not very convincing. It simply concludes that the arrangements between Humana Inc., its operating subsidiaries, and HCI constitute insurance. Furthermore, it is contrary to the cases cited above.

Dr. Plotkin and Mr. Stewart prepared a joint opinion. Their opinion is consistent with our decisions in Carnation and Clougherty and contains very persuasive reasoning. The analysis portion of the Plotkin-Stewart expert report is as follows:

Analysis

This case presents the question of whether payments made by a corporation to its wholly owned subsidiary in exchange for formal contracts of 'insurance' constitute deductible premiums for federal income tax purposes. The respondent has taken the position that such transactions are not deductible since they are devoid of any RISK TRANSFER (also referred to as risk shifting), an element which he believes to be critical to the definition of insurance for federal income tax purposes.

The respondent has requested us to analyze whether or not the various transactions between and among Humana, AMI, HCI, and * * *, labeled 'insurance' by the petitioner, can actually be considered 'insurance' from the standpoint of how the insurance and economic professions view them.

Commercial insurance is a mechanism for transferring the financial uncertainty arising from pure risks faced by one firm to another in exchange for an insurance premium. Such financial uncertainty is caused by the possibility of certain types of occurrences that may have only adverse financial consequences. A corporation such as Humana that places its risks in a captive insurance company that it owns, either directly or through a parent corporation, subsidiary, or a fronting company, is not relieving itself of this financial uncertainty. The reason for this is simply that such corporation, through its ownership position, still holds the benefits and burdens of retaining the financial consequences of its own risks. It has a dollar for dollar economic interest in the result of any 'insured' peril.

A term frequently used for the act of insuring is underwriting. An essential element of the concept of underwriting is the transference of uncertainty from one firm to another, generally from the one whose activities naturally give rise to the uncertainty to one whose investors are in the business of accepting such uncertainty for the potential profit they can earn thereby.

Thus, insurers, and the interests that own them, are risk takers. They assume the financial consequences of the risks for others in return for a premium payment. * * *

The essential element of an insurance transaction from the standpoint of the insured (e.g., Humana and its hospital network), is that no matter what insured perils occur, the financial consequences are known in advance. Thus the insured, for the price of its premium, is protected from such financial consequences, within the limits of its policy. By reason of its contract, the insured is indemnified against loss from a defined hazard or risk. In essence, the premium represents the substitution of a small, but certain 'loss', for a potentially large and uncertain loss,

To have a true transfer of risk, another risk-bearer must replace the insured. To speak of a transfer of risk to a fund or reserve established by the insured is merely to describe 'self-insurance'. A captive insurance subsidiary, such as HCI, represents a recognized form of risk retention or 'self-insurance'. Many scholars have noted that the very term, 'self-insurance', is a misnomer, since there cannot be any insurance without risk transfer.

Accordingly, a firm cannot insure itself. This does not mean, however, that a firm cannot or should not choose to retain the financial uncertainty of the hazards it faces, nor attempt to predict and minimize the financial consequences of its risks. Whether its portfolio of risks is large or small, there is always uncertainty concerning what will be the actual financial consequences of the events that may occur during some future time period. In fact, the larger the collection of risks, the greater is the uncertainty concerning the actual result. The only way a firm can relieve itself but only of the financial uncertainty is by entering into a contract whereby some other firm will assume that uncertainty. * * *

A firm placing its risks in a captive insurance company in which it holds a sole or predominant[12] ownership position, is not relieving itself of financial uncertainty. It is, through its ownership, retaining-the burdens and benefits of assuming the financial responsibility of its own risks. This concept has been recognized by scholars for at least twenty years:

It is apparent that the nature of the captive-insurance device involves not only the element of insurance through 'transfer' of risks, but also the notion of self-insurance since the 'owners' of the risks insured therein are the 'owners' of the insurer. The fortunes of the two entities are interlocked to the extent that the risks insured in the captive are not reinsured. In this sense, captive insuring can be considered a risk-retention device similar to self-insurance. In fact, if self-insurance involves the conduct of risk management 'according to all the sound principles and practices employed by insurance companies' it might be argued that captive insuring is the epitome of the self-insurance device ... (Robert S. Goshay, 'Captive Insurance Companies,' Risk Management, Ch. VI, Richard D. Irwin, Inc., Homewood, Illinois, 1964, pp. 80-121, at p. 85.)

---

12   The instant case presents only sole ownership of the captive insurance company. We express no opinion where the ownership of the captive insurance company is only predominant.

* * * The recognition and description of captive insurance as a form of risk retention and self-insurance permeates the theoretical and applied insurance and accounting literature. * * *

When a firm actually obtains insurance, the firm's financial costs associated with the insured peril are independent of whether or not the peril actually comes to pass, or the extent of the financial damage caused by the peril. Its costs, in fact, are equal to the insurance premium and KNOWN IN ADVANCE WITH CERTAINTY. Just the opposite obtains with any form of self-insurance, be it on the corporation's books or through the books of the firm's captive insurance subsidiary. The actual costs are a direct, dollar-for-dollar function of what perils in fact come to pass and what their financial consequences turn out to be.

* * *

A question that perplexes some when initially confronted with the captive insurance area is whether or not respondent has chosen to treat, either directly or indirectly, two separate legal entities as one single economic unit. One's first impression might be that, since a parent corporation can deal at arm's-length with a subsidiary in other areas besides insurance and have such transactions respected by respondent, 'insurance premiums' paid to a captive should not be treated any differently. The answer to this paradox lies in the unique nature of insurance transactions relative to other types of parent/subsidiary transactions.

True insurance relieves the firm's balance sheet of any potential impact of the financial consequences of the insured peril. For the price of the premiums, the insured rids itself of any economic stake in whether or not the loss occurs. * * * however as long as the firm deals with its captive, its balance sheet cannot be protected from the financial vicissitudes of the insured peril.[13]

---

[13]   For financial reporting purposes, Humana Inc. prepared consolidated financial statements which included all of its subsidiaries. Accordingly, its investment in HCI stock would be eliminated on the consolidated financial statements. The net effect is that after the elimination of intercompany accounts the assets of HCI are included in the consolidated financial statements. Furthermore, even if HCI were not included in the consolidated financial statements, Humana Inc. would properly account for its investment in HCI stock using the equity method. Accounting Principles Board Opinion No. 18, 'The Equity Method of Accounting for Investments in Common Stock,' AICPA (New York 1971). Accordingly, the investment of Humana Inc. in HCI stock would reflect the changes in the retained earnings of HCI.

On the other hand, if a parent sold its subsidiary a hotel, it is true that the ultimate fate of that hotel will be reflected on the balance sheet. However, whether or not the transferred property could accurately, for tax and other purposes, be described as a hotel is not a function of whether or not the parent's balance sheet reflects the ultimate fate of the property. This, however, is precisely opposite from the case of insurance. A transaction can be fairly described as insurance if, and only if, the parent's balance sheet is immunized from the financial consequences of the insured peril. * * *

It is well recognized that insurance premiums are accorded unique and favorable treatment within the Internal Revenue Code. The same is true for other specific economic activities, such as the depletion allowance accorded to oil wells. We believe that if company A sold company B a farm but in the contract described it as an oil well, company B would not be eligible for depletion allowances.

* * *

CONCLUSION

So long as the firm does not transfer to another the ultimate responsibility for the financial consequences of its risks, it remains the risk bearer and faces the uncertainty of each year's actual financial losses. The attempted placing of a firm's risks, directly or indirectly, in its 'insurance affiliates' did not accomplish a transference of risk, or constitute an insurance transaction as a matter of insurance theory or economic reality. We find our conclusion in complete accord with the clear theoretical and applied teachings of the economics, insurance theory, risk management, and captive self-insurance literatures.

In Beech Aircraft, the District Court commented favorably on the testimony of Dr. Plotkin, found it to be relevant, and overruled the taxpayer's objections to the testimony.[14] No court has refused to accept the testimony of Dr. Plotkin on captive insurance.

Dr. Plotkin testified in both of the brother-sister cases. The District Court, in Stearns-Roger, adopted the analysis of Dr. Plotkin. The Claims Court, in Mobil, based upon the opinion of Dr. Plotkin, concluded that the risk of loss was always with the parent corporation and was not shifted away from the parent by reason of payments among the brother-sister subsidiaries. The Claims Court commented upon the testimony of Dr. Plotkin as follows:

---

[14]   Beech Aircraft Corp. v. United States, an unreported case (D. Kan. 1984, 54 AFTR 2d 84-6173, 84-2 USTC par. 9803).

Dr. Irvin Plotkin, * * * was qualified as an expert in the economics of insurance. Dr. Plotkin testified that Mobil did not actually purchase insurance as the term is defined in the field of economics. Essentially, Dr. Plotkin testified that a wholly-owned subsidiary cannot insure its parent because there is no risk transference. The risk of loss remains within the economic unit. As a shareholder of a wholly-owned insurance affiliate, the parent company bears the risks of the subsidiary, suffers from losses sustained by the subsidiary, and benefits from gains realized by the subsidiary. * * * (8 Cl. Ct. at 563.)

Mr. Stewart, in his testimony in the instant case, agreed with Dr. Plotkin as to the shifting of risk. Mr. Stewart has imposing credentials, among them he was superintendent of insurance for the State of New York from 1967 through 1970. From a pragmatic standpoint he perceived no difference between the payments at issue and self insurance.

The joint opinion of Dr. Plotkin and Mr. Stewart proceeds from the proposition that there must be a transfer or shifting of risk for the transactions to represent insurance. This conforms to 'hornbook law' that a taxpayer cannot deduct as insurance premiums amounts set aside in its own possession to compensate itself for perils which are generally the subject of insurance. Stearns-Roger Corp. v. United States, 774 F.2d at 416; Carnation Co. v. Commissioner, 640 F.2d at 1013; Mobil Oil Corp. Commissioner, 8 Cl. Ct. at 566; Clougherty Packing Co. v. Commissioner, 84 T.C. at 958; Pan-American Hide Co. v. Commissioner, 1 B.T.A. 1249, 1250 (1925). Thus, a taxpayer cannot deduct as insurance premiums amounts which it sets aside as a reserve to cover future casualties.

If we decline to extend our holdings in Carnation and Clougherty to the brother-sister factual pattern, we would exalt form over substance and permit a taxpayer to circumvent our holdings by simple corporate structural changes. Assume that Corporation A incorporates a wholly owned captive insurance company, Corporation B, which insures the risks of A. Under our holdings in Carnation and Clougherty, A could not deduct the premiums it pays to B.

Let us alter the corporate structures to the brother-sister factual pattern. The shareholders of Corporation A exchange their stock for the stock of Corporation B, which was incorporated for the sole purpose of holding the stock of A. A is now the wholly owned subsidiary of B. A continues to be the operating corporation. B then incorporates a wholly owned captive insurance company, Corporation C. Corporation C insures the risks of Corporation A, the operating company. Corporations A and C are brother-sister corporations of a common parent, Corporation B.

If we do not extend the holdings of Carnation and Clougherty to the brother-sister factual pattern, the payments from Corporation A to Corporation C would be deductible as insurance premiums. Such a holding, of course, would be contrary to the decisions of the Tenth Circuit in Stearns-Roger and the Claims Court in Mobil, both of whom relied upon our decisions in Carnation and Clougherty.

Respondent again argues that we should adopt his 'economic family' concept which he articulated in Rev. Rul. 77-316, 1977-2 C.B. 53. We declined to adopt that concept in Carnation Co. v. Commissioner, 71 T.C. at 413, and also declined to adopt it in Clougherty Packing Co. v. Commissioner, 84 T.C. at 956. We again decline to adopt that concept because it does not tell all of the story. As we have seen from Crawford Fitting an 'economic family' may exist which results in the shifting of risk. Instead of applying a broad approach such as 'economic family' to captive insurance, we hold that it is more appropriate to examine all of the facts to decide whether or to what extent there has been a shifting of the risk from one entity to the captive insurance company.

We conclude that there was not the necessary shifting of risk from the operating subsidiaries of Humana Inc. to HCI and, therefore, the amounts charged by Humana Inc. to its subsidiaries did not constitute insurance. Accordingly, the amounts paid to HCI are not deductible as ordinary and necessary business expenses.

Decisions will be entered under Rule 155.

Reviewed by the Court.

STERRETT, SIMPSON, CHABOT, NIMS, PARKER, WHITAKER, HAMBLEN, COHEN, JACOBS, PARR, and WILLIAMS, JJ., agree with the majority opinion.

CONCURRENCE OF JUDGE WHITAKER

WHITAKER, J., concurring:

We are faced in this case with another aspect of the captive insurance problem-the deduction of insurance premiums between brother-sister corporations. The majority purports to decline as in Carnation Co. v. Commissioner, 71 T.C. 400, 413 (1978), affd. 640 F.2d 1010 (9th Cir. 1981) and Clougherty Packing Co. v. Commissioner, 84 T.C. 948, 956 (1985), on appeal (9th Cir., Dec. 13, 1985), to adopt respondent's 'economic family' concept. See Rev. Rul. 77-316, 1977-2 C.B. 53 at 54. However, the majority refers repeatedly with apparent approval to decisions of other courts, including the opinion of the Court of Appeals of the Ninth Circuit affirming our opinion in Carnation, all of which follow Carnation and adopt the economic family concept. The majority also quotes extensively with approval from the testimony of respondent's experts, Dr. Plotkin and Mr. Stewart, who have fully swallowed respondent's economic family concept. The dissenting opinion here as in the prior cases accuses the majority of having in fact adopted the economic family concept and charges us with failing to follow Moline Properties, Inc.

v. Commissioner, 319 U.S. 436 (1943). I think it unfortunate that we-the majority-have allowed respondent's buzzword-economic family-to produce so much strained rationalization that we appear to have lost sight of the real issue, whether or not the contracts in question are insurance contracts.

It bears emphasizing at the outset that what this Court has so far dealt with is a single affiliated group, including the insurance entity, consisting of one parent corporation and one or more wholly owned subsidiaries. The majority correctly notes (footnote 12) that our opinion is limited to the consequences of insuring with a wholly owned captive. I suggest what we have decided and all that we have decided in this case and its two predecessors is simply that on the particular facts of these three cases we do not have insurance for tax purposes. Here the only insurance relationship is that which is purportedly created between entities which are related to each other through a single parent with no unrelated persons being insured or having material interests in any of the entities involved. In so doing we have not 'pierced any corporate veil' or done violence to Moline Properties Inc.

There is also another equally compelling basis for our decision. Necessary elements of insurance are risk-shifting and risk-distributing. Helvering v. Le Gierse, 312 U.S. 531 (1941); Commissioner v. Treganowan, 183 F.2d 288 (2d Cir. 1950). These two decisions are fundamental to this insurance issue. In Helvering v. Le Gierse, supra the Supreme Court recognized that there were two parties to the contract-an insurance company and an insured individual who were distinct legal entities. There was a contract of insurance and a related annuity contract, each of which were legally binding contracts. As Justice Murphy said:

Considered together, the contracts wholly fail to spell out any element of insurance risk. It is true that the 'insurance' contract looks like an insurance policy, contains all the usual provisions of one, and could have been assigned or surrendered without the annuity. * * * The fact remains that annuity and insurance are opposites; in this combination the one neutralizes the risk customarily inherent in the other. * * * (312 U.S. at 541.)

The Second Circuit in Commissioner v. Treganowan, supra, defined risk-shifting as effected by a contract between the insurer and the insured, each of whom gambles on the risk. Risk-distributing on the other hand reduces the potential loss by spreading its cost throughout a group. In Humana as in Carnation and Clougherty, we looked at the facts and at the several corporate entities involved, and found neither risk-shifting nor risk-distributing. We have not invalidated the contracts; we simply found that the contracts involved were not contracts of insurance.

The majority here states 'Payments to a captive insurance company are equivalent to additions to a reserve for losses. * * * It has long been recognized that sums set aside as an insurance reserve are not deductible.[15] Again that is a correct analysis under these facts. If a single entity, party A, undertakes to indemnify an unrelated entity, party B, from a specific risk, at least superficially the risk has been shifted. But in order for the transaction to be economically sound for both parties, the premium would have to approximate the present value of the risk, equating to a reasonable self-insurance reserve. There has certainly been no distribution of the risk. However such a relationship might be characterized, it is not insurance. In the real world, this hypothetical transaction would not occur. Moreover, given that self-insurance reserves are not deductible, to characterize a contract between a parent and its wholly owned captive subsidiary, with no other insurance business, as insurance would exalt form over substance. For these two reasons, Carnation and Clougherty were inevitable. One does not need the economic family concept for this result. And given Carnation and Clougherty as correctly decided, the form over substance rationale is alone sufficient to prevent taxpayers from altering the result in the parent-subsidiary circumstance by the simple expedient of creating a sister insurance captive to insure its brother operating company. It requires very little further rationalization to reach the conclusion that in fact, as opposed to form, there is no risk shifting or risk distributing no matter where in the affiliated wholly owned group one places the captive insurance subsidiary.

I emphasize again that only in these factual contexts have we found that the purported insurance contract does not qualify as such for tax purposes. Whether or not the contract should be recognized as insurance for any other purpose is not an issue before us. In reaching this result we have not collapsed or looked behind the separate corporate existence of any party. As the Supreme Court did Le Gierse, we have merely applied to the facts before us the accepted definition of insurance and the well known 'form over substance' doctrine. That we may someday be called upon to determine how much dilution from 100-percent control or how much insurance business with unrelated entities is necessary to achieve risk-shifting and risk-distributing is a probable fact of life, but it should not interfere with our decision in this case.

STERRETT, CHABOT, NIMS, PARKER, HAMBLEN, JACOBS, and WILLIAMS, JJ., agree with this concurring opinion.

---

[15] It has been suggested with considerable logic that "The basic concept in a capture program * * * may even have grown out of the early defeats of the self-insurers.' Bradley and Winslow, 'Self-Insurance Plans and Captive Insurance Companies-A Perspective on Recent Tax Developments,' 4 Am. J. Tax Policy 217 at 233 (1985).

CONCURRENCE OF JUDGE HAMBLEN

HAMBLEN, J., concurring:

In Clougherty Packing Co. v. Commissioner, I expressed my concern about the 'economic family' concept.[16] Noting that respondent's assertion of the economic family concept did not square with Moline Properties v. Commissioner, 319 U.S. 436 (1943), I felt that the Moline Properties issue was injected unnecessarily into Clougherty by way of the economic family concept analogy. I could see little difference between the economic family concept described in Rev. Rul. 77-316, 1977-2 C.B. 53, and the determination made by the majority in Clougherty. However, I concluded that the Clougherty arrangement was not a true insurance arrangement as there was no risk distribution. Following a similar analysis, I concur only in the result of the majority opinion and agree in principle with Judge Whitaker's concurring opinion.

The majority cite proponents of the economic family concept as authority to support its determination. This, I feel, is neither appropriate nor necessary for the following reasons.

First, one has only to thumb through any text or hornbook on corporate tax law to see the arsenal available to respondent in related corporation transactions. Yet this plethora of available tools, whether codified or judicially developed, apparently is inadequate for respondent in this area, so he asserts an 'economic family' theory which has ominous ramifications within and beyond the captive insurance area.[17]

More importantly, under the economic family theory asserted by respondent, there seems to be no real distinction between disregarding transactions between related corporations and disregarding their separate status. However, I submit that, generally, transactions between ANY entities, related or unrelated, should be repudiated or recharacterized only if they are not legally or factually what they purport to be. The majority's reliance on financial reports to buttress its conclusion only fuels the economic family fire; it consolidates two entities for tax purposes which are not permitted to file consolidated tax returns and, without a basis for so doing, erodes the long-standing principle of Moline Properties v. Commissioner, supra.

---

[16]   See Hamblen, J., concurring, Clougherty Packing Co. v. Commissioner, 84 T.C. 948, 961 (1985).

[17]   For example, it has been noted that respondent's 'experts' have stated in another case that the economic family principle is dependent upon piercing the corporate veil. See Bradley and Winslow, 'Self Insurance Plans and Captive Insurance Companies-A Perspective on Recent Tax Developments, ' 4 Am. J. of Tax Policy 217, 248 n. 101 (1985).

For these reasons, I strongly believe that we should decide the issue solely on a lack of risk shifting and risk distribution basis. In this respect, there appears to be no tax avoidance scheme. The inter-corporate contractual arrangements are not determined to be shams. Indeed, a business purpose for the transactions is obvious because the entities could not obtain insurance coverage elsewhere.

If we are to abrogate the insurance transaction between these related entities, we should do so by simply saying, without more, that there is neither shifting nor distribution of risk and, consequently, no valid insurance arrangement. If we cannot say that, or must say more than that, then it seems to me that we have valid insurance transactions between separate, though related entities.

In sum, I believe that the economic family theory may conflict with fundamental principles of tax law by invoking attribution among related corporations where it has not been legislated by Congress.[18] I see no reason to give such a concept credence, as the majority is doing here. Consequently, I concur only in the result reached by the majority.

WHITAKER, J., agrees with this concurring opinion.

CONCURRENCE OF JUDGE KORNER

KORNER, J., concurring and dissenting in part:

So far as the majority opinion holds that the premiums paid to HCI by petitioner Humana, Inc. (the common parent corporation) for insurance ON ITSELF may not be deducted as insurance premiums, I agree that such an outcome is controlled by our holdings in Carnation Co. v. Commissioner, 71 T.C. 400 (1978), affd. 640 F.2d 1010 (9th Cir. 1981), and Clougherty Packing Co. v. Commissioner, 84 T.C. 948 (1985), on appeal (9th Cir. 1985). I therefore concur in that portion of the opinion.

With respect to the majority's holding that the same result obtains with respect to premiums paid by the Humana subsidiaries to HCI for comparable insurance on them and their employees, I dissent.

Neither Carnation nor Clougherty are authority for denying deductions for the amounts paid, as insurance premiums, by Humana Inc.'s subsidiaries to HCI. Said wholly-owned subsidiaries of Humana Inc. are related to HCI as brother-sister corporations. In Carnation, we found that Three Flowers (the wholly-owned offshore insurance subsidiary) was organized 'to carry on the business of insurance and reinsurance of various multiple line risks including those of petitioner (Carnation) and its subsidiaries.' 71 T.C.

---

18   See Bradley and Winslow, 4 Am. J. of Tax Policy at 246-255, supra.

at 402. However, the issue of the deductibility of insurance premiums were the insurance contract is between corporations related as brother-sister was not decided. It was stipulated that for purposes of the case all premiums were to be deemed as having been paid and deducted by Carnation.[19] In Clougherty, the wholly-owned subsidiary, Lombardy's, only business was the reinsurance of Clougherty's workers' compensation coverage. Clougherty was the taxpayer-petitioner. No subsidiaries of Clougherty related to Lombardy as brother-sister were involved.

In contrast with the factual situations presented in Carnation and Clougherty, the record herein shows that: (1) the wholly-owned subsidiaries of Humana Inc. were insured under the subject policies; (2) the subsidiaries are related to HCI as brother-sister, not as parent-subsidiary; (3) the amounts due under the subject policies, as premiums, were billed by HCI to Humana Inc. on a monthly basis; (4) Humana Inc. paid the total amount billed by HCI on a monthly basis; (5) later, the foregoing amounts were allocated and charged back by Humana Inc. to its appropriate subsidiaries; and (6) the subsidiaries are petitioners here.[20] See sec. 1.1502-77(a), Income Tax Regs. Moreover, respondent does not contend that the existence of the said subsidiaries as separate and viable tax entities should be ignored, or that they were organized in order to unlawfully avoid the payment of tax. Respondent similarly does not contend that the subsidiaries did not engage in any business activities.

I find the majority's holding with respect to the premiums paid by the Humana subsidiaries to HCI (the brother-sister situation) deficient in at least two important respects:

1. The majority relies heavily upon, and quotes extensively from the joint opinion of respondent's expert witnesses Plotkin and Stewart. A careful examination of that opinion, however, leads me to the conclusion that it gives no support to the position of the majority on the brother-sister question. As the quotations show, the thrust of the report is aimed at the parent-subsidiary question, concluding that there is no true insurance (hence no deductible premium) because there is no transfer of the risk of loss from the 'insured' parent to its wholly-owned subsidiary 'insurer.' The reasoning apparently is that the subsidiary's stock is shown as an asset on the parent's balance sheet. If the parent

---

[19]   Carnation and its subsidiary corporations that were required to file Federal income tax returns each filed separate Federal income tax returns rather than a consolidated return.

[20]   As stated in the majority's findings of fact, supra, Humana Inc. and its domestic subsidiaries filed consolidated Federal income tax returns for the years in issue. Respondent conceded that HCI was not a member of the affiliated group of corporations of which Humana Inc. was the common parent. HCI was not able to and did not file its income tax returns on a consolidated basis with Humana Inc. and its subsidiaries. Secs. 1501, 1504(a), 1504(b). HCI filed separate returns for all the pertinent years.

suffers an insured loss which the subsidiary (HCI in this case) has to pay, the assets of the subsidiary insurer will be depleted by the amount of the payment. This, in turn, will reduce the value of the subsidiary's shares as an asset of the parent (Humana), so that, in effect, the assets of the 'insured' parent are bearing the loss as far as true economic impact is concerned. As the experts' joint opinion (quoted by the majority) clearly puts it:

True insurance relieves the firm's balance sheet of any potential impact of the financial consequences of the insured peril. For the price of the premiums, the insured rids itself of any economic stake in whether or not the loss occurs. * * * however as long as the firm deals with its captive, its balance sheet cannot be protected from the financial vicissitudes of the insured peril.

* * *

CONCLUSION

So long as the firm does not transfer to another the ultimate responsibility for the financial consequences of its risks, it remains the risk bearer and faces the uncertainty of each year's actual financial losses. The attempted placing of a firm's risks, directly or indirectly, in its 'insurance affiliates' did not accomplish a transference of risk, or constitute an insurance transaction as a matter of insurance theory or economic reality. We find our conclusion in complete accord with the clear theoretical and applied teachings of the economics, insurance theory, risk management, and captive self-insurance literatures.

Accepting, arguendo, that this is an accurate statement and is in line with our reasoning in Carnation and Clougherty, it nevertheless provides no support to the majority's position in the brother-sister situation. Humana's insured subsidiaries own no stock in HCI, nor vice versa. The subsidiaries' balance sheets and net worth would in no way be affected by the payment of an insured claim by HCI.[21] It follows that when the Humana subsidiaries paid THEIR OWN premiums for THEIR OWN insurance, as the facts show, they shifted their risks to HCI. The rationale of Carnation and Clougherty thus does not apply, and such premiums should be allowable as deductions to the subsidiaries.

---

21 The majority, at footnote 13 of the majority opinion, states that Humana Inc. (the common parent), filed consolidated balance sheets for all of its subsidiaries (including HCI) for FINANCIAL reporting purposes. The effect, says the majority, is that the assets of HCI were included in the consolidated statements. I question whether this would be proper for TAX reporting purposes, where HCI was not and could not be a member of the consolidated returns which were filed. See my footnote 2, supra.

The majority further states that even if HCI was not properly includible in Humana's consolidated balance sheet for tax reporting purposes, nevertheless Humana would reflect its investment in HCI's stock under the 'equity' method. Ergo if HCI pays an insured claim against one of its brother/sister subsidiaries, its assets, and therefore the assets of Humana PARENT will decrease, and therefore Humana PARENT is the one who truly bears the loss. Consistent with this reasoning, is respondent prepared to allow a deduction to Humana PARENT when HCI pays an insured claim against one of the brother/sister hospital subsidiaries?

Upon what other basis can these premiums be disallowed? That is the subject of my next point of disagreement with the majority.

2. The majority in this case for the first time extends the rationale of Carnation and Clougherty to the brother-sister situation. In addition, the majority cites and relies upon Stearns-Roger Corp. v. United States, 774 F.2d 414 (10th Cir. 1985), and Mobil Oil Corp. v. United States, 8 Cl. Ct. 555 (1985). See also Beech Aircraft Corp. v. United States, 797 F.2d 920 (10th Cir. 1986). A reading of these cases shows that each of them, either explicitly or implicitly, has adopted the 'economic family' concept advanced by respondent in Rev. Rul. 77-316, 1977-2 C.B. 53, where it is said:

there is no economic shifting or distributing of risks of loss with respect to the risks carried or retained by the wholly owned * * * subsidiaries * * * The insuring parent corporation and its domestic subsidiaries, and the wholly owned 'insurance' subsidiary, through separate corporate entities, represent one economic family with the result that those who bear the ultimate economic burden of loss are the same persons who suffer the loss. To the extent that the risks of loss are not retained in their entirety by * * * or reinsured with * * * insurance companies that are unrelated to the economic family of insureds, there is no risk-shifting or risk-distributing, and no insurance, the premiums for which are deductible under section 162 of the Code.

Thus, the amounts paid by the rents, and their domestic subsidiaries, and retained by the insurance subsidiaries), respectively, are not deductible under section 162 of the Code as 'ordinary and necessary expenses paid or incurred during the taxable year.' Because such amounts remain within the economic family and under the practical control of the respective parent in each situation, there has been no amount 'paid or incurred.' * * *

In spite of its citation of, and reliance upon the above cases, the majority in the instant case (as in Carnation and Clougherty) again purports to refuse to accept respondent's economic family argument. Instead, the majority passes over the substantial issues which are raised with the airy statement that 'we hold that it is more appropriate to examine all of the facts to decide whether or to what extent there has been a shifting of the risk from one entity to the captive insurance company.'

I find the majority's attempted distinction here to be disingenuous and entirely unconvincing. What facts are there which support the conclusion here that there was no shifting of risk from the Humana subsidiaries to HCI: The subsidiaries, WHO PAID THEIR OWN PREMIUMS FOR THEIR OWN INSURANCE, had no ownership in HCI, the insurer, nor did HCI have any ownership in them. If we are to recognize HCI and the hospital subsidiaries as valid separate business entities, conducting active legitimate businesses and devoid of sham-neither respondent nor the majority herein say to the contrary-then how can we say that there was no shifting of risk from the hospital-subsidiaries/sisters to the insurer/brother (HCI), without violation the time-honored rule that each taxpayer is a separate entity for tax purposes? Moline Properties, Inc. v. Commissioner, 319 U.S. 436 (1943); Burnet v. Commonwealth Imp. Co., 287 U.S. 415 (1932). The only way it can be done is to ignore the separate entities of Humana, its hospital subsidiaries and HCI, to call them all one 'economic family' and to say that what happens to one happens to all of them. On the facts of the brother-sister situation presented here, I think that is what the majority is doing, and it ought to say so forthrightly. I would still disagree with such a position, but at least it would have the virtue of candor. Other than 'economic family,' I can think of no theory on which the result here can be rationalized, and the majority has not articulated any.

This Court has never adopted respondent's economic family theory,[22] and has expressed-justifiably-its concern regarding the adoption of such theory and its application to other areas of the tax law.[23] The theory of Helvering v. Le Gierse, 312 U.S. 531 (1941) may have been adequate to sustain the holdings in Carnation and Clougherty, where only a parent and its insurance subsidiary were involved. It cannot be stretched to cover the instant brother-sister situation, where there was nothing-equity ownership or otherwise-to offset the shifting of risk from the hospital subsidiaries to HCI. If the majority is to accomplish the fell deed here, 'a decent respect to the opinions of mankind requires that they should declare the causes which impel them'[24] to such a result.

SHIELDS, CLAPP, SWIFT, GERBER, WRIGHT, and WELLS, JJ., agree with this concurring and dissenting opinion.

---

[22] See Carnation Co. v. Commissioner, 71 T.C. 400, 409-410 (1978); Clougherty Packing Co. v. Commissioner, 84 T.C. 948, 956, 957, 959 (1985).

[23] Clougherty Packing Co. v. Commissioner, 84 T.C. at 959 (majority opinion); 962-964 (Hamblen, J., concurring); 964 (Jacobs, J., concurring).

[24] Jefferson, The Declaration of Independence (1776).

Opinion of Sixth Circuit

UNITED STATES COURT OF APPEALS, SIXTH CIRCUIT

HUMANA INC., Petitioner-Appellant,

v.

COMMISSIONER OF INTERNAL REVENUE, Respondent-Appellee.

[Names of counsel omitted.]

Before MARTIN and MILBURN, Circuit Judges, and HACKETT,* District Judge.

BOYCE F. MARTIN, Jr., Circuit Judge.

Humana Inc. and its wholly owned subsidiaries with which it files a consolidated federal income tax return appeal the decision of the United States Tax Court determining deficiencies against them with respect to their 1976-1979 fiscal years on the basis that: 1) sums paid by Humana Inc. to its captive insurance subsidiary, Health Care Indemnity, on its own behalf and on behalf of other wholly owned subsidiaries did not constitute deductible insurance premiums under the Internal Revenue Code § 162(a) (1954), and 2) such payments are not deductible under the Internal Revenue Code § 162 (1954) as ordinary and necessary business expenses as payments to a captive insurance company are equivalent to additions to a reserve for losses.

Humana Inc. and its subsidiaries operate hospitals whose insurance coverage was cancelled. Humana Inc. incorporated Health Care Indemnity, Inc., as a Colorado captive insurance company. In order to facilitate the incorporation of Health Care Indemnity, Humana Inc. also incorporated Humana Holdings, N.V., as a wholly owned subsidiary in the Netherland Antilles. The only business purpose of Humana Holdings was to assist in the capitalization of Health Care Indemnity.FN1[25] At the time of the initial capitalization, Health Care Indemnity issued 150,000 shares of preferred stock and

---

*   The Honorable Barbara K. Hackett, United States District Judge for the Eastern District of Michigan, sitting by designation.

[25]   Humana Incorporated owns 75% of Health Care Indemnity and Humana's Netherland affiliate owns 25%. Technically, therefore, Humana is not a 100% owner of Health Care Indemnity. However, the tax court stated, and both parties agreed, that the only business purpose of the offshore affiliate was to provide capital for Health Care Indemnity. Therefore, the court and both parties agreed to treat Health Care Indemnity as a wholly-owned subsidiary of Humana.

250,000 shares of common stock. Of these, Humana Holdings, the wholly owned Netherland subsidiary, purchased the preferred stock for $250,000.00 in cash (its entire capitalization) and Humana Inc. purchased 150,000 shares of Health Care Indemnity's common stock for $750,000.00 in the form of irrevocable letters of credit (as provided by Colorado statute).

Health Care Indemnity, the captive insurance subsidiary of Humana Inc., provided insurance coverage for Humana Inc. and its other subsidiaries. Humana Inc. paid to Health Care Indemnity amounts which it treated as insurance premiums. Humana Inc. allocated and charged to the subsidiaries portions of the amounts paid representing the share each bore for the hospitals each operated. The remainder represented Humana Inc.'s share for the hospitals which it operated. The total sums, $21,055,575.00, were deducted on a consolidated income tax return as insurance premiums.

The Commissioner, in accordance with the position outlined in Rev.Rul. 77-316, 1977-2 C.B. 52, disallowed the deductions and asserted deficiencies against Humana Inc. and the subsidiaries. Humana Inc. and its subsidiaries filed petitions in the tax court for redeterminations of the deficiencies assessed against them. On August 14, 1985, the tax court issued a memorandum opinion upholding the Commissioner's determination. Following a petition forreconsideration, the tax court withdrew that opinion. Humana Inc. requested full court review. On January 26, 1987, the tax court, after review by the entire nineteen member court, upheld the Commissioner. Humana Inc. and Subsidiaries v. Commissioner, 88 T.C. 197 (1987).

The opinion of the tax court contains a twelve member majority written by Judge Goffe, an eight member concurrence written by Judge Whitaker and joined by seven members of the majority, a two member concurring opinion written by Judge Hamblen and joined by Judge Whitaker, and a seven member dissent written by Judge Korner. The twelve member majority relied on its prior decisions in Carnation Company v. Commissioner, 71 T.C. 400 (1978), aff'd. 640 F.2d 1010 (9th Cir.1981), cert. denied, 454 U.S. 965, 102 S.Ct. 506, 70 L.Ed.2d 381 (1981) and Clougherty Packing Company v. Commissioner, 84 T.C. 948 (1985), aff'd. 811 F.2d 1297 (9th Cir.1987), and held 1) that sums paid by Humana Inc. to Health Care Indemnity on its own behalf (described as the "parent-subsidiary" issue) were not deductible as ordinary and necessary business expenses for insurance premiums, and 2) the sums charged by Humana Inc. to the operating subsidiaries (described as the "brother-sister" issue) were also not deductible on the consolidated income tax return as ordinary and necessary business expenses for insurance premiums. The majority reasoned that there was no insurance because the risks of loss were not shifted from Humana Inc. and its subsidiaries to Health Care Indemnity. In so holding, the majority specifically rejected adoption of the economic family concept argued by the Commissioner.

The tax court noted that the second issue, the brother-sister issue-whether the sums charged by Humana Inc. to its operating subsidiaries were deductible on the consolidated income tax returns as ordinary and necessary business expenses as insurance premiums-was an issue of first impression before the court. The court claimed that the issue had been decided in favor of denying the premiums as deductible in two other cases, Stearns-Roger Corp. v. United States, 774 F.2d 414 (10th Cir.1985) and Mobil Oil Corp. v. United States, 8 Cl.Ct. 555 (1985). The majority stated that Stearns-Roger and Mobil extended the rationale of Carnation and Clougherty to the "brother-sister" factual pattern. In holding that Humana Inc. did not shift the risk from the subsidiaries to Health Care Indemnity by charging its subsidiaries portions of the amounts paid representing the share each bore for the hospitals each operated, the tax court accepted the joint opinion of two experts, Dr. Plotkin and Mr. Stewart. Dr. Plotkin and Mr. Stewart stated:

> Commercial insurance is a mechanism for transferring the financial uncertainty arising from pure risks faced by one firm to another in exchange for an insurance premium.... The essential element of an insurance transaction from the standpoint of the insured (e.g. Humana and its hospital network), is that no matter what perils occur, the financial consequences are known in advance.... A firm placing its risk in a captive insurance company in which it holds a sole ... ownership position, is not relieving itself of financial uncertainty.... True insurance relieves the firm's balance sheet of any potential impact of the financial consequences of the insured peril.... [However] as long as the firm deals with its captive, its balance sheet cannot be protected from the financial vicissitudes of the insured peril.

Humana, 88 T.C. at 219-25 (1987).

The majority also declared that payments to a captive insurance company are equivalent to additions to a reserve for losses and, therefore, not deductible under the Internal Revenue Code § 162 (1954) as ordinary and necessary business expenses paid or incurred during the taxable years in issue. Stearns-Roger Corp. v. United States, 774 F.2d 414 (10th Cir.1985); Mobil Oil Corp. v. United States, 8 Cl.Ct. 555 (1985).

The eight member concurrence agreed with the majority's conclusion on both issues but felt uncomfortable with the majority's reliance on the expert witnesses, Dr. Plotkin and Mr. Stewart, whose theories rested heavily upon the economic family concept of captive insurance companies. They wrote to affirm that they were holding against Humana solely on the basis that the contracts between Humana Inc. and Health Care Indemnity and the contracts between Humana Inc.'s subsidiaries and Health Care Indemnity were not insurance contracts because of the lack of risk shifting. Humana, 88 T.C. at 231 (1987) (Whitaker, J., concurring).

A two member concurrence wrote to express concern about the "economic family" concept. They noted that the Commissioner's discussions of the economic family concept did not square with Moline Properties v. Commissioner, 319 U.S. 436, 63 S.Ct. 1132, 87 L.Ed. 1499 (1943). The Supreme Court in Moline Properties held that each corporate taxpayer was a separate entity for tax purposes. The two person concurrence felt that the Moline Properties issue was injected unnecessarily by way of the economic family concept analogy. The two member concurrence noted that the majority cites proponents of the economic family concept and felt that this was neither appropriate nor necessary. The two member concurrence stated that they "strongly believe that we should decide the issue solely on a lack of risk shifting and risk distribution basis." Humana, 88 T.C. at 237 (1987) (Hamblen, J., concurring).

The seven member dissent concurred in part with the majority that the premiums paid to Health Care Indemnity by Humana Inc. for insurance on itself may not be deducted as insurance premiums. They dissented with respect to the majority's holding that the same result applies to premiums paid by Humana Inc.'s subsidiaries to Health Care Indemnity for comparable insurance on them and their employees. The dissent stated that neither Carnation nor Clougherty decided the issue of deductibility of insurance premiums where the insurance contract was between corporations related as brother and sister. The dissent stated that the record in this case showed that 1) the wholly owned subsidiaries of Humana Inc. were insured under the subject policies, 2) the subsidiaries were related to Health Care Indemnity as brother-sister, not as parent-subsidiaries, 3) the amounts due under the subject policies as premiums were billed by Health Care Indemnity to Humana on a monthly basis, 4) Humana paid the total amount billed by Health Care Indemnity on a monthly basis, 5) later, the foregoing amounts were allocated and charged back by Humana, Inc. to its appropriate subsidiaries.

The dissent further noted that the majority rested heavily upon the joint opinion of the experts Plotkin and Stewart. However, these opinions gave no support to the position of the majority on the brother-sister question. The thrust of the Plotkin, Stewart testimony was aimed at the parent-subsidiary question, the reasoning being that the subsidiary's stock was shown as an asset on the parent's balance sheet. If the parent suffered an insured loss which a subsidiary had to pay, the assets of the subsidiary insurer would be depleted by the amount of the payment. This, in turn, reduced the value of the subsidiary shares as an asset of the parent. In effect, the assets of the insured parent were bearing the loss as far as the true economic impact was concerned. The dissent claimed that the reasoning presented by the experts provided no support for the majority's position in the brother-sister context. Humana, 88 T.C. at 243-44 (1987) (Korner, J., dissenting). Humana Inc.'s insured subsidiaries owned no stock in Health Care Indemnity, nor vice versa. The subsidiarys' balance sheets and net worth were in no way affected by the payment of an insured claim by Health Care Indemnity. When the subsidiaries paid their own premiums for their own insurance, they shifted their risks to Health Care Indemnity. The dissent argued that the rationale of Carnation and Clougherty thus did not apply. Id. at 247.

The dissent further noted that the cases cited by the tax court, Stearns-Roger, Mobil Oil, and Beech Aircraft v. United States, 797 F.2d 920 (10th Cir.1986), each explicitly or implicitly adopted the economic family concept. However, Health Care Indemnity and the hospital subsidiaries were valid separate business entities conducting active legitimate businesses devoid of sham. No facts stated the contrary. The dissent argued that to hold the insurance contracts between them invalid because they are one "economic family" and what happens to one happens to all of them ignored the separate entities of Humana Inc., its hospital subsidiaries, and Health Care Indemnity. Such a holding violated the time honored rule under Moline Properties that each taxpayer is a separate entity for tax purposes.

I.

We review de novo the legal standard applied by the tax court in determining whether Humana Inc.'s payments to its captive insurance company, Health Care Indemnity, for itself and on behalf of its subsidiaries constitute ordinary and necessary business expenses for insurance. Rose v. Commissioner, 868 F.2d 851 (6th Cir.1989). The tax court's findings of fact shall not be overturned unless clearly erroneous. Id. at 853.

The Internal Revenue Code § 162(a) (1954) allows a deduction for all ordinary and necessary business expenses paid or incurred during the taxable year in carrying on a trade or business. Insurance premiums in the case of a business are generally deductible business expenses. Treas.Reg. § 1.162-1(a) (1954). Although the term "insurance" is not self-defined by the Internal Revenue Code, the Supreme Court in Helvering v. Le Gierse, 312 U.S. 531, 61 S.Ct. 646, 85 L.Ed. 996 (1941), provided the test for defining "insurance" for federal tax purposes.

An insurance contract involves (1) risk shifting and (2) risk distribution. Helvering v. Le Gierse, 312 U.S. 531, 539, 61 S.Ct. 646, 649, 85 L.Ed. 996 (1941) (where an annuity contract completely neutralized the risk inherent in a life insurance contract when both contracts were considered together as one transaction). Risk shifting involves the shifting of an identifiable risk of the insured to the insurer. The focus is on the individual contract between the insured and the insurer. Risk distribution involves shifting to a group of individuals the identified risk of the insured. The focus is broader and looks more to the insurer as to whether the risk insured against can be distributed over a larger group rather than the relationship between the insurer and any single insured. Commissioner of Internal Revenue v. Treganowan, 183 F.2d 288, 291 (2nd Cir.), cert. denied, 340 U.S. 853, 71 S.Ct. 82, 95 L.Ed. 625 (1950).

We believe that the tax court correctly held on the first issue, the parent-subsidiary issue, that under the principles of Clougherty and Carnation the premiums paid by Humana Inc., the parent to Health Care Indemnity, its wholly owned subsidiary, did not constitute insurance premiums and, therefore, were not deductible. Humana Inc. did not shift the risk to Health Care Indemnity. As the Tenth Circuit stated in Stearns-Roger:

The comparison of the arrangement here made to self-insurance cannot be ignored. The parent provided the necessary funds to the subsidiary by way of what it called "premiums" to meet the casualty losses of the parent. The subsidiary retained these funds until paid back to the parent on losses···· In the case before us we must again consider economic reality. The sums were with the subsidiary for future use and would be included in the Stearns-Roger balance sheet. Again the risk of loss did not leave the parent corporation.

Stearns-Roger, 774 F.2d at 416-17. We believe the tax court also correctly held that if the subject payments made by the wholly owned subsidiaries were not deductible as insurance premiums, they likewise should be considered additions to a reserve for losses and not deductible under the Internal Revenue Code § 162 (1954) as ordinary and necessary business expenses. Stearns-Roger, 774 F.2d at 415; Mobil Oil, 8 Cl.Ct. at 567; Steere Tank Lines, Inc. v. United States, 577 F.2d 279, 280 (5th Cir.1978), cert. denied 440 U.S. 946, 99 S.Ct. 1424, 59 L.Ed.2d 634 (1979); Spring Canyon Coal v. Commissioner, 43 F.2d 78 (10th Cir.1930), cert. denied 284 U.S. 654, 52 S.Ct. 33, 76 L.Ed. 555 (1931). We find no error in fact or law with regard to this first issue.

With regard to the second issue, the brother-sister issue, we believe that the tax court incorrectly extended the rationale of Carnation and Clougherty in holding that the premiums paid by the subsidiaries of Humana Inc. to Health Care Indemnity, as charged to them by Humana Inc., did not constitute valid insurance agreements with the premiums deductible under Internal Revenue Code § 162(a) (1954). We must treat Humana Inc., its subsidiaries and Health Care Indemnity as separate corporate entities under Moline Properties. When considered as separate entities, the first prong of Le Gierse is clearly met. Risk shifting exists between the subsidiaries and the insurance company. There is simply no direct connection in this case between a loss sustained by the insurance company and the affiliates of Humana Inc. as existed between the parent company and the captive insurance company in both Carnation and Clougherty.

In so stating, we adopt the analysis of the Ninth Circuit in Clougherty. It dealt with the parent-subsidiary issue and held that Clougherty could not deduct payments as insurance to Lombardy, its captive insurance company, as there was no risk shifting. Its holding was explained as follows, 811 F.2d at 1305:

In reaching our holding, we do not disturb the legal status of the various corporate entities involved, either by treating them as a single unit or otherwise. Rather, we examine the economic consequences of the captive insurance arrangement to the "insured" party to see if that party has, in fact, shifted the risk. In doing so, we look only to the insured's assets, i.e., those of Clougherty.··· Viewing only Clougherty's assets and considering only the effect of a claim on those assets, it is clear that the risk of loss has not been shifted from Clougherty. (emphasis added).

Because the Ninth Circuit's analysis does "not disturb the separate legal status of the various corporate entities," we adopt the same line of reasoning to decide the brother-sister issue in the case before us. If we look solely to the insured's assets, i.e., those of the various affiliates of Humana Inc., and consider only the effect of a claim on those assets, it is clear that the risk of loss has shifted from the various affiliates to Health Care Indemnity.

The only open question is whether there was risk distribution, the second prong of the test for an insurance contract under Le Gierse. We hold that there was both risk shifting and risk distribution between the subsidiaries and the captive insurance company. The tax court, therefore, erred on this second "brother-sister" issue.

II.

A. Risk Shifting

We recognize, as we must, the separate corporate existence of the affiliates of Humana Inc. and that of Health Care Indemnity. As the Supreme Court stated in Moline Properties, "[S]o long as [its] purpose is the equivalent of business activity or is followed by the carrying on of business by the corporation, the corporation remains a separate taxable entity." Moline Properties, 319 U.S. at 439, 63 S.Ct. at 1134. See Clougherty, 811 F.2d at 1302 (where the Ninth Circuit stated that, "While Moline Properties concerned an attempt by the sole shareholder of a corporation to report on his personal return income attributable to the corporation, the rule it enunciates applies as well to a corporation and its subsidiaries."). See also National Carbide Corporation v. Commissioner, 336 U.S. 422, 429, 69 S.Ct. 726, 730, 93 L.Ed. 779 (1949) (where the Moline Properties doctrine was applied for federal income tax purposes even where a parent corporation controlled its wholly-owned subsidiary). We, therefore, look solely to the relationship between the affiliates and Health Care Indemnity and conclude the facts of this case support a finding of risk shifting as between the affiliates of Humana Inc. and Health Care Indemnity.

Health Care Indemnity met the State of Colorado's statutory minimum requirements for an insurance company, was recognized as an insurance company following an audit and certification by the State of Colorado, and is currently a valid insurance company subject to the strict regulatory control of the Colorado Insurance Department. The State of

Colorado has either approved or established the premium rate for insurance between the Humana affiliates and Health Care Indemnity. As a valid insurance company under Colorado law, Health Care Indemnity's assets cannot be reached by its shareholders except in conformity with the statute. Colorado Rev.Stat. 10-3-503.

Health Care Indemnity was fully capitalized and no agreement ever existed under which the subsidiaries or Humana Inc. would contribute additional capital to Health Care Indemnity. The hospital subsidiaries and Humana Inc. never contributed additional amounts to Health Care Indemnity nor took any steps to insure Health Care Indemnity's performance. It is also undisputed that the policies purchased by the hospital subsidiaries and Humana Inc. were insurance policies as commonly understood in the industry. The hospital subsidiaries and Humana Inc. entered into bona fide arms length contracts with Health Care Indemnity. Health Care Indemnity was formed for legitimate business purposes. Health Care Indemnity and the hospital subsidiaries conduct legitimate businesses and are devoid of sham. No suggestion has been made that the premiums were overstated or understated. Health Care Indemnity did not file its income tax returns on a consolidated basis with Humana Inc. and its subsidiaries. Humana Inc.'s insured subsidiaries own no stock in Health Care Indemnity, nor vice versa.

As noted, supra, the tax court majority cites Mobil Oil in support of its holding on the brother-sister issue. The court in Mobil Oil stated that the imposition of a tax must be based on economic reality and the incidence of taxation depends upon the substance of the transaction and the relationship of the parties. Mobil Oil, 8 Cl.Ct. at 567. The economic reality of insurance between a parent and a captive insurance company is that the captive's stock is shown as an asset on the parent's balance sheet. If the parent suffers an insured loss which the captive has to pay, the assets of the captive will be depleted by the amount of the payment. This will reduce the value of the captive's shares as an asset of the parent. In effect, the assets of the parent bear the true economic impact of the loss. The economic reality, however, of insurance between the Humana subsidiaries and Health Care Indemnity, where the subsidiaries own no stock in the captive and vice versa, is that when a loss occurs and is paid by Health Care Indemnity the net worth of the Humana affiliates is not reduced accordingly. The subsidiaries' balance sheets and net worth are not affected by the payment of an insured claim by Health Care Indemnity. In reality, therefore, when the Humana subsidiaries pay their own premiums under their own insurance contracts, as the facts show, they shift their risk to Health Care Indemnity.

The tax court majority has argued that Stearns-Roger and Mobil extend the rationale of Carnation and Clougherty to cover the brother-sister factual pattern of Humana in favor of denying deductions of payments by the Humana affiliate corporations. The tax court majority stated that "they likewise extend the rationale to the ⋯ brother-sister factual pattern presented in the case." Humana, 88 T.C. at 217.

Neither Carnation nor Clougherty themselves, nor Stearns-Roger nor Mobil Oil provide a basis for denying the deductions in the brother-sister issue. Carnation did not deal with a captive insurance company of a parent corporation insuring separate and distinct wholly owned affiliate corporations of that parent. Carnation dealt solely with the parent-subsidiary issue, not the brother-sister issue. Likewise, Clougherty dealt only with the parent-subsidiary issue and not the brother-sister issue. Nothing in either Carnation or Clougherty lends support for denying the deductibility of the payments in the brother-sister context.

Stearns-Roger and Mobil Oil also do not provide a basis for extending Carnation and Clougherty to cover the brother-sister situation because both clearly rest on the economic family argument that the tax court claimed to reject in Humana. The court in Mobil Oil made no distinctions between the various entities involved-Mobil, its domestic and foreign subsidiaries, and the various captive insurance companies. The court treated them all as one economic unit. The court cited for support cases resting on the economic family argument, looked only to the parent and stated that the "risk of loss remains with the parent," and thus there was no insurance. Mobil Oil, 8 Cl.Ct. at 570.

The Tenth Circuit in Stearns-Roger v. United States, 774 F.2d 414 (1985), rested its holding impliedly if not expressly on the economic family theory. On appeal pursuant to certification under § 1292(b), the Tenth Circuit affirmed the district court's holding, 577 F.Supp. 833, 838 (1984), in which the district court concluded:

Its [Glendale Insurance Company] only business is to insure its parent corporation which wholly owns it and ultimately bears any losses or enjoys any profits it produces. Both profits and losses stay within the Stearns-Roger "economic family." I conclude that since the agreement between Stearns-Roger and Glendale did not shift the risk of losses, it was not an insurance contract for federal tax purposes.[26]

The tax court cannot avoid direct confrontation with the separate corporate existence doctrine of Moline Properties by claiming that its decision does not rest on "economic family" principles because it is merely reclassifying or recharacterizing the transaction as nondeductible additions to a reserve for losses. The tax court argues in its opinion that

---

[26] The Carnation case involved an undercapitalized foreign captive, with a capitalization agreement running to the captive from the parent. Stearns-Roger, although involving an adequately capitalized domestic captive, involved an indemnification agreement running from the parent to the captive. A third case, Beech Aircraft, 797 F.2d 920 (10th Cir.1986), mentioned as support for the majority position, also involved an undercapitalized captive. These weaknesses alone provided a sufficient basis from which to find no risk shifting and to decide the cases in favor of the Commissioner. The Humana case contained no such indemnification agreement and Health Care Indemnity was adequately capitalized.

such "recharacterization" does not disregard the separate corporate status of the entities involved, but merely disregards the particular transactions between the entities in order to take into account substance over form and the "economic reality" of the transaction that no risk has shifted.

The tax court misapplies this substance over form argument. The substance over form or economic reality argument is not a broad legal doctrine designed to distinguish between legitimate and illegitimate transactions and employed at the discretion of the tax court whenever it feels that a taxpayer is taking advantage of the tax laws to produce a favorable result for the taxpayer. Higgins v. Smith, 308 U.S. 473, 476, 60 S.Ct. 355, 357, 84 L.Ed.406 (1940) (where the Court stated, "The Government urges that the principle underlying Gregory v. Helvering finds expression in the rule calling for a realistic approach to tax situations. As so broad and unchallenged a principle furnishes only a general direction, it is of little value in the solution of tax problems."). The substance over form analysis, rather, is a distinct and limited exception to the general rule under Moline Properties that separate entities must be respected as such for tax purposes. The substance over form doctrine applies to disregard the separate corporate entity where "Congress has evinced an intent to the contrary...." Clougherty, 811 F.2d at 1302. As the Court stated in Moline, 319 U.S. at 439, 63 S.Ct. at 1134, "A particular legislative purpose, such as the development of the merchant marine, ... may call for the disregarding of the separate entity, Munson S.S. Line v. Commissioner, 77 F.2d 849 [2nd Cir.1935], as may the necessity of striking down frauds on the tax statute, Continental Oil v. Jones, 113 F.2d 557 [10th Cir.1940]." However, as the Ninth Circuit pointed out in Clougherty, "Congress ... has remained silent with respect to the taxation of captive insurers...." 811 F.2d at 1302. In general, absent specific congressional intent to the contrary, as is the situation in this case, a court cannot disregard a transaction in the name of economic reality and substance over form absent a finding of sham or lack of business purpose under the relevant tax statute. Clougherty, 811 F.2d at 1302; Gregory v. Helvering, 293 U.S. 465, 469, 55 S.Ct. 266, 269, 79 L.Ed. 596 (1935); Higgins v. Smith, 308 U.S. 473, 477, 60 S.Ct. 355, 357, 84 L.Ed. 406 (1940).

In the instant case, the tax court found that Humana had a valid business purpose for incorporating Health Care Indemnity. Congress has manifested no intent to disregard the separate corporate entity in the context of captive insurers. In short, the substance over form or economic reality argument under current legal application does not provide any justification for the tax court to reclassify the insurance premiums paid by the subsidiaries of Humana Inc. as nondeductible additions to a reserve for losses. The test to determine whether a transaction under the Internal Revenue Code § 162(a) (1954) is legitimate or illegitimate is not a vague and broad "economic reality" test. The test is whether there is risk shifting and risk distribution. Only if a transaction fails to meet the above two-pronged test can the court justifiably reclassify the transaction as something other than insurance.

We have both risk shifting and risk distribution involved in the transactions between the Humana subsidiaries and Health Care Indemnity. The transactions between Health Care Indemnity and the separate affiliates of Humana, therefore, are properly within the statutory language of the Internal Revenue Code § 162(a) (1954) as interpreted in Le Gierse. As long as the transactions meet the purposes of the tax statute, Higgins, 308 U.S. at 477, 60 S.Ct. at 357, the substance of the transactions are valid and legitimate regardless of its form and regardless of the tax motivation on the part of the taxpayers involved, Gregory, 293 U.S. at 469, 55 S.Ct. at 267.

We, therefore, find no credence in the distinction between disregarding the particular transactions between the Humana affiliates and Health Care Indemnity and disregarding the separate entities. Absent a fact pattern of sham or lack of business purpose, a court should accept transactions between related though separate corporations as proper and not disregard them because of the relationship between the parties. As the Second Circuit stated in Kraft Foods Company v. Commissioner, 232 F.2d 118, 123-24 (2nd Cir.1956):

> [I]t is one thing to say that transactions between affiliates should be carefully scrutinized and sham transactions disregarded, and quite a different thing to say that a genuine transaction affecting legal relations should be disregarded for tax purposes merely because it is a transaction between affiliated corporations. We think that to strike down a genuine transaction because of a parent's subsidiary relation would violate the scheme of the statute and depart from the rules of law heretofore governing inter-company transactions.

Id. 123-24.

Finally, the tax court argues that if it did not deny the deductions in the brother-sister context, Humana Inc. could avoid the tax court's holding on issue one, the parent-captive issue, that insurance premiums paid by the parent to a captive insurance company are not deductible and accomplish the same purpose through its subsidiaries. Such an argument provides no legal justification for denying the deduction in the brother-sister context. The legal test is whether there has been risk distribution and risk shifting, not whether Humana Inc. is a common parent or whether its affiliates are in a brother-sister relationship to Health Care Indemnity. We do not focus on the relationship of the parties per se or the particular structure of the corporation involved. We look to the assets of the insured. Clougherty, 811 F.2d at 1305. If Humana changes its corporate structure and that change involves risk shifting and risk distribution, and that change is for a legitimate business purpose and is not a sham to avoid the payment of taxes, then it is irrelevant whether the changed corporate structure has the side effect of also permitting Humana Inc.'s affiliates to take advantage of the Internal Revenue Code § 162(a) (1954) and deduct payments to a captive insurance company under the control of the Humana parent as insurance premiums.

The Commissioner argues for us to adopt its economic family approach because this approach recognizes the economic reality of the transaction between Humana affiliates and the captive insurance company, Health Care Indemnity. We do not, however, as the government argues, look to Humana Inc., the parent, to determine whether premiums paid by the affiliates to Health Care Indemnity are deductible. To do so would be to treat Humana Inc., its affiliates and Health Care Indemnity as one "economic unit" and ignore the reality of their separate corporate existence for tax purposes in violation of Moline Properties. Even the tax court explicitly rejected the Commissioner's economic family argument. Humana, 88 T.C. at 230.FN3

Although the tax court in the present case disclaims reliance on the economic family theory, its holding appears ultimately premised on the same type of analysis. In effect the tax court holds that one corporate entity cannot shift risk of loss in an insurance transaction to another corporate entity if they are in the same affiliated group. This approach conflicts with the Moline Properties rule of separate corporate entities. As the eight member concurrence written by Judge Whitaker pointed out:

> However, the majority refers repeatedly with apparent approval to decisions of other courts, including the opinion of the Court of Appeals of the Ninth Circuit affirming our opinion in Carnation, all of which follow Carnation and adopt the economic family concept. The majority also quotes extensively with approval from the testimony of respondent's experts, Dr. Plotkin and Mr. Stewart, who have fully swallowed respondent's economic family concept.... For these reasons, I strongly believe that we should decide the issue solely on a lack of risk shifting and risk distribution basis.

Humana, 88 T.C. 197, 231 (1987) (Whitaker, J., concurring).

It is this argument that we consider more logically sound than the majority. We disagree, however, in the application of the argument and find the existence of risk shifting and risk distribution.

The Commissioner has also argued that even if we do not adopt the economic family argument, we should look through the form of the transaction between the Humana affiliates and Health Care Indemnity to the substance of the transaction and hold that in substance there was no risk shifting. It would appear that this is just another way of stating that transactions between affiliates for tax purposes shall be disregarded if devoid of business purposes or a sham. We have already discussed in detail this exception to Moline Properties, supra. However, if the Commissioner's form over substance or "economic reality" argument is an attempt to broaden the "sham" exception or fashion a new exception, we reject the argument.

B. Risk Distribution

Treating the Humana affiliates and Health Care Indemnity as separate entities and rejecting the economic family argument leads to the conclusion that the first prong of the Le Gierse test for determining "insurance" has been met-there is risk shifting between the Humana affiliates and Health Care Indemnity. However, we must also satisfy the second prong of Le Gierse and find risk distribution. As stated, supra, risk distribution involves shifting to a group of individuals the identified risk of the insured. The focus is broader and looks more to the insurer as to whether the risk insured against can be distributed over a larger group rather than the relationship between the insurer and any single insured. Commissioner of Internal Revenue v. Treganowan, 183 F.2d 288, 291 (2nd Cir.), cert. denied, 340 U.S. 853, 71 S.Ct. 82, 95 L.Ed. 625 (1950). There is little authority adequately discussing what constitutes risk distribution if there is risk shifting. Just recently, the tax court in Gulf Oil v. Commissioner, 89 T.C. 1010, 1035 (1987), noted that insurance must consist of both risk shifting and risk distribution and that the definition of an insurance contract depended on meeting both of the prongs.[27] With this we firmly agree. Risk transfer and risk distribution are two separate and distinct prongs of the test and both must be met to create an insurance contract. An arrangement between a parent corporation and a captive insurance company in which the captive insures only the risks of the parent might not result in risk distribution. Any loss by the parent is not subject to the premiums of any other entity. However, we see no reason why

---

[27]   The tax court noted in Gulf Oil, decided shortly after this Humana case, that if a captive insurance company insured unrelated interests outside the affiliated group of the captive insurance company, then there might be adequate risk transfer created by insuring the risks of independent third parties. The majority held that the addition of 2% of unrelated premiums is de minimis and would not satisfy the majority that the risk was transferred. However, if the premium income from unrelated parties was at least 50%, the majority stated that there would be sufficient risk transfer so that the arrangement would constitute insurance and premiums paid by the parent and affiliates to the captive insurance company would be deductible under the Internal Revenue Code § 162(a) (1954). It is unclear in the language employed by the tax court majority in Gulf Oil whether the appearance of unrelated third-party premiums constitutes risk shifting or risk distribution. The tax court majority refers to the appearance of unrelated third-parties as sufficient to constitute "risk transfer." If the appearance of unrelated third-parties creates "risk transfer" and by this the tax court means both risk shifting and risk distribution, the tax court majority ignores the fact that risk shifting and risk distribution are two separate and distinct prongs. The tax court majority cannot collapse the two prong test into one and claim that the appearance of unrelated third-parties creates enough risk transfer. Such is not the law. If the presence of unrelated third-parties goes to the question of risk distribution, then the tax court majority should never have reached that issue as its prior opinions, especially its opinion in Humana, stated that there can be no risk shifting as between a captive insurance company and a parent and its affiliated corporations where both are owned by a common parent, as was the situation in Gulf Oil. Thus the tax court has created its own conflict between its holding in Humana and its holding in Gulf.

there would not be risk distribution in the instant case where the captive insures several separate corporations within an affiliated group and losses can be spread among the several distinct corporate entities.

III.

In conclusion, we affirm the tax court on issue one, the parent-subsidiary issue. The contracts between Humana, Inc., the parent, and Health Care Indemnity, the wholly owned captive insurance company, are not insurance contracts and the premiums are not deductible under the Internal Revenue Code § 162(a) (1954). We reverse the tax court on issue two, the brother-sister issue. The contracts between the affiliates of Humana Inc. and Health Care Indemnity are in substance insurance contracts and the premiums are deductible. Under Moline Properties, we must recognize the affiliates as separate and distinct corporations from Humana Inc., the parent company, and, as such, they shifted their risk to Health Care Indemnity. Furthermore, we find there was risk distribution on the part of Health Care Indemnity given the number of separate though related corporations insured by Health Care Indemnity. Under no circumstances do we adopt the economic family argument advanced by the government.

Thus the Tax Court is affirmed on Issue One, Reversed on Issue Two and the case remanded for recomputation of the tax due.

Appendix M

Gulf Oil Corp. v. C.I.R.

914 F.2d 396 (3rd Cir. 1990).

United States Court of Appeals, Third Circuit.

GULF OIL CORPORATION, Appellant in No. 89-2049

v.

COMMISSIONER OF INTERNAL REVENUE.

COMMISSIONER OF INTERNAL REVENUE, Appellant in No. 89-2050

v.

GULF OIL CORPORATION.

[Names of counsel omitted]

Before SLOVITER and MANSMANN, Circuit Judges, and THOMPSON, District Judge.*

OPINION OF THE COURT

MANSMANN, Circuit Judge.

---

* Honorable Anne E. Thompson of the United States District Court for the District of New Jersey, sitting by designation.

Gulf Oil Corporation and the Commissioner of Internal Revenue cross-appeal several decisions of the U.S. Tax Court involving Gulf's corporate tax liability for tax years 1974 and 1975.

Gulf, both directly and through its foreign subsidiaries and affiliates, explores, develops, produces, purchases and transports crude oil and natural gas world-wide, and manufactures, transports and markets petroleum products. Gulf is an accrual method taxpayer using the calendar year as its tax year. During 1974 and 1975, Gulf was a Pennsylvania corporation with its principal office in Pittsburgh,[1] filing federal corporate income tax returns with the Internal Revenue Service in Philadelphia, Pennsylvania. During 1974 and 1975, Gulf and certain of its subsidiaries constituted an "affiliated group" as that term is defined in I.R.C. § 1504.[2] As the common parent, Gulf timely filed consolidated federal income tax returns for these tax years on behalf of itself and certain of its subsidiaries. We refer to this affiliated group variously as "Gulf" or as "the taxpayer."

The Commissioner determined federal income tax deficiencies of $80,813,428 and $166,316,320 for Gulf's tax years 1974 and 1975, respectively. Gulf challenged these deficiencies in the U.S. Tax Court, alleging numerous erroneous rulings by the Commissioner. Due to their complex and diverse nature, certain issues were severed and tried at a special trial session, resulting in seven Tax Court opinions, four of which are involved in this appeal.

The first issue, referred to by the parties as the "Worthless Properties" issue, involves the question of whether Gulf could take abandonment loss deductions pursuant to I.R.C. § 165 on geological strata which were found to be devoid of mineral deposits and, hence, were deemed worthless by the taxpayer, even though the entire lease was not abandoned. Gulf appeals from the Tax Court's determination that there was no abandonment.

The second dispute, referred to as the "Kuwait Nationalization" issue, presents several questions, the foremost of which is whether the value of the price discount under a five year crude oil supply agreement is ordinary income to the taxpayer or whether it was compensation by Kuwait for its nationalization of the taxpayer's interests and, hence, a capital gain. Gulf appeals from the Tax Court's determination that the price discount was not compensation for nationalization. The Commissioner appeals from the Tax Court's determination that the taxpayer could accrue and deduct, in tax year 1975, Kuwait income taxes related to the prospective five year crude oil supply agreement.

---

[1]   Gulf Oil Corporation is now known as Chevron U.S.A. Inc.

[2]   Except as noted, all statutory references are to the Internal Revenue Code of 1954 (26 U.S.C.) as amended and in effect during tax years 1974 and 1975.

The third problem, referred to as the "Captive Insurance" issue, presents cross-appeals by Gulf and by the Commissioner concerning the Tax Court's determination that the premiums paid by the taxpayer to its subsidiary insurance company were not deductible expenses and that the payments on losses by the subsidiary insurance company to other subsidiaries owned by Gulf were not constructive dividends to the parent corporation.

Finally, in the section referred to as the "Iran Agreement," upon the Commissioner's appeal, we must determine whether the Tax Court erred by concluding that Gulf possessed an economic interest in minerals in place pursuant to a 1973 Agreement. The Tax Court determined that the taxpayer possessed an economic interest and, therefore, was permitted to take a depletion allowance deduction for tax year 1974 and was further permitted to have a foreign tax credit for taxes paid to Iran.

We will address these issues seriatim, keeping in mind our scope of review. We exercise plenary review of the Tax Court's construction and application of the Internal Revenue Code. Pleasant Summit Land Corp. v. Comm'r, 863 F.2d 263, 268 (3d Cir.1988). With respect to disputes of fact, we may reverse the Tax Court's decision only if the findings are clearly erroneous. A finding is clearly erroneous when "there is evidence to support it, [but] the reviewing court on the entire evidence is left with the definite and firm conviction that a mistake has been committed." Anderson v. City of Bessemer City, N.C., 470 U.S. 564, 573, 105 S.Ct. 1504, 1511, 84 L.Ed.2d 518 (1985); Double H Plastics, Inc. v. Sonoco Prods. Co., 732 F.2d 351, 354 (3d Cir.1984). We are quite aware that we cannot reverse findings of fact simply because we would have decided the case differently. Anderson v. Bessemer City, 470 U.S. at 573, 105 S.Ct. at 1511. Our jurisdiction rests on 26 U.S.C. § 7482(a): United States Courts of Appeals have exclusive jurisdiction to review Tax Court decisions.

Under the appropriate standard of review for each issue, we are affirming in part and reversing in part the decisions of the U.S. Tax Court. Our reversing in part requires recomputation of Gulf's tax liability for these tax years. Thus, we will remand for a recomputation of Gulf Oil Corporation's 1974 and 1975 tax liability consistent with this opinion.

I. WORTHLESS PROPERTIES

[Discussion omitted. The court held that the taxpayer could not take abandonment loss deductions on certain offshore leases.]

II. KUWAIT NATIONALIZATION

[Discussion omitted. The court held that the value of price discount received by taxpayer under crude oil supply agreement with foreign government was taxable as ordinary income rather than capital gain.]

III. CAPTIVE INSURANCE

Both parties appeal from the Tax Court's decisions involving payments of insurance premiums by Gulf and its domestic affiliates to Gulf's wholly-owned foreign subsidiary, Insco, in tax years 1974 and 1975. Gulf deducted these insurance premiums as § 162 ordinary and necessary business expenses, but the Commissioner disallowed these deductions and instead determined that both premium payments from Gulf's foreign affiliates and claims paid by Insco to Gulf and its domestic affiliates represented constructive dividends to Gulf. The Tax Court-in a majority opinion and numerous concurring opinions-found that the insurance premiums paid by Gulf and its domestic affiliates that were ceded to Insco were not deductible insurance premiums. The court also held that neither the portions of the insurance premiums paid by Gulf's foreign affiliates that were ceded to Insco nor claims paid by Insco relative to the reinsurance of the risks of Gulf and its domestic affiliates were constructive dividends to Gulf. We will affirm on both issues.

A. Facts

The parties generally stipulated to the operative facts on the issues before the Tax Court, which the court set forth at length in its opinion of Gulf Oil Corp. v. Comm'r, 89 T.C. 1010 (1987). We repeat only those most important to our resolution.

Through the late 1960's, Gulf and its affiliates were able to obtain insurance coverage at acceptable rates from commercial insurers. The general policy of Gulf and its affiliates was to self-insure risks up to $1 million. For those risks in excess of $1 million, including catastrophic risks, i.e., risks in excess of $10 million, Gulf obtained insurance coverage from primary insurance carriers and reinsurers in both the United States and world-wide markets.

Several incidents occurred in the late 1960's[3] which caused commercial insurance carriers to increase the rates charged to the oil industry and either limit or altogether eliminate coverage for certain types of risks. Gulf decided that the higher rates for the coverages made available to it did not adequately reflect its claims history. Therefore, in late 1970, Gulf participated with several other major independent oil companies in the creation of Oil Insurance Ltd. (OIL).[4] Gulf also created Insco, Ltd., its own subsidiary insurance company authorized to conduct general insurance business under the laws of

---

[3]   These incidents included a refinery explosion in Louisiana and an oil spill off Santa Barbara, California.

[4]   OIL was formed as a petroleum industry mutual insurance company in 1971 for the purpose of providing catastrophic risk insurance coverage for its member-shareholders.

Bermuda.[5] Initial capitalization for Insco was authorized at $10 million. However, Insco originally issued 1,000 shares valued at $1,000 per share, of which only 12% was paid. Marsh & McLennan, Incorporated, an insurance brokerage and consulting firm, agreed to provide Insco with all underwriting and related services.

Generally, Gulf and its affiliates entered into insurance contracts with and paid premiums to third-party commercial carriers. Although Gulf and its affiliates paid premiums directly to third-party commercial carriers, a significant portion of the primary carrier's exposure was reinsured with Insco.[6] On December 20, 1973, Gulf executed guarantees in favor of American International Group, Inc. (AIG)[7] and of Oil Industry Association that obligated Gulf to indemnify these insurers should Insco be unable to meet its In 1975, Gulf shifted ownership of Insco to Transocean Gulf Oil Co., a wholly owned Gulf holding company incorporated in Delaware. Insco collected its shares of non-paid-up stock, while Transocean contributed $880,000 in capital. Simultaneously, Insco distributed 9,000 new shares at $1,000 par, which Transocean purchased as fully paid. This increased Insco's paid-in capital to $10 million. Gulf and its affiliates then began to place catastrophic risk coverage directly with Insco which, in turn, reinsured those risks. Gulf also commenced withdrawal from OIL over the minimum five-year period required. Also in 1975, Insco first began insuring risks of unrelated parties. Over subsequent years, Insco increased underwriting risks for unrelated parties and continued to underwrite additional risks of Gulf and its affiliates.

In tax years 1974 and 1975, Gulf reported ordinary and necessary business expense deductions pursuant to I.R.C. § 162 for insurance premiums, which the Commissioner challenged. The Commissioner disallowed $10,285,330 and $10,900,081, respectively, representing the amounts of insurance premium payments made by Gulf and its domestic affiliates to primary insurers that the insurers subsequently ceded to Insco. In addition, the Commissioner recharacterized, as constructive dividends, the amounts of insurance premium payments ($4,029,646 and $4,662,192, respectively) made by Gulf's foreign affiliates that were subsequently ceded to Insco. Finally, the Commissioner treated claims paid by Insco in these tax years ($1,001,441 and $3,059,194, respectively), relative to the reinsurance of the risks of Gulf and its domestic affiliates, as constructive dividends

---

5   Insco was incorporated on November 3, 1971. Gulf's management agreed that Insco would initially insure only certain foreign risks of domestic subsidiaries. Later, Insco was to provide further insurance, including coverage for Gulf's marine fleet and United States situs risks. Gulf contemplated that Insco would eventually offer insurance coverage to unrelated third parties.

6   Insco's assumed risks were limited to $10 million, but did not include the first $1 million of loss, which Gulf and its affiliates self-insured. Insco ceded the portion of the premiums it received attributable to catastrophic risks either to third-party reinsurers or to OIL.

7   Primary insurers for a substantial amount of the risks reinsured with Insco.

directly to Gulf or to Gulf through Transocean. However, the Commissioner also determined that Gulf and its domestic affiliates sustained deductible uninsured losses under I.R.C. § 165 for the same amounts, $1,001,441 and $3,059,194, respectively.

The Tax Court held that the portions of the insurance premiums paid by Gulf and its domestic affiliates that were ceded to Insco were not deductible insurance premiums. Gulf appeals, claiming the Tax Court committed legal error because the court allegedly based the decision on a "substance over form" analysis that ignores the separate existence of Gulf and its affiliates, including Insco.

The Tax Court rejected the Commissioner's position and found that insurance premiums paid by the foreign affiliates could not be considered constructive dividends under the test in Sammons v. Comm'r, 472 F.2d 449 (5th Cir.1972), since those payments were for the affiliates' benefit, i.e., providing risk coverage, rather than for a shareholder purpose. In addition, the claims paid by Insco to Gulf and its domestic affiliates were not constructive dividends since the claims were paid in consideration for the premiums paid.

The Commissioner appeals, contending that, under Helvering v. Le Gierse, 312 U.S. 531, 61 S.Ct. 646, 85 L.Ed. 996 (1941), the transaction at issue does not constitute "insurance" for federal tax purposes and must be considered as constructive dividends to Gulf.

B. Deductibility of Insurance Premiums Paid to Insurance Subsidiary

Under I.R.C. § 162(a), insurance premiums are deductible as ordinary and necessary business expenses. The premium is the means by which two unrelated parties measure the cost of the risk-shifting. Whereas insurance premiums are deductible expenses, amounts entered into self-insurance funds are not. Clougherty Packing Co. v. Comm'r, 811 F.2d 1297, 1300 (9th Cir.1987). As the Supreme Court stated in Le Gierse, both "[h]istorically and commonly insurance involves risk-shifting and risk-distributing." Le Gierse, 312 U.S. at 539, 61 S.Ct. at 649. Thus, to be permitted to take an insurance deduction, the relationship between the parties must actually result in a shift of risk. Id. at 540-41, 61 S.Ct. at 649-50.

Gulf asserts that it meets this standard because it created a separate legal identity in Insco for risk shifting and, in fact, Insco insured the risks of unrelated parties, evidence of risk distributing. (In tax year 1975, 2 percent of Insco's premium income came from unrelated parties.)

The threshold question we must address is whether Insco's insurance coverage to Gulf and its affiliates satisfies both the element of risk transfer and that of risk distribution, regardless of whether Insco insured risks of unrelated parties, if Gulf and its affiliates, both domestic and foreign, are each viewed as separate entities. "Where separate agreements are interdependent, they must be considered together so that their overall economic effect can be assessed." Clougherty Packing Co., 811 F.2d at 1301.

In Moline Properties v. Comm'r, 319 U.S. 436, 439, 63 S.Ct. 1132, 1134, 87 L.Ed. 1499 (1943), the Court held that a corporation must be recognized as a separate taxable entity if that corporation's purpose is the equivalent of a business activity or is followed by the carrying on of a business. The Court of Appeals for the Sixth Circuit relied on this proposition in Humana Inc. v. Comm'r, 881 F.2d 247, 252 (6th Cir.1989), when it held that fellow subsidiaries of a captive insurer, i.e. in a brother-sister relationship, could properly deduct insurance premium payments to that insurer.

In Humana, the Tax Court expressly recognized the legal, financial and economic substance of insurance provided by a wholly owned insurance subsidiary to its brother-sister affiliates. Humana Inc. v. Comm'r, 88 T.C. 197 (1987). Nonetheless, on appeal, the court of appeals suggested that a parent's insured loss paid by the insurance subsidiary would have a dollar-for-dollar impact on the parent's net worth. Although many of the facts in Humana are similar to those in this case, critical distinguishing facts exist. In contrast to the facts here, (1) the captive insurer in Humana was fully capitalized initially; (2) no agreement ever existed under which Humana, Inc. or any Humana subsidiary would contribute additional capital to the insurer; and (3) Humana, Inc. and the hospital subsidiaries never contributed additional amounts to the insurer nor took any steps to insure the insurer's performance. In contrast, Insco began as an undercapitalized subsidiary and Gulf executed guarantees in effect during the tax years at issue to protect its primary insurers, AIG and OIA, should Insco fail to meet its obligations as reinsurer. It is thus difficult to see that Gulf truly transferred the risk to Insco during the years in question.

We conclude that the Tax Court did not err in finding that the risk was not here appropriately shifted to the insurance subsidiary during 1974 and 1975. Gulf's arguments that it actually paid premiums to Insco, that Insco was required to establish and maintain appropriate reserves and to satisfy other regulatory requirements imposed by Bermuda law, that each insured had rights against Insco under insurance contracts, and that the source for payment of their claims included premiums paid by others and Insco's capital, do not address the crucial question of whether there was transfer of financial risk. Le Gierse, 312 U.S. at 540, 61 S.Ct. at 649, Clougherty Packing Co., 811 F.2d at 1300.

Our decision is consistent with previous opinions of the Tax Court. The Tax Court has held that payments to a captive subsidiary, designated as premiums, whether from the parent corporation or from other subsidiaries, did not represent payments for insurance. See Carnation Co. v. Comm'r, 71 T.C. 400 (1978), aff'd, 640 F.2d 1010 (9th Cir.1981);

Clougherty Packing Co., 84 T.C. 948 (1985); Humana v. Comm'r, 88 T.C. 197 (1987), aff'd in part, rev'd in part, 881 F.2d 247 (6th Cir.1989) (disallowing insurance premium deductions on the parent-subsidiary relationship, allowing brother-sister subsidiary to deduct the insurance premiums). Thus, the Tax Court has plainly held that where the captive was wholly owned by its parent, and the captive insured risks only within the affiliated group, the risk is not truly distributed.

We recognize that with regard to the tax year 1975, the majority of the Tax Court held that the 2% net premiums from unrelated parties was de minimis and did not demonstrate the existence of a true transfer of risk. One concurring judge of the Tax Court warns that the court's opinion will create a problem because at some point the majority's analysis will require a line to be drawn as to when third party premiums are no longer de minimis. He argued that, as far as risk transfer is concerned, there can be no true risk transfer when a captive insurance company is involved. In response, another concurring judge rejected that analysis as not invoking insurance law principles but relying, rather, on economic theory. The lone dissenter would have adopted the concurring "economic" theory, but disagreed with the majority's "overreaching" opinion.

We need not reach the issue which divided the judges of the Tax Court-whether the addition of unrelated insurance premiums into the insurance pool for tax year 1975 establishes risk transfer and justifies the deduction of insurance premiums paid by the unrelated party to the insurance pool. It is clear to us that, because of the guarantee to the primary insurers, Gulf and Insco did not truly transfer the risk, nor was there a de facto risk distribution to third parties, elements crucial to the allowance of a premium deduction.

C. Constructive Dividends

We turn now to the insurance premiums paid by Gulf's foreign affiliates to Insco and to the claims paid by Insco to Gulf and its domestic affiliates, which the Commissioner argues constitute constructive dividends to Gulf. His theory is that "where funds are transferred from one such sibling corporation to another, ⋯ the funds pass from the transferor to the common stockholder as a dividend and then to the transferee as a capital contribution." Sammons, 472 F.2d at 453.

In Sammons, the Court of Appeals for the Fifth Circuit formulated a two-part test to determine whether a transfer of property from one corporation to another corporation constitutes a constructive dividend to a common shareholder in both corporations. The first prong of the test is objective and requires a determination that there was a distribution of funds.

A transfer of funds by a corporation to another corporation which the former owns directly or indirectly can be a constructive dividend to the individual controlling stockholder only if (1) the funds are diverted from the parent-subsidiary corporate structure and come within the control of the stockholder, and (2) no adequate consideration for the diversion passes from the stockholder to the corporation, i.e., there must be a net distribution.

Sammons, 472 F.2d at 453-54. The second prong of the Sammons test is a subjective determination. Thus, a constructive dividend will be found where, in addition to the determination of distribution, "the business justifications [for the transfer] put forward are not of sufficient substance to disturb a conclusion that the distribution was primarily for shareholder benefit." Sammons, 472 F.2d at 452 (emphasis in original).

The Tax Court found that the second prong was not met since the insurance premium payments in question were for the benefit of the affiliates, i.e., the affiliates were provided risk coverage. In other words, there was an adequate business reason for the payment of funds, here risk insurance, by the affiliates to Insco. The benefit to Gulf was tangential, the same "benefit" it would have received if an outside third-party insurer were to insure the losses of Gulf's affiliates.

The Commissioner provides no strong reason, support or authority to compel us to overturn either the Tax Court's factual determination of an adequate business reason for the transfer or the legal conclusion that the payments in question do not constitute constructive dividends to Gulf.

D. Conclusion

The Tax Court did not err in denying a § 162 business expense deduction for insurance premiums paid to Gulf's captive insurance subsidiary (Insco) by Gulf and its domestic affiliates or in refusing to categorize the insurance premiums paid by Gulf's foreign affiliates to Insco and claims paid by Insco to Gulf's domestic affiliates as constructive dividends.

We will thus affirm the Tax Court's decision on these cross-appeals.

IV. IRAN AGREEMENT

[Discussion omitted. The court held that the taxpayer possessed economic interest in minerals in place pursuant to sale and purchase agreement with foreign government.]

V. CONCLUSION

Gulf Oil Corporation has filed a motion for a remand for recomputation under Rule 55 to calculate the 1977 and 1978 net operating loss carryback for Gulf's tax years 1974 and 1975. As a result of our decisions in these appeals, a remand is necessitated for both tax years. Therefore, the matters raised in the motion can properly be presented to the Tax Court on remand.

We will remand these appeals to the Tax Court for recalculation consistent with this opinion.

Appendix N

AMERCO, Inc. v. C.I.R.

979 F.2d 162 (9th Cir. 1992)

UNITED STATES COURT OF APPEALS, NINTH CIRCUIT.

AMERCO, INC.; Republic Insurance, Petitioners-Appellees,

v.

COMMISSIONER INTERNAL REVENUE SERVICE, Respondent-Appellant.

[Names of counsel omitted.]

Appeal from a Decision of the United States Tax Court.

Before POOLE, FERNANDEZ, and G. NELSON, Circuit Judges.

FERNANDEZ, Circuit Judge:

AMERCO and a number of its subsidiaries (AMERCO Group) purchased insurance policies from Republic Western Insurance Company (Republic) and deducted the premiums for income tax purposes. Republic was a subsidiary of AMERCO. The Commissioner of Internal Revenue (Commissioner) determined that because of the relationships among the parties the transactions did not constitute insurance. A notice of deficiency was issued by the Commissioner, and AMERCO petitioned the Tax Court for a redetermination. The Tax Court found that the transactions were insurance.[1] It, therefore, held against the Commissioner, who now appeals. We affirm.

---

[1]   AMERCO & Subsidiaries v. Commissioner, 96 T.C. 18 (1991).

BACKGROUND

The AMERCO Group constitutes the U-Haul system. AMERCO itself is a holding company which owns the stock of a number of subsidiaries. Among those subsidiaries are U-Haul International, Inc., the administrative clearing house, AMERCO Lease Co., which owns much of the U-Haul rental equipment, and numerous other rental companies, repair shops, manufacturing companies and service companies. Approximately 250 of these joined in AMERCO's consolidated returns for the tax years in question-1979-85.

Republic was incorporated in 1973. It is a third tier wholly owned subsidiary of AMERCO. It is a property and casualty insurance company, licensed in most states and the District of Columbia. Republic issued insurance policies to members of the AMERCO Group and to unrelated parties. Those policies were issued at normal commercial rates and were divided into a number of categories by the Tax Court. They included: (1) corporate policies issued to members of the AMERCO Group; (2) workers' compensation policies issued to members of the AMERCO Group; (3) U-Haul rental system policies, which covered members of the AMERCO Group, independent fleet owners, and truck rental customers; (4) SafeMove and SafeStor policies, which covered U-Haul rental customers; and (5) policies which covered risks entirely unconnected with the U-Haul system.

The Tax Court found that based upon gross premiums insurance written for the AMERCO Group itself, related business, was from 26 percent to 48 percent of Republic's total insurance business. Insurance written for others, unrelated business, constituted the remaining 74 percent to 52 percent.

The Commissioner took the position that the transactions between the AMERCO Group and Republic could not be insurance because Republic is a wholly owned subsidiary of AMERCO and is, therefore, a member of the same economic family as the AMERCO Group. As a result, the Commissioner contended, there could be no risk-shifting or risk-distributing and, absent those, insurance could not exist. The Commissioner takes the same position before us.

JURISDICTION AND STANDARD OF REVIEW

The Tax Court had jurisdiction pursuant to 26 U.S.C. § 6213. We have jurisdiction pursuant to 26 U.S.C. § 7482.

Whether the transactions constitute insurance is a question of law subject to de novo review. Clougherty Packing Co. v. Commissioner, 811 F.2d 1297, 1299 (9th Cir.1987) (based upon stipulated facts it is a question of law whether payments to a captive insurer constitute deductible insurance premiums). Whether certain insurance policies issued by Republic are related or unrelated business is a question of fact reviewed for clear error. See Pomarantz v. Commissioner, 867 F.2d 495, 497 (9th Cir.1988). Although a presumption exists that the Tax Court correctly applied the law, no special deference is given to Tax Court decisions. Clougherty, 811 F.2d at 1299.

DISCUSSION

It is common ground that insurance premiums constitute ordinary and necessary business expenses which can be deducted in arriving at taxable income. See 26 U.S.C. § 162; Treas.Reg. § 1.162-1(a) (as amended in 1988). On the other hand, amounts placed by a company into a self insurance reserve fund cannot be deducted; any deductions must await an actual payment out of that reserve. See Clougherty, 811 F.2d at 1300.

The question before us is an intermediate one: Can insurance premiums paid to a wholly owned subsidiary be deducted or are they more like amounts paid into a self insurance reserve? In order to answer that question it is necessary to determine the nature of insurance, and, more particularly, its nature for income tax purposes. Then, we must see if transactions between members of a corporate family and a subsidiary insurance company can meet that definition.

A. Definition of Insurance.

In setting forth definitions of insurance, we do not start afresh. Rather, we look to a line of cases starting with Helvering v. Le Gierse, 312 U.S. 531, 61 S.Ct. 646, 85 L.Ed. 996 (1941). In Le Gierse, an estate tax case, the Supreme Court described insurance as follows:

> We think the fair import of subsection (g) [the estate tax section] is that the amounts must be received as the result of a transaction which involved an actual "insurance risk" at the time the transaction was executed. Historically and commonly insurance involves risk-shifting and risk-distributing. That life insurance is desirable from an economic and social standpoint as a device to shift and distribute risk of loss from premature death is unquestionable. That these elements of risk-shifting and risk-distributing are essential to a life insurance contract is agreed by courts and commentators.

312 U.S. at 539, 61 S.Ct. at 649.

We have often referred to this definition, with particular emphasis on the risk-shifting and risk-distributing aspect. See Clougherty, 811 F.2d at 1301; Carnation Co. v. Commissioner, 640 F.2d 1010, 1012 (9th Cir.), cert. denied, 454 U.S. 965, 102 S.Ct.

506, 70 L.Ed.2d 381 (1981). In this case, the Tax Court identified three principles at the heart of the Le Gierse definition: "(1) [t]hat an insurance transaction must involve 'insurance risk;' (2) that insurance involves risk-shifting and risk-distributing; and (3) that, in the absence of a statutory definition, 'insurance' is to be defined in its commonly accepted sense." 96 T.C. at 38. It supplemented these with the reflection that "matters of Federal income taxation must be resolved with principles of Federal income taxation borne in mind." Id. We agree with this formulation, which supplements what we have said before. While the Tax Court avoided calling this a definition, we do not think that the three articulated principles places it at odds with our prior cases. Rather, they underscore the fact that many considerations can come into play when one attempts to decide whether a deduction of a purported insurance premium will be allowed.

Here, as in other cases, the focus is on risk-shifting and risk-distributing, but that does not mean that additional factors could not be important at times. Here, as the Tax Court determined, there was an insurance risk involved-the AMERCO Group undoubtedly faced potential hazards from its operations which constituted insurable risks. By the same token, there could be no real doubt that Republic was engaged in the insurance business in the commonly accepted sense. The Commissioner does not contest those determinations. Thus, we must turn to an analysis of risk-shifting and risk-distributing.

B. Risk-Shifting and Risk-Distributing.

Courts have not spilled a great deal of ink in defining risk-shifting as opposed to risk-distributing. That is probably because in most instances the facts which demonstrated that one did not exist also demonstrated that the other did not. See Carnation, 640 F.2d at 1013. Nevertheless, it is fair to say that "'[r]isk-shifting' means one party shifts his risk of loss to another, and 'risk-distributing' means that the party assuming the risk distributes his potential liability, in part, among others. An arrangement without the elements of risk-shifting and risk-distributing lacks the fundamentals inherent in a true contract of insurance." Beech Aircraft Corp. v. United States, 797 F.2d 920, 922 (10th Cir.1986); see also Robert E. Keeton and Alan I. Widiss, Insurance Law § 1.3(b)(2) (1988).

(1) Risk-Shifting.

In the germinal case of Le Gierse, the Court described a classic situation where no risk-shifting could take place. There the 80-year-old insured purchased both an insurance policy on her life and an annuity. The premiums were fixed in a way that assured she would retain all of the risk of her own untimely death. The insurance company assumed none of the risk attendant upon that event, and the only result of the combined transactions would have been to remove assets from her taxable estate. Not surprisingly, the Court found that no insurance existed, even though the company itself was, no doubt, an insurance company which had written an insurance policy. In effect, there was no risk-shifting, and, for that matter, no risk-distributing.

We confront the same sort of problem when a parent purchases insurance from its wholly owned subsidiary, and that subsidiary is a captive insurance company. By "captive insurance company" we mean one which is organized for the purpose of insuring the liabilities of the parent and its affiliates. See Clougherty, 811 F.2d at 1298 n. 1.

Since at least 1977 the Commissioner has taken the position that where the only insurance written by a captive insurance company is for the parent and its affiliates, there is no risk-shifting and hence no insurance. See Rev.Rul. 77-316, 1977-2 C.B. 53. The reason is, the Commissioner says, that they represent one economic family unit so that the risk of loss is still borne by that unit no matter what happens. That approach is not entirely without merit. Nevertheless, it presents a difficulty with the general tax law principle of treating subsidiary corporations as if they were truly separate entities. See Moline Properties, Inc. v. Commissioner, 319 U.S. 436, 439, 63 S.Ct. 1132, 1134, 87 L.Ed. 1499 (1943). We have discussed that difficulty previously. Clougherty, 811 F.2d at 1302-05. While in Clougherty we pointed out that looking to the realities of a transaction between corporations and their subsidiaries does not necessarily run afoul of Moline, we also found it unnecessary to accept the economic family concept for the purpose of deciding the case then before us. Id. at 1305. The reason we did not need to accept the economic family theory is also the reason that we and other courts have hitherto refused to allow the deduction of premiums paid to captive insurance companies. In those cases, not unlike Le Gierse, in economic reality the transaction was not insurance.

In Clougherty itself, for example, the parent set up and capitalized the captive insurance company. The parent then purchased insurance from an unrelated company which immediately reinsured most of the loss with the captive. We agreed that deduction of the portion of the premium ceded to the captive should be disallowed. 811 F.2d at 1307.

In our earlier decision in Carnation we were faced with the same kind of situation. There, too, the parent, Carnation Corporation, created a captive insurance company. There, too, the parent insured with an unrelated entity which, in turn, reinsured most of the risk with the captive. There, too, we disallowed the premium payment. 640 F.2d at 1013.

In both Clougherty and Carnation we determined that there had been no shifting of the risk from the parent to the captive. As a matter of economic reality every dollar paid out by the captive was a dollar out of the parent's pocket from whence it came in the first place. In fact, the arrangement was little different from a reserve fund held by the parent itself; only corporate formalities distinguished it. Those were not enough. We could as easily have said that there was no risk-distributing either because the only risks involved were those of the parent. In Carnation we did say just that. 640 F.2d at 1013.

Cases from other circuits have reached the same conclusion when faced with this simple captive problem and for much the same reasons. For example, in Stearns-Roger Corp. v. United States, 774 F.2d 414 (10th Cir.1985), the parent created a captive which was wholly owned by it and one of its subsidiaries. The parent capitalized the captive and the captive only wrote insurance for the parent. The court found no risk-shifting. In reality, the parent was self-insured. Id. at 416. Similarly, in Beech Aircraft the captive insurance company wrote insurance almost exclusively for the parent-.5 percent was written for others. 797 F.2d at 921-22. The court found that for practical purposes Beech paid its own claims. Id. at 922; see also Mobil Oil Corp. v. United States, 8 Cl.Ct. 555, 561, 567-68 (1985) (parent's premium deduction disallowed although some portion of captive's premium came from others); cf. Humana Inc. v. Commissioner, 881 F.2d 247, 257 (6th Cir.1989) (parent's insurance premium could not be deducted but those of brother-sister corporations could be).

Thus, although many cases, including ours, have disallowed premium deductions in captive insurance company situations, none have found it necessary to rely upon the Commissioner's economic family theory. When courts have been required to consider it, they have noted its difficulties and have not followed it. See Sears Roebuck & Co. v. Commissioner, 972 F.2d 858, 861 (7th Cir.1992); Ocean Drilling & Exploration Co. v. United States, 24 Cl.Ct. 714, 729 (1991); AMERCO, 96 T.C. at 41 and cases cited. We see no reason to follow it now.

That, however, leaves the question of what distinguishes this case from those which have come before. Of course, the major distinction is that Republic does a substantial unrelated insurance business. The Tax Court found that made all the difference in the world. The Commissioner contends that it really makes none at all. We agree with the Tax Court.

In Rev.Rul. 88-72, 1988-2 C.B. 31, 32, the Commissioner essentially took the position that the mere fact that outside insurance business was done by a captive could have no effect on risk-shifting from the parent or its subsidiaries to the captive. That was based, in part, on the Commissioner's economic family theory. It was also based on the Commissioner's view of the nature of insurance.

The Tax Court has determined that when a parent purchases a policy from a captive which has a larger pool of risks from others, the parent has, indeed, shifted its risk to the captive insurer. Of course, the Commissioner is not wholly wrong, for it is undoubtedly true that a decrease in the value of the captive can result in a decrease in the value of what the parent holds-the captive's stock. But that is too narrow a focus because there is much more in the insurer's pool than the parent's premium dollars. To put it another way, as the Tax Court noted in a related case, "risk transfer and risk distribution are two sides of the same coin which as an integrated whole constitute 'insurance.'" Harper Group v. Commissioner, 96 T.C. 45, 59 (1991). That is to say, when the pool consists of a substantial amount of dollars, and risk, from those outside the parent and its affiliates, there is a true shift of the risk, even though the parent could suffer somewhat if the captive made a payment on account of an insured's loss. In a real sense, the parent's risk has been placed with the captive and thence spread among all of those in the pool.

The Commissioner claims that this improperly collapses the ideas of risk-shifting and risk-distributing. What the Commissioner does not recognize, however, is the fact that the pool itself would not exist were it not for those who have purchased policies from the insurer. The existence of that pool enables every insured to have its risk spread among all of the participants. The parent's situation is no different.

Indeed, it would be more accurate to say that the Commissioner appears to conflate actual insurance risk and speculative risk. The insurance risk is the possibility that a particular event for which an insured will be held liable will occur. Of course, from the standpoint of the insured there can be no profit from that risk. The only possible outcomes are loss or no loss. It is that risk which must be transferred to the insurer if true insurance is to be involved.

Speculative risk, on the other hand, is merely investment risk, and it can produce profit or loss. An insurance company, for example, may earn or lose money based upon the outcome of its investment, underwriting, adjusting, and management activities. When it does, the value of its stock will increase or decrease, and if the parent owns that stock it, too, will suffer gain or loss.

The Commissioner argues, in effect, that because the parent retains speculative risk it cannot have transferred the insurance risk. That argument has weight in the case of a captive insurer which writes insurance entirely, or almost entirely, for the parent. In that event, the insurance risk is not transferred because the parent is in the same economic position whether it holds a policy or not. In addition, because only the parent's money is in the pool, the parent has no speculative risk other than that involving its own funds, wherever they are.

On the other hand, when there is unrelated insurance business, there is a pool to which the parent's own risk can be transferred, and the mere fact that a payment from that larger pool may affect the value of the insurer is not dispositive. Again, there would be no pool at all if insurance were not being sold to others.

Nor can we accept the Commissioner's position that there is no insurance unless all effects of a possible risk of loss have been removed from the insured. That overbroad position flies in the face of the reality of the insurance market. It takes no real account of mutual insurance companies, where policyholders suffer losses each time an amount is paid out of the pool, whether that amount is for their own insurance risk or someone else's. It also fails to take account of the well-known phenomenon of retrospectively rated policies, where the insured will often ultimately bear a large part of the insurance risk. See Sears Roebuck, 972 F.2d at 862.[2] Perhaps it would not be amiss to note that, at bottom, one can never eliminate all of one's risk-there is always a possibility that the insurance company will become insolvent.

In fine, we are satisfied that a parent and its subsidiaries can shift risk to a captive insurer, where that insurer has significant unrelated business. In this case, the Tax Court determined that if only AMERCO were looked at, its share of Republic's business was under one percent and if the whole AMERCO Group were considered, the share was from 26 percent to 48 percent of that business. That, said the court, left sufficient unrelated business to create a true pool and to allow for true risk-shifting. In that determination, the Tax Court did not err.

(2) Risk-Distributing.

As we have already pointed out, risk-distribution looks at the transaction from the standpoint of the insurer. Here, where a substantial part of the insurer's business comes from sources unrelated to the parent and its subsidiaries, it was proper for the Tax Court to decide that there was sufficient risk distribution. The distribution aspect is rather apparent. As the Tax Court found, Republic's "insurance business was diverse, multifaceted, and ... involved a substantial amount of outside risks. More of the money in its pool came from outside unrelated insureds than came from AMERCO & Subsidiaries." 96 T.C. at 41. That determination was not clearly erroneous.[3]

CONCLUSION

As precedent requires, we have discussed this case from the standpoint of risk-shifting and risk-distributing. However, we also agree with the Seventh Circuit that discussions of this

---

2   At argument the Commissioner stated that retrospectively rated policies may not be insurance. We need not decide that issue here. The argument, however, does seem to underscore the Commissioner's very limited view of what does constitute insurance. That view bespeaks an exceedingly narrow concept of when a corporation is entitled to deduct expenses which are typically considered ordinary and necessary in the conduct of its business.

3   The Commissioner attacks a number of the Tax Court's factual determinations regarding the allocation of Republic's premium income between related and unrelated insureds. We have reviewed the Commissioner's contentions and find no clear error in the Tax Court's determinations.

area might seem less abstruse if we asked ourselves a somewhat different question: "Suppose we ask not 'What is insurance?' but 'Is there adequate reason to recharacterize this transaction?,' given the norm that tax law respects both the form of the transaction and the form of the corporate structure.... For whether a transaction possesses substance independent of tax consequences is an issue of fact...." Sears Roebuck, 972 F.2d at 864. The Seventh Circuit held that, because nothing of substance would differ from the purchase of insurance from an unrelated insurance company, a trier of fact could conclude that the captive-Allstate-had furnished the parent-Sears-with insurance. Here, for the same reasons, we are satisfied that a trier of fact could, as the Tax Court did, conclude that the captive-Republic-furnished the parent-AMERCO-and the AMERCO Group with insurance. Here, as there, the captive performed all of the functions of an insurer. The decision of the Tax Court was not clearly erroneous when viewed from this vantage point.

At any rate, we conclude that it is possible to have a true insurance transaction between a corporation and its wholly owned subsidiary insurance company if that captive company does substantial unrelated business. Likewise, it is possible for other members of the corporate group to have true insurance transactions with the captive company in that instance.[4] When that is so, the insurance premiums paid by the parent and its subsidiaries are deductible.

AFFIRMED.

---

[4]   We need not, and do not, decide whether brother-sister corporations can deduct premiums, even in the absence of business unrelated to the corporate family. See Humana, 881 F.2d at 252-57.

Appendix O

Sears, Roebuck and Co. v. C.I.R.

972 F.2d 858 (1992)

UNITED STATES COURT OF APPEALS, SEVENTH CIRCUIT.

SEARS, ROEBUCK AND CO. and Affiliated Corporations, Petitioner-Appellant, Cross-Appellee,

v.

COMMISSIONER OF INTERNAL REVENUE, Respondent-Appellee, Cross-Appellant.

[Names of counsel omitted.]

Before BAUER, Chief Judge, EASTERBROOK, Circuit Judge, and NOLAND, Senior District Judge.[*]

EASTERBROOK, Circuit Judge.

Several subsidiaries of Sears, Roebuck & Co. sell insurance. One, Allstate Insurance Co., underwrote some of the risks of the parent corporation. Two others wrote mortgage insurance, promising to pay lenders if borrowers defaulted. Because Sears and all other members of the corporate group file a consolidated tax return, disputes about the tax consequences of these transactions affect the taxes of the entire group. The Commissioner of Internal Revenue assessed the group with deficiencies exceeding $2.5 million for the tax years 1980-82. Whether the group owes this money depends on the proper characterization of the two kinds of transaction.

---

[*] Hon. James E. Noland, of the Southern District of Indiana, sitting by designation. This opinion was in press on August 12, 1992, the date of Judge Noland's death.

An insurer may deduct from its gross income an amount established as a reserve for losses. 26 U.S.C. § 832. Until 1986 it could deduct the entire reserve; today it must discount this reserve in recognition of the fact that a dollar payable tomorrow is worth less than a dollar today. Tax Reform Act of 1986 § 1023, 100 Stat. 2085, 2399 (1986). These transactions occurred before 1986, and in any event we deal with the existence rather than the size of the deduction. Allstate created and deducted reserves to cover casualties on policies it issued to Sears. The Commissioner disallowed these deductions (and made some related adjustments), reasoning that the shuffling of money from one corporate pocket to another cannot be "insurance." The Tax Court disagreed. It distinguished captive subsidiaries (which write policies for the parent corporation but few or no others) from bona fide insurance companies that deal with their corporate parents or siblings at market terms. 96 T.C. 61 (1991).

The two subsidiaries underwriting mortgage insurance estimated losses as of the time the underlying loans went into default. The Commissioner contended that these insurers could not establish deductible loss reserves until the lenders obtained good title to the mortgaged property, because the insurance policies made a tender of title a condition precedent to the insurers' obligation to pay. The Tax Court agreed with this conclusion, rejecting the insurers' argument that the Internal Revenue Code permits them to deduct loss reserves required by state law, as these reserves were.

The judges of the Tax Court split four ways. Judges Körner, Shields, Hamblen, Swift, Gerber, Wright, Parr, Colvin, and Halpern joined Judge Cohen's opinion for the majority. Judges Chabot and Parker would have ruled for the Commissioner on both issues; Chief Judge Nims and Judge Jacobs would have ruled for Sears on both issues. Judge Whalen concluded that the majority had things backward: that Sears should have prevailed on the mortgage insurance issue but lost on the subsidiary issue. We join Chief Judge Nims and Judge Jacobs.

I

Allstate is a substantial underwriter, collecting more than $5 billion in premiums annually and possessing more than $2 billion in capital surplus. During the years at issue, Allstate charged Sears approximately $14 million per year for several kinds of insurance. Some 99.75% of Allstate's premiums came from customers other than Sears, which places 10% to 15% of its insurance with Allstate. The Commissioner's brief concedes that "[p]olicies issued to Sears by Allstate were comparable to policies issued to unrelated insureds. With respect to the execution, modification, performance and renewal of all of the policies in issue, Allstate and Sears observed formalities similar to those followed with respect to the insurance policies issued by Allstate to unrelated insureds. In addition, the premium rates charged by Allstate to Sears were determined by means of the same underwriting principles and procedures that were used in determining the premium rates charged to unrelated insureds, and were the equivalent of arm's-length rates." The Tax Court made similar findings, although not nearly so concisely.

Allstate, founded in 1931, has been selling insurance to Sears since 1945. Everyone, including the Commissioner, has taken Allstate as the prototypical non-captive insurance subsidiary. Until 1977 the Internal Revenue Service respected transactions between non-captive insurers and their parents. In that year the Commissioner decided that a wholly owned subsidiary cannot "insure" its parent's operations, even if the subsidiary's policies are identical in terms and price to those available from third parties. Rev.Rul. 77-316, 1977-2 C.B. 53. Examples given in this revenue ruling all dealt with captives that had no customers outside the corporate family. After issuing the ruling the Service continued to believe that subsidiaries engaged in "solicitation and acceptance of substantial outside risks" could provide insurance to their parents. G.C.M. 38136 (Oct. 12, 1979). But in 1984 the General Counsel reversed course, G.C.M. 39247 (June 27, 1984), and the Commissioner later announced that all wholly owned insurance subsidiaries should be treated alike. Rev.Rul. 88-72, 1988-2 C.B. 31, clarified, Rev.Rul. 89-61, 1989-1 C.B. 75. Our task is to decide whether this is correct. We therefore disregard details, which may be found in the Tax Court's opinion. Like the Commissioner, we deem immaterial the nature of the risks Allstate accepted, the terms the parties negotiated, and the precise deductions taken.

If Sears did no more than set up a reserve for losses, it could not deduct this reserve from income. United States v. General Dynamics Corp., 481 U.S. 239, 107 S.Ct. 1732, 95 L.Ed.2d 226 (1987). Firms other than insurance companies may deduct business expenses only when paid or accrued; a reserve is deductible under § 832 only if the taxpayer issued "insurance." "Self-insurance" is just a name for the lack of insurance-for bearing risks oneself. According to the Commissioner, "insurance" from a subsidiary is self-insurance by another name. Moving funds from one pocket to another does nothing, even if the pocket is separately incorporated. If Subsidiary pays out a dollar, Parent loses the same dollar. Nothing depends on whether Subsidiary has other customers; there is still a one-to-one correspondence between its payments and Parent's wealth. So although Allstate may engage in the pooling of risks, and thus write insurance, Sears did not purchase the shifting of risks, and thus did not buy insurance. Unless the transaction is insurance from both sides-unless it "involves risk-shifting [from the client's perspective] and risk-distributing [from the underwriter's]", Helvering v. Le Gierse, 312 U.S. 531, 539, 61 S.Ct. 646, 649, 85 L.Ed. 996 (1941)-it is not insurance for purposes of the Internal Revenue Code. The Commissioner asks us to pool the corporate family's assets to decide whether risk has been shifted. This is the "economic family" approach of Rev.Rul. 77-316, which the Service sometimes supplements with a "balance sheet" inquiry under which a transaction is not insurance if it shows up on both sides of a corporation's balance sheet.

No judge of the Tax Court has ever embraced the IRS's "economic family" approach, which is hard to reconcile with the doctrine that tax law respects corporate forms. Molien Properties, Inc. v. CIR, 319 U.S. 436, 63 S.Ct. 1132, 87 L.Ed. 1499 (1943). Although the Commissioner may recharacterize intra-corporate transactions that lack substance independent of their tax effects, cf. Gregory v. Helvering, 293 U.S. 465, 55 S.Ct. 266, 79 L.Ed. 596 (1935); Yosha v. CIR, 861 F.2d 494 (7th Cir.1988)-which supports disregarding captive insurance subsidiaries-the "economic family" approach asserts that all transactions among members of a corporate group must be disregarded. Even the ninth circuit, which in citing Rev.Rul. 77-316 favorably has come the closest to the Commissioner's position, has drawn back by implying that subsidiaries doing substantial outside business cannot be lumped with true captives into a single pot. Carnation Co. v. CIR, 640 F.2d 1010 (9th Cir.1981); Clougherty Packing Co. v. CIR, 811 F.2d 1297, 1298 n. 1 (9th Cir.1987).

What is "insurance" for tax purposes? The Code lacks a definition. Le Gierse mentions the combination of risk shifting and risk distribution, but it is a blunder to treat a phrase in an opinion as if it were statutory language. Zenith Radio Corp. v. United States, 437 U.S. 443, 460-62, 98 S.Ct. 2441, 2450-51, 57 L.Ed.2d 337 (1978). Cf. United States v. Consumer Life Insurance Co., 430 U.S. 725, 740-41, 97 S.Ct. 1440, 1448-49, 52 L.Ed.2d 4 (1977). The Court was not writing a definition for all seasons and had no reason to, as the holding of Le Gierse is only that paying the "underwriter" more than it promises to return in the event of a casualty is not insurance by any standard. Life insurance passes outside a decedent's estate, making it advantageous to turn (taxable) assets of the estate into insurance proceeds. Less than a month before her death, an elderly woman bought a policy denominated life insurance. The policy named a death benefit of $25,000 and carried a premium of $23,000. As part of the package, the "insurer" required the beneficiary to buy an annuity contract for $4,000. If the beneficiary died immediately, the insurer was $2,000 to the good; if she lived, the premiums were more than enough to fund the promised annuity payment and death benefit. So no risks were being spread, transferred, pooled, whatever. As the Court observed, there was no insurance risk; the buyer of the policy expected to die soon, and the issuer expected to turn the proceeds over to the heirs, keeping an administrative fee for the service of removing the assets from the estate. Le Gierse, like Gregory and Yosha, shows that substance prevails over empty forms. Sears, by contrast, had insurable risks. The Commissioner does not deny that if Sears had purchased from Hartford or Aetna the same policies it purchased from Allstate, these would have been genuine "insurance." Forms there were, but not empty ones-and taxes usually depend on form, as the Commissioner trumpets whenever this enlarges the revenue. E.g., Howell v. United States, 775 F.2d 887 (7th Cir.1985). Distinctions with little meaning to the populace-for example, income at 11:59 p.m. on December 31 versus income at 12:01 a.m. on January

1, or wages plus the promise of a pension versus higher wages used to purchase an annuity-produce large differences in tax.

Doubtless a casualty that leads Allstate to reimburse Sears does not bring cash into the corporate treasury the same way a payment from Hartford would. A favorable loss experience for Sears cuts Allstate's costs, and thus augments the group's aggregate wealth, by more than the same reduction in losses would produce if Hartford issued the policy. Yet the Commissioner does not push this as far as he could. Corporate liability is limited by corporate assets. Corporations accordingly do not insure to protect their wealth and future income, as natural persons do, or to provide income replacement or a substitute for bequests to their heirs (which is why natural persons buy life insurance). Investors can "insure" against large risks in one line of business more cheaply than do corporations, without the moral hazard and adverse selection and loading costs: they diversify their portfolios of stock. Instead corporations insure to spread the costs of casualties over time. Bad experience concentrated in a single year, which might cause bankruptcy (and its associated transactions costs), can be paid for over several years. See generally David Mayers & Clifford W. Smith, Jr., On the Corporate Demand for Insurance, 55 J. Bus. 281 (1982). Much insurance sold to corporations is experience-rated. An insurer sets a price based on that firm's recent and predicted losses, plus a loading and administrative charge. Sometimes the policy is retrospectively rated, meaning that the final price is set after the casualties have occurred. Retrospective policies have minimum and maximum premiums, so the buyer does not bear all of the risk, but the upper and lower bounds are set so that almost all of the time the insured firm pays the full costs of the losses it generates. Both experience rating and retrospective rating attempt to charge the firm the full cost of its own risks over the long run, a run as short as one year with retrospective rating. The client buys some time-shifting (very little in the case of retrospective rating) and a good deal of administration. Insurers are experts at evaluating losses, settling with (or litigating against) injured persons, and so on. A corporation thus buys loss-evaluation and loss-administration services, at which insurers have a comparative advantage, more than it buys loss distribution. If retrospectively rated policies, called "insurance" by both issuers and regulators, are insurance for tax purposes-and the Commissioner's lawyer conceded for purposes of this case that they are-then it is impossible to see how risk shifting can be a sine qua non of "insurance."

The Commissioner insists that "shifting risk to third-party insureds" is an essential ingredient of insurance, but what does this mean? Take term life insurance. One thousand persons at age 30 pay $450 each for a one-year policy with a death benefit of $200,000. In a normal year two of these persons will die, so the insurer expects to receive $450,000 and disburse $400,000. Of course more may die in a given year than the actuarial tables predict. But as the size of the pool increases the law of large numbers takes over, and the ratio of actual to expected loss converges on one. The absolute size of the expected variance increases, but the ratio decreases.

Risk-averse buyers of insurance shuck risk. Risk-neutral insurers match risks. No third party gets extra risk. Each person's chance of dying is unaffected; the financial consequences of death are shared. Joseph E. Stiglitz, professor of economics at Stanford, one of the leading students of risk and insurance, and an expert witness for Sears, put things nicely in saying that insurance does not shift risk so much as the pooling transforms and diminishes risk. See Richard A. Posner, Economic Analysis of Law 103 (4th ed. 1992). Insurance companies, with diversified investors and oodles of potential claims, are effectively risk-neutral. So everyone gains. The insureds willingly pay the loading charge to reduce their financial variance. The investors in the underwriters make a profit.

Convergence through pooling is an important aspect of insurance. Allstate puts Sears's risks in a larger pool, performing one of the standard insurance functions in a way that a captive insurer does not. More: Allstate furnishes Sears with the same hedging and administration services it furnishes to all other customers. It establishes reserves, pays state taxes, participates in state risk-sharing pools (for insolvent insurers), and so on, just as it would if Sears were an unrelated company. States recognize the transaction as "real" insurance for purposes of mandatory-insurance laws (several of the policies were purchased to comply with such laws for Sears's auto fleet, and for workers' compensation in Texas). From Allstate's perspective this is real insurance in every way. It must maintain the reserves required by state law (not to mention prudent management). Sears cannot withdraw these reserves on whim, and events that affect their size for good or ill therefore do not translate directly to Sears's balance sheet. It therefore does not surprise us that the Tax Court, while accepting the Commissioner's view that true captives do not write insurance, believes that insurance affiliates with substantial business from outside the group are genuine insurers. E.g., Gulf Oil Corp. v. CIR, 89 T.C. 1010, 1025-27 (1987) (dictum), aff'd in relevant part, 914 F.2d 396 (3d Cir.1990); AMERCO v. CIR, 96 T.C. 18 (1991) (52% to 74% writing for unrelated parties); Harper Group v. CIR, 96 T.C. 45 (1991) (30% writing for unrelated parties). So, too, courts of appeals have allowed the Commissioner to recharacterize "captive" cases as self-insurance without extending this principle to firms with substantial outside business. Beech Aircraft Corp. v. United States, 797 F.2d 920 (10th Cir.1986); Stearns-Roger Corp. v. United States, 774 F.2d 414 (10th Cir.1985). One court has held that fraternal corporations may write genuine "insurance" for each other, although they do no business outside the corporate group. Humana Inc. v. CIR, 881 F.2d 247 (6th Cir.1989).

Power to recharacterize transactions that lack economic substance is no warrant to disregard both form and substance in the bulk of cases. The Tax Court has given up the effort to find a formula, instead listing criteria such as insurance risk, risk shifting, risk distribution, and presence of forms commonly accepted as insurance in the trade. 96 T.C. at 99-101 (this case); Harper, 96 T.C. at 57-58 (opinion by Judge Jacobs describing this as a "facts and circumstances" test); AMERCO, 96 T.C. at 38 (opinion by Judge Körner rejecting any unified "test" and remarking that the considerations "are not independent or exclusive. Instead, we read them as informing each other and, to the extent not fully consistent, confining each other's potential excesses.").

No set of criteria is a "test." Lists without metes, bounds, weights, or means of resolving conflicts do not identify necessary or sufficient conditions; they never prescribe concrete results. Perhaps a list is all we can expect when the statute is silent and both sides of a dispute have solid points. For the Commissioner is right to say that Sears does not buy insurance in the same sense as a natural person buys auto insurance, and that it transfers less risk when buying a policy from Allstate than when buying the same policy from Nationwide. Sears is right to say that Allstate sells Sears a product that passes for insurance in the industry, identical to what Allstate sells to its other clients and having economic consequences differing from a self-insurance reserve. Perhaps disputes of this kind do little more than illustrate the conundrums inherent in an effort to collect a tax from corporations, as opposed to a tax measured by the changes in wealth of corporate investors (or measured by their withdrawals for consumption, so as to encourage investment). The experts who labored during this trial to define "insurance" all would have agreed that this dispute is an artifact of the corporate income tax, which by divorcing taxation from real persons' wealth, income, or consumption is bound to combine tricky definitional problems with odd incentives.

Suppose we ask not "What is insurance?" but "Is there adequate reason to recharacterize this transaction?", given the norm that tax law respects both the form of the transaction and the form of the corporate structure. It follows from putting the matter this way that the decision of the Tax Court must be affirmed. For whether a transaction possesses substance independent of tax consequences is an issue of fact-something the Commissioner harps on when she prevails in the Tax Court. E.g., Yosha, 861 F.2d at 499 (citing cases). The transaction between Sears and Allstate has some substance independent of tax effects. It increases the size of Allstate's pool and so reduces the ratio between expected and actual losses; it puts Allstate's reserves at risk; it assigns claims administration to persons with a comparative advantage at that task. These effects are no less real than those of loans and interest payments within corporate groups-which the Commissioner usually respects even though they are occasionally recharacterized as contributions to capital. E.g., National Farmers Union Service Corp. v. United States, 400 F.2d 483 (10th Cir.1968); Crosby Valve & Gage Co. v. CIR, 380 F.2d 146 (1st Cir.1967). Hartford is a subsidiary of ITT, as Allstate is of Sears. Suppose Sears were to buy from Hartford the same policies it obtained from Allstate, and Allstate were to serve ITT's needs. Then even the Commissioner would concede that both ITT and Sears had "insurance," yet nothing of substance would differ-not given the Commissioner's concession that Allstate wrote policies with standard commercial terms at competitive premiums. A trier of fact may, and did, conclude that Allstate furnished Sears with insurance.

II

PMI Mortgage Insurance Company, another part of the Sears group, writes mortgage insurance. PMI Mortgage Insurance and its own subsidiary, PMI Insurance Company (collectively PMI), insure lenders against the risk that borrowers will not pay. The Tax Court's opinion marshals the facts, 96 T.C. at 73-85, which are unnecessary to recount at length. Two dominate: (1) The insured risk is a borrower's default in payment. (2) Mortgage insurers insist that the lender try to collect from borrowers or realize on the collateral; until the lender has foreclosed on or otherwise obtained title to the property securing the loan (which also fixes the amount of the loss), the insurer does not pay. The last statement is a simplification. Sometimes PMI compromises with the lender in advance of foreclosure, but the policy does not require PMI to pay until the lender has good title.

Lenders must tell PMI about defaults and the steps they have taken to collect. PMI establishes reserves for losses when one of the following occurs: (a) the property has been conveyed to the lender but not sold to a third party; (b) the property is in the process of foreclosure; or (c) the loan has been in default for four months or more. PMI also estimates the number of loans for which one of these three things has occurred but not been reported. Such reserves for incurred but not reported (IBNR) casualties are staples of the insurance business, and the Commissioner does not contest the establishment of IBNR reserves, provided that an identical reported event would support a loss reserve deductible under § 832.

Obviously not all of these events will lead to obligations on the insurance. Borrowers may catch up on overdue payments and retire their loans. Property sold at foreclosure may generate proceeds adequate to cover the outstanding balance of the loan. Insurers, including PMI, therefore discount their reserves to reflect their experience (and the industry's). PMI discounted too heavily, as things turned out. For 1982 PMI established year-end reserves of $35.9 million. The amounts disbursed in later years on account of these defaulted loans came to $51.5 million. So its reserve was too small. But the Commissioner believes that PMI's reserves were too big for tax purposes. She limited the loss reserve deduction to $19.5 million for 1982, making comparable cuts for other years, and the Tax Court sustained her decisions. The court held that an "insurer cannot incur a loss until the insured has suffered the defined economic loss, to wit, after the lender takes title to the mortgaged property and submits a claim for loss." 96 T.C. at 114. By this time, of course, there is no need for a "reserve"; payment is a current obligation. The court's approach does not affect the taxes of insurers in a steady state but substantially increases the taxes of those with growing businesses (or growing losses) by postponing the time when the losses may be deducted.

Sears contests this decision on two grounds: first, that § 832 does not limit loss deductions to casualties that have reached the point of being payable; second, that the Tax Court erred in deciding when an insurer's obligation attaches. Judge Whalen (joined in this respect by Chief Judge Nims and Judge Jacobs) agreed with the former argument, concluding that the majority's holding "is a radical departure from the annual statement method of accounting, which section 832 and its predecessors have required property and casualty insurance companies to use in reporting underwriting and investment income for Federal income tax purposes since 1921." 96 T.C. at 114-15.

The "annual statement method of accounting" to which Judge Whalen referred is prescribed by the National Association of Insurance Commissioners, a body comprising state insurance regulators that has filed a brief as amicus curiae in support of Sears. The NAIC's annual statement requires property and casualty insurers to take certain things into income and prescribes reserves. A mortgage insurer must include in its reserves the three categories of losses that PMI used, plus reserves for IBNR losses. The Commissioner concedes that PMI complied with the NAIC's requirements. Federal agencies such as the Federal Housing Administration engaged in guaranteeing loans account for loss reserves exactly as PMI did. The insurance regulators believe that PMI erred, if at all, in understating its loss reserves. No surprise here. State regulators strive to assess and preserve the solvency of insurers. Accurate estimates of losses are essential to the former task, and high estimates contribute to the latter by requiring insurers to obtain additional capital or curtail the writing of new policies. Regulators therefore favor generous estimates of losses, while the federal tax collector prefers low estimates. The majority of the Tax Court stressed this when concluding that PMI could not follow the NAIC's method: "The objectives of State regulation ⋯ are not identical to the objectives of Federal income taxation. State insurance regulators are concerned with the solvency of the insurer⋯. In contrast, Federal tax statutes are concerned with the determination of taxable income on an annual basis." 96 T.C. at 110.

Generalities about what "[f]ederal tax statutes are concerned with" do not control concrete cases. Section 832 is no ordinary rule. It expressly links federal taxes to the NAIC's annual statement:

> (a) In the case of [a property or casualty] insurance company ⋯ the term "taxable income" means the gross income as defined in subsection (b)(1) less the deductions allowed by subsection (c).
>
> (b)(1) The term "gross income" means the sum of—
>
> ⋯
>
> (A) the combined gross amount earned during the taxable year, from investment income and from underwriting income as provided in this subsection,

computed on the basis of the underwriting and investment exhibit of the annual statement approved by the National Association of Insurance Commissioners·····

...

(b)(3) The term "underwriting income" means the premiums earned on insurance contracts during the taxable year less losses incurred and expenses incurred.

...

(b)(5)(A) The term "losses incurred" means losses incurred during the taxable year on insurance contracts computed as follows:

(i) To losses paid during the taxable year, deduct salvage and reinsurance recovered during the taxable year.

(ii) To the result so obtained, add all unpaid losses ··· outstanding at the end of the taxable year and deduct all unpaid losses ··· outstanding at the end of the preceding taxable year.

This quotation includes changes made in 1988, but these do not affect the current dispute. Section 832(b)(1)(A) requires an insurer to use "the underwriting and investment exhibit of the annual statement approved by the National Association of Insurance Commissioners" to determine its "gross income." Contrary to usual notions of "gross income," this concept in § 832 does not denote all inflows of revenue. Instead it refers to "premiums earned" (a premium is not "earned" until the period for which it purchases coverage occurs) less "losses incurred." For purposes of § 832, then, "gross income" is a version of net earned income. Both the "premiums earned" and "losses incurred" go into determining "gross income"-which is to be "computed on the basis of the underwriting and investment exhibit of the annual statement approved by the National Association of Insurance Commissioners". State insurance commissioners' preferences about reserves thus are not some intrusion on federal tax policy; using their annual statement is federal tax law. See Brown v. Helvering, 291 U.S. 193, 201, 54 S.Ct. 356, 360, 78 L.Ed. 725 (1934): "[T]he deductions allowed for additions to the reserves of insurance companies are technical in character and are specifically provided for in the Revenue Acts. These technical reserves are required to be made by the insurance laws of the several States."

True enough, the definition of loss reserves in § 832(b)(5) does not refer to the annual statement. Yet subsection (b)(5) losses are a component of subsection (b)(1) income, which is to be computed according to the NAIC's statement. It is scarcely possible to use the statement when determining one but not the other. Although it is not impossible-almost nothing is impossible in tax law-divorcing (b)(5) losses from the annual statement computations would make no sense in terms of the structure of the statute or its genesis. Subsection (b)(5) prescribes a method of toting up losses derived almost verbatim from the annual statement used in 1921, when Congress enacted the provision.

If annual statements were to depart from an effort to approximate actual "losses" then subsections (b)(1) and (b)(5) might come into conflict. This occurred when states required insurers to mark up their loss reserves by a percentage. The Commissioner objected to the deduction of these marked up losses, issuing regulations in 1943 and 1944 requiring insurers to use experience, and not formulas prescribed by state rules, as the basis of loss reserves. Modified versions of these regulations are still in force but no longer present the insurers with conflicting state and federal demands. In 1950 the NAIC came 'round to the Commissioner's point of view, changing its annual statement so that both federal and state governments require insurers to reserve "only actual unpaid losses ··· stated in amounts which, based upon the facts in each case and the company's experience with similar cases, represent a fair and reasonable estimate of the amount the company will be required to pay." Treas.Reg. 1.832-4(b). Charles W. Tye, The Convention Form and Insurance Company Tax Problems, 6 Tax L.Rev. 245 (1951), narrates the history of this dispute and the details of its resolution. PMI used actual cases to generate its loss reserves, and in the event underestimated losses; it complied with both the NAIC's requirements and the Treasury's regulations. Having followed the NAIC's annual statement approach, PMI is entitled to deduct the loss reserves so computed.

For what it is worth, we believe that PMI would be entitled to prevail under the regulation independent of the requirements of the NAIC's annual statement. The regulation says "actual unpaid losses" but omits any requirement that these losses be quantified and immediately payable. Once an obligation is quantified, an accrual-basis taxpayer may deduct it. Yet § 832 and the regulation suppose that insurers may deduct losses denied to any old accrual-basis taxpayer, a supposition the Supreme Court confirmed in General Dynamics when holding that an employer paying for its employees' medical care without an insurer's intermediation could not deduct IBNR expenses (in this context, the cost of medical services already rendered to employees but for which the employer did not have bills in hand).

Consider some standard issues in establishing reserves. A policy of auto insurance requires the issuer to pay if its insured is at fault in a collision. An accident occurs during December. May the insurer add to its reserves? The liability is not fixed, for the insurer is not legally obliged to pay until a court determines that its policy-holder was at fault (or the underwriter so concedes), and even then the firm may not be called on to pay if the loss turns out to be less than the deductible or the victim collects from his own carrier, which decides not to pursue the other driver's carrier. It may take years before the amount of the loss is quantified and the negligent driver is identified. Yet reserves established for such a case meet the regulatory definition of actual, case-based losses, and it would be insane of an insurer not to establish reserves for such casualties. Or consider health insurance. An insured has a heart attack on December 31. Medical care will be required over the next months (or years), and the insurance policy conditions the obligation to pay on receipt of a physician's bill at rates usual and customary in the vicinity (with a provision for arbitration if the fee seems high or the medical services unnecessary). Once again it may be some time before services have been rendered and billed at rates agreeable to the carrier. Does it follow that the insurer must wait till it receives the bill before establishing a reserve? At oral argument counsel for the Commissioner answered "yes," but the Commissioner cannot mean it, for this answer collapses all distinction between "reserves" and bills payable by return mail. Cf. Harco Holdings, Inc. v. United States, 969 F.2d 440, 442 (7th Cir.1992).

Just so with the Tax Court's conclusion about mortgage insurance. It has confused quantification of the loss, which does not occur until the lender tenders title, with the occurrence of the covered loss. Perhaps it seems artificial to speak of a borrower's failure to make a few payments as a "loss." The borrower may catch up, or the sale of the property may reimburse the lender. Default is not an immediate casualty in the sense that a collision between two automobiles crushes the cars (and people) on the spot, and it does not portend outlays with the high probability that a myocardial infarction does. Yet the acid test is whether the default leaves the insurer responsible for payment. Let us suppose that PMI issues a policy for 1982 only, and the borrower omits the last four payments of the year. The lender neglects to renew the policy (or purchase a substitute) for 1983. Eventually the lender forecloses and sends PMI a bill. Must PMI pay? The answer is yes; the default is the event triggering coverage under the policy. (Neither the Commissioner nor the Tax Court disagrees with PMI's representations about its obligations under the policy.) Thus to state its statutory "gross income" for 1982 accurately, PMI must take into income the premiums earned during 1982 and exclude a reserve for losses attributable to those premiums, including the bills that will straggle in during future years on account of defaults that began in 1982. The Tax Court's observation that federal law calls for "determination of taxable income on an annual basis", 96 T.C. at 110, turns out to support PMI, once we see that default is the event triggering coverage under the policy and leaving the insurer on the hook, waiting to see how things turn out, even if it never receives another penny in premiums.

Corporate taxation teems with artificial and formal distinctions, and the taxation of insurers has more than its share of them. Whether § 832 is attributable to some finely honed sense of the economics of the insurance business or to political pressure is not for us to say. Provisions of the Internal Revenue Code do not conflict with "tax policy," as the Commissioner seems to believe. They are tax policy and are to be enforced. Usually this enlarges the revenue. E.g., Holywell Corp. v. Smith, 503 U.S. 47, 112 S.Ct. 1021, 117 L.Ed.2d 196 (1992); INDOPCO v. CIR, 503 U.S. 79, 112 S.Ct. 1039, 117 L.Ed.2d 226 (1992). An Internal Revenue Service eager to dish out the medicine of literalism must be prepared to swallow it. Sears is entitled to prevail on both branches of this case. The judgment of the Tax Court is affirmed with respect to the Allstate dispute and reversed with respect to the PMI dispute. The case is remanded for the redetermination of the deficiency in accord with this opinion. The Tax Court is free to consider the

Commissioner's argument, which it did not need to reach before, that PMI's returns for 1980 and 1981 did not use a proper case-based method of approximating its loss reserves.

NOLAND, Senior District Judge, concurring in part and dissenting in part.

While I join the majority's opinion on the insurance premiums issue, finding the same to be well-reasoned, I must respectfully dissent on the mortgage guarantee insurance issue for the reason stated in Tax Court Judge Mary Ann Cohen's fifty-three (53) page majority opinion[1] (approximately twelve (12) pages of which were dedicated to this issue). As Judge Cohen states in her opinion:

> "In common understanding, an insurance contract is an agreement to protect the insured (or a third-party beneficiary) against a direct or indirect economic loss arising from a defined contingency." Allied Fidelity Corp. v. Commissioner, 66 T.C. 1068, 1074 (1976), affd. 572 F.2d 1190 (7th Cir.1978). The defined contingency in this case was the insured's loss on the mortgage loan. It follows that the insurer cannot incur a loss until the insured has suffered the defined economic loss, to wit, after the lender takes title to the mortgaged property and submits a claim for loss.

Sears, Roebuck & Co. v. Commissioner, 96 U.S.T.C. 61, 113-114 (T.C.1991). Judge Cohen's analysis regarding the timing of the insurer's loss, i.e., the taxable event, is compelling.

---

[1]   Judge Cohen authored the majority opinion. Two (2) of the judges on the Tax Court, Judges Wells and Ruwe, did not participate in the consideration of the Court's opinion. Judge Whalen authored a dissenting opinion signaling his disagreement with the majority on both issues. Chief Judge Nims, joined by Judge Jacobs, concurred with respect to the insurance premiums issue and dissented with respect to the mortgage guarantee insurance issue. Judge Chabot, joined by Judge Parker, concurred with respect to the mortgage insurance issue and dissented with respect to the insurance premiums issue. Thus, only three (3) members of the Tax Court dissented with respect to the mortgage guarantee insurance issue.

Appendix P

Ocean Drilling & Exploration Co. v. U.S.

988 F.2d 1135 (Fed.Cir. 1993).

UNITED STATES COURT OF APPEALS, FEDERAL CIRCUIT.

OCEAN DRILLING & EXPLORATION COMPANY, (on behalf of itself and its consolidated subsidiaries), Plaintiff-Appellee,

v.

The UNITED STATES, Defendant-Appellant.

[Names of counsel omitted.]

Before NIES, Chief Judge, ARCHER and CLEVENGER, Circuit Judges.

PER CURIAM.

The United States appeals the judgment of the United States Claims Court[1] in Ocean Drilling & Exploration Co. v. United States, 24 Cl.Ct. 714 (1991). The issues appealed by the government are: (1) whether the Claims Court erred in holding that payments made by Ocean Drilling & Exploration Company (ODECO) (on behalf of its operating subsidiaries) to Mentor Insurance Limited (Mentor), a wholly-owned subsidiary of ODECO, constituted true insurance premiums that are deductible as business expenses under section 162 of the Internal Revenue Code of 1954, as amended (IRC),[2] and (2) if properly classified as insurance premiums, whether Mentor's income from insuring the

---

1   The Claims Court was renamed the Court of Federal Claims on October 29, 1992. Federal Courts Administration Act of 1992, Pub.L. No. 102-572, § 902(a), 106 Stat. 4506.

2   All references are to the Internal Revenue Code of 1954, as amended, because the tax years involved in this proceeding are 1974 and 1975. See 26 U.S.C. §§ 162, 951-953 (1988).

drilling rigs of ODECO's subsidiaries located in waters of the outer continental shelf of the United States constituted income from the insurance of United States risks within the meaning of sections 951-953 of the IRC.

We adopt the analysis and holding on these issues as set forth in the Claims Court's opinion, which is attached as an appendix. Accordingly, the judgment of the Claims Court is

AFFIRMED.

APPENDIX

OPINION OF THE UNITED STATES CLAIMS COURT

NETTESHEIM, Judge.

This tax refund case, before the court after trial, calls for resolution of two questions: first, whether payments by a parent company to its wholly-owned Bermuda insurer during tax years 1974 and 1975 constitute a reserve for losses as opposed to insurance premiums that qualify as a business deduction for federal income tax purposes; second, if the payments constitute insurance, whether the premiums were for insurance of property located in the United States and therefore taxable income.

FACTS

The following facts were developed at trial. Plaintiff Ocean Drilling and Exploration Company ("ODECO" or "plaintiff") was incorporated in 1953 to take advantage of business opportunities that resulted from the opening up of the Gulf of Mexico to oil and gas exploration.[3] Murphy Oil Corporation ("Murphy") and private investors provided the funds to establish plaintiff. The objectives of plaintiff were to build offshore drilling rigs and to invest the profits earned from this undertaking to establish an oil and gas reserve base. Plaintiff achieved these objectives and during the years at issue in this case, 1974 and 1975, operated as a holding company, with subsidiaries conducting its business. Plaintiff's principal lines of business during that period were offshore contract drilling, exploration for and production of oil and gas, underwater diving services, and insurance.

Richard E. Roberson, Jr., testified as to the development and business operations of plaintiff and its insurance subsidiary, Mentor Insurance Limited ("Mentor"). Mr.

---

3   ODECO brought this suit on behalf of itself and its subsidiaries with which it filed consolidated federal income tax returns in 1974 and 1975. Plaintiff in this decision refers only to ODECO.

Roberson's knowledge derives from his experience as an internal auditor at Murphy from 1962 to 1965; controller for plaintiff from 1965 to 1977; vice-president for plaintiff from 1974 to 1977; and controller for Mentor from 1968 through the years at issue in this case. Currently, Mr. Roberson is employed by plaintiff as vice-president of finance. He returned to ODECO in 1986 after serving in executive positions with two other oil companies between 1977 and 1983 and as a financial consultant between 1983 and 1986.

Mr. Roberson described at length the type of drilling rigs owned by plaintiff and its subsidiaries and insured by Mentor. Plaintiff designed the first rig capable of operating as a mobile drilling rig in the Gulf of Mexico.[4] Prior to the advent of mobile rigs, exploration companies had to construct artificial islands, also known as platforms, and use conventional land rigs on these sites. If oil was not discovered, the platform had to be torn down. Mobile drilling rigs reduced the cost of exploration; they could be moved from one location to another, thereby avoiding the cost of constructing and tearing down platforms. The mobile drilling rigs at issue in this case were operating in the Outer Continental Shelf area of the Gulf of Mexico.

During the 1960's plaintiff faced difficulties insuring its drilling rigs. At that time the drilling rig business was written predominately by the Lloyd Syndicate ("Lloyd's"), with the London Market serving as an ancillary market to Lloyd's. As the technology of drilling rigs developed rapidly, Lloyd's adjusted its insurance rates in an attempt to cover itself against potential losses from the new drilling rigs. Because of the limited experience in insuring the new rigs and a number of substantial losses on these rigs, insurance rates increased sharply. By the end of the 1960's, rates were as high as 10 percent of the value of insured vessels, and plaintiff was unable to obtain full coverage of its rigs through the existing insurance market. In response to this dilemma, plaintiff analyzed its history of premiums and losses and determined that establishment of a captive insurer could alleviate the problems that plaintiff faced in the insurance market. In 1968 plaintiff established Mentor as a wholly-owned subsidiary incorporated in Bermuda.

The initial capitalization for Mentor was $12,000.00, the minimum amount of capitalization required to organize a company in Bermuda. Plaintiff increased the capital contribution to Mentor to $200,000.00 by the end of 1968. In a December 19, 1968 meeting of Mentor's board of directors, the chairman of the board stated that this increase in capital was necessary for the insurance business that Mentor was undertaking. In June 1969 plaintiff increased Mentor's capitalization to $950,000.00. At the time Mentor was increasing its insurance of plaintiff's risks and considering insuring the risks of companies

---

4   Previously there had been limited use of a mobile drilling rig in the bays and lakes of south Louisiana.

unrelated to plaintiff. Mentor increased its capitalization because of its concern that it be adequately capitalized and able to attract unrelated entities to insure with Mentor.

The capitalization of Mentor remained at $950,000.00 through the years 1974 and 1975, despite Mentor's purchase of another insurance company in 1975.[5] Through 1975 Mentor was never asked by the Government of Bermuda to increase its capital, nor was it informed that it did not meet the capital requirements of Bermuda. For 1974 the capital surplus (share capital + retained earnings + minority interests) of Mentor amounted to $12,508,417.00; the net earned premiums (accounted for premiums net of commissions and reinsurance) were $5,335,617.00; the losses paid were $2,527,640.00; and the reserves for losses (liabilities) were $2,512,030.00. For 1975 the capital surplus was $15,943,790.00; the net earned premiums were $12,310,711.00; the losses paid were $7,946,191.00; and the reserves for losses were $6,427,834.00. Mentor's capitalization during 1974 and 1975 was adequate to cover any losses that might be presented to Mentor for payment.[6]

Mentor maintained offices in Bermuda from the time of its inception in 1968. Initially, Mentor shared an office and employees with Universal Marine Insurance Co., Ltd. ("Universal Marine"), a company not affiliated with plaintiff. This share arrangement between Mentor and Universal Marine was a common practice among insurers in Bermuda. Mentor entered into the arrangement prior to underwriting any insurance and concluded the arrangement in 1973 due to the increased business of both companies.

When the arrangement between Mentor and Universal Marine was instituted, Mentor's books were transferred to Bermuda. A chartered accountant kept Mentor's books, and Anthony Robert Gwinnell, an employee of both Mentor and Universal Marine in

---

5   Mentor purchased Enterprise Insurance ("Enterprise") on January 1, 1975, for $1,375,000.00 and thereby assumed the insurance obligations of Enterprise. Prior to acquiring Enterprise, Mentor acted as an agent for Enterprise. Its activities as agent entailed underwriting risks for Enterprise and then ceding the risks to Enterprise by way of reinsurance. Enterprise had been a subsidiary of Murphy, a 51.8-percent owner of plaintiff, but had not underwritten risk for Murphy. Thus, the purchase of Enterprise by Mentor did not increase the amount of related business Mentor was insuring.

6   Francis James Carter, the underwriter for Mentor during 1974 and 1975, testified that the capitalization of Mentor was sufficient to cover potential losses of insured companies. He stated that it was normal in the insurance business for net earned premiums to be as much as two and one-half times greater than the amount of capital surplus and that Mentor's ratio of net earned premiums to capital surplus of less than one to one was very conservative. Mr. Carter concluded that Mentor's conservative ratio, combined with the fact that Mentor's capital surplus was considerably greater than its reserve losses, indicated that Mentor was sufficiently capitalized to pay off any claims. The court concurs with the assessment of Mr. Carter that Mentor was adequately capitalized in 1974 and 1975.

Bermuda, underwrote insurance for Mentor.[7] Mr. Gwinnell was employed by Mentor and Universal Marine from December 1968 to February 1971. His position with Mentor required that Mr. Gwinnell establish an underwriting seat for Mentor in Bermuda. He was also responsible for the placement of investments for Mentor, but plaintiff determined how funds would be invested during Mr. Gwinnell's tenure with Mentor.

When plaintiff hired Mr. Gwinnell, plaintiff explained to him that Mentor initially would insure risks of plaintiff and that, if such endeavor proved successful, Mentor would begin underwriting risks for unrelated parties. Consequently, the first policies Mr. Gwinnell wrote for Mentor were those of plaintiff, followed by those of unrelated parties from 1970 onward. The reinsurance of Mentor's policies began in 1969 as a measure to protect the policies written by Mentor.

In his position with Mentor, Mr. Gwinnell rejected submissions for insurance that he deemed undesirable or bad for business. The rates charged by Mentor to plaintiff and third parties were not established or approved by plaintiff. Plaintiff negotiated through its brokerage house, Marsh & McLennan Inc. ("Marsh & McLennan"), the rates it would pay for insurance by Mentor. Plaintiff paid Marsh & McLennan for insurance obtained for itself and its subsidiaries with Mentor and other insurers. Marsh & McLennan then paid the insurers directly, and plaintiff charged its subsidiaries for their share of the insurance.

Subsequent to the conclusion of the arrangement with Universal Marine, Mentor retained its own accountant and underwriter in Bermuda. Mentor compensated them with funds from accounts in Bermuda. Mentor also retained both legal counsel, Conyers, Dill & Pearman, and a certified public accounting firm, Peat, Marwick, Mitchell & Co., in Bermuda. Operations conducted in Bermuda by Mentor included hiring, firing, budgeting, underwriting, and expanding business. To execute these practices, Mentor had five to six employees in Bermuda during 1974 and 1975.

The underwriter for Mentor during 1974 and 1975 was Francis James Carter. Mr. Carter, an impressive and informative witness, testified as to the operations of Mentor during his tenure in Bermuda. Mr. Carter started working for both Mentor and Universal Marine in 1971 after working for Lloyd's for eleven years. In 1971 Mentor had a capital surplus of greater than $2 million, and Mr. Carter was expected to underwrite a general account for Mentor. When the arrangement between the two insurance companies ended in 1973, Mr. Carter worked exclusively for Mentor until 1978. In 1974 Mr. Carter was promoted to vice-president and director of Mentor. In this position he was responsible

---

7   The deposition of Mr. Gwinnell, now deceased, was taken on August 1, 1978, in a previous action between the parties. Designated portions of Mr. Gwinnell's deposition were admitted into evidence.

for the entire running of the office, including underwriting, budgeting, expanding business, hiring and firing of employees, and generally managing Mentor.

Mr. Carter knew of no Mentor funds loaned to or commingled with funds of plaintiff or its subsidiaries. Mentor refrained from undertaking such transactions because the resulting arrangements would have reflected negatively on Mentor's financial stability. From 1973 until the time Mr. Carter left Mentor, the investment decisions of Mentor were under the control of Mentor's accountant, Collin O'Conner, who worked with plaintiff's treasury department on investment decisions. Investment guidelines were established by Mentor's board of directors in accordance with plaintiff's investment criteria.

Premiums paid to Mentor for insurance coverage were placed in Mentor's accounts. Mentor maintained a premium loss account of approximately $2-$3 million in Bermuda during 1974 and 1975 to cover operating expenses and policyholders' claims. Funds in excess of this amount were maintained in accounts outside Bermuda. Investment of Bermuda funds consisted primarily of high grade certificates of deposit. Plaintiff's treasury department, or, specifically, Odie Vaughan, managed the investment of Mentor's other funds within the guidelines established by Mentor's board of directors. Mr. Vaughan was treasurer of both plaintiff and Mentor.[8]

Mentor's funds were separate from plaintiff's funds through 1975; Mentor never loaned money to plaintiff or its subsidiaries;[9] Mentor's funds were never used as collateral for

---

[8]   Defendant in its post-trial brief stated that Mentor's "main" bank account was located in the Whitney National Bank, New Orleans, Louisiana. This was not established at trial. Mr. Vaughan "thought" that premiums were received by Mentor at the Whitney account in New Orleans, which he believed to be the main account. However, Mr. Carter definitively testified that Mentor collected premiums in Bermuda. Because it was established at trial that Mentor's funds were not commingled with plaintiff's funds, the court does not deem essential to its decision the determination of the location of either the collection of premiums or the main account of Mentor.

[9]   Defendant's assertion in its post-trial brief that Mentor loaned money to plaintiff is unfounded. The evidence that defendant offers as proof of its assertion does not indicate that Mentor loaned money to plaintiff. Plaintiff's accounts receivables noted that Mentor Insurance Company (U.K.) Limited, owned 70 percent by Mentor and 30 percent by plaintiff, owed plaintiff $34,095.05 at the start of both 1975 and 1976 and that plaintiff owed Mentor approximately $36,000.00 at the beginning of 1976. The accounts receivable documents did not specify the items represented by these amounts. This is not proof that Mentor loaned funds to plaintiff. The court finds credible the testimony of Messrs. Roberson, Carter, and Vaughan that Mentor to their knowledge did not loan money to plaintiff. Because the court believes these principal employees of Mentor and plaintiff would have known if Mentor had loaned funds to plaintiff, the court finds that no loans were made to plaintiff by Mentor.

plaintiff's loans; Mentor never invested in any of plaintiff's non-insurance subsidiaries; and Mentor's investment funds were not commingled with plaintiff's investment funds. The only guarantee by plaintiff of amounts payable under a Mentor policy of insurance was for a policy issued to Ben ODECO Limited ("Ben ODECO") in 1977.[10] However, for both tax years 1974 and 1975, plaintiff included the revenue and income of Mentor on its Consolidated Statements of Income and included Mentor as an asset on its Consolidated Balance Sheets.

Mentor's business was not completely separate from plaintiff's business.[11] Mentor was required to obtain approval from plaintiff's board of directors for certain facets of its business, including approval of its operating budget, approval of letters of credit over a certain amount, approval of large claims, and approval of capital expenditures.[12] Furthermore, Mentor had directors and officers who were employees of plaintiff and its affiliates. In 1974 four of Mentor's seven officers were employees of plaintiff or its affiliates, and in 1975 four of Mentor's eight officers were employees of plaintiff. The treasurer for both plaintiff and Mentor, Mr. Vaughan, is an example of an individual with loyalties to both plaintiff and Mentor.

With respect to the payment of large claims, plaintiff's approval was required only in instances where Mentor had approved a payment that could severely drain the premium loss account. If Mentor did not approve payment of a claim, Mentor's decision was not subject to review by plaintiff.

---

10   Ben ODECO was a joint venture between ODECO and Ben Line Streamers. Ben ODECO owned and operated drilling barges and purchased insurance through Ben Line Streamers and through ODECO via Marsh & McLennan. Mentor's arrangement with Marsh & McLennan resulted in Mentor's insuring a small portion of the risk of Ben ODECO.

11   Defendant in its post-trial brief stated that Mentor was required to insure risks of North American Reinsurance Company ("North American") as part of an agreement between plaintiff and North American. This fact was not established at trial. Mr. Carter testified that Mentor's business relationship with North American was one of reciprocity or goodwill trading and that he believed this business represented only two out of hundreds of treaties written by Mentor. Such evidence is not sufficient to validate defendant's implication that plaintiff determined what business Mentor would write. In actuality, this implication was specifically negated at trial by the testimony of Mr. Carter that he determined whether to underwrite the risks of North American.

12   Mentor's submission of its budget to plaintiff's board of directors for approval was a part of an aggregate budget submitted by plaintiff and its subsidiaries to the board for approval. In addition to the budget process, plaintiff had an authorization for expenditure ("AFE") process that applied primarily to its contract drilling and oil and gas operations. Under this process expenditures, depending on the amount, had to be approved by a manager, the president, or the board. Thus, when Mentor paid off on a claim, the subsidiaries of plaintiff insured by Mentor had to go through the AFE process before spending the money received from Mentor.

Mr. Vaughan testified as to his responsibilities as treasurer for both plaintiff and Mentor during 1974 and 1975. Although he acted as treasurer for both entities, Mr. Vaughan was considered an employee of plaintiff. The work performed for Mentor was done under a fee arrangement. Mr. Vaughan was responsible for the administrative functions with respect to the receipt, disbursement, and investment of money of both plaintiff and Mentor. Mr. Vaughan knew of no Mentor funds commingled with plaintiff's funds, loaned to plaintiff, or used as collateral for plaintiff's loans. When plaintiff owed a subsidiary money or a subsidiary owed plaintiff money, a check would be issued for the amount owed, rather than merely noting the transfer of funds in their books.

Charles Niederer[13] was a second individual affiliated with both plaintiff and Mentor. Prior to August 1974, Mr. Niederer occupied the position of insurance manager for Murphy. This position entailed the purchasing of insurance and the general management of insurance operations for Murphy. Mr. Niederer held a similar position with plaintiff from August 1974 until January 1977, when he became vice-president of insurance for plaintiff. Mr. Niederer's positions with Mentor included vice-president of Mentor from May 1969 to April 1974 and director and chairman of the board of directors of Mentor from April 1974 through the years at issue. As chairman of the board, Mr. Niederer received reports from Mr. Carter on the underwriting business transacted by Mr. Carter. While Mr. Carter actually determined what business to underwrite within the guidelines established by the board, Mr. Niederer maintained an active role overseeing such business. His active role stemmed from his ardent interest in Mentor's business and from his personal relationship with some of the parties acquiring insurance from Mentor.[14]

Mentor's business entailed writing direct insurance for plaintiff and writing reinsurance for unrelated companies. Mentor's insurance of risks of plaintiff's subsidiaries consisted of two types of policies. One type of policy covered the full value of the property insured for plaintiff. The second type of policy was a first-loss policy that covered the first $1 million of a loss. Plaintiff purchased first-loss policy insurance for property that it had insured with Oil Insurance Limited ("OIL") and for which there existed a $1 million

---

13   Mr. Niederer is now deceased.

14   The rates charged by Mentor to plaintiff were based on the commercial rates in London. In 1974 and 1975, the rates Mentor charged to plaintiff were the London rates modified to reflect plaintiff's experience. Mentor's typical policy for plaintiff was a joint policy with an unrelated insurer that would underwrite 5 to 20 percent of the risk of plaintiff. In addition to co-insuring plaintiff's policies, Mentor reinsured a portion of plaintiff's risk. During 1974 and 1975, Mr. Carter determined what risk Mentor would accept within the guidelines established by Mentor's board of directors. Mr. Carter could decline to insure the risks of plaintiff. When a claim for loss was submitted to Mentor by plaintiff, Mentor appointed an experienced sur-veyor to verify the validity of the claim. This same procedure of verification was used by Mentor for claims by unrelated parties that Mentor reinsured as a lead underwriter.

deductible per occurrence.[15] Thus, if there was an event that caused damage to one or more ships, Mentor would be liable for the first $1 million of loss and OIL would be liable for the balance of the loss.

With respect to business of Mentor unrelated to plaintiff for the years 1974 and 1975, respectively, the net premiums received from Highlands Insurance Company ("Highlands") accounted for 57 percent and 56 percent of all net premiums received from unrelated business.[16] Mentor's ratios of incurred claims to net premiums for Highlands during 1974 and 1975 were 138.4 percent and 112.4 percent, respectively, indicating that incurred claims exceeded net premiums. The corresponding ratios for all unrelated business of Mentor were 123.4 percent and 101 percent, while those ratios for business of plaintiff were 15.1 percent for 1974 and 13.9 percent for 1975, indicating that plaintiff's net premiums exceeded its incurred claims. These underwriting statistics do not reveal whether Mentor ultimately suffered a loss from its unrelated business during 1974 and 1975, since they do not take into account money earned from investment of premiums.[17]

The Internal Revenue Service (the "IRS") in its audit of plaintiff for tax years 1974 and 1975 determined that premiums received by Mentor from plaintiff and its consolidated United States subsidiaries amounted to self insurance. The IRS proposed for disallowance as a business expense the amount of $1,433,214.00 for 1974 and $1,744,194.00 for 1975. In addition, the IRS developed an alternative position in the event that the premiums were allowed as a deduction. The IRS determined that premiums earned from drilling rigs operating over the Outer Continental Shelf of the Gulf of Mexico were premiums on property located in the United States. The IRS determined that such premiums not already included as income by plaintiff amounted to $1,333,617.00 for 1974 and to

---

[15] OIL, a Bermuda insurance company, was created by several major oil corporations. Plaintiff joined OIL in 1971 through plaintiff's parent company Murphy.

[16] When William Nolan, a senior vice-president of Highlands, wrote to Mentor to request letters of credit, he addressed the correspondence to Mr. Niederer, who was responsible for acquiring insurance for plaintiff, not to Mr. Carter, who was vice-president of Mentor at the time. Mr. Carter testified that this was due to Mr. Nolan's incompetence and offered as further proof of such incompetence the fact that Mr. Nolan had incorrectly stated Mentor's name. (Mr. Nolan wrote "MENTOR INSURANCE COMPANY" rather than Mentor Insurance Limited.) Mr. Carter admitted that Mentor needed to obtain the approval of plaintiff to issue letters of credit over a certain amount. Defendant in its post-trial brief asserted that Mr. Nolan was correct in writing to Mr. Niederer, since Mr. Niederer had the authority to approve Mentor's providing the requested letters of credit. The only point the court finds relevant with respect to this matter is that letters of credit for large amounts could not be issued by Mentor without plaintiff's approval.

[17] Defendant, in its post-trial brief, concluded that this evidence indicated that the earned surplus of Mentor for 1974 and 1975 was derived solely from premiums paid by plaintiff. The term "earned surplus" was not defined at trial or in defendant's post-trial brief.

$1,257,876.00 for 1975. The IRS proposed that these amounts be included as income under Internal Revenue Code, 26 U.S.C. ("I.R.C.") § 953 (1970), a provision requiring taxpayers to include as income premiums earned from insurance of United States risks.

Edward K. Dwyer testified as to the derivation and accuracy of the IRS's figures. Mr. Dwyer was employed by plaintiff from July 1973 to July 1984, initially as tax manager and subsequently as tax director. Mr. Dwyer was responsible for tax planning, complying with tax laws, handling IRS audits, working with outside and in-house tax counsel, and filing of federal income tax returns for plaintiff and its subsidiaries. Mr. Dwyer was involved in, and had the responsibility for, IRS audits of the tax returns of plaintiff and its subsidiaries for tax years 1969-1975. The tax returns were compiled from the workpapers of outside auditors, from the workpapers of earlier years, and from supplemental material obtained from plaintiff and its subsidiaries. In auditing plaintiff and its subsidiaries, the IRS examined the workpapers used to prepare the tax returns and scrutinized thoroughly inter-company dealings. Mr. Dwyer reviewed the assessments made by the IRS for tax years 1974 and 1975 and determined that the amounts assessed for disallowance of a business expense and for premiums earned on property located in the United States were complete and accurate representations of what the IRS purported them to be-that is, he agreed that the amounts assessed for disallowance were the premiums received by Mentor from plaintiff and its consolidated United States subsidiaries and that the amounts assessed for premiums earned on United States risks were the premiums earned from drilling rigs operating over the Outer Continental Shelf of the Gulf of Mexico that had not been included as income by plaintiff.[18]

In addition, Mr. Dwyer testified that the tax returns for 1974 and 1975 were completed in accordance with the "70/30 Rule" [sic] that appears in the Treasury Regulations for I.R.C. § 953. The rule provides that if an asset is in the United States for not more than 30 percent of the days of a period, such asset shall not be considered to be located in the United States and that if an asset is in the United States for more than 50 percent of the days of a period, such asset shall be considered to be located in the United States. Treas.Reg. § 1.953-2 (1964).

DISCUSSION

I. Risk shifting and risk distributing

The first issue to be addressed is whether payments by plaintiff to its subsidiary insurer constitute insurance, thus qualifying as a business deduction for federal income tax purposes.

---

[18]   Mr. Dwyer did not comment on the legal contentions of the IRS that such amounts were income. Rather, he verified the accuracy of the derivation of the numbers.

I.R.C. § 162(a) allows as a deduction from taxable income "all the ordinary and necessary expenses paid or incurred during the taxable year in carrying on any trade or business." Insurance premiums are considered an ordinary and necessary business expense. Treas.Reg. § 1.162-1(a) (1973). Over the last ten years, several courts have addressed the issue of whether premiums paid by a parent company to a subsidiary insurer constitute insurance. These courts based their findings on this issue on the Supreme Court's definition of insurance in Helvering v. Le Gierse, 312 U.S. 531, 61 S.Ct. 646, 85 L.Ed. 996 (1941). In Le Gierse the Supreme Court stated that "insurance involves risk-shifting and risk-distributing...." 312 U.S. at 539, 61 S.Ct. at 649. The Court in Le Gierse did not provide definitions for risk-shifting and risk-distributing, and consequently lower courts differ on their interpretations of these terms.

1. Courts also have differed on the significance of treating the parent company and the subsidiary insurer as separate entities on the question of whether payments to a subsidiary insurer constitute insurance. Under Moline Properties, Inc. v. Commissioner, 319 U.S. 436, 438-39, 63 S.Ct. 1132, 1133-34, 87 L.Ed. 1499 (1943), a corporation with a legitimate business purpose must be treated as "a separate taxable entity." Thus, Moline Properties stands for the proposition that a parent corporation and its subsidiary corporation be accorded treatment as separate taxable entities. National Carbide Corp. v. Commissioner, 336 U.S. 422, 69 S.Ct. 726, 93 L.Ed. 779 (1949). The courts disagree on the role of this requirement in determining whether payments to a subsidiary insurer constitute a valid business deduction for the parent corporation.

The focus in the case at bar differs from that of some of the earlier cases involving a parent company and its subsidiary insurer. The primary issue in this case involves the effect of business unrelated to the parent that a subsidiary insurer underwrites in determining whether a parent's payments to its subsidiary constitute insurance. The following discussion of prior case law indicates that this issue was not a central focus of any court's decision until earlier this year. However, analysis of the prior case law is helpful in understanding the development of a definition for what is meant by "insurance" in tax law. The cases discussed below are not binding precedent on the Claims Court.

Carnation Co. v. Commissioner, 640 F.2d 1010 (9th Cir.), cert. denied, 454 U.S. 965, 102 S.Ct. 506, 70 L.Ed.2d 381 (1981), involved a subsidiary insurance company, incorporated in Bermuda, and wholly-owned by its parent. The subsidiary wrote insurance solely for the parent company and its subsidiaries. The parent company, Carnation Company, purchased insurance from an unrelated insurer and the subsidiary insurer then reinsured the unrelated insurer for 90 percent of Carnation's liability. As part of the agreement with the unrelated insurer, the parent company agreed to capitalize the subsidiary insurer for up to $3,000,000.00 at either the subsidiary's request or the parent's election.[19]

---

[19]   The initial capital contribution was $120,000.00.

In assessing whether risk shifting and risk distribution took place, the Ninth Circuit looked to "the substance of the transaction." 640 F.2d at 1013. The court analyzed the insurance, reinsurance, and capitalization agreements together and determined that the agreements operated to neutralize risk in the instances of reinsurance by the subsidiary insurer. In addition, the court noted that Rev.Rul. 77-316, 1977-2 C.B. 53, situation 2, stated on facts identical to those before the court that "there ... [was] no risk shifting or risk distribution with respect to the risks carried or retained by the wholly owned subsidiary····." Carnation, 640 F.2d at 1013.[20] The court did not attempt to define "insurance" except to say that it involves risk shifting and risk distribution. Without discussing how risk is shifted or distributed, the court concluded that the agreements neutralized risk to the extent of reinsurance and that the separate corporate status of the subsidiary and parent had no bearing on whether the risk was shifted away from the parent.

Stearns-Roger Corp. v. United States, 774 F.2d 414 (10th Cir.1985), involved an insurance company, incorporated under state captive insurance laws. Under these laws the captive insurer could insure only risks of the parent company, its subsidiaries, its affiliates, and associated companies. The parent company, Stearns-Roger Corporation, and one of its wholly-owned subsidiaries owned all the stock of the captive insurer. The parent company provided initial and subsequent capital to the captive insurer and indemnified the captive insurer for up to $3,000,000.00 for losses that it might suffer. The captive company insured risks of the parent, the parent's subsidiaries and affiliates, and participants in projects where the parent had assumed such participants' risks. The parent company paid for this coverage by the captive company.

The Tenth Circuit in Stearns-Roger did not attempt to define "insurance" beyond stating that it must involve risk shifting or risk distribution. The court focused on the effects of the parent's payments to the captive insurer to resolve whether the payments amounted to insurance. The court asserted that it did not ignore the separate corporate status of the captive and parent companies and that this status was not inconsistent with its findings. The court determined that the parent company's assets were diminished by any casualty loss and, thus, that the economic reality of the situation was that the risk of loss did not leave the parent company. The parent did not receive insurance for its payments, the court concluded, because the parent did not shift its risk of loss. The court noted that it did not consider the indemnity agreement in its analysis.

Mobil Oil Corp. v. United States, 8 Cl.Ct. 555 (1985), involved four insurance companies, owned indirectly by one company, Mobil Oil Corporation ("Mobil"). The loci of incorporation for the affiliate insurers included the Bahamas, Bermuda, and the

---

20   The revenue ruling is not applicable to the present case as it specifically deals with situations where the subsidiary insurer writes no unrelated business.

United Kingdom. The affiliate insurers wrote insurance for the parent, its affiliates, and for unrelated parties.

To determine if insurance existed, the Claims Court in Mobil analyzed whether Mobil had sufficiently transferred the risk of loss. The court assessed the economic substance of the transaction and determined that any losses or profits realized by the insurance affiliates would be reflected on Mobil's financial statements. The court concluded that this did not amount to a transfer of risk of loss by Mobil. The court stated that "[i]nsurance through a wholly-owned insurance affiliate is essentially the same as setting up reserve accounts. The risk of loss remains with the parent and is reflected on the balance sheet and income statements of the parent...." 8 Cl.Ct. at 567. The court determined that its holding did not disregard the separate status of parent and affiliate insurer, but, rather, was "an example of reclassification of a transaction." Id. The court did not address the issue of what impact the writing of unrelated business by the affiliate insurer might have on the determination of whether the payments by Mobil amounted to insurance.

In Beech Aircraft Corp. v. United States, 797 F.2d 920 (10th Cir.1986), the insurance company was incorporated in Bermuda and was primarily owned by Beech Aircraft Corporation ("Beech Aircraft") and its affiliates. All but 0.5 percent of the insurer's business was insurance issued Beech Aircraft. The premium paid by Beech Aircraft supplemented by the interest the premium would earn equaled the liability of the insurer to Beech Aircraft. The Tenth Circuit stated that Stearns-Roger "bears directly on" and "for all practical purposes, is dispositive of" the case before the court. 797 F.2d at 923. The court in Beech Aircraft assessed the economic reality of the transaction and determined that Beech Aircraft paid for any losses sustained by the insurer and that no shifting of risk occurred. The court held that the separate corporate status of Beech Aircraft and the insurer did not prevent a finding that risk of loss did not shift. The court did not discuss any effects of unrelated business.

Clougherty Packing Co. v. Commissioner, 811 F.2d 1297 (9th Cir.1987), involved a wholly-owned subsidiary incorporated in Colorado under state captive insurance laws. The parent company, Clougherty Packing Company ("Clougherty"), purchased insurance from an unrelated insurer which then reinsured the first $100,000.00 of each claim against Clougherty with the subsidiary insurer. The subsidiary insurer's only business was reinsurance of the parent company. The Ninth Circuit in Clougherty defined "insurance" as involving risk shifting and risk distributing. The court stated that "[i]f the insured has shifted its risk to the insurer, then a loss by or a claim against the insured does not affect it because the loss is offset by the proceeds of an insurance payment...." 811 F.2d at 1300. With respect to risk distributing, the court stated that "[i]nsuring many independent risks in return for numerous premiums serves to distribute risk····" Id. The court determined that risk shifting did not take place and, therefore, did not address the issue of risk distributing.

According to the Ninth Circuit, the insurance and reinsurance contracts were interdependent; interdependent agreements must be considered together to determine their economic effect. The court examined the assets of the insured party, not the insurer's assets or "some aggregation of the two," to see if the risk of adverse economic consequences was divested from the insured by the agreements. 811 F.2d at 1305. Because the insurer's "income and net worth f[e]ll dollar for dollar by the amount of the loss" claimed by the parent and because the insurer did no business other than the parent's, the stock of the insurer declined by the amount of the claim. Id. The court maintained that, consequently, the assets of the insured fell by the amount of the claim: The insured was the owner of the insurer's assets and the reduction in value of the insured's assets was the same as it would have been if the parent had self-insured. Thus, the court concluded that risk of loss did not shift.

The court stated that its holding did not conflict with Moline Properties since only the assets of the insured were analyzed to determine if risk shifted. The Ninth Circuit reiterated its holding in Carnation, that Rev.Rul. 77-316 does not conflict with Moline Properties. The court pointed out that other courts had addressed the captive insurer issue and none had determined that "a policy provided by a wholly-owned subsidiary that exists solely for the purpose of providing insurance to its parent constitutes insurance, or that such a conclusion violates Moline Properties." 811 F.2d at 1303.

Humana Inc. v. Commissioner, 881 F.2d 247 (6th Cir.1989), involved an insurancecompany incorporated in Colorado under state captive insurance laws. The insurer provided coverage for the parent company and its subsidiaries. The parent company, Humana Incorporated ("Humana"), purchased insurance for itself and its subsidiaries from the captive insurer and then charged its subsidiaries for their share of coverage. Humana owned 75 percent of the insurer, and a wholly-owned subsidiary of Humana owned 25 percent of the insurer.

The Sixth Circuit, relying on Le Gierse, stated that an insurance contract involves risk shifting and risk distribution: "Risk shifting involves the shifting of an identifiable risk of the insured to the insurer···· Risk distribution involves shifting to a group of individuals the identified risk of the insured····" 881 F.2d at 251. The court then separately analyzed the premiums paid by the parent and the premiums paid by the subsidiaries. It concluded that the rationale of Clougherty and Carnation applied to the parent's premiums and, consequently, that these premiums did not constitute insurance. With respect to the premiums paid by the subsidiaries, the court determined that Moline Properties required that the separate corporate status of the subsidiaries and the insurer be maintained. Adopting the analysis in Clougherty, the Sixth Circuit examined the effect of a claim on the assets of the insured. The court considered the insured to be the subsidiaries and not the parent under Moline Properties. When the insurer paid a claim, the assets of the subsidiaries were not affected and, thus, the risk of loss transferred from the insured to the insurer.

The court stated that it did not look to the assets of the parent because to do so would be to treat the parent, its subsidiaries, and the insurer "as one 'economic unit' and ignore the reality of their separate corporate existence for tax purposes in violation of Moline Properties." 881 F.2d at 256. The court noted that "absent specific congressional intent to the contrary, ⋯ a court cannot disregard a transaction in the name of economic reality and substance over form absent a finding of sham or lack of business purpose under the relevant tax statute." Id. at 255 (citations omitted).

After determining that risk shifting occurred, the court stated that risk distribution must also be present for insurance to exist. The court concluded that risk distribution was present since several corporations were insured and losses could be spread among them. Thus, the court ruled that the premiums paid by the subsidiaries of Humana constituted insurance because both risk shifting and risk distribution occurred.

Gulf Oil Corp. v. Commissioner, 914 F.2d 396 (3d Cir.1990), an appeal from the United States Tax Court, involved a subsidiary insurer incorporated in Bermuda. The insurer was undercapitalized until 1975 when the parent company, Gulf Oil Corporation ("Gulf"), transferred ownership of the insurer to Gulf's wholly-owned holding company, which provided additional capital to the insurer. Gulf and its affiliates paid premiums to third-party commercial carriers. These carriers then reinsured a significant portion of their liability to Gulf and its affiliates with the subsidiary insurer. Gulf executed guarantees to the third-party commercial carriers obligating Gulf to indemnify them should the subsidiary insurer be unable to meet its obligations to them. All of the subsidiary's premium income came from related parties except for 2 percent in one of the two tax years involved.[21]

The Third Circuit discussed the necessity of risk shifting and risk distribution for insurance to exist and noted that interdependent agreements must be considered together. The court determined that the undercapitalization of the insurer and the guarantees executed by the parent indicated that risk did not shift. The court viewed Humana as distinguishable on the basis that Humana did not involve an undercapitalized insurer or guarantees executed by the parent company.

The court noted that the Tax Court in prior decisions held that risk does not transfer in circumstances where a wholly-owned subsidiary does not insure parties unrelated to the

---

[21]   The tax years at issue in the litigation were 1974 and 1975.

parent company. In the present case, the Tax Court was divided over the effects of unrelated business on risk shifting. The appeals court stated that it need not reach this issue since it was clear that "because of the guarantee to the primary insurers, Gulf and Insco [the subsidiary insurer] did not truly transfer the risk, nor was there a de facto risk distribution to third parties, elements crucial to the allowance of a premium deduction." 914 F.2d at 412.

Subsequent to Gulf the Tax Court established a three-step analysis to determine if insurance existed in cases wherein the subsidiary insurer did business for parties unrelated to the parent and its affiliates. These cases are Sears, Roebuck & Co. v. Commissioner, 96 T.C. 61, 1991 WL 4979 (1991), as modified, 96 T.C. 671, 1991 WL 61250 (1991); The Harper Group v. Commissioner, 96 T.C. 45, 1991 WL 4980 (1991); and AMERCO v. Commissioner, 96 T.C. 18, 1991 WL 4981 (1991). The Tax Court analysis, based on Le Gierse, involves "presence of insurance risk," "risk shifting and risk distributing," and "commonly accepted notions of insurance."

With respect to "presence of insurance risk" the Tax Court stated the following:

> Basic to any insurance transaction must be risk. An insured faces some hazard; an insurer accepts a premium and agrees to perform some act if or when the loss event occurs. If no risk exists, then insurance cannot be present. "Insurance risk" is required; investment risk is insufficient. If parties structure an apparent insurance transaction so as to effectively eliminate the effect of insurance risk therein, insurance cannot be present.

AMERCO, 96 T.C. at 38-39. With respect to "risk shifting and risk distributing," the Tax Court stated that while Le Gierse established that insurance requires risk shifting and risk distributing, Le Gierse did not define these terms. The Tax Court relied on the Tenth Circuit's decision in Beech Aircraft for the following definition: "'Risk-shifting' means one party shifts his risk of loss to another, and 'risk-distributing' means that the party assuming the risk distributes his potential liability, in part, among others." Harper, 96 T.C. at 58-59, and AMERCO, 96 T.C. at 40 (quoting Beech Aircraft, 797 F.2d at 922). With respect to the third requirement of "commonly accepted notions of insurance," the Tax Court did not discuss how to apply the requirement. The court dealt with this requirement by applying the facts of each case to determine if insurance existed in a commonly understood manner.

Sears involved a wholly-owned subsidiary insurer of Sears, Roebuck and Co. ("Sears"). The subsidiary insurer, Allstate Insurance Company ("Allstate"), was licensed in 40 states. While the subsidiary insured 10-15 percent of the parent company's risk, the premiums received from this business only amounted to 0.25 percent of the premiums earned by the subsidiary insurer for the years in issue. The other 99.75 percent of the subsidiary's premiums were received from policyholders unrelated to the parent.

The Tax Court, employing its three-step analysis, concluded that payments by Sears to the subsidiary constituted insurance. The court found that the claims involved-claims relating to injuries to persons on the parent's premises or by the parent's vehicles-established the presence of insurance risk. Risk shifting existed in both form and substance: in form because insurance contracts were written; premiums were transferred; losses were paid; and the subsidiary insurer was a separate, viable entity financially capable of meeting its obligations-in substance because the insurer's business relationship with its parent was the same as its business relationship with unrelated insured parties. The scope of the subsidiary's business demonstrated the presence of risk distribution. Finally, the court determined insurance to be present, in the commonly accepted sense, based on the arrangements between the parent and subsidiary being understood as insurance for non-tax purposes and there being no justification to look at such arrangements differently for tax purposes.

Harper involved a subsidiary insurer incorporated in Hong Kong. The parent company, The Harper Group ("Harper"), was a holding company that owned several subsidiaries. The subsidiary insurer shared facilities and employees with another subsidiary of the parent. The subsidiary insurer provided insurance to the parent's domestic and foreign subsidiaries and to customers of two of the parent's subsidiaries. The customers were parties unrelated to the parent, and the premiums received from these unrelated parties approximated 30 percent of the subsidiary's premiums for the years in issue.

The Tax Court in Harper concluded through its three-step analysis that premiums received by the subsidiary insurer from related parties constituted insurance. The court determined insurance risk to exist, stating that the transfer of risk to the insurer and the exposure of the insurer were "real, not illusory." 96 T.C. at 58. The court found risk shifting to exist based on the following facts: Insurance contracts were written; premiums were paid; claims were paid; related parties' premiums were negotiated at arm's length; and the subsidiary insurer was a separate entity, regulated under the laws of Hong Kong and financially capable of meeting its obligations. The court considered that risk distribution existed, finding that unrelated business approximating 30 percent was sufficient to provide risk distribution. Finally, the court determined insurance to exist in the commonly accepted sense, listing as relevant factors the following: The subsidiary insurer was organized and operated as an insurance company and was regulated by Hong Kong insurance law, the insurer's capitalization was adequate, premiums were negotiated at arm's length, and the policies issued by the insurer were valid and binding.

AMERCO involved a subsidiary insurer incorporated in Arizona. The parent Company, AMERCO, was a holding company with one to three employees during the years at issue.

AMERCO filed consolidated tax returns with approximately 250 of its subsidiaries. These subsidiaries were a primary component of the U-Haul rental system. The subsidiary insurer was not included in AMERCO's consolidated returns. The subsidiary insurer had gross written premiums attributable to parties unrelated to the parent in the range of 52 to 74 percent during the seven years at issue.

The Tax Court concluded that the premiums paid by parties related to AMERCO constituted insurance. The court determined that risk existed, stating that the insured parties faced potential hazards. The court found there to be technical risk shifting and risk shifting in substance: technical because insurance contracts were written; premiums were paid; claims were paid; and the insurer was a separate, viable entity, financially capable of meeting its obligations, licensed and operating under many states' insurance laws-in substance because of the substantial business the insurer wrote for parties other than AMERCO. Risk distribution was present based on the diverse, multifaceted, and substantial unrelated business of the insurer. Finally, the court found that insurance existed in the commonly accepted sense, emphasizing the technical and substantive nature of the transactions and the state regulators' view of such transactions as insurance.

2. The case law demonstrates the different issues that have been presented to courts on the overriding question of whether payments by a parent to a subsidiary insurer constitute insurance. A consensus on a precise definition of insurance does not emerge from these opinions. At trial plaintiff presented an expert witness to define "insurance." Defendant did not tender such a witness. Dr. Neil A. Doherty testified for plaintiff as an expert on the economics of insurance. Dr. Doherty is a professor at the Wharton School at the University of Pennsylvania where he primarily teaches classes on insurance and risk management. He has written several books and numerous articles for academic journals on the topic of insurance. Dr. Doherty testified as an expert witness in the trilogy of Tax Court cases discussed above.

Dr. Doherty described insurance as "an institution whereby a number of individuals or firms transfer their premiums and their exposures to loss to a common fund, and the common fund is then available to pay for the losses of whoever might suffer them." He stated that the risk dimension that is being transferred is the unpredictability or variability of loss and not the expected loss or long run average cost.[22] Under the statistical principle of the law of large numbers, risk or variability is reduced by increasing the number of policies in a common fund.

---

[22]   The expected loss is the average loss expected to occur over a period of time. The insurance company charges a premium that will cover the expected loss. Thus, the risk of the expected loss theoretically is not transferred, since the insured pays an amount through a premium that covers the expected loss.

Dr. Doherty asserted that when the only business of a captive insurer is that of insuring its parent, the risk for the parent is the same as it would be if the parent had self-insured by setting aside funds to cover possible losses. In neither case is risk reduced for the parent; the two scenarios therefore did not conform to Dr. Doherty's definition of insurance. He then demonstrated that when a captive insurer underwrites insurance for both its parent and unrelated parties, risk is lower for the parent than it would be if the parent was self-insured. Under the axiom of the law of large numbers, risk is reduced when the number of policyholders is increased by the captive insurer.[23]

In his analysis Dr. Doherty distinguished between ownership risk and policyholder risk. He described the latter as the risk the parent transferred to the subsidiary. Ownership risk, he asserted, is the investment risk or the level of risk that exists after combining all the policies written by the insurer. Dr. Doherty illustrated that the policyholder risk and the ownership risk would be the same only if an insurer did not write any unrelated business. He demonstrated how the ownership risk is reduced the greater the amount of unrelated business that is written by the insurer. Dr. Doherty described the owner as the one that takes the equity interest in the profit or loss of the pool after the insurance function of the arrangement is completed. He stated that the capital of the company serves as a second line of defense to cover losses if premiums are not sufficient to pay out claims.

It was Dr. Doherty's expert opinion that the premiums paid by plaintiff and its subsidiaries to Mentor constituted insurance. He stated that the percentage of unrelated business by Mentor was economically significant in terms of risk reduction. He determined that unrelated business was approximately 44 percent of Mentor's business for 1974 and 66 percent for 1975. According to the witness, the risk reduction created by this unrelated business was sufficient to qualify the premiums paid to Mentor by plaintiff and its subsidiaries as insurance.[24]

This court must adhere to the principles of Le Gierse and Moline Properties in reaching a decision. Plaintiff and Mentor must be considered as separate entities in evaluating whether the transactions between the two companies resulted in risk shifting and risk distributing.

---

[23] Dr. Doherty noted an additional distinction between a captive insurer's underwriting only for its parent and a captive insurer's underwriting for unrelated parties. He stated that when unrelated parties are involved, the parent company does not have the same level of control over the insurer's funds, since such funds must be available to meet all the parties' claims and thus are not available to the parent to spend in whatever manner it wishes.

[24] Dr. Doherty also determined that Mentor was adequately capitalized, but stated that this was not a crucial factor to his determination of whether the premiums by plaintiff and its subsidiaries constituted insurance. In his view, inadequate capitalization would not negate the existence of insurance, but, rather, would reduce its effectiveness, since there would be greater risk to the policyholders than in the case of adequate capitalization.

However, if the business operations of Mentor are a sham, Mentor's "corporate form may be disregarded." Moline Properties, 319 U.S. at 439, 63 S.Ct. at 1134. Furthermore, even if plaintiff and Mentor are separate entities, if plaintiff retained the risk of the losses against which it insured, plaintiff's premiums amounted to a reserve for losses, and plaintiff would not be entitled to deduct such premiums from taxable income. Beech Aircraft, 797 F.2d at 922 (citing United States v. Newton Livestock Auction Market, Inc., 336 F.2d 673, 676 (10th Cir.1964), and Spring Canyon Coal Co. v. Commissioner, 43 F.2d 78, 79 (10th Cir.1930), cert. denied, 284 U.S. 654, 52 S.Ct. 33, 76 L.Ed. 555 (1931)).

3. The court turns first to the issue of whether the separate status of Mentor was a sham. Defendant attempted at trial to establish that Mentor's operations were controlled by plaintiff and that Mentor's existence was therefore a sham. Defendant was unsuccessful in this endeavor and in post-trial closing argument abandoned the contention that Mentor was a sham. Nevertheless, the court believes it useful to elaborate on the facts that demonstrate Mentor's valid business existence. These facts establish two of the three factors found by the Tax Court to illustrate the existence of insurance: "presence of insurance risk" and "commonly accepted notions of insurance."

Several factors contribute to recognizing Mentor as a valid insurance company. The parties that insured with Mentor, both plaintiff and unrelated parties, truly faced hazards. Events such as hurricanes and accidents were real possibilities and could result in losses to the insured parties. The business underwritten by Mentor was understood to be insurance provided by Mentor. Insurance contracts were written and premiums were paid. Unrelated parties purchased reinsurance from Mentor. Unrelated parties co-insured a portion of the direct insurance Mentor wrote for plaintiff. Unrelated parties reinsured policies that Mentor wrote for plaintiff. Premiums charged to plaintiff and unrelated parties were based on the commercial rates in London. The validity of claims was established before payments were made on them. Claims were paid from funds of Mentor that were maintained separately from plaintiff's funds. Mentor's capitalization was adequate, and the policies it entered into were valid and binding. Mentor's business operations were separate from plaintiff's.[25] Cumulatively, these facts indicate that Mentor's existence as an insurance company was valid and not a sham.

Having established Mentor was not a sham, the next question to be addressed is whether plaintiff shifted its risk to Mentor through its arrangements with Mentor. In order to determine if risk is shifted, it is necessary to identify the risk that is shifted in the

---

[25]   Defendant questioned the separate status of Mentor and plaintiff based, in part, on the overlap in several key employees and officers and on plaintiff's control over the investment of some of Mentor's funds. Defendant cited no case law supporting the proposition that either factor would serve to negate the separate status of plaintiff and Mentor. Having examined all the factors, the court finds that Mentor's business operations were separate from those of plaintiff.

insurance context. The case law previously discussed does not delve into the connotation given to risk by the various courts. The Tax Court asserts that insurance risk must be present, but does not define the risk that parties insure against. The Tax Court's assertion that there must be the chance of an event occurring that will cause a loss to the insured party addresses the issue of whether the business is a sham rather than the definition of risk. The other courts use terms such as "risk of loss" or "risk of adverse economic consequences," without elaborating on their meaning. Thus, the prior case law does not provide a definitive answer to the question of the risk that is shifted by insured parties.

The court found Dr. Doherty's testimony helpful on this point. Dr. Doherty explained how insurance operates and clarified what the risk element is that insurance premiums guard against. Insurance protects against the variability of loss. An insured party pays a premium that is expected to cover the average loss. Therefore, the insured party does not transfer the cost of the average loss, since the insured party pays that amount to the insurer. What the insured party transfers to the insurer when it pays premiums is the cost of variability in losses. The risk that the insured transfers to the insurer is the variability of loss, not the complete loss from an event, such as a hurricane or an accident, since the insured pays a premium that covers the average cost of the complete loss.

Plaintiff paid premiums to Mentor, and Mentor thereby became liable for claims of loss on the insured property. When plaintiff experienced a loss, a claim was filed with Mentor and Mentor paid the claim out of its own funds, funds that were separate from plaintiff's funds. However, because Mentor was a subsidiary of plaintiff, any expense of Mentor, such as payment of a claim, would reduce the assets of plaintiff. If this court were to rely on Stearns-Roger or Mobil, this fact alone would be sufficient to find that risk did not transfer from plaintiff to Mentor. Both Stearns-Roger and Mobil concluded that risk did not transfer from parent to subsidiary because the parents' assets were diminished by casualty losses when the subsidiary paid off a claim on the loss.[26] The court does not

---

26 The other cases discussed above that did not find transfer of risk did not base their conclusions solely on the existence of the parent/wholly-owned subsidiary relationship and can be distinguished from the present case. The finding of no risk transfer in Carnation was based, in part, on the parent company's agreement to further capitalize the insurer. No such agreement is present here. The finding of no risk transfer in Beech Aircraft was based on the fact that the liability of the insurer for the parent's losses could not exceed the amount paid in premiums by the parent, supplemented by interest. That situation is not present here. Clougherty made specific reference to the fact that assets of the parent were reduced by the exact amount of the casualty loss experienced by the parent because no outside business was written by the insurer. Thus, Clougherty distinguishes itself from the present case. To the extent Humana determined risk transfer to not be present, it based its findings on Clougherty and Carnation, and is distinguishable for the same reasons as these cases. The finding of no risk transfer in Gulf was based on the insurer's being undercapitalized and on the presence of guarantees by the parent. These factors are not present here. (The court does not consider one guarantee executed by plaintiff after the years in issue to be evidence of guarantees by plaintiff for the years in issue.)

consider these decisions to offer the correct approach to the present case. To follow Stearns-Roger or Mobil would be to ignore the effect that unrelated business underwritten by Mentor has on the level of risk.

Unrelated business operated to reduce the amount of risk to which plaintiff was exposed. When plaintiff purchased insurance from Mentor, plaintiff transferred to Mentor a certain level of risk or a certain amount of variability of loss. Because Mentor had unrelated business, this level of risk was not retained by plaintiff, the parent of Mentor. The considerable amount of unrelated business, approximately 44 and 66 percent during the years in issue, caused a significant reduction in risk. Plaintiff as the parent of Mentor thus shouldered a level of risk significantly lower than the level of risk that it initially transferred to Mentor. Consequently, the risk transferred to Mentor and the risk ultimately borne by plaintiff were not the same, and plaintiff's premiums constituted the transfer of risk.

If the level of risk plaintiff initially had transferred and the level of risk plaintiff ultimately had shouldered were virtually the same, plaintiff's risk effectively would not have transferred. However, this situation is not present in the case at bar, and plaintiff's payment of premiums to Mentor did amount to a transfer of risk. The court does not address the question of what amount of unrelated business is necessary to result in transfer of risk. The court notes that the Tax Court found transfer of risk in situations where unrelated business was 30, 52 to 74, and 99 percent. The percentage of unrelated business present here, 44 and 66 percent, is within the range of unrelated business found by the Tax Court's decisions to constitute transfer of risk.

Unlike this court's analysis, the Tax Court's discussions of risk transfer did not focus solely on the amount of unrelated business. The Tax Court's decisions concluded that risk shifting occurred based on some of the following factors: Insurance contracts were written; premiums were paid; claims were paid; the insurer operated as a separate, viable entity, financially capable of meeting its obligations; the insurer wrote substantial unrelated business; and the insurer was regulated under insurance laws. The only factor in this list not established at trial was that Mentor was regulated under insurance laws.[27] The court does not find that the absence of this factor negates the existence of insurance. Although during the years at issue, the Bermuda law under which Mentor was regulated was general corporation law, rather than specifically insurance law, Mentor effectively was

---

[27]   Defendant argued that the terms of business were different for plaintiff and unrelated parties since plaintiff's policies were for direct insurance and unrelated parties' policies were for reinsurance. Defendant's contention is not persuasive. Direct insurance and reinsurance are both considered insurance, and the premiums charged on both types of policies were based on commercial rates in London. The court finds that Mentor underwrote business for plaintiff and unrelated parties on the same terms.

regulated by the insurance industry itself.[28] Unrelated parties would reinsure and co-insure with Mentor only if they viewed Mentor as financially sound, since they would be liable if Mentor was unable to meet its obligations. Thus, Mentor was required to maintain financial stability if it desired to undertake business with unrelated parties. Mr. Carter's testimony on this point was unimpeachable. The significant amount of unrelated business underwritten by Mentor during the years in issue illustrates Mentor's success in meeting the industry's standards of a viable business. Because the factors that led the Tax Court to conclude that risk shifting occurred in its decisions are also present in this case, the court finds risk shifting to be present under the Tax Court's analysis, in addition to being present under this court's own analysis.[29]

Since risk shifting was present, the next question to be addressed is whether risk distribution occurred. Risk distribution involves spreading the risk of loss among policyholders. Mentor had unrelated business of approximately 44 and 66 percent for the two years at issue. This amount of unrelated business sufficiently spreads risk so as to constitute risk distribution. The court notes that the Tax Court found risk distribution to exist in Harper where unrelated business approximated only 30 percent.

Since risk shifting and risk distributing were present, the court finds that insurance exists as outlined in Le Gierse. Thus, the payments by plaintiff to Mentor constituted insurance and were allowed to be deducted from taxable income.

4. Other arguments raised by defendant were considered and found to be without merit. Defendant's argument regarding the inconsistency of Humana with Federal Circuit law is deemed irrelevant to this decision because this court does not rely on Humana. Nevertheless, the court notes that it does not agree with defendant's assertion that plaintiff and the subsidiaries with which it filed a consolidated return must be treated as a single entity under Exxon Corp. v. United States, 785 F.2d 277 (Fed.Cir.1986), despite Moline Properties. Exxon, in stating that those who file a consolidated return must be treated as a single entity, quotes American Standard, Inc. v. United States, 220 Ct.Cl.

---

28 From evidence presented at trial, it appeared that Bermuda did not have laws specific to regulating insurance until after the years in issue.

29 The court did not find convincing defendant's distinctions of the Tax Court's cases. The factors that the Tax Court relied on in concluding that risk shifting occurred are present in this case, except for regulation by insurance laws. Each of the three Tax Court cases; Sears, Harper, and AMERCO, listed some, but not all, of the factors listed above. The court does not read the Tax Court cases as creating specific criteria that must exist for risk shifting to occur between a parent and a subsidiary. Rather, the Tax Court's intention was to examine all the factors of a particular case together to determine if risk shifting was present. This court analyzed all the facts of this case and determined that risk shifting occurred within the Tax Court's meaning of risk shifting.

411, 602 F.2d 256 (1979). 785 F.2d at 280. American Standard specifically states with respect to the proposition quoted in Exxon, "The single entity framework does not mean that all items of income, deductions, and credit for the affiliated corporations are combined into single accounts as if the corporations were one. The consolidated return regulations, in fact, primarily deal with the affiliated corporations as separate corporate entities…." American Standard, 220 Ct.Cl. at 418, 602 F.2d at 261. Thus, American Standard and Exxon do not require disregarding the separate status of affiliated entities and do not conflict with Moline Properties. Furthermore, to the extent they might, Moline Properties as a Supreme Court decision would override such contrary decisions by lower courts.

This court also views as without merit defendant's argument that plaintiff's payments to Mentor are not deductible under Commissioner v. Lincoln Savings & Loan Ass'n, 403 U.S. 345, 91 S.Ct. 1893, 29 L.Ed.2d 519 (1971), based on their serving to create or enhance a separate asset for plaintiff. The funds in Lincoln Savings that were determined to constitute an asset are clearly distinguishable from the premiums paid by plaintiff. In Lincoln Savings the funds that were determined to be an asset were a "prepayment with respect to future premiums," 403 U.S. at 348, 91 S.Ct. at 1896; if such funds were converted to actual premiums or "used to pay losses," the funds became deductible. Id. at 358, 91 S.Ct. at 1900. In the present case the payments by plaintiff were actual premiums, not prepayments of future premiums. Furthermore, the insured parties in Lincoln Savings had a "property interest" in the funds constituting future premiums, earned a return on the funds, and in certain situations could receive funds back. Id. at 355, 91 S.Ct. at 1899. Plaintiff's payments were placed into a pool of funds used to pay claims of the insurer, and plaintiff did not maintain a property interest in these payments.

II. Insurance of United States risks

The second issue to be addressed is whether the court's determination that plaintiff's premiums to Mentor constituted insurance results in plaintiff's owing taxes because the premiums received by plaintiff's subsidiary, Mentor, were for insurance of property located in the United States.[30]

Under I.R.C. § 951 a United States shareholder must include in gross income his pro rata share of a controlled foreign corporation's subpart F income. I.R.C. § 952(a)(1) includes as subpart F income "the income derived from the insurance of United States risks (as determined under section 953)." I.R.C. § 953(a) provides the following:

---

[30]   References in the discussion below to sections of the Internal Revenue Code are to the sections as they existed in 1974 and 1975, unless otherwise noted.

(a) General rule.

For purposes of section 952(a)(1), the term "income derived from the insurance of United States risks" means that income which—

(1) is attributable to the reinsurance or the issuing of any insurance or annuity contract—

(A) in connection with property in, or liability arising out of activity in, or in connection with the lives or health of residents of, the United States....[31]

Under I.R.C. §§ 951-953, if the premiums paid by plaintiff to Mentor were for insurance of property located in the United States or for liability arising out of activity in the United States, these premiums should have been included in plaintiff's gross income for the years in which the payments were received by Mentor. The insured property at issue was located over the Outer Continental Shelf of the Gulf of Mexico. Plaintiff and defendant disagree as to whether the Outer Continental Shelf is a part of the United States for purposes of I.R.C. § 953(a).

I.R.C. § 7701 sets forth general definitions for the Internal Revenue Code. Section 7701(a)(9) provides the following:

(a) When used in this title, where not otherwise distinctly expressed or manifestly incompatible with the intent thereof—

....

(9) United States.

The term "United States" when used in a geographical sense includes only the States and the District of Columbia.

The regulations for section 953 provide, in pertinent part: "For purposes of section 953(a), the term 'United States' is used in a geographical sense and includes only the States and the District of Columbia...." Treas.Reg. § 1.953-2 (1964). Thus, section 7701(a)(9) and the regulation applicable to section 953 do not include the Outer Continental Shelf as a part of the United States. If the court were to rely solely on section 953, its applicable regulation, and section 7701, the court would conclude that plaintiff's payments were not insurance of United States risks.

---

31   In 1986 Congress amended I.R.C. §§ 952-953 and substituted "insurance income" for "income derived from the insurance of United States risks." Thus, the issue addressed in this opinion, the meaning of United States risks, is not relevant for insurance income earned subsequent to the effective date of the 1986 amendment. "The product of a judge's labor in tax cases frequently is as ephemeral as the subject is arcane." Anon. Judge.

302 Adkisson's Captive Insurance Companies

Defendant contends that the court must look beyond section 953 and its pertinent regulation to I.R.C. § 638 and its regulations. Section 638 was enacted in 1969 and provides, in pertinent part, as follows:

> Continental shelf areas.
>
> For purposes of applying the provisions of this chapter (including sections 861(a)(3) and 862(a)(3) in the case of the performance of personal services) with respect to mines, oil and gas wells, and other natural deposits—
>
> (1) the term "United States" when used in a geographical sense includes the seabed and subsoil of those submarine areas which are adjacent to the territorial waters of the United States and over which the United States has exclusive rights, in accordance with international law, with respect to the exploration and exploitation of natural resources....

Defendant argues that I.R.C. § 638 operates to include the Outer Continental Shelf as a part of the United States for purposes of section 953. According to defendant, reference to "this chapter" in section 638 is a reference to Chapter 1 of the Internal Revenue Code, encompassing I.R.C. §§ 1-1399, and the language "with respect to the exploration and exploitation of natural resources" in section 638 refers to any activity relating to exploration and exploitation, including insurance of mobil drilling rigs. In support of its position that section 638 is intended to apply to insurance activities, defendant cites an example in the Treasury Regulations for section 638 that indicates insurance income from a platform attached to the Outer Continental Shelf "is income derived from the insurance of United States risks, within the meaning of section 953(a)(1)(A)." Treas.Reg. § 1.638-1(f) (1973).

Plaintiff responds that I.R.C. § 638 operates to include the Outer Continental Shelf as a part of the United States only when the activity involved is the actual exploration and exploitation of natural resources or the personal services performed on mines, oil and gas wells, and other natural deposits. Plaintiff asserts that the language of section 638 clearly reinforces its contention and, furthermore, that the legislative history of section 638 illustrates that the intention of Congress through enactment of section 638 was to determine the source of income from actual mining activities. The report of the Senate Committee on Finance states with respect to enactment of section 638:

> Present law.-Present law is not explicit as to whether for purposes of the exploration for, or exploitation of, natural resources in the continental shelf area of a country over which the country exercises tax jurisdiction under the principles of international law, that area is considered for U.S. tax purposes as a part of the country.
>
> General reasons for change.-The development of natural resources in the continental shelf areas of the world makes the status of these areas for tax

purposes of increasing importance. This status is important, for example, in determining the source of income from mining activities conducted in continental shelf areas.···· Accordingly, the committee believes it appropriate to clarify the status of continental shelf areas with regard to the application of the income tax provisions of the code to natural resource activity.

Explanation of provision.---- [W]ith respect to mines, oil and gas wells and other natural deposits, the term "United States" when used in a geographical sense includes the seabed and subsoil of the submarine areas adjacent to the territorial waters of the United States ··· with respect to the exploration and exploitation of natural resources.

[W]ages or salaries received for personal services performed on a mine or oil or gas well located or being developed on the Continental Shelf of the United States constitute income from sources within the United States.

S.Rep. No. 91-552, 91st Cong., 1st Sess., reprinted in 1969 U.S.Code Cong. & Admin.News 1645, 2027, 2223 (emphasis added).

Courts "must defer to Treasury Regulations that 'implement the congressional mandate in some reasonable manner.'" Commissioner v. Portland Cement Co. of Utah, 450 U.S. 156, 169, 101 S.Ct. 1037, 1045, 67 L.Ed.2d 140 (1981) (quoting United States v. Correll, 389 U.S. 299, 307, 88 S.Ct. 445, 449, 19 L.Ed.2d 537 (1967)); Thomas Int'l Ltd. v. United States, 773 F.2d 300, 303 (Fed.Cir.1985), cert. denied, 475 U.S. 1045, 106 S.Ct. 1261, 89 L.Ed.2d 571 (1986) (quoting Portland). Where there is a doubt as to the meaning of the statutory language "an examination of the legislative history, for whatever illumination it may shed, is necessary." Ellis First Nat'l Bank of Bradenton v. United States, 213 Ct.Cl. 44, 55-56, 550 F.2d 9, 15 (1977). "In the interpretation of statutes levying taxes it is the established rule not to extend their provisions, by implication, beyond the clear import of the language used, or to enlarge their operations so as to embrace matters not specifically pointed out. In case of doubt they are construed most strongly against the government, and in favor of the citizen." Estate of Renick v. United States, 231 Ct.Cl. 457, 463, 687 F.2d 371, 376 (1982) (quoting Gould v. Gould, 245 U.S. 151, 153, 38 S.Ct. 53, 53, 62 L.Ed. 211 (1917) (citations omitted)).

The court carefully examined the above statutes and regulations to determine the applicability of I.R.C. § 638 to § 953. The court concludes that rules of statutory interpretation support a construction that section 638 does not affect section 953. First, the specific references in the legislative history to "purposes of the exploration for, or exploitation of, natural resources," "source of income from mining activities," "natural resource activity," and "personal services performed" are references to mining activities and to personal services performed at mining sites, not to insurance activities. Second, it is unlikely that the statutory language "this chapter" is intended to be so broad as to include any type of activity that relates to mining in I.R.C. §§ 1-1399. Persuasive to this end is the fact that the statute specifically states that "this chapter" includes "the performance of personal services." This reference would not have been necessary were section 638 to apply to all activities that have any relationship to mining in Chapter 1, since the performance of personal services is a part of Chapter 1. Third, because insurance activity is more remote to mining activity than personal service activity conducted at the site of exploration, it seems likely that if Congress had intended for section 638 to apply to insurance activity, Congress would have made specific reference to that activity since Congress made specific reference to personal service activity. Fourth, I.R.C. § 953, and not section 638, explicitly relates to insurance activity. Moreover, the accompanying regulation to section 953, even after amendment in 1980, maintained that the United States includes only the States and the District of Columbia.[32] Fifth, the sections of the Internal Revenue Code that precede section 638, I.R.C. §§ 611-636, are related to actual mining activities, not to insurance activities. Finally, if there is a doubt as to the meaning of the provisions of the Internal Revenue Code, the doubt "must be resolved in favor of the taxpayer." Citizens Nat'l Bank of Waco v. United States, 213 Ct.Cl. 236, 255, 551 F.2d 832, 843 (1977) (citing Porter v. Commissioner, 288 U.S. 436, 442, 53 S.Ct. 451, 453, 77 L.Ed. 880 (1933), and United States v. Merriam, 263 U.S. 179, 188, 44 S.Ct. 69, 71, 68 L.Ed. 240 (1923)). Thus, if a doubt exists as to the applicability of section 638 to insurance activities, it must be resolved against the IRS position in order to favor plaintiff taxpayer. Although the court does not consider this last factor determinative, the foregoing factors, cumulatively, fully support the conclusion that I.R.C. § 638 is not applicable to section 953. The premiums paid to Mentor by plaintiff were not for insurance of United States risks since the insured property was located over the Outer Continental Shelf which is not a part of the United States for purposes of I.R.C. § 953.[33]

CONCLUSION

Based on the foregoing, plaintiff has established its entitlement to a refund of federal corporate income taxes. The parties shall file a stipulation as to the amount of refund by February 28, 1992, after which the Clerk of the Court shall enter judgment accordingly. Plaintiff shall have its costs.

IT IS SO ORDERED.

---

32   The example provided in the regulations to section 638, indicating section 638 is to apply to insurance activity, cannot override the regulations to section 953.

33   Having determined for the reasons given above that the premiums paid by plaintiff were not for insurance of United States risks, the court need not address the other issues raised by plaintiff, including the role of the Outer Continental Shelf Lands Act, 43 U.S.C. §§ 1331-1343 (1970) (originally enacted in 1953). It is noted that, to the extent possible, tax questions should be resolved within the Internal Revenue Code itself, without reference to other statutes.

Appendix Q

Malone & Hyde, Inc. v. C.I.R.

62 F.3d 835 (6th Cir. 1995)

UNITED STATES COURT OF APPEALS, SIXTH CIRCUIT.

MALONE & HYDE, INC., and Subsidiaries, Petitioner-Appellee,

v.

COMMISSIONER OF INTERNAL REVENUE, Respondent-Appellant.

No. 94-1607, Decided Aug. 18, 1995

[Names of counsel omitted.]

Before: LIVELY, NELSON, and SILER, Circuit Judges.

LIVELY, Circuit Judge.

In this case the Commissioner of Internal Revenue assessed an income tax deficiency against a corporate taxpayer based on the Commissioner's denial of a portion of a claimed deduction for insurance premiums paid by the corporation to a wholly-owned insurance subsidiary. The United States Tax Court reversed the Commissioner's determination in part, allowed the deduction in issue here, and directed a recomputation of the corporation's income tax liability for the years in question.

I.

The facts were stipulated.

In the mid-1970s, Malone & Hyde, a Tennessee corporation engaged in the wholesale food distribution business, began to look for less expensive insurance coverage for itself and its operating subsidiaries. After contacting an independent consulting firm in the business of developing and managing captive insurance programs, Malone & Hyde decided to create an insurance subsidiary to reinsure selected risks. In 1977 Malone & Hyde established a wholly-owned Bermuda insurance subsidiary, Eastland Insurance, Ltd. (Eastland), to provide reinsurance for itself and its subsidiaries.

Eastland was capitalized at $120,000 when Malone & Hyde purchased all 120,000 shares of common stock issued by Eastland at $1 par value. This capitalization met the minimum requirements of Bermuda law. Eastland's officers and directors, who also served as Malone & Hyde's officers, determined that the initial activity of the company would only include reinsurance of the risks of Malone & Hyde and its subsidiaries. During the years in question, Eastland did not insure the risks of any unrelated third party.

After incorporating Eastland to provide reinsurance services, Malone & Hyde selected Northwestern National Insurance Company (Northwestern), a large casualty insurance company located in Milwaukee, Wisconsin, as its primary insurer. On July 1, 1978, Malone & Hyde obtained from Northwestern a master insurance policy for itself and its wholly-owned operating subsidiaries and divisions covering workers' compensation, automobile liability, and general liability.

By prearrangement, on July 11, 1978, Eastland executed a reinsurance agreement with Northwestern. The agreement provided that Malone & Hyde and its subsidiaries and divisions insured their risks with Northwestern, and Northwestern in turn reinsured the first $150,000 of coverage per claim with Eastland. Under the terms of the reinsurance agreement, Eastland provided Northwestern with an irrevocable letter of credit dated June 23, 1978, in the amount of $250,000 to cover any amounts unpaid under the reinsurance agreement. At this time, Eastland had no assets other than its paid-in capital of $120,000. The letter of credit was amended in February of 1980 to increase the amount to $600,000, effective as of January 1, 1980.

In consideration for the policies issued in favor of it by Northwestern, Malone & Hyde executed "hold harmless" agreements in favor of Northwestern in July and October of 1978. Under these documents, Malone & Hyde agreed that in the event Eastland defaulted on its obligations as reinsurer of Northwestern, Malone & Hyde would shield Northwestern completely from any liability.

During the tax years 1979 and 1980, Malone & Hyde paid Northwestern $2,613,354 and $3,047,507 respectively, for insurance coverage and then charged the subsidiaries for their shares of the premiums. After retaining amounts for commissions, taxes, and third-party reinsurance premiums, Northwestern paid Eastland a reinsurance premium of

$1,982,369 for the tax year 1979 and $2,343,648 for the tax year 1980. During 1979 and 1980, the insurance provided to Malone & Hyde covered 1,782 and 1,836 vehicles respectively. The workers' compensation insurance covered 6,700 to 7,100 employees, and the general liability insurance covered all the physical facilities owned and operated by Malone & Hyde and its subsidiaries and divisions.

Northwestern determined the overall premiums to be charged to Malone & Hyde based on actuarial methods and information provided by the company. The risk management department of Malone & Hyde's subsidiary, Hyde Insurance Agency, Inc., determined the internal allocation of these overall premiums among Malone & Hyde's various subsidiaries and divisions, based primarily on past premiums and losses for the preceding three years. The total amounts billed to and paid by the eight subsidiaries for insurance were $172,413 for 1979 and $218,900 for 1980. This allocation method had been in use for several years before Eastland was formed.

Malone & Hyde filed consolidated tax returns with the eight insured subsidiaries for the years 1979 and 1980. The company claimed deductions for the entire insurance premiums paid by Malone & Hyde to Northwestern. On audit, the Commissioner disallowed all premiums paid by Malone & Hyde to Northwestern which Northwestern in turn paid to Eastland as reinsurance premiums. The disallowed reinsurance premiums totaled $2,002,393 for tax year 1979 and $2,367,321 for 1980. Malone & Hyde contested the disallowance in the tax court.

II.

The tax court issued two decisions in this case, the second decision following a motion for reconsideration.

Following a trial on November 20, 1986, the tax court held that Malone & Hyde was not entitled to deduct as business expenses under section 162 of the Internal Revenue Code of 1954 (I.R.C.), 26 U.S.C. § 162(a), those portions of the amounts it paid to Northwestern as insurance premiums that were in turn paid ("ceded") by Northwestern to Eastland as reinsurance premiums.

Malone & Hyde filed a motion for reconsideration and requested permission to supplement the record on the "brother-sister" issue in light of Humana, Inc. v. Commissioner, 881 F.2d 247 (6th Cir.1989), rev'g in part and aff'g in part, 88 T.C. 197, 1987 WL 49269 (1987). In Humana, deciding the brother-sister issue for the first time, this court held that insurance premiums paid to a captive insurance subsidiary on behalf of the parent's other subsidiaries were deductible as ordinary and necessary business expenses. Although Malone & Hyde did not raise the brother-sister issue at the original trial, the tax court granted Malone & Hyde's Motion for Supplementation of Findings and Reconsideration of Opinion. A further trial took place on June 26, 1990. In the second trial, the taxpayer argued that the instant case fell squarely within the Humana holding. The Commissioner argued in response that a number of factors in the present case (the hold harmless agreements, the irrevocable letters of credit, and Eastland's thin capitalization) distinguished this case from Humana.

In a supplemental opinion on December 14, 1993, the tax court ruled in favor of Malone & Hyde on the brother-sister issue. The tax court outlined a three-part test for determining whether a transaction involved "insurance" for income tax purposes: (1) whether the transaction involves "insurance risks"; (2) whether there is risk shifting and risk distribution; and (3) whether there is "insurance" in its commonly accepted usage. (JA at 99)

First, the tax court held that the Malone & Hyde subsidiaries faced real insurance risks. Second, in determining whether the subsidiaries transferred these risks to Eastland, the tax court concluded that it was required under Humana to "look only at the insured's assets and the impact that a claim of loss would have on them." (JA at 107) The tax court held that the subsidiaries transferred their insurance risks because "their financial obligations regarding sustained losses ended with payment of their insurance premiums." (JA at 107)

Because the Humana balance sheet test looked only to the insured subsidiaries' assets, the tax court reasoned that the existence of the hold harmless agreements and the letters of credit in this case did not change its decision. The court concluded that, from the subsidiaries' perspective, these agreements provided additional assurance that their insured losses would be paid. The court did not accept the Commissioner's argument that Eastland's thin capitalization demonstrated the lack of real risk shifting, finding that Eastland's capitalization met Bermuda's minimum requirements. The court went on to reason that the separate corporate status of Eastland could not be disregarded in the name of "economic reality" or "substance over form" absent a finding of sham or lack of business purpose. Additionally the court concluded that there were a sufficient number of subsidiaries insuring risks to achieve adequate risk distribution in this case.

Finally, the court found the third prong of its test met since the agreements between the subsidiaries and Eastland constituted insurance in the commonly accepted sense. Consequently, the tax court held that under the reasoning of Humana, the insurance payments indirectly made by Malone & Hyde's operating subsidiaries to their sibling Eastland were deductible as insurance premiums under § 162(a). The Commissioner appealed this decision.

III.

Section 162(a) of the Internal Revenue Code creates a deduction for "all the ordinary and necessary expenses paid or incurred during the taxable year in carrying on any trade or business." The tax court's determination that payments paid by Malone & Hyde and its subsidiaries to Eastland were ordinary and necessary business expenses is subject to de novo review. Humana, 881 F.2d at 251; Rose v. Commissioner, 868 F.2d 851, 853 (6th Cir.1989) (holding that a court "review[s] de novo the legal standard applied by the tax court in determining whether or not a transaction is a sham").

Typically, premiums paid by a business for insurance are considered deductible business expenses. Treas.Reg. § 1.162-1(a) (1954); Humana, 881 F.2d at 251. In contrast, sums set aside for the payment of anticipated losses through reserves or otherwise, as a plan for self-insurance, are not deductible business expenses.

The term "insurance" is not defined in the Internal Revenue Code. However, the Supreme Court in Helvering v. Le Gierse, 312 U.S. 531, 61 S.Ct. 646, 85 L.Ed. 996 (1941), established a test for identifying insurance for federal income tax purposes. Under the Le Gierse test, unless the transaction involves both "risk shifting" (from the insured's perspective) and "risk distribution" (from the insurer's perspective), it is not insurance for the purposes of the Internal Revenue Code. Id. at 539, 61 S.Ct. at 649. Risk shifting involves the transfer from the insured to the insurer of one or more risks which present uncertainty. Humana, 881 F.2d at 251. We are not concerned in this case with the element of risk distribution; the Commissioner only contests the finding that there was risk shifting.

Although Le Gierse involved estate taxes, courts generally have based their decisions in cases involving liability insurance furnished by captive subsidiaries upon the Le Gierse approach. See, e.g., Gulf Oil Corp. v. Commissioner, 914 F.2d 396, 411 (3d Cir.1990); Stearns-Roger Corp. v. United States, 774 F.2d 414, 415 (10th Cir.1985); Carnation Co. v. Commissioner, 640 F.2d 1010, 1012 (9th Cir.), cert. denied, 454 U.S. 965, 102 S.Ct. 506, 70 L.Ed.2d 381 (1981). But see Sears, Roebuck and Co. v. Commissioner, 972 F.2d 858, 861, 863 (7th Cir.1992) (In Le Gierse "[t]he Court was not writing a definition for all seasons and had no reason to····").

In Humana, 881 F.2d at 247, this court applied the Supreme Court's test in Le Gierse to determine the deductibility of insurance premiums paid by a parent corporation and its operating subsidiaries to a captive insurance subsidiary. The Humana court concluded that, based on the facts of that case, risk shifting was present in the "brother-sister" situation since the premiums paid by the insured subsidiaries sufficiently insulated them from the insured-against risks.

IV.

In this case the tax court reached a different conclusion in its second decision solely on the basis of the intervening decision in Humana. The basic reasoning of its two decisions concerning the elements of "insurance" was unchanged; the different result in the second decision related only to the "brother-sister" relationship between the insurance subsidiary (Eastland) and Malone & Hyde's other subsidiaries. Thus, we examine the Humana decision and then discuss the parties' arguments.

A.

At the time of its dispute with the Internal Revenue Service, Humana Inc. (Humana) and its subsidiaries operated an extensive chain of for-profit hospitals in the United States and abroad. The insurance coverage of the hospitals operated by both the parent company and its subsidiaries was cancelled. In order to obtain protection, Humana incorporated Health Care Indemnity, Inc. (HCI) as a Colorado captive insurance company. Together, Humana and a non-operating subsidiary purchased stock in HCI for $1 million. HCI was treated, for tax purposes, as a wholly-owned subsidiary of Humana. HCI provided insurance coverage to Humana and its subsidiaries, and Humana paid to HCI premiums for the insurance coverage afforded hospitals operated by Humana and its subsidiaries. Humana allocated and charged to the subsidiaries portions of the premiums it paid to HCI representing the share each bore for the hospitals operated. Humana claimed the total amounts paid to HCI as an ordinary and necessary business deduction on its consolidated income tax returns. Humana, 881 F.2d at 248-49. After the Commissioner denied the deductions and assessed deficiencies for the years 1976-1979, Humana filed suit in the tax court, which upheld the Commissioner's determination.

On appeal this court determined that the payments made by Humana to HCI for its own coverage did not constitute insurance premiums. Id. at 251-52. With respect to the payments made to HCI for coverage provided to Humana's operating subsidiaries, however, the court determined that there had been "risk shifting" under Le Gierse and that Humana was entitled to deduct the amounts charged to these subsidiaries under § 162(a). The court rejected the "economic family"[1] theory relied upon by some courts and explicitly adopted the approach used in Clougherty Packing Co. v. Commissioner, 811 F.2d 1297 (9th Cir.1987). Humana, 881 F.2d at 252-53. Based on Clougherty, the Humana court reasoned that it must look only to the effect of a claim on the insured's assets to determine whether that party shifted its risks. Id. at 252. The court reasoned that this approach, unlike the

---

1   The Internal Revenue Service first articulated its "economic family" theory in Revenue Ruling 77-316, 1977-2 C.B. 53. The Service ruled that insurance arrangements between related corporations are not true insurance but "self-insurance." This conclusion was based on the premise that the corporations participating in the captive insurance arrangement "though separate entities, represent one economic family with the result that those who bear the ultimate economic burden of corporate loss are the same persons who suffer the loss." Id. (emphasis added) Basically, the "economic family" approach mandates that all transactions among members of a corporate group must be disregarded.

economic family argument, was consistent with the Supreme Court's holding in Moline Properties v. Commissioner, 319 U.S. 436, 63 S.Ct. 1132, 87 L.Ed. 1499 (1943), that a court must not disregard the separate legal status of various companies where the companies have a valid business purpose and are not sham corporations.

In finding that the subsidiaries shifted the risks of loss to the captive, the court noted, "There is simply no direct connection in this case between a loss sustained by the [captive] insurance company and the affiliates of Humana···." Humana, 881 F.2d at 252. The court also concluded that a court should not look to the parent to determine whether a subsidiary shifted its risk of loss, since to do so treats the parent and its subsidiaries as one "economic unit" in contravention of Moline Properties. Id. at 256.

Although the court's test for risk shifting focused on the insured's balance sheet, the court explicitly noted that the Humana captive met Colorado's statutory minimum requirements for an insurance company and was recognized as a valid insurance company following an audit and certification by the state. Id. at 253. In finding that the captive was "devoid of sham," the court further pointed out that the captive "was fully capitalized and no agreement ever existed under which the subsidiaries or Humana Inc. would contribute additional capital to [the captive]." Id. Further, Humana and its subsidiaries "never contributed additional amounts to [the captive] nor took any steps to insure [the captive's] performance." Id. The court then distinguished the cases relied upon by the Commissioner as involving undercapitalized captives which often had indemnification agreements running from the parent to the captive. In a footnote accompanying this portion of the text, the court stated:

> The Carnation case involved an undercapitalized foreign captive, with a capitalization agreement running to the captive from the parent. Stearns-Roger, although involving an adequately capitalized domestic captive, involved an indemnification agreement running from the parent to the captive. A third case, Beech Aircraft Corp. v. U.S., 797 F.2d 920 (10th Cir.1986), mentioned as support for the majority position, also involved an undercapitalized captive. These weaknesses alone provided a sufficient basis from which to find no risk shifting and to decide the cases in favor of the Commissioner. The Humana case contained no such indemnification agreement and Health Care Indemnity [the captive] was adequately capitalized.

Humana, 881 F.2d at 254 n. 2. (emphasis added)

B.

On appeal the parties urge different interpretations of this court's holding in Humana.

The Commissioner argues that she does not rely on the economic family concept. Rather, she contends, there are critical differences between Humana and the present case that require the present case to be analyzed in light of these differences. When this analysis is undertaken, the Commissioner asserts, it is clear that the present case involves a scheme that contains the same "weaknesses" referred to in Humana 's footnote 2, weaknesses that "alone provide [ ] sufficient basis from which to find no risk shifting."

Malone & Hyde replies that footnote 2 referred only to the premium Humana paid for its own coverage and did not relate to the court's determination of the brother-sister issue. Malone & Hyde asserts that "Humana requires that one look solely to the insured's assets and consider the effect on those assets of a claim filed with an insurance company subsidiary." (Brief at 10) Consequently, Malone & Hyde contends that the letters of credit and hold harmless agreements in this case are "irrelevant" for the purpose of applying this court's balance sheet test adopted in Humana. Malone & Hyde argues that because the risk of loss was shifted away from the subsidiaries' assets, the premiums paid by those subsidiaries constitute valid insurance payments, deductible as business expenses on the consolidated tax returns. Malone & Hyde also dismisses the Commissioner's argument as premised on the discredited economic family argument, which is untenable under the Moline Properties doctrine.

V.

A.

This court clearly applied the Le Gierse analysis in Humana. But it did so only after finding that Humana's use of a Colorado captive insurance company was not a sham and that it served a legitimate business purpose.

We believe the tax court put the cart before the horse in this case. It should have determined first whether Malone & Hyde created Eastland for a legitimate business purpose or whether the captive was in fact a sham corporation. A taxpayer is "free to arrange his financial affairs to minimize his tax liability." Estate of Stranahan v. C.I.R., 472 F.2d 867, 869 (6th Cir.1973). Thus, "the presence of tax avoidance motives will not nullify an otherwise bona fide transaction." Id. However, the establishment of a tax deduction is not, in and of itself, an "otherwise bona fide transaction" if the deduction is accomplished through the use of an undercapitalized foreign insurance captive that is propped-up by guarantees of the parent corporation. The captive in such a case is essentially a sham corporation, and the payments to such a captive that are designated as insurance premiums do not constitute bona fide business expenses, entitling the taxpayer to a deduction under § 162(a).

In contrast to the situation in Humana, Malone & Hyde had no problems obtaining insurance from an unrelated insurance carrier. Humana, a hospital chain with enormous risk exposure, found itself without coverage when its insurance was cancelled. It faced an obvious dilemma and acted in a legitimate manner in seeking to find an answer. Malone & Hyde was not responding to any such crisis when it created Eastland. Rather, it departed drastically from the norm, and without any legitimate reason, devised the circuitous scheme for realizing tax deductions heretofore described.

In addition, Humana created HCI as a fully capitalized insurer under Colorado law, subject to regulatory control of that state's insurance commission. In contrast, Eastland undertook to reinsure the first $150,000 of each claim against Malone & Hyde, while operating on the extremely thin minimum capitalization required by Bermuda law. The record does not indicate that Bermuda exercised oversight similar to that which Colorado exercised over Humana's captive insurer. At the time, Malone & Hyde had more than 6,000 employees eligible for workers' compensation, about 1,800 vehicles including heavy-duty over-the-road trucks, and a plethora of buildings and other physical facilities.

Given the apparent inability of Eastland to pay a significant volume of claims, it was perfectly reasonable for Northwestern to demand protection from Malone & Hyde if it was to be the primary insurer, though retaining only a small part of the total premiums. This brings us to the third important factual distinction between Humana and the present case-the hold harmless agreements Malone & Hyde furnished Northwestern on two occasions. Under these documents, Malone & Hyde agreed that in the event Eastland defaulted on its obligations as reinsurer of Northwestern, Malone & Hyde: (1) would not pursue against Northwestern any claim arising out of the policies; and (2) would hold Northwestern harmless and defend Northwestern against any claims or judgments under the policies from any third party. (JA at 88-89, 212, 214)

B.

Two of the three differences discussed above reveal that Malone & Hyde's scheme contains the very "weaknesses" the Humana court referred to as "alone provid[ing] a sufficient basis from which to find no risk shifting" in footnote 2. On the other hand, Humana's scheme involved none of these "weaknesses." Humana, 881 F.2d at 254 n. 2. The presence of these "weaknesses" in this case indicates that the captive insurance scheme established by Malone & Hyde was not an "otherwise bona fide transaction," but a sham.

Interestingly, none of the three cases mentioned in the footnote concerned both undercapitalized captive insurers and guarantees running from the insured to the primary insurer. Yet, the Humana court found the presence of either one of the "weaknesses" sufficient to support a judgment for the Commissioner in the cited cases.

Carnation v. Commissioner, the first case cited in the footnote, involved a wholly-owned insurance subsidiary organized under Bermuda law with $120,000 of paid-in capital. As in the present case, an unrelated commercial insurer issued a policy to Carnation Corp., and the wholly-owned foreign subsidiary of Carnation agreed simultaneously to reinsure 90% of the primary insurer's liability under Carnation's policy. In return, the unrelated insurer ceded to the Carnation subsidiary 90% of the premium it received from Carnation. There was no letter of credit or other guarantee, but Carnation agreed to capitalize the Bermuda subsidiary up to $3 million on its own election or upon request of the insurance subsidiary. Carnation, 640 F.2d at 1012. In upholding the Commissioner's deficiency determination, the Carnation court held that the key to the decision was that the outside insurer would not have entered into the agreement, considering the subsidiary's undercapitalization, without the undertaking by Carnation to increase that capitalization by a factor of 25. The agreements were interdependent, and it was necessary to consider them together. Id. at 1013.

Stearns-Roger, the second case cited in the footnote, involved an adequately capitalized subsidiary incorporated under the same Colorado statute used by Humana. Nevertheless, the parent company agreed to indemnify its subsidiary against claims up to $3 million. Responding to the taxpayer's argument that the Commissioner and the court were applying the economic reality test, the court stated:

> The result we here reach is not inconsistent with the fact that the parent and the subsidiary are separate corporate entities. Moline Properties v. Commissioner, 319 U.S. 436, 63 S.Ct. 1132, 87 L.Ed. 1499 (1943). The separation is not ignored instead the focus must be on the nature and consequences of the payments by the parent and the Supreme Court's requirement that there must be a shift of risk to have insurance. There is no question that the parent paid the subsidiary, but the consequence of the payments sought to be deducted nevertheless still left the parent with its losses. The parent did not for its money receive "insurance." Many intercorporate transfers of funds are recognized, but in the circumstances before us nothing was received by the parent company in return. No insurance resulted.

Stearns-Roger, 774 F.2d at 416.

The facts in Beech Aircraft, the third case cited in footnote 2, presented yet another variation. Based on all the facts, the Beech Aircraft court agreed with the Commissioner and the tax court-there was no risk shifting because, in the end, the parent company stood to be required to pay claims. The court stated it did not overlook the separate corporate existence of the insurance subsidiary in violation of Moline. Beech Aircraft, 797 F.2d at 923.

Gulf Oil Corp. v. Commissioner, 914 F.2d 396 (3d Cir.1990), was decided after this court decided Humana. We have no doubt, however, that Gulf Oil would have been included in footnote 2 if it had been decided before Humana. The facts in Gulf Oil are strikingly similar to those in the present case. A parent with extensive exposure formed a Bermuda subsidiary with $120,000 capitalization. Gulf and its affiliates purchased a wide range of insurance from commercial carriers who reinsured their risks with Gulf's foreign insurance subsidiary and ceded portions of the premiums to the subsidiary. Id. at 410. Gulf executed agreements with the unrelated carriers guaranteeing indemnification to those carriers in the event of default by the captive insurer. Id.

In disallowing deductions for the premiums, the court of appeals in Gulf Oil recognized and distinguished Humana. The court also stated that it was following the reasoning of Clougherty Packing Co. v. Commissioner, 811 F.2d 1297 (9th Cir.1987), relied upon and adopted by this court in Humana. The Clougherty court stated, "Where separate agreements are interdependent, they must be considered together so that their overall economic effect can be assessed." Clougherty, 811 F.2d at 1301. The Clougherty court dismissed the argument that it was relying on the economic family concept in considering the "overall effect" of the interdependent agreements. Id. at 1305.

VI.

If Humana's scheme had involved a thinly-capitalized captive foreign insurance company that ended up with a large portion of the premiums paid to a commercial insurance company as primary insurer, and had included a hold harmless agreement from Humana indemnifying the unrelated insurer against all liability, we believe the result in Humana would have been different. This court accepted the bona fides of the transaction in Humana and recognized the premiums paid to the captive insurance company as deductible business expenses since Humana established the captive to address a legitimate business concern (the loss of insurance coverage), and the captive was not a sham corporation; the captive in Humana was fully capitalized, domestically incorporated, and established without guarantees from the parent or other related corporations. Because Humana acted in a straightforward manner, without any evidence of an intent to create an unwarranted tax deduction based on payments that largely ended up in its subsidiary's coffers, this court accepted the bona fides of the transaction before examining the brother-sister issue.

We disagree with Malone & Hyde's contention that footnote 2 in Humana refers only to the question of whether Humana's premium payments for its own coverage, as opposed to the coverage extended its subsidiaries, involved risk shifting. Footnote 2 clearly applies to the fundamental and decisive question of whether there was risk shifting from any insured-parent or subsidiary-to the captive insurer. When the entire scheme involves either undercapitalization or indemnification of the primary insurer by the taxpayer claiming the deduction, or both, these facts alone disqualify the premium payments from being treated as ordinary and necessary business expenses to the extent such payments are ceded by the primary insurer to the captive insurance subsidiary.

It is true that Eastland operated as an insurance company. As the tax court found, it "established reserve accounts, paid claimed losses only after the validity of those claims had been established, and was profitable." (JA at 111) For purposes of determining the correct tax treatment of premiums paid to Eastland by Malone & Hyde, however, we cannot be blind to the realities of the case. The "interdependent" separate agreements, when considered together, Clougherty, 811 F.2d at 1301, indicate an arrangement under which there was no risk shifting. Under the hold harmless agreement, the ultimate risk for workers' compensation, auto liability, and general liability remained with Malone & Hyde. This being so, the transactions did not result in Malone & Hyde or the subsidiaries receiving "insurance" from Eastland within the meaning of that term under the Internal Revenue Code.

The judgment of the tax court is REVERSED and the case is REMANDED for re-entry of the original judgment for the Commissioner pursuant to the tax court's first opinion.

Appendix R

Kidde Industries, Inc. v. U.S.

40 Fed.Cl. 42 (Ct.Cl. 1997)

UNITED STATES COURT OF FEDERAL CLAIMS.

KIDDE INDUSTRIES, INC., Plaintiff,

v.

The UNITED STATES, Defendant.

No. 447-88T, Dec. 31, 1997.

[Names of counsel omitted.]

OPINION

ANDEWELT, Judge.

I.

In this tax refund action, plaintiff, Kidde Industries, Inc. (Kidde), seeks a refund for income taxes it allegedly overpaid for tax years 1977 and 1978. This action is before the court after trial on two of the four counts presented in plaintiff's amended complaint. The first count, Count II, raises issues concerning the proper tax treatment of premiums paid by a parent company for insurance ultimately provided by a wholly owned subsidiary, i.e., where the parent company's insurance is provided by a "captive insurer." The second count, Count IV, alleges that plaintiff is entitled to certain work incentive (WIN) tax credits.

II.

Turning first to the "captive insurer" issue, during the 1970s, Kidde was a broad-based, decentralized conglomerate with approximately 15 separate operating divisions and 100 wholly owned subsidiaries, each of which Kidde treated as an independent profit center. Prior to 1977, Kidde had insurance agreements with Travelers Insurance Company (Travelers) under which Travelers provided master insurance policies covering workers' compensation and automobile and general (including products) liability. Each Kidde division and subsidiary had the option either to participate in these master policies or to "opt out" if it could secure coverage from another insurer on a more cost-effective basis. Kidde's divisions and subsidiaries generally chose to participate in the Travelers program, but some did not.

In 1976, in the midst of a products liability insurance crisis in which many insurance companies either ceased or significantly restricted their coverage of products liability in the United States, Travelers informed Kidde that it would not renew Kidde's products liability insurance policy for 1977. Given the general reluctance of insurance companies to offer products liability coverage, Kidde determined that in order to secure such insurance from a new provider, Kidde would have to offer these insurers the entire package that Travelers previously had provided, not just products liability. Most of the insurance companies Kidde approached refused to quote any price for insurance that included products liability coverage and those that did extend offers quoted rates that were so high as to be unacceptable to Kidde. Some offers, in effect, would have required Kidde to pay virtually all of its products liability claims.

Kidde responded to the limited availability of products liability insurance by seeking the aid of outside firms and consultants, including American International Group (AIG), a large multi-national insurance conglomerate. The plan that Kidde and these outside sources developed and implemented involved Kidde incorporating in Bermuda a wholly owned insurance subsidiary. On December 22, 1976, Kidde incorporated Kidde Insurance Company Ltd. (KIC) with an initial capital of $1 million. Kidde then purchased workers' compensation and automobile and general (including products) liability insurance from two subsidiaries of AIG, National Union Fire Insurance Company and American Home Assurance Company (hereinafter collectively referred to as National). National, in turn, entered "facultative reinsurance agreements" with KIC pursuant to which KIC reinsured a portion of the risks National had insured for Kidde. These National-KIC agreements involved National covering Kidde's workers' compensation and automobile and general (including products) liability claims and KIC assuming the first $1 million of each workers' compensation and automobile and general liability claim, and the first $2.5 million of each products liability claim. As with its prior policies with Travelers, Kidde allowed its divisions and subsidiaries either to participate in the National program or to "opt out" and secure coverage from other insurers.

In sum, because of the products liability insurance crisis, Kidde could not convince an established insurance company to provide, at a satisfactory price, all of the insurance Travelers previously had provided. Kidde was able, however, to acquire from National insurance equivalent in scope to that provided by Travelers but only upon the condition that Kidde create a wholly owned subsidiary with which National would reinsure a significant portion of that insurance. On January 1, 1977, National issued two master insurance policies covering the Kidde divisions and subsidiaries that opted to participate in the program. National and KIC did not enter the "facultative reinsurance agreements" pursuant to which KIC reinsured a portion of the risks National insured for Kidde under these policies until April 1977.

III.

For 1977 and 1978, Kidde paid National premiums of $11,624,819 and $13,671,100, respectively. National then ceded $9,461,017 and $11,509,432 of these premiums, respectively, to KIC for reinsurance.[1] National determined the premiums that it charged Kidde based in part on underwriting data supplied by Kidde's divisions and subsidiaries, including payroll data for workers' compensation, sales data for general liability, and number of cars for automobile liability. Kidde used these same data to allocate the total premiums among its divisions and subsidiaries. For 1977 and 1978, Kidde allocated approximately 60 percent of its total payments to National to its subsidiaries and the remaining 40 percent to its divisions.

The only insurance KIC provided during 1977 was that provided under the above-described reinsurance agreement it entered with National. In 1978, 1979, and 1980, KIC had one additional insurance client, Theurer Atlantic, Inc., whose premiums constituted

---

[1]   FN1. The following table shows the differences between Kidde's payments to National and National's payments to KIC for 1977 and 1978.

	1977	1978
Kidde's Payment to National	$11,624,819	$13,671,100
Payment for National's Retained Risk	595,000	300,000
Issuing Fee	414,726	534,844
Claims Services	350,000	380,000
Engineering Services	105,000	90,000
Taxes	699,076	856,823
	=========	=========
Subtotal	2,163,802	2,161,667
National Payment to KIC	9,461,017	11,509,433

less than one percent of KIC's insurance premiums for each of those years.[2] KIC first actively sought third-party reinsurance business in 1980 and in connection with this effort capitalized $9 million of its retained earnings, bringing its total capital to $10 million. KIC's third-party business rose to 17 percent of KIC's total premium income in 1981, over 30 percent in 1982, and in excess of 50 percent in 1983, 1984, and 1985.

For tax years 1977 and 1978, Kidde filed federal income tax returns on a consolidated basis covering all of its divisions and wholly owned subsidiaries. In calculating its taxable income for these years, Kidde deducted from its gross income the entirety of its payments to National, including the full amount National ceded to KIC for reinsurance. The Internal Revenue Service (ORS) allowed Kidde a full deduction for the amount of Kidde's payments that National kept for itself (i.e., did notcede to KIC). With respect to the premiums National ceded to KIC, the IRS allowed Kidde a deduction in the amount of the claims KIC actually paid to Kidde's divisions and subsidiaries plus the amount KIC accrued for liabilities for workers' compensation claims. The IRS disallowed the remaining $6,916,047 of Kidde's payments that National ceded to KIC for 1977 and $6,751,033 for 1978. The IRS's disallowance of these payments is the subject of Count II of the instant complaint.

IV.

Pursuant to I.R.C. § 162(a), when calculating the amount of income taxes due, corporations may deduct from their income "all the ordinary and necessary [business] expenses." Pursuant to Treas. Reg. § 1.162-1(a), "insurance premiums" are considered an ordinary and necessary business expense. Hence, if the disputed payments to National are properly characterized as "insurance premiums," then these payments are fully deductible from Kidde's income. The IRS did not so categorize these payments and instead treated these payments, in effect, as constituting reserves that Kidde had set aside to pay future claims, i.e., as a form of self insurance. Where a corporation reserves certain funds for the payment of future claims, the tax laws allow a deduction in a particular tax year only for the claims against that reserve that are actually paid or accrue in that year. Anesthesia Service Medical Group, Inc. v. Commissioner, 825 F.2d 241, 242 (9th Cir.1987).

Neither the Internal Revenue Code nor treasury regulations define the term "insurance," and the lack of a precise definition has resulted in extensive litigation concerning the proper tax treatment of payments made by parent corporations directly or indirectly to captive insurers. See, e.g., Malone & Hyde, Inc. v. Commissioner, 62 F.3d 835, 838 (6th

---

2   Prior to 1978, Theurer was a wholly owned Kidde subsidiary and participated in the National insurance program. After Kidde divested its interest in Theurer, KIC provided insurance directly to Theurer for which Theurer paid premiums of $100,000 for 1978 and 1979 and $90,000 for 1980.

Cir.1995); Sears, Roebuck and Co. v. Commissioner, 972 F.2d 858, 861-62 (7th Cir.1992); Gulf Oil Corp. v. Commissioner, 914 F.2d 396, 411-12 (3rd Cir.1990); Humana, Inc. v. Commissioner, 881 F.2d 247, 251 (6th Cir.1989); Clougherty Packing Co. v. Commissioner, 811 F.2d 1297, 1300 (9th Cir.1987); Mobil Oil Corp. v. United States, 8 Cl.Ct. 555, 564 (1985). In Ocean Drilling & Exploration Co. v. United States, 988 F.2d 1135, 1137 (Fed.Cir.1993), the Court of Appeals for the Federal Circuit, whose precedent is binding on this court, articulated its analysis for determining whether payments to a captive insurer "constitute[ ] true insurance premiums that are deductible as business expenses under section 162."[3] Unlike the instant case, where Kidde made its payments to a third-party insurer which in turn reinsured with Kidde's wholly owned subsidiary, Ocean Drilling involved the parent taxpayer making payments directly to its wholly owned captive insurer subsidiary. Therein, the substantive discussion of the deductibility of insurance payments to captive insurers began with the overall guideline that the court "must adhere to the principles of [Helvering v. Le Gierse, 312 U.S. 531, 61 S.Ct. 646, 85 L.Ed. 996 (1941) and Moline Properties, Inc. v. Commissioner, 319 U.S. 436, 63 S.Ct. 1132, 87 L.Ed. 1499 (1943)], in reaching a decision." In Le Gierse, the Supreme Court stated that "insurance involves risk-shifting and risk-distributing." 312 U.S. at 539, 61 S.Ct. at 649. Moline Properties, discusses the tax treatment of corporations and enunciates the general rule that absent an exception, such as where the arrangement is a "sham," a corporation should be viewed as "a separate taxable entity" from its shareholder. 319 U.S. at 438-39, 63 S.Ct. at 1133-34. Bringing together the requirements of Le Gierse and Moline Properties, the Federal Circuit in Ocean Drilling explained:

> Plaintiff and [its captive insurer] must be considered as separate entities in evaluating whether the transactions between the two companies resulted in risk shifting and risk distributing. However, if the business operations of [the captive insurer] are a sham, [the captive insurer's] "corporate form may be disregarded." Moline Properties, 319 U.S. at 439, 63 S.Ct. at 1134. Furthermore, even if plaintiff and [the captive insurer] are separate entities, if plaintiff retained the risk of the losses against which it insured, plaintiff's premiums amounted to a reserve for losses, and plaintiff would not be entitled to deduct such premiums from taxable income.

988 F.2d at 1150-51.

---

[3]   The Federal Circuit appended the decision of the lower court and stated that it adopted the analysis therein as its own.

V.

A.

Defendant contends that plaintiff cannot prevail under the standard articulated in Ocean Drilling because during the tax years in issue, a binding indemnity agreement between Kidde and National was in effect pursuant to which Kidde retained the risk of losses with respect to the insurance policies that National had issued to Kidde. Plaintiff responds that although a document entitled "Indemnity Agreement" existed, the document never took effect.

The terms of the "Indemnity Agreement," if in effect, would, as defendant contends, have resulted in Kidde retaining the pertinent risks. Article I of the document lists the specific insurance policies that National would issue to Kidde and Articles II and III provide for indemnification as follows:

ARTICLE II

[Kidde] will indemnify [National] against all liability including but not limited to:

(a) all losses

(b) all loss expenses

(c) all other expenses

(d) all reserves

that [National] may incur by reason of its issuance of the insurance policies listed in Article I hereof, or in defending or prosecuting any suit, action or other proceeding either in connection therewith, or in obtaining or attempting to obtain a release from liability in respect thereof.

[Kidde] covenants that it will pay over to [National] all sums of money which [National] shall pay or become liable to pay by reason of the foregoing and will make such payment to [National] as soon as [National] shall make demand therefor.

ARTICLE III

[Kidde] undertakes to guarantee to [National] the payment of the amounts due under Article II hereof and will provide [National] the following:

A clean irrevocable Letter of Credit acceptable to [National] in favor of [National] in the amount of one million U.S. dollars ($1,000,000).

Plaintiff does not dispute that the "Indemnity Agreement," if in effect, would place the ultimate risk of loss with Kidde. Plaintiff also acknowledges that Kidde officials signed and forwarded the indemnity agreement to National. Plaintiff argues, however, that the "Indemnity Agreement" was not in effect for all or at least part of the tax years in issue.

B.

Plaintiff initially argues that Kidde officials revoked the offer contained in the "Indemnity Agreement" before it was accepted by National and, in any event, that the parties never considered the "Indemnity Agreement" to be part of their business understanding. To support this argument, plaintiff notes that the parties did not find a signed copy of the "Indemnity Agreement" in their files. But the evidence submitted at trial, considered as a whole, weighs heavily to support a contrary conclusion that National representatives signed the "Indemnity Agreement" and returned the signed copies to Kidde, and that both parties considered the agreement to be an important part of their insurance relationship until they decided to void the agreement.

Kidde did not consider self insurance a viable option and was determined to have new insurance in effect on January 1, 1977, when its products liability insurance with Travelers' lapsed. National and Kidde, however, did not have sufficient time by that date to complete their negotiations with respect to the details of their insurance relationship. The "Indemnity Agreement," including the $1 million "Letter of Credit," enabled Kidde to convince National to issue the insurance policies prior to completion of these negotiations. The "Indemnity Agreement" assured National that it would be protected against loss until the parties could satisfactorily negotiate the details of their insurance relationship.

Indeed, even if there were no products liability crisis at the time Kidde approached National, National still would have had reason to be concerned about reinsuring with KIC a portion of its liability under the Kidde policies. KIC was newly created and had no experience in insurance. Perhaps most significantly, KIC was significantly undercapitalized by United States standards. Although KIC had premiums of $9 million in the first year, its initial capital was only $1 million, resulting in a premium-to-capital ratio of approximately 9:1. Insurance regulators within the United States generally insist on a premium-to-capital ratio of no more than 3:1.[4] Given this undercapitalization,[5] it is not surprising, and indeed to be expected, that before issuing the insurance to Kidde, National would have insisted that Kidde provide some additional security with respect to KIC's performance under the KIC-National reinsurance agreement. The "Indemnity Agreement" provided such security by permitting National to terminate the insurance

---

[4]   Plaintiff argues that KIC's initial capital exceeded the minimum required in Bermuda. But satisfying Bermuda standards does not mean that a reinsurer such as National seeking to share risk would have considered such capitalization to be adequate. Indeed, KIC's capitalization was below the ratio followed by some other Bermuda captive insurers and was below the minimum requirement adopted into Bermuda law in 1980.

[5]   Indeed, KIC's $1 million capitalization was equal to its potential liability for a single automobile or general liability claim against Kidde.

arrangement without suffering any possible loss in the event the parties were unable to negotiate satisfactorily the details of their insurance relationship. In this regard, the crucial nature of the signed "Indemnity Agreement" to National was underscored by the testimony of Robert King, who had primary responsibility within AIG for establishing the National-Kidde insurance relationship. King testified that the "Indemnity Agreement" provided National the "level of comfort" it needed to issue the Kidde insurance policies at a time when KIC was not in a position itself to assume the risk in a manner satisfactory to AIG.

C.

After January 1, 1977, National and Kidde had ongoing negotiations, for a substantial period of time, concerning the remaining details of their insurance relationship. In April 1977, National and KIC entered into "facultative reinsurance agreements" pursuant to which KIC reinsured a portion of the risks National had insured for Kidde. Plaintiff argues that assuming the "Indemnity Agreement" was in fact executed, the agreement nevertheless was intended only to protect National on a temporary or interim basis until KIC was ready to begin business. Hence, plaintiff argues, if the "Indemnity Agreement" ever went into effect, Kidde and National intended it to be superseded when National and KIC entered the "facultative insurance agreements" in April 1977.

The court agrees that National and Kidde reasonably could not have viewed the "Indemnity Agreement" as a long-term commitment. National and Kidde intended to establish an insurance relationship and, by holding Kidde ultimately responsible for any losses National suffered, the "Indemnity Agreement" was fundamentally inconsistent with the existence of any true insurance relationship. But, although the April 1977 "facultative reinsurance agreements" set forth some terms between the parties, they did not address National's concerns about KIC's undercapitalized status. These agreements did not offer National any security, beyond KIC's assets, to ensure that KIC would fulfill its reinsurance obligations thereunder. Thus, in an effort to address this concern, National and Kidde continued negotiations after National and KIC entered the "facultative reinsurance agreements." During the course of these often adversarial negotiations, National continually requested that Kidde provide a parental guarantee pursuant to which Kidde would guarantee KIC's obligations under the reinsurance agreement. Replacing the "Indemnity Agreement" with such a parental guarantee would change the parties' legal relationship in that the "Indemnity Agreement" did not include KIC and under that agreement, Kidde's obligation to cover National's losses was not limited to the reinsurance aspect of the National-Kidde insurance policy.

Upon first impression, it seems unusual for an insurance arrangement to be in place for such a long period of time without the parties having worked out the final details of their insurance relationship. But at trial, plaintiff's witnesses explained that it was typical in the insurance industry for insurance to be issued with an understanding by both parties that the precise terms would later be determined through good faith negotiations. In this case, the continued existence of the "Indemnity Agreement" gave National leverage to ensure that Kidde would continue to negotiate in good faith. Indicative of the continued existence of the signed "Indemnity Agreement" and the leverage it provided National is a September 27, 1977, letter from Robert King to a representative of Kidde's insurance broker, Fred S. James and Company, which states: "We still hold the objectionable Indemnity Agreement for which Fred. S. James and Kidde diligently described as a thorn in the side."

D.

Ultimately, National agreed to void and return the signed "Indemnity Agreement" to Kidde because National became convinced that KIC's financial status and the "facultative reinsurance agreements" and letters of credit received from KIC were sufficient to support a standard insurer-reinsurer relationship. The court cannot, however, determine from the record the precise date on which the parties agreed that the signed "Indemnity Agreement" no longer would be in effect. Defendant argues that because plaintiff bears the burden of proof, the absence of clarity in the record as to the precise date on which the agreement was voided requires that plaintiff's claim fail. But the trial record, taken as a whole, supports a finding that by at least June 1, 1978, the parties had agreed that the "Indemnity Agreement" no longer would control.

KIC's gain of experience in the reinsurance business apparently resulted in an increase in KIC's net assets during 1977 and 1978. As a result, on or about May 3, 1978, National decided no longer to pursue a parental guarantee from Kidde. National decided instead that it would be satisfied if KIC provided a letter of credit from a major United States bank. This determination by National is crucial. Having decided that a letter of credit from KIC would be adequate to protect National's financial interests, it would follow that it was neither necessary nor reasonable for National to maintain the "Indemnity Agreement" in force. As explained above, the parties did not view the "Indemnity Agreement" as a long-term agreement but rather only as controlling until the parties completed negotiations as to the details of their insurance relationship. Once National became convinced that KIC's assets combined with the letter of credit from a major United States bank were sufficient to ensure that KIC would perform its obligations, National was beyond the point that it needed the "level of comfort" to which King referred at trial. Hence, at this point in time, the purpose behind the "Indemnity Agreement" ceased to exist. Because National and Kidde were interested in a long-term insurance relationship, it is reasonable to conclude that upon deciding that KIC's assets and letter of credit were sufficient to protect its financial interests, National would have proceeded in due course to remove the "thorn" from Kidde's side and render the

"Indemnity Agreement" void. The court concludes that National would have returned the signed "Indemnity Agreement" and rendered it void by at least June 1, 1978.

Hence, for tax year 1977 and tax year 1978 up through May 31, Kidde retained the risk of losses with respect to the insurance policies that National had issued to Kidde. Thus, under Ocean Drilling, Kidde's payments to National that National ceded to KIC during these periods amounted to reserves for future claims and Kidde is not entitled to deduct that amount from its taxable income.

VI.

The next issue to address is the tax treatment of the disputed payments to National between June 1 and December 31, 1978. As described above, if the payments are properly characterized as "insurance premiums" under Treas. Reg. § 1.162-1(a), then these payments are properly deductible from Kidde's income.

A.

The court will begin its analysis with a discussion of the Supreme Court's decision in Moline Properties. In Moline Properties, a corporation sold real property that it owned and the sole stockholder of the corporation sought to treat the gains from that sale as income taxable to the stockholder rather than to the corporation, i.e., to ignore the corporate existence as a mere fiction. The Supreme Court refused to treat the gains as individual income and instead insisted that the corporation be considered a distinct entity notwithstanding the fact that the shareholder owned 100 percent of the corporation's stock. The Court explained:

> The doctrine of corporate entity fulfills a useful purpose in business life. Whether the purpose be to gain an advantage under the law of the state of incorporation or to avoid or to comply with the demands of creditors or to serve the creditor's personal or undisclosed convenience, so long as that purpose is the equivalent of business activity or is followed by the carrying on of business by the corporation, the corporation remains a separate taxable entity....

> To this rule there are recognized exceptions. A particular legislative purpose ... may call for the disregarding of the separate entity, as may the necessity of striking down frauds on the tax statute. In general, in matters relating to the revenue, the corporate form may be disregarded where it is a sham or unreal. In such situations, the form is a bald and mischievous fiction.

319 U.S. at 438-39, 63 S.Ct. at 1134 (citations omitted) (footnotes omitted).

As the court in Ocean Drilling suggested, Moline Properties has been an important focus in court decisions addressing the tax treatment of purported insurance premiums paid to captive insurers. This is so because Moline Properties generally requires that the captive insurer not be treated as the alter ego of its parent but rather as a distinct taxable corporate entity.

Consistent with Moline Properties, when applying the tax laws to captive insurers, courts initially have sought to determine whether the arrangement among the captive insurer, the parent, and any third-party companies should be classified as a "sham." If the court determines that the corporate arrangement is a sham, then the inquiry ends and the payments to the captive insurer are treated as nondeductible reserves rather than "insurance premiums." Next, either as part of this analysis of whether a sham exists, or as part of a separate analysis of whether the payments to the captive insurer otherwise should be characterized as "insurance premiums," courts have analyzed whether the arrangement among the parties is consistent with commonly accepted notions of insurance. If the arrangement is not consistent with commonly accepted notions of insurance, then the payments are not deductible from income.[6] Finally, assuming the arrangement is not a sham and is otherwise consistent with commonly accepted notions of insurance, courts generally have proceeded to apply the definition of "insurance" provided in Le Gierse and determine whether risk shifting and risk distributing are present.

B.

Turning to the sham exception in Moline Properties, the totality of the evidence indicates that Kidde's creation of KIC was not a sham and that Kidde had legitimate business reasons for creating a captive insurer subsidiary that had nothing to do with the tax advantages that would result from paying insurance premiums rather than self insurance. First, in order to conduct business in the over 40 states in which Kidde's divisions and subsidiaries operated, Kidde was required to possess certificates of insurance as evidence of primary casualty coverage. Apparently, Kidde potentially could have satisfied this requirement through self insurance, but setting up such a program to satisfy state requirements would have taken more time than Kidde had available before its Travelers policy expired. Second, securing insurance from National rather than self insurance enabled Kidde to maintain existing prices and policies for catastrophic insurance. Kidde had in effect catastrophic insurance with third-party insurers which covered claim amounts above the limits contained in the Travelers policy of up to $400 million per

---

6   Such a conclusion does not mean that an interrelationship among the parties is irrelevant to this analysis. The fundamental issue in captive insurance cases is whether payments to the captive insurer should be classified as "insurance premiums" and whether the ownership relationship among the corporations involved has been relevant to this analysis, particularly, as explained below, when assessing whether risk shifting and risk distributing are present.

claim. Apparently, writers of catastrophic insurance required that the amount of the claims that fall below the catastrophic level be covered under a separate insurance policy. This would ensure that another established insurance company would be analyzing and seeking to uncover deficiencies in any claim for which the catastrophic insurer may be liable. Finally, creating a captive insurer furthered the aim of Kidde to form an insurance subsidiary that would provide insurance or reinsurance to unrelated third parties and serve as a separate profit center for Kidde. The fact that KIC moved fairly quickly into reinsurance with third parties supports the conclusion that when Kidde established KIC, or at least by June 1, 1978, Kidde had hoped one day to operate KIC as an insurance subsidiary that ultimately would have third-party clients. As described above, after 1980, KIC began writing a significant amount of insurance for unrelated third parties.

One factor courts have considered in determining whether a sham exists is the capitalization and financial condition of the captive insurer. See Malone, 62 F.3d at 839. As described above, during the period at issue here, between June 1 and December 31, 1978, KIC's total financial position was adequate to fulfill KIC's obligations under its agreement with National. The best evidence of the adequacy of KIC's overall financial position is that without any parental guarantee or other distinct financial support from Kidde, National was willing to reinsure with KIC claims on which National was primarily liable.

C.

Next, the court will turn to the question of whether the arrangement among KIC, Kidde, and National is consistent with commonly accepted notions of insurance. Based on the record as a whole, the court concludes that the arrangement is sufficiently consistent so as not to disqualify the disputed payments to National from being treated as "insurance premiums."

The written agreements between Kidde and National, and National and KIC are fully consistent with commonly accepted notions of insurance in that each allocates a risk, i.e., the risk that in the future one of the parties to the agreement will face uncertain and variable claims against it. In the Kidde-National agreement, Kidde agreed to pay National a specified premium and National in turn agreed to assume the risk with respect to undetermined future claims against Kidde. In the National-KIC "facultative reinsurance agreements," National agreed to pay KIC a specified premium and KIC in turn agreed to assume primary responsibility for certain future claims against Kidde over which National had assumed responsibility in the Kidde-National agreement. The respective premiums set out in these agreements apparently were generally established through means typically used in the insurance industry, which are based primarily on predictions as to the amount of future claims.

The Kidde-National-KIC arrangement also conforms to commonly accepted notions of insurance when viewed from the perspective of a claimant presenting a claim against Kidde. KIC contracted with National to accept, process, evaluate, and pay certain claims against Kidde. Those filing claims against Kidde apparently interacted with KIC representatives in essentially the same way as claimants interact with representatives of any other reinsurance company. Defendant's contention that the Kidde-National-KIC arrangement is inconsistent with commonly accepted notions of insurance does not focus on the wording of the respective agreements, the methods of establishing premiums, or the presentation of claims by claimants. Rather, defendant focuses on the organization of KIC and certain other aspects of its operation.

Defendant's argument that the organization and operation of KIC is inconsistent with commonly accepted notions of insurance focuses on KIC's incorporation in Bermuda, the control Kidde exercised over KIC, and the comparatively small amount of traditional insurance functions KIC performed. As to incorporation in Bermuda, Kidde chose to incorporate KIC in Bermuda in part because Bermuda has far less regulation of insurance companies than the United States. Indeed, after its incorporation, KIC intentionally sought to avoid United States regulation. KIC never applied for business in the United States and the president of KIC, who was also the risk manager at Kidde, traveled to Bermuda from his United States office to sign pertinent documents. As to Kidde's control over KIC, the officers of KIC were primarily officers of Kidde, and these officers controlled KIC's activities, including the investment of funds. Next, as to the functions KIC performed, defendant argues that KIC was virtually an invisible company which existed primarily on paper. KIC had minimal contacts in Bermuda. It had no employees and no separate offices in Bermuda and operated in Bermuda through a management company specializing in managing captive insurance companies. The management company prepared a limited amount of documents annually for KIC. KIC contracted with third parties, primarily companies related to AIG, for most of the typical functions performed by insurance companies, including, as noted above, the processing of insurance claims.

Clearly, KIC's organization and certain aspects of its operation are different than many United States insurance companies. It is not apparent, however, that these differences, by themselves, should render nondeductible payments that otherwise would be classified as deductible insurance premiums. With respect to KIC's incorporation in Bermuda, any corporation, including insurance corporations, generally can be expected to base its decision as to where to incorporate and where to locate its employees on a determination as to which choices will result in maximum profits for the corporation. Hence, an insurance corporation's decision to incorporate in Bermuda because of a more favorable regulatory environment and to locate its employees elsewhere would not be inherently inconsistent with commonly accepted notions of insurance. Indeed, courts, including the

Federal Circuit in Ocean Drilling, have allowed deductions for payments to captive insurers incorporated in Bermuda.

As to Kidde's control over KIC, staffing KIC with Kidde employees suggests that Kidde not only wanted to take advantage of the expertise of its own employees in overseeing KIC's operation but also wanted to keep firm control over KIC's day-to-day operations. But assuming that such a close relationship between the insured and insurer is relatively rare, Kidde's aims would not be inherently inconsistent with KIC creating what amounts to a traditional insurer-insured relationship with respect to future claims against Kidde. As to KIC "contracting out" most typical insurance functions, it would not seem unreasonable for KIC to do so when KIC first entered the insurance business. Through such contracts, a new entrant into the industry could eliminate uncertainty as to the cost of performing certain services and thereby secure greater predictability as to its operational costs.

D.

The court will now address perhaps the most difficult area of the inquiry-application of the reference in Le Gierse to insurance being characterized by risk shifting and risk distributing. The risk to which Le Gierse refers is the risk that in the future a corporation will face uncertain and variable claims against it. See Ocean Drilling, 988 F.2d at 1151; Sears, Roebuck, 972 F.2d at 862. Risk shifting involves the transfer of that risk from the insured to the insurer. In exchange for the insured paying a specified premium, the insurer agrees to process and pay all claims against the insured that are covered under the insurance policy. Hence, in effect, the insured shifts the risk to the insurer that the total amount of the claims against it (including the costs of processing) will exceed the premium paid.

Insurance companies have expertise in estimating and administering claims and seek to set the premiums charged so as to reflect the expected losses that will result from future claims. Although insurance companies may be able to predict such costs with reasonable accuracy over extended periods of time, for shorter periods, such as year to year, the total cost of these claims will vary from the expectation, i.e., vary from the average. In some years the total cost of claims may exceed the expected amount, i.e., the average yearly cost calculated over a longer period of time, and in other years the costs may be less than the expected amount. Thus, by agreeing to provide insurance for a fixed premium for a particular year, the insurer assumes the risk that the total cost of claims for that year will exceed the expected amount. See Ocean Drilling, 988 F.2d at 1151.

Risk distribution addresses this risk that over a shorter period of time claims will vary from the average. Risk distribution occurs when particular risks are combined in a pool with other, independently insured risks. By increasing the total number of independent, randomly occurring risks that a corporation faces (i.e., by placing risks into a larger pool), the corporation benefits from the mathematical concept of the law of large numbers in that the ratio of actual to expected losses tends to approach one. In other words, through risk distribution, insurance companies gain greater confidence that for any particular short-term period, the total amount of claims paid will correlate with the expected cost of those claims and hence correlate with the total amount of premiums collected.

In concluding that risk shifting and risk distributing were present in Ocean Drilling, the court relied upon a factor not present in the instant case-the captive insurer issued insurance to unrelated third parties during the tax years in issue. With respect to risk shifting, the court concluded that "[u]nrelated business operated to reduce the amount of risk to which [the insurer] was exposed." Id. at 1152. With respect to risk distribution, the court stated: "Risk distribution involves spreading the risk of loss among policyholders. [The captive insurer] had unrelated business of approximately 44 and 66 percent for the two years at issue. This amount of unrelated business sufficiently spreads risk so as to constitute risk distribution." Id.

E.

Given the decision in Ocean Drilling, the issue presented herein is whether the disputed payments to National can be classified as "insurance premiums" notwithstanding KIC's lack of significant unrelated business. Humana, 881 F.2d 247, involved a fact situation in many ways similar to the instant action. Humana, like Kidde, was a large corporation that operated a variety of businesses, some within the parent corporation and others through wholly owned subsidiaries. Humana created a captive insurance subsidiary and purchased insurance from that captive insurer covering future claims against itself and its wholly owned, separately incorporated subsidiaries. Like Kidde, Humana allocated the total premiums among its subsidiaries according to the risk each subsidiary posed.

In determining the deductibility of the disputed payments in Humana, the Court of Appeals for the Sixth Circuit distinguished between the payments that covered future claims against Humana's own operations and the payments that covered future claims against the operations of Humana's separately incorporated subsidiaries. The court allowed a deduction for the payments covering claims against the subsidiaries, but not the payments covering claims against the businesses that Humana operated within its own corporate structure. In denying a deduction for the payments that related to the captive insurer assuming responsibility for future claims against the parent corporation, the Sixth Circuit, citing Clougherty, 811 F.2d 1297, concluded that the agreements did not produce any risk shifting and amounted to no more than Humana setting aside a reserve for future claims against it. In concluding that no risk shifting occurred, the court focused on the parent's assets and concluded that there was no net change in the value of the parent's assets when the captive insurer assumed responsibility to pay future claims against the parent. The court explained:

> The economic reality of insurance between a parent and a captive insurance company is that the captive's stock is shown as an asset on the parent's balance sheet. If the parent suffers an insured loss which the captive has to pay, the assets of the captive will be depleted by the amount of the payment. This will reduce the value of the captive's shares as an asset of the parent. In effect, the assets of the parent bear the true economic impact of the loss.

Humana, 881 F.2d at 253. Because Humana suffered the full economic impact of a payment of a claim by its wholly owned captive insurer subsidiary, the court reasoned that the arrangement did not result in the parent divesting itself of any risk, and hence no risk shifting occurred and no insurance existed under the requirements of Le Gierse.

If the Sixth Circuit had maintained this narrow focus on the net assets of Humana when it evaluated the payments to the captive insurer relating to future claims against Humana's wholly owned subsidiaries, then the court also would have concluded that these payments should not be classified as "insurance premiums." Because Humana owned 100 percent of these separately incorporated subsidiaries, Humana's net assets would not be affected by a contractual arrangement pursuant to which one of its wholly owned subsidiaries agreed to pay future claims against another wholly owned subsidiary. For example, a $1,000 payment on a claim against one of its subsidiaries would result in a $1,000 decrease in Humana's net assets regardless of which subsidiary paid the claim. Thus, when viewed from the perspective of Humana, the various contractual arrangements did not produce any shifting of risk away from Humana. Humana would face essentially the same risk before and after entry of the contracts rendering the captive insurer responsible for future claims against the wholly owned subsidiaries.

The Sixth Circuit, however, did not maintain this narrow focus on Humana's net assets when determining the deductibility of payments covering future claims against the wholly owned subsidiaries. Rather, the court interpreted Moline Properties as precluding a focus on the parent corporation when evaluating the tax status of payments by the wholly owned subsidiaries because such a focus would improperly treat the various distinct corporations as a single economic unit. The court interpreted Moline Properties to require, when assessing whether risk shifting and risk distributing is present, a focus on the net assets of the distinct corporation that is purchasing the protection rather than the parent. The court explained:

> The economic reality, however, of insurance between the Humana subsidiaries and [Humana's captive insurer], where the subsidiaries own no stock in the captive and vice versa, is that when a loss occurs and is paid by [the captive

insurer] the net worth of the Humana affiliates is not reduced accordingly. The subsidiaries' balance sheets and net worth are not affected by the payment of an insured claim by [the captive insurer]. In reality, therefore, when the Humana subsidiaries pay their own premiums under their own insurance contracts, as the facts show, they shift their risk to [the captive insurer].

Id.

F.

Herein, both parties argue that this court should reject the split result in Humana. Defendant argues that the court should deny an "insurance premium" deduction both for the payments covering the subsidiaries that are separately incorporated as well as the payments for the divisions that operate within Kidde's own corporate structure. Plaintiff argues that both types of payments should qualify for an "insurance premium" deduction.

Defendant's argument relies in part upon the testimony of defendant's expert, Professor Gregory Niehaus. Professor Niehaus testified in effect that modern economic theory views a corporation as a nexus of contracts among individual stakeholders and evaluates corporate decisions based on how the individual stakeholders are affected. Consistent with this approach, Professor Niehaus argued that corporations do not bear risk but rather individual stakeholders bear risk. Hence, defendant argues, in determining whether risk shifting or risk distributing occurred herein, the court should focus on the individual shareholders of Kidde, and the risk faced by these shareholders is not affected when one subsidiary assumes legal responsibility for the claims against the other subsidiaries.

Professor Niehaus' position, to the extent it presents a purely economic analysis, is straightforward and makes eminent sense. The modern theory of the corporation which looks at corporations as fictional entities, provides an excellent analytic framework in which to evaluate the economic effects of a corporate action.[7] Corporations are owned by their shareholders and from the shareholders' perspective herein, the insurance arrangement did not result in the shareholders securing the benefits of risk shifting or risk distribution. Because the shareholders in effect own 100 percent of Kidde, KIC, and each

---

[7]   Defendant relies upon the following statement of the theory:

Stripped to its essentials, the corporation is simply a legal fiction which serves as a nexus of contracts. Individuals and organizations-employees (including managers), investors, suppliers, customers-contract with each other in the name of a financial entity, the corporation.

William H. Meckling and Michael C. Jensen, Reflections on the Corporation as a Social Invention, J. Applied Corp. Fin. 9.

of Kidde's other wholly owned subsidiaries, the shareholders' financial position would be the same whether, for example, a $1,000 claim is paid by Kidde, KIC, or some other wholly owned Kidde subsidiary. Hence, shifting responsibility for claims to different points within the overall Kidde structure would not shift any risk away from the shareholders or distribute any risk the shareholders face to a larger pool.

A problem with Professor Niehaus' argument, however, arises in the transition from abstract economic theory to application of existing tax laws and case precedent. Contrary to the modern theory of corporations, the tax laws do not view corporate actions from the perspective of the corporate shareholders and do not treat corporations as fictitious entities that can be ignored. Instead, the tax laws treat corporations as distinct and substantive legal entities which are taxed separate and apart from the entities that own them. "Moline Properties stands for the proposition that a parent corporation and its subsidiary corporation be accorded treatment as separate taxable entities." Ocean Drilling, 988 F.2d at 1144. Indeed, in Moline Properties, the Supreme Court specifically rejected the taxpayer's request, in effect, to treat the corporation as a fiction and to treat the assets owned by the corporation as though they were owned by the corporate shareholder. The teaching of Moline Properties in effect is that the incorporation of a business brings with it certain benefits and certain burdens and once the business is incorporated, the benefits accrue and the burdens must be borne. See Moline Properties, 319 U.S. at 438-39, 63 S.Ct. at 1133-34.

Hence, for purposes of assessing income taxes, Moline Properties requires this court to treat Kidde and its separately incorporated subsidiaries as distinct from one another as well as distinct from Kidde shareholders. When these separately incorporated subsidiaries are so treated, the contractual arrangement pursuant to which KIC assumed responsibility for the subsidiaries' future claims would involve the shifting of risk away from these subsidiaries in the same way as if the subsidiaries secured insurance from an independent third-party insurer. As explained in Humana, 881 F.2d at 253, the wholly owned subsidiaries have no ownership interest in the parent's captive insurer and hence would not suffer any additional loss if payments by the captive insurer of future claims against the subsidiaries exceeded the amount of premiums the captive insurer received. For example, because a $1,000 claim against a Kidde subsidiary paid by KIC would not result in a corresponding decrease in that subsidiary's net worth, the risk as to that claim was shifted from the subsidiary, through National, to KIC. Similarly, when viewed from the perspective of that subsidiary, risk distribution also took place in that KIC distributed the risk faced by that subsidiary in a pool with the risks of other entities in which the subsidiary did not have an ownership interest. Because risk shifting and risk distributing are present, consistent with Le Gierse, Moline Properties, and Humana, Kidde's payments to National covering future claims against its wholly owned subsidiaries are properly treated as "insurance premiums."[8]

G.

This brings the court to the issue of the tax treatment of the payments Kidde made to National covering future claims against the divisions that operate within Kidde's own corporate structure. Plaintiff does not dispute that Kidde's divisions would suffer a dollar-for-dollar loss in net asset value for every dollar KIC paid on a claim against Kidde. Relying in part upon the testimony of and a report co-authored by its expert Dr. Michael Powers, however, plaintiff contends that this court's determination that the payments covering future claims against Kidde's wholly owned subsidiaries are deductible as "insurance premiums" dictates that the court also treat in the same way the payments pertaining to future claims against the divisions that operate within Kidde's structure and not as separate corporate subsidiaries. Plaintiff argues that the court should view the crucial issue to be whether the operation of KIC is properly characterized as the equivalent of a self-insurance reserve for Kidde or rather as a separate viable entity, financially capable of meeting its insurance obligations. Plaintiff then argues that the fact that distinct corporate entities accounted for approximately 60 percent of KIC's business during the tax years in issue is itself sufficient to show that KIC was operating as a viable insurance company and that it is not relevant that these entities were wholly owned subsidiaries of Kidde. In a related argument, plaintiff contends that because the wholly owned subsidiaries had the option to select other insurers, KIC was subject to market forces in its pricing and thus was operating like a traditional insurance company rather than simply as a loss reserve for Kidde.

The problem with plaintiff's argument is that it ignores Ocean Drilling's interpretation of Le Gierse as requiring risk shifting and risk distributing for payments to be classified as "insurance premiums." ("[E]ven if plaintiff and [the captive insurer] are separate entities, if plaintiff retained the risk of the losses against which it insured, plaintiff's premiums amounted to a reserve for losses, and plaintiff would not be entitled to deduct such premiums from taxable income." 988 F.2d at 1150-51.) With respect to risk shifting and risk distribution, as generally noted above, the Federal Circuit in Ocean Drilling

---

8   In its post-trial brief, defendant presents the alternative argument that the court need not focus on the shareholders' interests to conclude that no risk shifting occurred, but rather could focus on Kidde's interests. By focusing on the parent's interests to determine whether payments by a wholly owned subsidiary involve risk shifting, defendant's argument is substantially identical to the economic family argument rejected in Humana, 881 F.2d at 252. As with the modern theory of the corporation, the economic family argument has appeal as a general theory for evaluating economic effects but fails to recognize the legal significance of incorporation in the manner required by Moline Properties.

defined the relevant risk that is transferred in an insurance relationship as the "variability of loss," i.e., the risk that the amount of the loss suffered will exceed the average or expected amount of loss. Id. at 1151-52. The court then explained the relationship between risk shifting and risk distribution as follows:

> Unrelated business operated to reduce the amount of risk to which plaintiff was exposed. When plaintiff purchased insurance from [its captive insurer], plaintiff transferred to [the captive] a certain level of risk or a certain amount of variability of loss. Because [the captive insurer] had unrelated business, this level of risk was not retained by plaintiff, the parent.... The considerable amount of unrelated business, approximately 44 and 66 percent during the years in issue, caused a significant reduction in risk. Plaintiff as the parent ... thus shouldered a level of risk significantly lower than the level of risk that it initially transferred to [the captive insurer]. Consequently, the risk transferred to [the captive] and the risk ultimately borne by plaintiff were not the same, and plaintiff's premiums constituted the transfer of risk.

> If the level of risk plaintiff initially had transferred and the level of risk plaintiff ultimately had shouldered were virtually the same, plaintiff's risk effectively would not have transferred.

* * * * * *

> Since risk shifting was present, the next question to be addressed is whether risk distribution occurred. Risk distribution involves spreading the risk of loss among policyholders. [The captive insurer] had unrelated business of approximately 44 and 66 percent for the two years at issue. This amount of unrelated business sufficiently spreads risk so as to constitute risk distribution.

Id. at 1152-53.

Hence, the Federal Circuit determined that risk shifting cannot be established simply by showing that the captive insurer was a separate corporation that was legally responsible for claims against the parent. Rather, the court distinguished between two concepts-the level of risk transferred to the captive insurer and the level of risk ultimately shouldered by the parent. If the risk ultimately shouldered by the parent is less than the risk transferred, then the required risk shifting occurred. If the two levels of risk are the same, however, then no risk shifting occurred even though the captive insurer has become legally responsible for the parent's claims. The Federal Circuit rested its position that the parent shifted risk, i.e., shifted the variability of loss, on its conclusion that "[b]ecause [the captive insurer] had unrelated business, [the] level of risk [transferred] was not retained by the parent." Id. at 1152.

In Ocean Drilling, for example, a $1,000 claim against the parent paid by the captive insurer would result in a $1,000 decrease in the parent's net assets whether or not the captive insurer also offered insurance to unrelated corporations. The question then becomes how this unrelated business operates to change the variability of loss faced by the parent. The Federal Circuit's answer appears to lie in the parent, through the arrangement involving the captive insurer, placing the risks faced by the parent into a pool with other independently insured risks. As explained above, pursuant to the mathematical law of large numbers, the variability of loss decreases when risks are combined with other independent risks. Hence, from the parent's perspective, when risks faced by the parent become the responsibility of a wholly owned subsidiary, and the subsidiary in turn combines those risks with other independent risks of corporations unrelated to the parent, the net effect is that the parent will shoulder less risk because it has a lower variability of loss than it faced before it entered the arrangement with its subsidiary.

There is no analogous decrease in risk where, as in the instant case, the risks combined by the captive insurer involve essentially only future claims against the parent and its wholly owned subsidiaries. Because the parent owns the subsidiary corporations, its net assets, as reflected on its balance sheet, would decrease dollar for dollar with any loss suffered by any one of those subsidiaries. Hence, herein, prior to entering the agreement that led to KIC assuming responsibility for future claims against Kidde's divisions and subsidiaries, Kidde's risk profile, i.e., the risks that Kidde potentially shouldered, included all claims against itself or any of its wholly owned subsidiaries. Kidde's risk profile did not change after KIC became responsible for these claims. Kidde's net assets would still decrease dollar for dollar with any payment made by KIC and Kidde would not benefit from any decrease in its variability of loss because Kidde did not combine its risk with substantial risks of unrelated business.

Thus, when viewed from the perspective of the parent, when its captive insurer combines the risks of the parent and/or its wholly owned subsidiaries with sufficient unrelated risks from unrelated corporations, the net effect is to decrease the variability of loss and hence, under the analysis of Ocean Drilling, to accomplish some shifting of risk. On the other hand, if the only risks in the pool are essentially those of the parent and its wholly owned subsidiaries, the parent has not changed the variability of loss it faces and hence has not shifted any risk.

This court acknowledges that at first blush it appears inconsistent to classify payments made by Kidde's wholly owned subsidiaries as "insurance premiums" and not to classify payments made by Kidde's divisions in the same way when KIC appears to have provided the same services to both. But as interpreted in Ocean Drilling, Le Gierse requires risk shifting and risk distributing for a relationship to involve insurance. Because, as explained above, Kidde did not shift any risk to KIC, the premiums it paid amounted merely to a reserve fund to pay future claims. The wholly owned subsidiaries, on the other hand, did

338 Adkisson's Captive Insurance Companies

shift risk to KIC. Thus, although viewing the arrangement from KIC's perspective may suggest that KIC was performing the same functions for Kidde and its subsidiaries, when viewed from the perspectives of Kidde and the other subsidiaries, the entities whose tax responsibility is under inquiry here, KIC was not performing the same functions. The subsidiaries were utilizing KIC to shift risk but Kidde was not.

This split result also is consistent with Moline Properties. Moline Properties requires the court to treat each corporation as a distinct taxable entity. This court achieves that end by making tax determinations based on the perspective of the corporations involved. As described above, from Kidde's perspective, the purported insurance relationship between Kidde and KIC covering Kidde's divisions did not produce risk shifting or risk distribution. From the perspective of the separately incorporated subsidiaries, their payments did produce risk shifting and risk distribution.

H.

Next, plaintiff presents two alternative arguments to support its position that Kidde achieved risk shifting and risk distribution. First, plaintiff notes that unlike the parent in Humana, Kidde made its payments to an independent third-party insurer, National, rather than to its captive insurer. This difference is compelling, plaintiff argues, because if Kidde transferred responsibility for future claims to National rather than KIC, then risk shifting occurred because National was a separate corporation in which Kidde had no ownership interest.

As generally described above, however, National's willingness to provide insurance to Kidde and its subsidiaries was conditioned upon National reinsuring a portion of that liability with KIC. From the beginning, the parties understood that KIC, rather than National, would be responsible for these claims and that Kidde's payments relating to such coverage would be ceded to KIC. In this regard, as described above, by June 1, 1978, both parties were convinced that KIC's assets were sufficient to provide such coverage without a parental guarantee. In addition, the IRS, in effect, considered the extent to which National maintained ultimate liability for the claims when it determined the amount of Kidde's payments that would be classified as insurance premiums. When determining the appropriate amount to cede to KIC for reinsurance, National would have factored into its calculations any possibility that KIC would not be able to meet its contractual burdens and would have withheld, i.e., not ceded, an appropriate amount to account for that risk. Because the entire amount of Kidde's payments that National retained were classified as insurance premiums, Kidde did receive a deduction for payments that correspond to National's maintaining ultimate responsibility for future claims.

Plaintiff's final argument rests on KIC having entered into reinsurance agreements subsequent to 1980 with third parties not related to Kidde. Plaintiff contends that it was predictable during the period in issue here that certain claims against Kidde that arose during that time would not have been reported and paid until 1981 or thereafter. For such claims, plaintiff argues, risk shifting and risk distribution are present because by the time the claims were resolved, KIC had entered reinsurance agreements with unrelated third parties and hence those claims ultimately were pooled with claims against unrelated corporations. But assuming that the pooling of claims in later years can be used to demonstrate the required risk shifting and risk distributing in earlier years, plaintiff has failed to demonstrate the precise amount of those claims that remained unresolved after 1980. Hence, plaintiff has not established that any risk shifting that did occur in later years was sufficient to warrant classifying all or any specific portion of the payments in issue as insurance premiums. In any event, it would not be appropriate, when assessing whether the payments in issue involved risk shifting and risk distributing, to rely upon third parties that purchased reinsurance from KIC for the first time after 1980. Assuming that it was apparent in 1978 that certain claims against Kidde would remain unresolved in 1980, it was not similarly predictable that by 1981 or any time thereafter KIC would enter into significant insurance relationships with unrelated third parties. Hence, it was not possible at the close of tax year 1978 to conclude that Kidde's arrangement covering claims arising during that year would shift and distribute risk to any significant extent.

VII.

[Discussion of WIN tax credits omitted.]

Conclusion

For the reasons set forth above, for tax year 1978, plaintiff is entitled to deduct from its income its payments to National covering the period June 1 through December 31, 1978, that National in turn ceded to KIC to cover claims against Kidde's wholly owned subsidiaries. Plaintiff is not entitled to deduct from its income its payments to National covering any period prior to June 1, 1978, with respect to its subsidiaries. For tax years 1977 and 1978, plaintiff is not entitled to deduct from its income any of its payments to National with respect to the divisions within Kidde's own corporate structure. As to WIN tax credits for 1977 and 1978, plaintiff "first filed" its claim prior to the March 11, 1987, deadline and hence is entitled to such a refund. Accordingly, on or before February 2, 1998, the parties shall file a stipulation as to the amount due plaintiff pursuant to this decision.

IT IS SO ORDERED.

Appendix S

United Parcel Service v. C.I.R.

254 F.3d 1014 (11th Cir. 2001)

UNITED STATES COURT OF APPEALS, ELEVENTH CIRCUIT

UNITED PARCEL SERVICE OF AMERICA, INC., Petitioner-Appellant,

v.

COMMISSIONER OF INTERNAL REVENUE, Respondent-Appellee.

No. 00-12720, June 20, 2001

[Names of counsel omitted.]

Appeal from a Decision of the United States Tax Court.

Before WILSON and COX, Circuit Judges, and RYSKAMPFN,[*] District Judge.

COX, Circuit Judge:

The tax court held United Parcel Service of America, Inc. (UPS) liable for additional taxes and penalties for the tax year 1984. UPS appeals, and we reverse and remand.

I. Background

UPS, whose main business is shipping packages, had a practice in the early 1980s of reimbursing customers for lost or damaged parcels up to $100 in declared value.[1] Above

---

[*]   Honorable Kenneth L. Ryskamp, U.S. District Judge for the Southern District of Florida, sitting by designation.

[1]   These facts synopsize the high points of the tax court's long opinion, which is published at 78 T.C.M. (CCH) 262, 1999 WL 592696.

that level, UPS would assume liability up to the parcel's declared value if the customer paid 25¢ per additional $100 in declared value, the "excess-value charge." If a parcel were lost or damaged, UPS would process and pay the resulting claim. UPS turned a large profit on excess-value charges because it never came close to paying as much in claims as it collected in charges, in part because of efforts it made to safeguard and track excess-value shipments. This profit was taxed; UPS declared its revenue from excess-value charges as income on its 1983 return, and it deducted as expenses the claims paid on damaged or lost excess-value parcels.

UPS's insurance broker suggested that UPS could avoid paying taxes on the lucrative excess-value business if it restructured the program as insurance provided by an overseas affiliate. UPS implemented this plan in 1983 by first forming and capitalizing a Bermuda subsidiary, Overseas Partners, Ltd. (OPL), almost all of whose shares were distributed as a taxable dividend to UPS shareholders (most of whom were employees; UPS stock was not publicly traded). UPS then purchased an insurance policy, for the benefit of UPS customers, from National Union Fire Insurance Company. By this policy, National Union assumed the risk of damage to or loss of excess-value shipments. The premiums for the policy were the excess-value charges that UPS collected. UPS, not National Union, was responsible for administering claims brought under the policy. National Union in turn entered a reinsurance treaty with OPL. Under the treaty, OPL assumed risk commensurate with National Union's, in exchange for premiums that equal the excess-value payments National Union got from UPS, less commissions, fees, and excise taxes.

Under this plan, UPS thus continued to collect 25¢ per $100 of excess value from its customers, process and pay claims, and take special measures to safeguard valuable packages. But UPS now remitted monthly the excess-value payments, less claims paid, to National Union as premiums on the policy. National Union then collected its commission, excise taxes, and fees from the charges before sending the rest on to OPL as payments under the reinsurance contract. UPS reported neither revenue from excess-value charges nor claim expenses on its 1984 return, although it did deduct the fees and commissions that National Union charged.

The IRS determined a deficiency in the amount of the excess-value charges collected in 1984, concluding that the excess-value payment remitted ultimately to OPL had to be treated as gross income to UPS. UPS petitioned for a redetermination. Following a hearing, the tax court agreed with the IRS.

It is not perfectly clear on what judicial doctrine the holding rests. The court started its analysis by expounding on the assignment-of-income doctrine, a source rule that ensures that income is attributed to the person who earned it regardless of efforts to deflect it elsewhere. See United States v. Basye, 410 U.S. 441, 450, 93 S.Ct. 1080, 1086, 35

L.Ed.2d 412 (1973). The court did not, however, discuss at all the touchstone of an ineffective assignment of income, which would be UPS's control over the excess-value charges once UPS had turned them over as premiums to National Union. See Comm'r v. Sunnen, 333 U.S. 591, 604, 68 S.Ct. 715, 722, 92 L.Ed. 898 (1948). The court's analysis proceeded rather under the substantive-sham or economic-substance doctrines, the assignment-of-income doctrine's kissing cousins. See United States v. Krall, 835 F.2d 711, 714 (8th Cir.1987) (treating the assignment-of-income doctrine as a subtheory of the sham-transaction doctrine). The conclusion was that UPS's redesign of its excess-value business warranted no respect. Three core reasons support this result, according to the court: the plan had no defensible business purpose, as the business realities were identical before and after; the premiums paid for the National Union policy were well above industry norms; and contemporary memoranda and documents show that UPS's sole motivation was tax avoidance. The revenue from the excess-value program was thus properly deemed to be income to UPS rather than to OPL or National Union. The court also imposed penalties.

UPS now appeals, attacking the tax court's economic-substance analysis and its imposition of penalties. The refrain of UPS's lead argument is that the excess-value plan had economic substance, and thus was not a sham, because it comprised genuine exchanges of reciprocal obligations among real, independent entities. The IRS answers with a before-and-after analysis, pointing out that whatever the reality and enforceability of the contracts that composed the excess-value plan, UPS's postplan practice equated to its preplan, in that it collected excess-value charges, administered claims, and generated substantial profits. The issue presented to this court, therefore, is whether the excess-value plan had the kind of economic substance that removes it from "shamhood," even if the business continued as it had before. The question of the effect of a transaction on tax liability, to the extent it does not concern the accuracy of the tax court's fact-finding, is subject to de novo review. Kirchman v. Comm'r, 862 F.2d 1486, 1490 (11th Cir.1989); see Karr v. Comm'r, 924 F.2d 1018, 1023 (11th Cir.1991). We agree with UPS that this was not a sham transaction, and we therefore do not reach UPS's challenges to the tax penalties.

II. Discussion

I.R.C. §§ 11, 61, and 63 together provide the Code's foundation by identifying income as the basis of taxation. Even apart from the narrower assignment-of-income doctrine-which we do not address here-these sections come with the gloss, analogous to that on other Code sections, that economic substance determines what is income to a taxpayer and what is not. See Caruth Corp. v. United States, 865 F.2d 644, 650 (5th Cir.1989) (addressing, but rejecting on the case's facts, the argument that the donation of an income source to charity was a sham, and that the income should be reattributed to the donor); United States v. Buttorff, 761 F.2d 1056, 1061 (5th Cir.1985) (conveying income to a trust controlled by the income's earner has no tax consequence because the assignment is insubstantial); Zmuda v. Comm'r, 731 F.2d 1417, 1421 (9th Cir.1984) (similar). This economic-substance doctrine, also called the sham-transaction doctrine, provides that a transaction ceases to merit tax respect when it has no "economic effects other than the creation of tax benefits." Kirchman, 862 F.2d at 1492.[2] Even if the transaction has economic effects, it must be disregarded if it has no business purpose and its motive is tax avoidance. See Karr, 924 F.2d at 1023 (noting that subjective intent is not irrelevant, despite Kirchman's statement of the doctrine); Neely v. United States, 775 F.2d 1092, 1094 (9th Cir.1985); see also Frank Lyon Co. v. United States, 435 U.S. 561, 583-84, 98 S.Ct. 1291, 1303, 55 L.Ed.2d 550 (1978) (one reason requiring treatment of transaction as genuine was that it was "compelled or encouraged by business or regulatory realities"); Gregory v. Helvering, 293 U.S. 465, 469, 55 S.Ct. 266, 267, 79 L.Ed. 596 (1935) (reorganization disregarded in part because it had "no business or corporate purpose").

The kind of "economic effects" required to entitle a transaction to respect in taxation include the creation of genuine obligations enforceable by an unrelated party. See Frank Lyon Co., 435 U.S. at 582-83, 98 S.Ct. at 1303 (refusing to deem a sale-leaseback a sham in part because the lessor had accepted a real, enforceable debt to an unrelated bank as part of the deal). The restructuring of UPS's excess-value business generated just such obligations. There was a real insurance policy between UPS and National Union that gave National Union the right to receive the excess-value charges that UPS collected. And even if the odds of losing money on the policy were slim, National Union had assumed liability for the losses of UPS's excess-value shippers, again a genuine obligation. A history of not losing money on a policy is no guarantee of such a future. Insurance companies indeed do not make a habit of issuing policies whose premiums do not exceed the claims anticipated, but that fact does not imply that insurance companies do not bear risk. Nor did the reinsurance treaty with OPL, while certainly reducing the odds of loss, completely foreclose the risk of loss because reinsurance treaties, like all agreements, are susceptible to default.

The tax court dismissed these obligations because National Union, given the reinsurance treaty, was no more than a "front" in what was a transfer of revenue from UPS to OPL. As we have said, that conclusion ignores the real risk that National Union assumed. But even if we overlook the reality of the risk and treat National Union as a conduit for transmission of the excess-value payments from UPS to OPL, there remains the fact that OPL is an independently taxable entity that is not under UPS's control. UPS really did lose the stream of income it had earlier reaped from excess-value charges. UPS genuinely

---

2   Kirchman, which is binding in this circuit, differs in this respect from the oft-used statement of the doctrine derived from Rice's Toyota World, Inc. v. Comm'r, 752 F.2d 89, 91-92 (4th Cir.1985). Rice's Toyota World, unlike Kirchman, requires a tax-avoidance purpose as well as a lack of substance; Kirchman explicitly refuses to examine subjective intent if the transaction lacks economic effects.

could not apply that money to any use other than paying a premium to National Union; the money could not be used for other purposes, such as capital improvement, salaries, dividends, or investment. These circumstances distinguish UPS's case from the paradigmatic sham transfers of income, in which the taxpayer retains the benefits of the income it has ostensibly forgone. See, e.g., Zmuda v. Comm'r, 731 F.2d at 1417 (income "laundered" through a series of trusts into notes that were delivered to the taxpayer as "gifts"). Here that benefit ended up with OPL. There were, therefore, real economic effects from this transaction on all of its parties.

The conclusion that UPS's excess-value plan had real economic effects means, under this circuit's rule in Kirchman, that it is not per se a sham. But it could still be one if tax avoidance displaced any business purpose. The tax court saw no business purpose here because the excess-value business continued to operate after its reconfiguration much as before. This lack of change in how the business operated at the retail level, according to the court, betrayed the restructuring as pointless.

It may be true that there was little change over time in how the excess-value program appeared to customers. But the tax court's narrow notion of "business purpose"-which is admittedly implied by the phrase's plain language-stretches the economic-substance doctrine farther than it has been stretched. A "business purpose" does not mean a reason for a transaction that is free of tax considerations. Rather, a transaction has a "business purpose," when we are talking about a going concern like UPS, as long as it figures in a bona fide, profit-seeking business. See ACM P'ship v. Comm'r, 157 F.3d 231, 251 (3d Cir.1998). This concept of "business purpose" is a necessary corollary to the venerable axiom that tax-planning is permissible. See Gregory v. Helvering, 293 U.S. 465, 469, 55 S.Ct. 266, 267, 79 L.Ed. 596 (1935) ("The legal right of a taxpayer to decrease the amount of what otherwise would be his taxes, or altogether avoid them, by means which the law permits, cannot be doubted."). The Code treats lots of categories of economically similar behavior differently. For instance, two ways to infuse capital into a corporation, borrowing and sale of equity, have different tax consequences; interest is usually deductible and distributions to equityholders are not. There may be no tax-independent reason for a taxpayer to choose between these different ways of financing the business, but it does not mean that the taxpayer lacks a "business purpose." To conclude otherwise would prohibit tax-planning.

The caselaw, too, bears out this broader notion of "business purpose." Many of the cases where no business purpose appears are about individual income tax returns, when the individual meant to evade taxes on income probably destined for personal consumption; obviously, it is difficult in such a case to articulate any business purpose to the transaction. See, e.g., Gregory, 293 U.S. at 469, 55 S.Ct. at 267 (purported corporate reorganization was disguised dividend distribution to shareholder); Knetsch v. United States, 364 U.S. 361, 362-65, 81 S.Ct. 132, 133-35, 5 L.Ed.2d 128 (1960) (faux personal loans intended to generate interest deductions); Neely v. United States, 775 F.2d 1092, 1094 (9th

Cir.1985) (one of many cases in which the taxpayers formed a trust, controlled by them, and diverted personal earnings to it). Other no-business-purpose cases concern tax-shelter transactions or investments by a business or investor that would not have occurred, in any form, but for tax-avoidance reasons. See, e.g., ACM P'ship, 157 F.3d at 233-43 (sophisticated investment partnership formed and manipulated solely to generate a capital loss to shelter some of Colgate-Palmolive's capital gains); Kirchman, 862 F.2d at 1488-89 (option straddles entered to produce deductions with little risk of real loss); Karr, 924 F.2d at 1021 (façade of energy enterprise developed solely to produce deductible losses for investors); Rice's Toyota World, Inc. v. Comm'r, 752 F.2d 89, 91 (4th Cir.1985) (sale-leaseback of a computer by a car dealership, solely to generate depreciation deductions). By contrast, the few cases that accept a transaction as genuine involve a bona fide business that-perhaps even by design-generates tax benefits. See, e.g., Frank Lyon, 435 U.S. at 582-84, 98 S.Ct. at 1302-04 (sale-leaseback was part of genuine financing transaction, heavily influenced by banking regulation, to permit debtor bank to outdo its competitor in impressive office space); Jacobson v. Comm'r, 915 F.2d 832, 837-39 (2d Cir.1990) (one of many cases finding that a bona fide profit motive provided a business purpose for a losing investment because the investment was not an obvious loser ex ante).

The transaction under challenge here simply altered the form of an existing, bona fide business, and this case therefore falls in with those that find an adequate business purpose to neutralize any tax-avoidance motive. True, UPS's restructuring was more sophisticated and complex than the usual tax-influenced form-of-business election or a choice of debt over equity financing. But its sophistication does not change the fact that there was a real business that served the genuine need for customers to enjoy loss coverage and for UPS to lower its liability exposure.

We therefore conclude that UPS's restructuring of its excess-value business had both real economic effects and a business purpose, and it therefore under our precedent had sufficient economic substance to merit respect in taxation. It follows that the tax court improperly imposed penalties and enhanced interest on UPS for engaging in a sham transaction. The tax court did not, however, reach the IRS's alternative arguments in support of its determination of deficiency, the reallocation provisions of I.R.C. §§ 482 and 845(a). The holding here does not dispose of those arguments, and we therefore must remand for the tax court to address them in the first instance.

III. Conclusion

For the foregoing reasons, we reverse the judgment against UPS and remand the action to the tax court for it to address in the first instance the IRS's contentions under §§ 482 and 845(a).

REVERSED AND REMANDED.

RYSKAMP, District Judge, dissenting:

I respectfully dissent. Although I agree with the majority's recitation of the facts as well as its interpretation of the applicable legal standard, I find that its reversal of the tax court is contrary to the great weight of the evidence that was before the lower court. The majority, as well as the tax court below, correctly finds that the question before the Court is whether UPS's insurance arrangements with NUF and OPL are valid under the sham-transaction doctrine. Under the sham-transaction doctrine, UPS's transaction ceases to merit tax respect when it has no "economic effects other than the creation of tax benefits," Kirchman v. Comm'r, 862 F.2d 1486, 1492 (11th Cir.1989), or has no business purpose and its sole motive is tax avoidance. See Karr v. Comm'r, 924 F.2d 1018, 1023 (11th Cir.1991). Thus the question before the Court is not strictly whether UPS had a tax avoidance motive when it formulated the scheme in question, but rather whether there was some legitimate, substantive business reason for the transaction as well. There clearly was not.

As the tax court articulated in great detail in its well-reasoned 114-page opinion, the evidence in this case overwhelmingly demonstrates that UPS's reinsurance arrangement with NUF and OPL had no economic significance or business purpose outside of UPS's desire to avoid federal income tax, and was therefore a sham transaction. First, the tax court based its decision upon evidence that the scheme in question was subjectively motivated by tax avoidance. For example, the evidence showed that tax avoidance was the initial and sole reason for the scheme in question, that UPS held off on the plan for some time to analyze tax legislation on the floor of the United States House of Representatives, and that a letter sent to AIG Insurance from UPS detailing the scheme claimed that AIG would serve in merely a "fronting" capacity and would bear little or no actual risk. The evidence thus showed that this scheme was hatched with only tax avoidance in mind.

Second, the tax court based its decision on overwhelming evidence that UPS's scheme had no real economic or business purpose outside of tax avoidance. For example, the evidence showed that NUF's exposure to loss under the plan (except in the very unlikely event of extreme catastrophe) was infinitesimal, and that UPS nevertheless continued to fully bear the administrative costs of the EVC program. NUF was only liable for losses not covered by another insurance policy held by UPS, yet UPS still collected the EVC's and deposited the money into UPS bank accounts, still processed EVC claims, and continued to pay all EVC claims out of UPS bank accounts (while collecting the accrued interest for itself). All NUF really did in the scheme was collect over $1 million in fees and expenses before passing the EVC income on to OPL, which was of course wholly owned by UPS shareholders. In essence, NUF received an enormous fee from UPS in exchange for nothing.

Moreover, the tax court systematically rejected every explanation of the scheme put forth by UPS. UPS claimed that the scheme was meant to avoid violation of state insurance laws, yet the evidence showed no real concern for such laws and that in fact UPS was well aware that federal preemption of these state laws likely made its old EVC plan legal. UPS claimed that it intended OPL to become a full-line insurer someday, yet the evidence showed that it was nevertheless unnecessary to specifically use EVC income for such a capital investment. UPS claimed that elimination of the EVC income allowed it to increase its rates, yet one of its own board members testified that this explanation was untrue. I also note that UPS's claim that OPL was a legitimate insurance company fails in light of the fact that OPL was charging a substantially inflated rate for EVCs. Evidence in the tax court showed that in an arms-length transaction with a legitimate insurance company, EVC rates would have been approximately half those charged by UPS (and in turn passed on to OPL), providing further evidence that the transaction was a sham. In sum, UPS failed to show any legitimate business reason for giving up nearly $100 million in EVC income in 1984.

For these reasons, I would affirm the holding of the tax court and find that UPS's arrangement with NUF and OPL was a sham transaction subject to federal tax liability.

Index

978-0-595-42237-1
0-595-42237-3